A DROP OF TREASON

A DROP OF TREASON

Philip Agee and His
Exposure of the CIA

JONATHAN STEVENSON

THE UNIVERSITY OF CHICAGO PRESS

CHICAGO AND LONDON

The University of Chicago Press, Chicago 60637
The University of Chicago Press, Ltd., London
© 2021 by Jonathan Stevenson
Published 2021
Printed in the United States of America

30 29 28 27 26 25 24 23 22 21   1 2 3 4 5

ISBN-13: 978-0-226-35668-6 (cloth)
ISBN-13: 978-0-226-35671-6 (e-book)
DOI: https://doi.org/10.7208/chicago/9780226356716.001.0001

Library of Congress Cataloging-in-Publication Data

Names: Stevenson, Jonathan, 1956– author.
Title: A drop of treason : Philip Agee and his exposure of the CIA /
Jonathan Stevenson.
Other titles: Philip Agee and his exposure of the CIA
Description: Chicago ; London : The University of Chicago Press,
2021. | Includes bibliographical references and index.
Identifiers: LCCN 2020051819 | ISBN 9780226356686 (cloth) |
ISBN 9780226356716 (ebook)
Subjects: LCSH: Agee, Philip. | United States. Central Intelligence
Agency—Officials and employees—Biography. | Intelligence
officers—United States—Biography. | Traitors—United States—
Biography.
Classification: LCC JK468.I6 S748 2021 | DDC 327.12730092—dc23
LC record available at https://lccn.loc.gov/2020051819

♾ This paper meets the requirements of ANSI/NISO Z39.48-1992
(Permanence of Paper).

For Sharon

All men should have a drop of treason in their veins,
if nations are not to go soft like so many sleepy pears.

REBECCA WEST, *THE MEANING OF TREASON*

These were fabled people. These were tricky times.

KEVIN BARRY, *NIGHT BOAT TO TANGIER*

Contents

1

A Geopolitically Charmed Life

Philip Agee remains unique in the annals of US intelligence in that he went from being the consummate intelligence insider—nobody is more entrenched than a Central Intelligence Agency case officer in the field—to being a thoroughgoing outsider, and did so by choice. Agee has continued to be, with the exception of Aldrich Ames, the United States' most hated erstwhile spy. Within the CIA, his "was taken as one of the most harmful, worst betrayals that we [have] suffered, and the hostility to him was greater than it was towards almost anybody else," notes Glenn Carle, himself a CIA whistleblower with respect to "enhanced interrogation."[1] While Agee did assert the natural right of purportedly noble individuals to speak truth to power against the agency's cult of secrecy and insularity, what really set him apart from other angry spies was the way in which history in the making—the full sweep of contemporaneous events—wormed its way into his head and helped motivate and consolidate his turn, however he might later be judged.

When Agee left the CIA in 1969, it was still a relatively young organization, having been officially created by the National Security Act of 1947. But it was built on the rather unsteady foundations of the wartime Office of Strategic Services (OSS)—which had been, despite the legendary status it inspired then and continues to enjoy owing to the charitableness of nostalgia, an erratic seat-of-the-pants enterprise. The Cold War, of course, created a crucial demand for intelligence, prompted exponential growth in the CIA's personnel strength and budget, and afforded the agency immense traction and clout within the United States' national security bureaucracy. Furthermore, during the Eisenhower administration CIA Director Allen Dulles—fully supported by his older brother, Secretary of State John Foster Dulles—burnished its reputation with covert action that secured US-friendly regimes in Iran (1953), Guatemala (1954), and the Congo (January 1961). Yet the agency had performed poorly in the Korean War and embarrassed itself with the failed Bay of Pigs invasion of Cuba in April 1961. Rightly or wrongly, in the mid- to late 1960s its intelligence assessments were partially blamed for the United States' ongoing frustrations in Vietnam. By the early 1970s, the CIA was an underconfident institution, worried about its place in an open democracy and less sanguine than it appeared about the stalwartness of its second generation of officers.

In fact, a fair number of intelligence officers who were Agee's rough contemporaries were experiencing disillusionment. Some, of course, were imperturbable cold warriors for whom the twinned ends of planting capitalist democracy and extirpating Marxist-Leninist communism justified any effective means. Others took a more nuanced view, subscribing to the American mission in general. Conceding that US institutions—including the CIA—made mistakes that ranged from mere operational errors to major strategic ones, they resolved to remain part of the system for lack of any better alternative. For them, becoming malcontents or whistleblowers or, beyond that, traitors, were not viable options; they had careers as professional patriots that they were not about to upend. Recrimination and reconsideration might someday be warranted, but not while they were busy doing what had to be done for themselves as well as their country. Then there were irrepressibly disaffected intelligence officers. What they had seen in the world of shadows they had chosen to inhabit had intolerably unsettling psychological effects. Some simply opted out of the intelligence business, leaving behind what they perceived as a somehow wrongheaded or just bad life, choosing never to talk about it or address it further. They might have had particular experiences that were disillusioning and upsetting, such as recruiting an agent who wound up dead. Or they might have developed a broader philosophical sense that convincing vulnerable, needy people to commit treason—the meat and drink of spycraft—was either immoral or, in the martial countries that were the focus of the agency's attention, futile. Among officers leaving the CIA before retirement age, this variety was perhaps the most common. Very few felt compelled to do something about the putative iniquity of American spying. As David Corn has observed, "It's very rare that someone decides to confront that institution, expose what they think is wrong about it, and bring it to a halt."[2]

Agee was just that rare. His turn shocked and traumatized the CIA, which characterized him as its first defector.[3] Its institutional loathing of Agee, and its wariness of his story as precedent, have endured. To this day the CIA is sensitive to the public disclosure of information about Agee's activities. The Philip Agee Papers— the various and sundry documents that he accumulated between the time of his resignation from the CIA and his death in January 2008, central to the composition of this book—have been held at New York University's Tamiment Library/Robert F. Wagner Labor Archives since 2010, his wife Giselle Roberge Agee having donated them to the library. The papers were in his Havana apartment when he died in January 2008, and Michael Nash, then the Tamiment Library/Wagner Archives' associate curator, supervised their transport from Cuba to the United States. Owing to US restrictions on direct flights between the two countries, he arranged for the documents to be flown to Montreal by DHL and then transferred over land to New York. Unsurprisingly, the CIA and other government agencies got wind of these arrangements. When the flight stopped to refuel in Cincinnati, the CIA, the FBI, and other national security officials seized the papers, combed through all of them, and confiscated an appreciable number of documents before allowing the shipment to proceed to Montreal. They also appeared to tear out and retain a significant number of pages from Agee's datebooks from several years—especially in the 1990s and 2000s, when Agee was spending much of his time in Cuba—and to confiscate his 1980, 1989, 2002, 2003, and 2005 datebooks in their entirety.*

Agee was the only publicly disaffected American intelligence officer to confront the CIA on full-fledged ideological grounds and to oppose American strategy and foreign policy on a wholesale basis. He left the agency after twelve years as a case officer in Latin America, at least in part over his disenchantment with what he perceived as the CIA's undermining of liberal democracy to serve American eco-

---

* The US agencies indicated in writing the number of documents they had removed but did not specifically identify them. New York University initiated a lawsuit to have the documents released but eventually dropped it. The US government also sought to fine Michael Nash for circumventing federal licensing requirements but eventually relented. To the extent that Agee himself wished to eliminate documentary evidence of post-CIA activities inconsistent with his public representations, he might have culled his own files accordingly. The documents Agee obtained via his Freedom of Information Act (FOIA) request in the 1970s, which the US agencies left in place, remain the most probative primary materials on the relationship between Agee and the CIA. Where cited, I specify their location in the Agee Papers and indicate that they were obtained by FOIA request. Many of those documents have been declassified and are available on the CIA's website. I submitted wide-ranging FOIA requests regarding Agee to the CIA, the FBI, and the Department of State in 2010 and 2015. Although the agencies provided little that Agee had not obtained himself or which they had not already declassified and made publicly available, the FBI did furnish several newly disclosed documents that shed some light on its investigations of Agee; these are duly cited, mostly in chapter 7. The other agencies also provided a few scattered documents of interest, also cited. Since this book focuses on Agee's point of view, I have relied on secondary sources to account for the attitudes of other well-known figures rather than consulting any available collections of their papers or the like. Among the people who knew Agee well and were still alive as I was researching this book, his second wife, Giselle Roberge Agee, was fully cooperative. His first wife, Janet, passed away in 2006. Philip Agee Jr. was initially inclined to cooperate in my research for this book but backed away after a substantive exchange of e-mails and one meeting, perhaps concerned that the book might question Agee's motives and national loyalty. Christopher, Agee's youngest son, did not respond to my inquiries. Several of Agee's classmates from Jesuit High School in Tampa and from Notre Dame were forthcoming, as were Melvin Wulf, his longtime lawyer; Lynne Bernabei, the attorney who represented him in his libel action against Barbara Bush; and Michael Opperskalski, a left-wing journalist based in Cologne whom Agee befriended in the 1980s when he lived in West Germany. Others in his life who may have still been with us as I composed the book I was unable to find.

nomic and political interests. He later resolved to subvert that effort by writing a book—entitled *Inside the Company: CIA Diary*—setting forth his political and philosophical grievances, published first in the United Kingdom in early 1975 and about six months later in the United States. It would take him five years to write and would become the urtext of spy tell-all books. Unlike most other vocally unhappy CIA officers, he also declined to submit the book to the CIA for vetting and redaction, violating his agency employment agreement. Unlike any other such officers, he published the names of some 400 clandestine CIA officers, agents, and fronts. (A CIA "officer" is a US government civil servant employed by the agency. A CIA "agent" is an outside party clandestinely recruited by the CIA to advance CIA objectives.)

Published in 1975—the so-called Year of Intelligence—*Inside the Company* scandalized the agency, enraged its top management as well as its rank and file, and compromised its operations in the Western Hemisphere. The book and Agee's campaign to expose intelligence operatives and operations drew bipartisan opprobrium among American politicians—Barry Goldwater wanted Agee's citizenship revoked, and Joe Biden said he should go to jail.[4] For the rest of his life, Agee would continue, albeit with diminishing returns, his efforts to undermine CIA covert operations and other aspects of what he considered objectionable US policies.

There have been quite a few former intelligence officers who have turned against the CIA or some other federal intelligence agency. But Agee set himself apart from other government dissidents. Perhaps the most prominent one of that period was Daniel Ellsberg, who in 1971 published the Pentagon Papers—a classified study of the Vietnam War that revealed, among other things, the Johnson administration's undisclosed expansion of the war in spite of growing evidence of its military futility. In a 2016 piece in the *New Yorker*, Malcolm Gladwell drew a perceptive distinction between Ellsberg and Edward Snowden, who in 2013 exposed the breadth and depth of the National Security Agency's digital surveillance capabilities and practices. Gladwell pointed out that Ellsberg really remained a dedicated security professional—an insider who exposed secrets to show that the US government was ill-serving its own agenda and to spur remedial action.[5]

At least at the time he leaked the Pentagon Papers, Ellsberg was a whistleblower in the true and original sense: a conscientious patriot and dedicated institutionalist addressing a transgression in the government's execution of policy by using the only effective recourse—namely, public exposure—that he could discern. He and those like him stayed inside the envelope of the loyal opposition, if sometimes only barely. Some combination of the cumulative value of well-intentioned and narrowly targeted disclosures like Ellsberg's and the cumulative damage of broadly destructive ones like Agee's impelled Congress to pass the Whistleblower Protection Act of 1989, which, as amended, in effect expanded the lane for insiders to lodge complaints about legally or ethically questionable policy implementation by protecting those who stayed in that lane. This statutory scheme has encouraged legitimate whistleblowing complaints of significant consequence in American affairs of state—notably, in 2019, that of a CIA officer alarmed by President Donald Trump's apparent withholding of foreign assistance to Ukraine for his personal political gain, which led to Trump's impeachment.

The label "whistleblower" aptly applies to, say, William Binney, a former National Security Agency (NSA) intelligence officer who registered concerns about its surveillance program through designated channels. It does not comfortably describe Snowden, who by contrast was essentially a young contractor with digital aptitude who saw the World Wide Web in idealistic terms. He had no deep fealty to the US intelligence and security apparatus, and in his exposure acted as an interloper looking to compromise rather than cure it.[6] In a generally meticulous, peer-reviewed 2019 article, Kaeten Mistry casts Agee merely as the *primus inter pares* whistleblower and "insider dissident" among other "anti-imperial" intelligence officers, one who both nourished and was nourished by a substantial if informal transnational support network.[7] The network and the synergy existed, but the term "whistleblower" is certainly too tame to apply to Agee, and the label "anti-imperial" too bold to describe the additional disaffected government employees—including Ellsberg,

Frank Snepp, and John Stockwell—whom Mistry mentions. While there was no statute protecting whistleblowers in Agee's day, even if there had been it wouldn't have been a sufficient outlet for him. His grievances were wholesale, involving the CIA's entire raison d'être and the American project writ large. He was part of the opposition, but he was no longer loyal. Calling Agee a whistleblower thus seems to constitute at least a modest category mistake—a venial sin of overinclusion.[8] (He is also not a mere "leaker." Indeed, one recent book on that subject does not even mention him, leaping from Ellsberg to Snowden.[9]) Agee was in some ways less of an outsider than Snowden, but in paramount respects more of one. While he was a career intelligence officer who had some appreciation going in that he would have to get his hands dirty, he crucially differed from Snowden in that he did not see the governance problem he had uncovered as a narrow one that could be fixed by self-restraint at the margins; Agee objected to the American Project writ large.

Over the CIA's history, numerous spies have aired their complaints publicly, but Agee was among the first. Most, like Ellsberg, have harbored grievances about the execution of a particular program or institutional culture with an eye to fixing a generally defensible system. Victor Marchetti, once a very senior agency analyst, resigned in 1969—shortly after Agee did—and published his book, *The CIA and the Cult of Intelligence*, a year before Agee published *Inside the Company*. Marchetti impugned the agency's overall effectiveness and its arrogation of covert control; he was for a while somewhat sympathetic with Agee, but he acknowledged the need for a reoriented CIA.[10] Former CIA analyst Frank Snepp thought the Americans withdrew from South Vietnam too shambolically in 1975, selling out Vietnamese locals who had helped them, but he chafes at suggestions that he and Agee are remotely equivalent.[11] John Stockwell, another ex–case officer, illuminated the counterproductive nature of CIA support for military operations in "secret wars," but he didn't dump on the entire American enterprise even though he became a friend of Agee.[12]

More recent critics from within have had even narrower, smaller-bore grievances and less time for Agee. For instance, Glenn Carle, a senior CIA case officer, resigned and chronicled the inefficacy, cruelty, and immorality of the CIA's "enhanced interrogation"—that is, torture—program for al-Qaeda suspects.[13] He considers someone like Stockwell a mere "malcontent" with some legitimate complaints, himself a pro-American idealist, Agee (or Snowden) a near-sociopathic traitor. "I oppose torture. I strongly support the mission of, and most of the officers in, the Agency. However many errors the United States makes in policy choices and operational acts, that doesn't in any way affect my loyalty to and support for the overall mission of the CIA in U.S. foreign policy."[14] He and most other disaffected ex-CIA officers have not undergone sweeping ideological conversions.

Agee raised the alarm not about a particular practice or policy but rather about the CIA's to him dubious role as an undemocratic enforcer of a democratic nation's interests. He is the only former case officer to systematically expose the identities of intelligence officers and assets to the public, damaging their careers and theoretically jeopardizing their lives. But he is more complicated than a mere villain. He is a figure of profound ambivalence and considerable subtlety, and a more sympathetic character than the likes of the mercenary, soulless Ames, though that is an admittedly low bar. Since November 2016, Agee has become a more resonant and ominous figure. American politics and government have arguably reached their lowest point: lower than the escalating Vietnam years of a Johnson administration that at least spawned sixties idealism, lower than the apocryphal "malaise" of the Jimmy Carter years, even lower than the post-9/11 paranoia, grandiosity, and ineptitude of George W. Bush's presidency. The election of a true American abomination—especially one intent on gutting the legacy of a largely admirable predecessor—presents many Americans with a country of which it is hard to be proud. And it makes salient the question of what national and international circumstances might prompt a person—particularly one whose very profession is applied patriotism—to turn against his or her government. The one epoch in the past seventy-five years almost as bleak as the tenure of Donald Trump was the sordidly deflating post-Watergate period, when Agee decided to expose CIA officers and agents. It was a veritable golden age of intelligence officer disaffection, yielding Snepp, Stockwell, and others.

Certainly another Agee could emerge. Reality Winner, a former Air Force intelligence and NSA contract linguist prosecuted under the Espionage Act in 2018 for leaking an intelligence report confirming Russia's hack of the 2016 election, acted partly on the basis of her progressive politics and dislike of Trump. Jeffrey Sterling's travails with the CIA stemmed from what he perceived as systemic racial discrimination. These people were not mere whistleblowers. Agee and those of his vintage walked what Graham Greene—himself a British intelligence officer during the Second World War—famously called "the giddy line midway." Greene appropriated the notion from Robert Browning's long poem "Bishop Blougram's Apology." The relevant lines are these:

> Our interest's on the dangerous edge of things
> The honest thief, the tender murderer,
> The superstitious atheist, demirep
> That loves and saves her soul in new French books–
> We watch while these in equilibrium keep
> The giddy line midway.

In contemporary American vernacular, "giddy" suggests giggly or overeager, but Browning—and Greene—understood the word to mean, in its Victorian sense, vertiginous. Greene applied this part of the poem, which he called "an epigraph for all the novels I have written," particularly to spies, including the legendary MI6 mole Kim Philby, with whom he remained ambivalently sympathetic. Greene considered disloyalty quite human, and therefore forgivable. Novelist and journalist Lawrence Osborne has commented that holding "the giddy line midway"—that is, wavering between duty and transgression—describes many of Greene's protagonists and encapsulates "the enigma of betrayal" that so fascinated him.[15] It also describes Philip Agee pretty well. For at least three years, he harbored doubts about the agency's agenda, contemplated abandoning it, yet dutifully prosecuted its mission; then he liberated himself along an almost equally unstable tangent until, at length, he became a dedicated dissident and an agitator for life.

AMERICAN GRAFFITI

A white Christian American male born in 1935, like Philip Burnett Franklin Agee, was likely to feel he had a geopolitically charmed life. He would have been too young to have risked his life in World War II, and he'd have fallen just short of military age for the Korean War too. His father had been too old for the big one, so his family was intact. The United States had entered that war a reluctant, even resentful, isolationist nation and emerged from it the greatest among the great powers. The Soviet Union was a formidable enemy, but it was also a starkly alien one that was easy to oppose with enduring alacrity. America also had a head start in the Cold War militarily, economically, and ideologically. Yet, in the nuclear age, major wars that called on all of a great power's resources seemed too dangerous—too inhuman—to undertake except as a last resort. As young American men of Agee's vintage came of age, in the early 1950s, most would feel privileged to be frontline soldiers in what would largely be a war of ideas, fought more with guile than bullets. If you wanted to be part of the fight in the Cold War, to be a true patriot, you could do so without putting yourself too directly in the way of lethal harm. You could become a spy.

So it was for Agee, and become a spy was what he did. He was descended from Huguenot nobility who fled anti-Protestant religious persecution in France to the Netherlands after Louis XIV revoked the Edict of Nantes in 1685. The first of his ancestors to emigrate to America, in the 1690s, was Mathieu Agé. He settled in Virginia, and all of the Agee men preceding Philip had been born there.[16] Agee himself was born in Takoma Park, Maryland, on January 19, 1935. When he was two, his family decamped to Tampa, Florida. His father, William Burnett Franklin Agee, known as Bill and born in Roanoke, was a self-made man who did not complete high school. Bill and his father—Philip Agee's grandfather—parlayed a small laundering and dry cleaning business into a citywide enterprise that included linen supply and uniform rental. MacDill Air Force Base was nearby, and Bill Agee expanded the company in considerable part by meeting its demand for clean uniforms. Socially well-connected, the Agees lived in a large and well-appointed home in the Palma Ceia neighborhood southwest of the downtown area, right next to the golf course of the Palma Ceia Golf & Country Club.

At some point, Agee's forebears had converted to Catholicism. Bill Agee and Helen Agee (née O'Neill) were solidly Catholic, and Agee was an altar boy at Christ the King Catholic Church. By the time the son entered high school, the father was a millionaire, which meant something in the late 1940s. He was also a proverbial pillar of the community. The Agees belonged to the Tampa Yacht & Country Club and the University Club as well as the Palma Ceia Golf & Country Club. Bill was a founder and board member of the Tampa and Florida Laundrymen's Association, and a member of the Tampa Merchants' Association, the Tampa Round Table, the Tampa Chamber of Commerce, the American Red Cross, and the Hillsborough County Tuberculosis Association. He served as president of the Tampa Rotary Club. He was an especially enthusiastic member of the Ye Mystic Krewe of Gasparilla, a community outreach and cultural enrichment organization founded in 1904 and "dedicated to enriching the vitality and imagination of Tampa and the surrounding community," and he reveled in showing photographs of himself marching in a pirate costume in the YMKG's massive annual parade. He was also an accomplished fisherman, yachtsman, and painter.[17] Philip Agee had one sibling, his older sister Barbara, who married and went by Barbara Agee Steelman. She was a talented pianist, attended the Juilliard School in New York, and eventually taught music at Florida State University. Barbara lived in Orlando in her later years and died in 1999 at age sixty-six.[18] She evidently had little contact with her brother as an adult.

Philip Agee went to Jesuit High School, an independent Catholic secondary school in Tampa, which hosted a substantial Cuban immigrant community in its Ybor City neighborhood, northeast of the downtown area. The antagonism between the United States and

Cuba's communist government was at the root of Agee's grievances against the CIA. But when he was in high school, in the late 1940s and early 1950s, Fidel Castro's revolutionary movement had not yet taken hold in Cuba. It would not begin until July 1953, would not gain cross-class support until early 1957, and would not dislodge Cuban President Fulgencio Batista until January 1959.[19] Before that, most Cubans who immigrated to the United States did so for economic rather than political reasons. Although Agee might have been aware of Batista's indifference to Cuba's widespread poverty, his flamboyant and expensive tastes, and his courtship of American organized crime, the few Cuban-American students that Jesuit High drew in from Ybor City would not have imbued Agee with any acute anticommunist sentiment.

He was a model student, participating in several clubs—including the Key Club (promoting community leadership), the Sodality Club (promoting Catholic fraternity), the Masque Club (drama), and the National Forensics League (debate)—and getting elected to student government. Like his sister, he played the piano. Agee played football and basketball and ran track, but Jesuit was a small school— his class size was only thirty-six—and most of the students were on sports teams; he was by no means a major jock. He graduated with honors in 1952 and was near the top of his class academically. In his senior yearbook, a narrative history of his class acknowledged his elite status, his achievement having accelerated during his junior and senior years: "JAMES LAMBERT led the class all four years. But keen was the competition to unseat him and many came close to doing it. JERRY ROBBINS and PAUL ANTINORI were always threatening, and in later years TOM MULLEN and PHIL AGEE were to come near doing it."[20]

Timothy Twomey was a close high school friend of Agee's whose father served as Tampa's city attorney for eighteen years. He remembers Agee wistfully and to an extent idealized him back in the day. "He was anything but an egghead. He was outgoing and as popular with the ladies as with the men."[21] In the senior class will, Agee bequeathed to Louis Lambert his "dreamy smile (a hit with all the fair sex)."[22] At the same time, Agee was "highly intelligent" and "witty."

Though upper middle class, Twomey and Agee were not snobs: after school, they hung around more with students from Plant High School, the public secondary school, than with Jesuit enrollees. Agee had conventionally centrist American views and, according to Twomey, would engage a "hippie type" they knew later, at the University of Florida, in political debate and just "eat him alive." Clearly Agee did not drift too far from his parents' moderate conservative position on the political spectrum. He also possessed the kind of mischievous streak popularly associated—think *American Graffiti*—with fifties youth. Twomey recalled that while cruising Tampa's Bay Shore Boulevard in Agee's vintage 1930s Plymouth, Agee would veer the car up onto the sidewalk just for shock value. During the winter holiday season, they would also insinuate themselves into publicly displayed life-size "Christmas cards," posing with mocked-up choir members and the like. Not wild, exactly, but playful. "He was a fun-loving guy," Twomey insisted. He also noted Agee's gameness in participating keenly in sports even though, except as a runner, he was not a gifted athlete, never starting on a varsity team but practicing hard every day.[23] Calibrated naughtiness notwithstanding, Agee was basically a square.

Twomey became a businessman, running a port management firm out of Charleston, South Carolina, and representing steamship companies including major carriers like Maersk. When *Inside the Company* came out, he had not seen Agee since shortly before he went into the CIA. Politically a moderate conservative, Twomey was "just floored," "stunned," and "could not believe" the anti-American sentiments Agee expressed. He found himself "wondering what in the world could have happened to him that would have twisted him so dramatically" and was compelled to read the book very carefully in hopes of getting the answer. He noted, forty years later, that Agee did not express dissatisfaction with US foreign policy until several hundred pages into the text, yet by its end seemed happy to ruin lives by revealing the names of hundreds of intelligence officers and agents. "Page after page after page. My God," he exclaimed. Twomey did not decipher the explanation he'd hoped to uncover. Agee had been "anything but a crazy, wild, reckless person." But he still marveled at Agee's wit, recalling his quip, in response to a US official's observation that his running a travel agency from Cuba was illegal, that running a stop sign was illegal, too.[24]

Agee struck other high school classmates as a rather aloof young man and not a campus luminary. "I don't remember Phil palling around with anybody," recalled Donald Hess, a classmate and fellow member of the debate team, in 2016. "I think he wasn't really comfortable with people. He was, if not a loner, at least a semi-loner." Hess rated Agee "smart, sharp, and quick," though "quiet." A political liberal, Hess was glancingly sympathetic with Agee's turn against the CIA but not terribly interested in his plight and understood why many considered him a traitor. When he heard about his former classmate's troubles following the publication of *Inside the Company*, he essentially shrugged and did not read the book. "Phil was not the kind of warm, fuzzy guy that you would cry over at his funeral. The signals he sent out suggested that you weren't welcome."[25] Judging by the testimony of Twomey and Hess, Agee had the ability to project both warmth and remove. Case officers need at once to gain the confidence of potential agents and to stave off their suspicions, so this dual quality would have served Agee well in his career. But it also suggested a man with an agenda sometimes at odds with his outward behavior.

While Agee was an upperclassman at Tampa Jesuit, Wisconsin Senator Joseph McCarthy's popularity as the nation's principal extirpator of communism was peaking. Although his inquisitions were generally in line with a national presumption that the Soviet Union was comprehensively targeting and rampantly infiltrating American institutions and society, his Gallup poll "favorable" ratings never exceeded 50 percent. In June 1954, as Agee finished his sophomore year at the University of Notre Dame, McCarthy's star fell after Army lawyer Joseph Welch epically chastised him during televised Senate committee hearings for gratuitously smearing a young lawyer at his firm. President Eisenhower considered the senator a demagogue, and Agee's father was an Eisenhower Republican. Agee himself would not have resisted McCarthy's defrocking. He was likely developing a more tempered and nuanced view of the Soviet threat than typical of even a slightly older person. John Foster Dulles's near-religious characterization of the Cold War as a Manichean confrontation between Christianity and "godless communism" and his messianic zeal in confronting it were giving way to a measured and technocratic approach, a more refined version of containment and deterrence. McCarthyism revealed that the Soviet threat was highly susceptible to exaggeration and political exploitation. That threat remained a standing challenge, to be sure, but one requiring considered and objective assessment and hard choices.[26]

Historians have properly revised the mythical portrayal of 1950s as a halcyon, ideologically static decade.[27] But most of its participants tended to see it that way and act accordingly, oblivious to liminal influences uncovered later. The Soviet-American confrontation stayed fervidly pitched, as Dulles sought to deter Soviet expansion of seemingly all varieties with the threat of nuclear "massive retaliation." The CIA lurched well beyond intelligence collection with covert operations culminating in outright coups in Iran and Guatemala. This generally blinkered and semipanicked tenor was understandable and forgivable—nobody knew how to manage nuclear weapons since they were unprecedented, and the United States had never before faced a strategic challenge of the magnitude posed by the Soviet Union. These factors would have suppressed or attenuated any liberal impulses in college students of Agee's ilk: middle class and with a comfortable social station that adherence to political norms would secure. Yet they were not the elite Ivy Leaguers anointed in 1945 as the stewards of America's postwar geopolitical preeminence, the inheritors of those, in Dean Acheson's phrase, "present at the creation." Their unstinting loyalty could be presumptively assured but not guaranteed in perpetuity.

THE FIFTIES AT NOTRE DAME

Though Agee was perhaps not the most pious of Catholics, the religion certainly took hold in his thinking and outlook. In high school, he was a member of the relatively small Sodality Club, which aimed to foster brotherhood among Catholics, consolidate their spirituality, and promote Catholic charity. Participation in the club involved daily prayers and devotions, mass once a week, and meetings with other sodalist groups including an annual convention. For his undergraduate studies, Agee chose Notre Dame. It is not a Jesuit institution, but it is of the equally devout Congregation of Holy Cross order and during Agee's time on campus was governed by Holy Cross priests. There Agee continued along the path of high achievement and keen political and civic engagement. He was elected to the Student Senate, joined the International Relations Club, was on the advisory council for the College of Arts and Letters, and would graduate cum laude in philosophy. John Manion, a classmate and close college friend, noted that Agee "was meetinged to death; he was always going to a meeting."[28] Agee was also a member of the Confraternity of Christian Doctrine and briefly considered becoming a priest.[29]

Notre Dame was renowned for its vision of Catholicism as an international force for good. At the college, this notion was manifested in two distinct and to a significant extent divergent types. On one hand, there were those who amounted to anticommunist missionaries like Tom Dooley, a legendary 1948 graduate, doctor, naval officer, and humanitarian whose charitable work with refugees in Indochina in the 1950s reputedly helped firm up US influence and stave off the ideological advance of communism. On the other, there were those who aspired to improving lives without ulterior geopolitical motives, colonial or neo-imperial, consistent with the Catholic liberation theology that was arising in Latin America in the 1950s. Agee felt the pull of both types. But his slow subsequent evolution, which would cross the liberalizing moment in 1962–65 of the Second Vatican Council under Pope John XXIII—Vatican II—suggests that Catholic liberation theology was the influence that ultimately roosted. Tim Rutten, a sympathetic journalist, would report his discovery, through post-CIA conversations with Agee, that they "had similar backgrounds: socially concerned Catholic families, Jesuit friends and an interest in liberation theology."[30]

The Korean War was under way as Agee's class of about 1,450 males entered Notre Dame as freshmen in 1952, but it was not controversial in the epochal way that the Vietnam War was a generation later. The university administration was fixed firmly in the political mainstream, and political differences within the faculty were muted. Donald Brophy, a classmate of Agee's, does not recall ever hearing a single voice on campus opposing the war in principle. Brophy remembered that, walking on campus for the first time and approaching the domed Main Building, he spotted a vaguely familiar figure among a small crowd of people on the steps. As he neared the crowd, he saw that the man was Dwight Eisenhower, then the Republican nominee for president. Brophy later learned that several professors had issued a statement supporting Adlai Stevenson, twice Eisenhower's Democratic opponent—most faculty members in those years were conservative theologically but mildly liberal politically—and identifying themselves as Notre Dame faculty. The Eisenhower campaign complained that the university was taking a partisan stance. Theodore M. Hesburgh—then in the first year of his long and storied tenure as president of Notre Dame—vowed that the professors did not speak for the university and shrewdly invited Eisenhower to a photo opportunity with the golden dome, ensuring the school's bona fides with the political camp of most of its alumni.[31]

The majority of faculty and students at Notre Dame acquiesced to the US government's rationale for the United States' intervention in Korea. "For most of us, the American presence in Korea was taken as a response to naked aggression by North Korea," according to Brophy. "In addition, it was a struggle carried on in the name of the United Nations, which gave it further justification. It wasn't just an American war. Of course by 1952, when my class entered Notre Dame, the war had been going on for quite some time and the American people were getting weary of the seeming stalemate. Eisenhower won the '52 election in part because he promised to go to Korea after the election and see what he could do. The only expressed unhappiness came from the right-wing hawks who supported MacArthur and complained because Truman called it a 'police action' instead of a war, and because the U.S. and the UN finally settled for something less than total victory."[32] McCarthyism was peaking, with Joseph Welch's scolding still nearly two years away. The Rosenbergs had been convicted and faced execution. Many freshmen signed up for ROTC to maintain a patriotic facade while avoiding being drafted and sent to Korea. Late afternoons saw massed units of undergraduates in uniform, marching. Agee, however, was not among them. Brophy himself quit ROTC before his junior year, after the Korean armistice was signed.

Despite the omnipresent Cold War backdrop, the Notre Dame campus mood did not rise (or descend) to the level of patriotic extremism or jingoism. Notre Dame students almost universally supported America's role in the Cold War. They tended to identify strongly as Catholics. Many, for instance, were steeped in images of Cardinal Jozsef Mindszenty being tortured, tried, and imprisoned in Hungary, and they exulted in his release from prison during the Hungarian Revolution of 1956.[33] The Catholic strain in Notre Dame students was manifested in a couple of different ways. The first was piety, practiced by those who see religion as a spiritual path advanced by a relationship with God. The Notre Dame campus—while all-male and fairly jock-heavy—resonated with this trait back in the 1950s, certainly more so than it does today. Daily mass attendance was high; there were chapels in every residence hall. A religious bulletin was slipped under each student's door three times a week. It wasn't unusual for students, while strolling back from class, to stop into Sacred Heart Church for a short, silent "visit."

Then there was a more subtle social-action strain of Catholicism, reflected in those who saw religion as a moral imperative to care for the community and the world in general, as articulated in the New Testament's Beatitudes (Matt. 5:3–12). A person might embrace this aspect of Catholicism without being especially or overtly pious.[34] The democratic socialist writer Michael Harrington took this path. Though he later claimed to be an atheist, he was a longtime editor for the *Catholic Worker* and wrote *The Other America*, which helped inspire President Lyndon Johnson's war on poverty. Another social-action adherent was Martin McLaughlin, who at Notre Dame joined a cell of Catholic Action, a fledgling international movement that centered on worker rights and antipoverty initiatives.[35] Dooley, who was Harrington's high school classmate in St. Louis and attended

Notre Dame from 1944 to 1948, exhibited both strains. He presented himself as socially conscious, setting up jungle hospitals in Southeast Asia, as well as personally pious, recalling in lectures upon his return to his alma mater how he relished praying at Notre Dame's Grotto.

Agee was not a dedicated churchgoer but appeared to be at least a social-action Catholic, as he later testified to the value he placed in Catholic social teaching in his books. For example, in the mid-1980s, he would provisionally attribute his dissidence to his Jesuit training in high school:

> Years later after being asked many times why I decided to write a book, I wondered if the Jesuits had something to do with it. Perhaps it was something from those early formative years. I remembered how they drilled into you the moral dimension, i.e., the need always to perceive and act on the difference between how things are and how they ought to be, how as an individual I am, and how I should or could be. My duty was to try to close the gap. I'd like to blame the Jesuits, they're an easy target, both for my decision to enter the CIA and for my decision to speak out. Activists, that's what they make of their kids.[36]

Agee's major was philosophy—a course of study that, at Notre Dame, was then strongly oriented toward Catholic teachings, including both the Aristotelian natural theology of St. Thomas Aquinas and Catholic liberation theology. Agee certainly would have absorbed a smattering of modern Catholic social teachings, for which his Jesuit high school training would have supplied him with a solid foundation. But while there was general acknowledgment in the 1950s that in nearly all of Latin America an entrenched Catholic Church worked hand-in-glove with repressive governments, Latin America, however sad, was also far away and of marginal concern— an attitude Brophy in retrospect attributed partly to racism. As he remembered it sixty years later, liberal and conservative students alike tended to accept government statements that communists were threatening to take over certain countries, and they regarded such impending takeovers uncritically as sufficient justification for right-wing coups. "We were proud that 'our side' had found a way to oust troublemakers."[37] The CIA-engineered coups in Iran in 1953 and Guatemala in 1954 didn't noticeably tweak any nerves, nor did resolute American opposition to Castro's attacks on and ultimate ouster of Batista in Cuba, America's eventual *bête noire*. José Napoleon Duarte—who would become the strongman president of El Salvador, recipient of comprehensive Reagan administration support, and CIA asset in the 1980s—was an engineering graduate of Notre Dame.

Nevertheless, the domestic ferment of the 1950s—evidence of its often ignored strain of social dynamism—certainly would have encouraged in Agee a latent social activism susceptible to being triggered by the more pitched social protest of the 1960s. The civil rights movement was just gaining momentum during Agee's Notre Dame years. *Brown v. Board of Education*, the school desegregation case, was decided in 1954. The Montgomery, Alabama, bus boycott began in late 1955. Lunch counter sit-ins were popping up nationally. Eisenhower sent federal troops to Little Rock to desegregate the city's Central High School in 1957, the year following Agee's college graduation. Although the Notre Dame student body was lily-white, there was a substantial reservoir of sympathy for African Americans. While large-scale student protests hadn't arisen there, political discussion was abundant: Catholics, too, had suffered from discrimination in an earlier American era. Yet the second, politically normalized incarnation of the Ku Klux Klan had been extraordinarily strong in Indiana during the 1930s—its enrollment was higher there than in any other state—and white-robed Klansmen not infrequently demonstrated outside the university gates in those days.[38]

Hesburgh was appointed to the Civil Rights Commission in 1957 and served with distinction through two presidents. At the same time, stiff-backed pacifism was very low on the Catholic agenda during the 1950s. Cardinal Francis Spellman was still visiting the troops overseas, blessing their guns and tanks. Thomas Merton, at his monastery in Kentucky, was beginning to write about pacifism, but it hadn't gained much traction among young Catholics. They might have admired the poet Robert Lowell for citing his Catholicism as the reason for being a conscientious objector during World War II, but Brophy could remember no classmates planning to go that route.[39] There was general agreement that the United States and other nuclear powers needed to "control" atomic energy and use it for "peaceful purposes," beating swords into ploughshares. And there was dismay among left-leaning students and faculty when John Foster Dulles in the late fifties spoke of taking the United States to the "brink of war." But opposition to brinkmanship was not the same as agitating to ban the bomb. In any case, most students let it pass.

Over virtually any American college campus, the Cold War cast a bigger shadow in the 1950s than it did in any other epoch. Among other factors, nuclear deterrence had not yet reached the stable if perverse equilibrium of mutual assured destruction, and the prospect of a nuclear first strike, implicit in the peremptory doctrine of "massive retaliation," loomed very large. Owing to the tension and fear that this brooding reality created, existential dread developed in the United States during Agee's college years. On an Ivy League campus, it tended to engender steely determination. But at Notre Dame it was more likely to breed youthful nervousness and uncertainty.

THE CIA BY DEFAULT

Notre Dame students also acquiesced in the CIA's recruiting presence on campus. It was discreet and not prominently in evidence, at least until activists in the sixties and seventies—including Agee—exposed and condemned it. It was common knowledge that national security and law-enforcement agencies liked to recruit Catholic college graduates because they were so dependably anticommunist. But it was the celebratedly upright, uptight, and middle-class FBI—and not the opaque and patrician CIA—that looked hardest at Catholic university students. From the early 1940s, the bureau recruited heavily from Jesuit institutions on the view that they cultivated the kind of "Christian manhood" required of the ideal G-man.[40]

At Notre Dame, as in high school, Agee excelled academically and was elected to the student government. As a senior he was chairman of the Washington's Birthday exercises, when the university gave its Patriots Award to General Curtis LeMay—the commander of the Air Force's Strategic Air Command, the United States' main nuclear force.[41] LeMay's aggressive and unyielding attitude had earned him the nicknames "Old Iron Pants," "Big Cigar," "The Iron Eagle," and later "Bombs Away LeMay." Agee graduated cum laude, thirteenth in his class. As Twomey indicated and Manion confirmed, his demeanor was bluff and cheerful, and at times a little jaunty and mischievous, but never to the point of risking his standing as a sturdily decent, even exemplary, young man. He had a medium build, thick, dark hair, heavy eyebrows, a wide mouth, and thin lips. His look was neat and squared-away and might have approached handsome. Broadly, he fit the evolving profile of the case officer.

Yet Agee did not sign up for an interview when the CIA came to Notre Dame in spring 1956. A campus recruiter, apparently prompted by a family friend in the agency who had encouraged Agee to consider a CIA career, tracked him down anyway. The recruiter had been fully briefed about Agee's background and accomplishments, including student government and academic honors, and encouraged him to consider a career in the agency. Agee demurred in favor of the University of Florida College of Law, which had already accepted him. Over the summer, he returned to Tampa to work in the family laundry business. He told Twomey about the CIA's overture at Notre Dame, and about his law school plan. "I knew that would never last," said Twomey in 2016. "Phil was much too bright and had much too much on the ball to last in the law business. Not that there's anything wrong with that because it's very lucrative, but Phil had better things to do."[42]

In the event, he found law school dull and superficial and stayed only three months. Going into the family's business, though it would have been comfortable, did not excite him either; he had rejected business administration as a college major, preferring philosophy. But, having tentative ideas about marrying Janet Wasserberger, whom he had started dating during college, he wanted some stability. So Agee revived the CIA contact and was approved for the CIA's Junior Officer Trainee Program (subsequently renamed the

Career Trainee Program). He was "happy" when he opened the letter by which he was provisionally accepted, according to John Manion, who was in his room with him at the time. "It was a coveted job, and a cause for joy."[43]

His satisfaction notwithstanding, Agee's decision to join the agency in 1956 was nothing like a revelatory epiphany nor the logical outcome of a personal moral and political crusade. There was no eureka moment. Rather, what was clearly an ambivalent, tentative, and protracted decision on Agee's part reflects a brand of patriotism that was highly calculated and calibrated. He was interested in world affairs as a child of the Cold War and thought it was right to serve his country. There was still a draft, and though it was somnolent in the wake of the Korean War, the prospect of its reenergization hovered ominously over the eligible population and spurred voluntary enlistment. Agee wanted to avoid the scut work and grunt combat that draftees were apt to endure. CIA training and cover for the Directorate of Operations involved Officers' Candidate School and abbreviated military service (for Agee, in the Air Force) that would fulfill any statutory military obligation.[44] He also had a more affirmative and emotional reason. Agee's second wife, Giselle Roberge Agee, would meet and get to know Agee in Paris. She would see how the city catered to his cosmopolitan tastes and witness him sustain a post-CIA life of considerable intrigue. From her later standpoint, he must have found the prospect of life as a spy "very glamorous."[45]

Twomey, who was completing his undergraduate degree at the University of Florida, saw quite a bit of Agee during the semester he attended the law school and registered the abruptness of his departure for the military. Twomey considered Agee a preternaturally talented person and didn't believe Agee was going to settle for a regimented career in the Air Force any more than he believed his friend was going to be a sedate Tampa lawyer. "There was no way in hell that Phil Agee was going into the Air Force. I remembered the CIA comment that he'd made to me, that they'd offered him a job. So I said to myself, 'if Phil Agee is in the Air Force, he's in the CIA.'"[46] From Twomey's vantage, Agee made sense as a spy.

The upshot is that it was more Agee's romantic temperament and self-regard than his religious or political commitment to the American way that conditioned him for service in the CIA. In his own recollection, he is cagey as to his initial motivation. He admits that it was not the image of the prototypical gentleman spy who served his country out of noblesse oblige that attracted him, as a Notre Dame student, to the CIA. But he does claim that his operative role model was Tom Dooley, then seen as a pious, social-action Catholic. In a later manuscript provisionally entitled "The CIA for Beginners: 100 Questions," he noted that when Dooley came to the university to speak in 1955, his "fire and brimstone" religious appeal to "fight communism" so moved Agee that he "entered the CIA the following year to join the fight."[47]

This inspirational account does not really square with Agee's desultory decision process and initial lack of enthusiasm. But it's easy to see how Agee might have talked himself into elevating Dooley's influence as a matter of post hoc justification. Lionized with the help of his autobiographical book *Deliver Us From Evil*, published in 1956, Dooley was a popular hero—the seventh-most admired man in the world, according to a 1957 Gallup poll.[48] His early death from cancer at age thirty-four, in 1961, gave him the whiff of the martyr. President Kennedy awarded him a posthumous Medal of Freedom and cited Dooley as a foundational example for the Peace Corps. A statue of Dooley still stands in the Grotto along with an engraved letter he wrote to Hesburgh. The Dr. Tom Dooley Society of Notre Dame awards current Notre Dame students and graduates stipends to participate in international medical mission trips. He was then, and to some extent remains, a formidable figure. But his legend was built before Graham Greene had written *The Quiet American* and before the dubiousness of American intrigue in Indochina had fully registered.

There is an additional layer of irony, perhaps calculated, to Agee's placing Dooley on a pedestal. In 1979, Jim Winters, in *Notre Dame Magazine*, revealed that Dooley's charitable work with refugees in Vietnam and Laos in the 1950s—first as a naval officer, then as a civilian doctor under the auspices of the International Rescue Committee—was part of a covert CIA counterinsurgency effort orchestrated by the legendary Edward Lansdale. In particular, Dooley apprised US intelligence officers of troop movements, ammunition shipments, and villagers' statements: an "ambiguous legacy."[49] In 1983, ex-CIA dissident Ralph McGehee, who would become a friend of Agee, also detailed his own personal knowledge of Dooley's duplicity about communist atrocities and broader involvement in CIA psychological operations in his book *Deadly Deceits*.[50] Eight years later, a targeted takedown by Diana Shaw in the *Los Angeles Times* argued that the US government had pressured Dooley into spreading disinformation on pain of revealing his homosexuality. Shaw argued credibly that Dooley's claims, especially about his post-military good works, were self-serving exaggerations, his reports of communist atrocities outright lies, and his media blitz shamelessly deceptive self-promotion.[51]

INTO THE FRAY

Given Agee's ambivalence at the time of his recruitment and his enigmatic attempt to cast Dooley as a role model, it is at least clear that Agee lacked the confident secular swagger of the anointed that characterized men like Allen Dulles, Desmond FitzGerald, Frank Wisner, and other legends of the agency's first generation. He recalled that he left college and embarked on his CIA career with some cultural trepidation. He wondered what it would be like "to live without the religion and discipline of the university" but still intent on living "the virtuous life of the good Catholic" in "constant fear" of dying "by accident with a mortal sin on my soul," condemned to "eternity in hell." He found consolation in his association with institutions: "After having to take all those courses on religion the only person to blame, if I really don't make it, will be me. It is the discipline and religion that makes Notre Dame men different, and after four years of training I ought to be able to do better."[52] He had Catholicism, Notre Dame, and now the CIA to gird him to the world's challenges.

As the 1950s proceeded, America's vaunted postwar status did start to show fissures. The United States' nuclear monopoly, of course, was gone by 1949, its exclusive possession of thermonuclear weapons by 1955. All the while, however, a tacit assumption prevailed that the United States would always outpace an intellectually decadent Soviet Union in designing and implementing military technology such that Moscow could not match it. In October 1957, shortly after Agee entered the CIA's Junior Officer Trainee Program to become a case officer, the Soviets' launch of the *Sputnik I* satellite, which technologically implied a Soviet intercontinental ballistic missile capability, put the lie to that assumption. The United States now had a technological and scientific peer-competitor as its principal strategic adversary, and its eventual victory in the Cold War did not seem as certain as it had before. Instantly, any discretionary room for doubt in the American strategic project among mainstream citizens shrank. The garden-variety American's instinct for total, unquestioning fidelity to nation was reinforced.

Agee's loyal disposition in particular would have intensified by virtue of his strong performance as a CIA career trainee. His training period, including six months of operational orientation and exercises at the agency's fabled "Farm" at Camp Peary, Virginia, ran from 1956 through 1960. His supervisor's Training and Evaluation Report from July 1957 portrayed an enthusiastic initiate, whose zealousness for the agency's mission if anything needed to be constrained and grounded. "Mr. Agee's overall presentation of substantive material was forceful and effective," he wrote. "In a few instances gaps in his knowledge and facts were evident, but these did not lower the quality of his overall performance." The section entitled "Report of Observations, Judgments, and Impressions" stated that "Mr. Agee has a tendency to make . . . statements which have no basis in fact. In one instance he missed the real point of the problem. However, his interest and enthusiasm were high at all times. Perhaps he could profit from further training in objective analysis."[53] As he gained experience, his judiciousness came to match his verve: Agee's performance evaluations were invariably above average. He was up to the job and often enjoyed it, and he didn't leave the agency on the mere pretext of an ideological change of heart.

2

The Young Spy

Given his background and practical motivations, Agee would have gone into the agency not as a crusading patrician leader—of which then–CIA Director Allen Dulles was the prototype—but rather as a dutiful middle-class follower. In the long run, this status probably made him more susceptible to subversive attitudes: many case officers of his vintage were ideologically rigidified by the idea that spying for America was a matter of noblesse oblige.

The CIA, formally established as an independent federal agency by the National Security Act of 1947, sprang from the wartime Office of Strategic Services (OSS) led by William "Wild Bill" Donovan, a Medal of Honor recipient in World War I and Wall Street lawyer. He was the OSS's first and only director, serving from 1942 until the organization was disbanded in 1945. Although he never officially worked for the CIA, he trained many of its first-generation officers, and his legacy loomed large figuratively as well as literally. His statue graces CIA headquarters at Langley. Donovan was an Irish-American from Buffalo, New York, and a self-identified and fairly observant Catholic. He brought to the OSS a strong sense of mission. But he was not so much interested in Catholic doctrine or rituals as he was sensitized to Catholicism's social costs. He was seriously considered to be Herbert Hoover's attorney general but rejected on the view that an Irish Catholic would not support Prohibition. A predominantly Protestant society seemed fearful of the Catholic Church's permeating mode of social and political influence. And in fact this cast of mind informed what Donovan called a "religious approach" to intelligence work. During World War II, he cultivated operational OSS relationships with American Catholic leaders and with the publicly neutral Vatican itself (including Pope Pius XII). He came to regard the sociopolitical salience of religion writ large as a ubiquitous and cost-free diplomatic tool and military weapon, with its mastery by the CIA essential. A kind of Catholic fervor may have impelled Donovan himself: before the Second World War he had been an outspoken advocate of Catholic public service. But his religion manifested itself in OSS and later CIA spycraft as an operational imperative to co-opt and manipulate believers of any powerful religion or sect—Christians, Jews, Muslims, Hindus, or Buddhists; Catholics or Protestants, Sunnis or Shi'ites—that is, psychological warfare in the service of American interests. Donovan's priority was a "generalizable theory of religion, something that could be applied to a variety of people and places around the world." Accordingly, even in the CIA's early years, there did not appear to be a strongly Catholic complexion to its internal or operational culture.[1] Agee therefore would not have apprehended an especially Catholic-friendly agency.

The OSS's spies had been drawn mainly from Ivy League universities (famously and proverbially Yale)—a predominantly though not exclusively Protestant milieu—and the practice carried over to the CIA itself. Frank Wisner spearheaded the agency's first big recruiting drive in 1948, even before Congress formally blessed the agency in May 1949. He was tasked to enlist thousands of spies to staff thirty-six overseas CIA stations within six months, yet his search ranged only "from the Pentagon to Park Avenue to Yale and Harvard and Princeton, where professors and coaches were paid to spot talent."[2] Well into its first decade, CIA recruitment continued to rely to a considerable degree on the informal "tap on the shoulder" from a campus talent spotter, just as MI6 recruitment had in the United

Kingdom.³ The "classic CIA resume of the 1950s" was "Groton, Yale, Harvard Law."⁴

The first two directors of central intelligence, Roscoe H. Hillenkoetter and Walter Bedell Smith, were both former career military officers, but their stints at the CIA were short and discordant. Succeeding Smith was Allen Dulles, a Wall Street lawyer and OSS alumnus who had gone to Princeton. In his long, powerful, and ultimately destructive tenure, Dulles became the avatar for proactive US intelligence that went well beyond intelligence collection to covert action, orchestrating regime changes in Iran, Guatemala, the Dominican Republic, and Congo during his eight years at the helm and entrenching a kind of elitist lawlessness in the CIA's ethos—what David Talbot has called a durable "philosophy about the boundless authority of the national security system's 'splendid watchmen.'"⁵ Among these watchmen were the owlishly paranoid James Angleton, a Yale graduate and also a Catholic, who dominated CIA counterintelligence for almost thirty years, and Desmond FitzGerald, a Harvard graduate who headed the Directorate of Plans late in Agee's intelligence career.

As the agency's ranks expanded by an order of magnitude, from a postwar level in the low thousands to a mid–Cold War mobilization strength into the tens of thousands, however, the Ivy League and the military became an inadequate recruiting pool. Exacerbating the problem was a precipitous downturn in morale at the end of the Korean War. In wartime operations the agency had performed very poorly and at considerable cost to its agents, many of whom died. Military recruits in particular were leaving the agency unhappy. A group of disaffected CIA officers conducted an internal poll indicating that many others, after being promised an ennobling career and an exciting lifestyle, shared their sense of futility and inertia.⁶ This was the CIA's first crisis of confidence, and it came surprisingly early in light of the strong sense of mission the Soviet challenge would have imbued in first-generation intelligence officers. It was not made public, and there is no indication that prospective career intelligence officers were aware of the downturn in patriotic spirit.

Combined with the increasing demands of containment, though, it meant that the list of campuses visited by the agency had to expand.

Among the colleges on the expanded list, Notre Dame would have had strong appeal to CIA recruiters. The Catholic Church had taken a firm anticommunist stance from the late nineteenth century. In 1946, American Catholics had become influential as US delegates to the World Student Congress, and they would play key roles in forming the National Student Association (NSA), a confederation of student governments. Of four delegates, two were from Notre Dame. Martin McLaughlin, a former Army Air Corps intelligence officer, was then a doctoral candidate there, and Vince Hogan was a 1942 graduate of the school. The CIA clandestinely funded the NSA's international programs from the late 1940s until 1967, and McLaughlin would himself become a senior CIA officer and later a deputy assistant secretary of state.[7] Ted Shackley, the storied CIA fixer who would be assigned to control the damage that Agee would do to the agency's Latin American networks, went to the University of Maryland. But such connections were utilitarian rather than lineal. During the 1950s, there remained at the CIA a residual culture of a conspiratorial boys' club of privileged, Ivy League, white Anglo-Saxon Protestants.

Agee's assignment to a CIA station in Latin America was in some ways overdetermined. While he had upper-middle-class advantages as the son of a wealthy self-made entrepreneur and a student at Notre Dame, he didn't have the kind of pedigree that Dulles, Angleton, and FitzGerald presented. His familiarity with the Cuban-American community in Tampa might have tilted his prospective field assignment toward Latin America. And he had joined the CIA before Castro came to power with the intellectual and operational assistance of the Argentine revolutionary Ernesto "Che" Guevara and before Cuba loomed as a forward extension of Soviet power. Within what was then known as the Directorate of Plans (later the Directorate of Operations), the Western Hemisphere division was still considered an intelligence backwater compared to Europe or Asia. The Ivy League cream of the recruiting crop tended to be assigned to stations in those locales, the B-team elsewhere.

Agee himself said it was "embarrassing" that the Western Hemisphere was "looked down upon" as "the gumshoe division" because its senior leadership consisted of "a fraternity of ex-FBI officers who had come into the CIA in 1947 when the CIA took over FBI intelligence work in Latin America."[8] Thus, Agee's professional grooming by C. Harlow Duffin, the CIA Latin America desk chief back at headquarters, and his assignment to Quito, Ecuador, might have been expected in 1956, the year of Agee's induction. Far less predictable was Latin America's abrupt elevation in geopolitical importance after 1959.

In January of that year, while Agee was still completing operational training at Camp Peary—The Farm—stateside, the Cuban Revolution culminated in Castro's overthrow of Batista. Castro nationalized industries and adopted distinctly anti-American rhetoric. Beyond that, the Cuban Revolution proved infectious throughout the region among wide swaths of people who had long been plagued by falling wages, denial of access to land, and stillborn agrarian reforms. Masses of supporters greeted Castro and Guevara when they toured Latin American universities in 1959 and 1960.[9] Most critically for the US government and the CIA, the Komitet Gosudarstvennoy Bezopasnosti, or KGB—the principal Soviet intelligence agency— saw the Cuban Revolution as a tool for hammering away at American hegemony in the region.[10] Agee himself had a distinct sense of both the Western Hemisphere cadre's second-class citizenship within the CIA and the geopolitical forces that were about to elevate it to the first: "The problem is that the glory for super-spooky achievements is enjoyed mostly by . . . old hands from Berlin and Vienna. We'll see how they treat us after Castro gets thrown out!"[11]

By the time Agee undertook his first field assignment in Quito on December 6, 1960, Cuba had established a nascent but growing economic and military alliance with the Soviet Union. The significance of these events was not lost on John F. Kennedy, who had been elected president four weeks earlier. In his celebrated inaugural address, JFK identified "a new generation of Americans" and exhorted them to be altruistic ("ask not . . .") in advancing an extroverted, active, and alert America ("pay any price . . ."). He also reached back to the Monroe Doctrine, framing Latin America for particular concern and consideration in the context of the United States' traditional hemispheric hegemony: "To our sister republics south of our border, we offer a special pledge—to convert our good words into good deeds—in a new alliance for progress—to assist free men and free governments in casting off the chains of poverty. But this peaceful revolution of hope cannot become the prey of hostile powers. Let all our neighbors know that we shall join with them to oppose aggression or subversion anywhere in the Americas. And let every other power know that this Hemisphere intends to remain the master of its own house." Kennedy's soaring rhetoric chimed with at least an idealized version of service in the CIA as a singularly noble calling "to bear the burden of a long twilight struggle."[12]

A week later, the Joint Chiefs of Staff predicted that Castro's ascendance would have "disastrous consequences to the security of the Western Hemisphere" while the CIA judged Cuba "an opportunity of incalculable value" to Moscow.[13] The radicalization of the Left, of course, confirmed right-wing elements' fears of socialist infiltration and induced them to dig in. Most of them welcomed the CIA's close assistance. The Cuban Revolution had swung to the Far Left, and the State Department and the American business community feared that Cuba would try to extend its revolution to other countries in the hemisphere, which might result in the nationalization of private assets. The CIA's "top priority" throughout Latin America was clear: "to seal off Cuba from the continent." In Quito, Agee said in his book, "our orders are to do everything possible to force Ecuador to break diplomatic and economic relations with Cuba, and also to weaken the Communist Party there, no matter what the cost."[14]

In a perversely serendipitous way, Agee found himself on the Cold War's critical new front. Left-wing populist José Maria Velasco Ibarra, running as an independent, had been elected president for the fourth time a few months before Agee arrived in Quito, defeating the right-wing incumbent, though his supporters held only a strong plurality of seats in the legislature, just short of a majority. Military coups had cut short Velasco's previous terms. While his inability to stay in office reflected his authoritarian tendencies and dearth of administrative competence, his political resilience stemmed from his rhetorical skill and mass populist appeal. He famously declared, "Give me a balcony, and I will become president."[15] And so he did, five times. This time, he had stressed his nationalist opposition to the Rio Protocol, a 1942 agreement between Ecuador and Peru whereby disputed land covering 77,000 square miles was awarded to Peru, of which the United States was a guarantor along with Argentina, Brazil, and Chile. Velasco declared the protocol null and void in his inauguration speech and took an aggressive stance on continuing boundary disputes between Ecuador and Peru, increasing tensions between Washington and Quito.

Moreover, Ecuador was the second-poorest country in Latin America. With gross inequality in both wealth and land distribution, and the population divided between the wealthy middle class on the coast and the rural poor in the mountains, it was highly susceptible to revolutionary impulses and Cuban infiltration. Velasco had tasked Manuel Araujo Hidalgo, the powerful left-wing minister of government, to purge the military, the national police force, and some civilian departments of supporters of the previous government, many of whom were CIA liaison contacts. Expressly anti-American, Araujo was an ardent supporter of the Cuban Revolution and stronger diplomatic relations between Ecuador and Cuba. He impeded US efforts to disrupt those relations and believed Ecuador should consolidate diplomatic and economic links with the Soviets. Bob Weatherwax, a CIA officer who had helped supervise a police response to a demonstration in which five Velasco supporters had been killed, had been temporarily sent home at the new government's urging. On Agee's fourth day in Quito, mobs attacked the US embassy there.[16]

Agee himself was galvanized, and all-in. Kennedy's Alliance for Progress, under which the United States would provide funding for Latin American countries to address social and economic problems with a view to spreading free-market democracy, made sense to the young spy.[17] So did the prescribed technocratic requirements for economic growth, such as agrarian, fiscal, and administrative reform, stable export markets, and industrialization. But what really captivated him were the clandestine means of assuring Ecuador's political fealty to the American strategy and its estrangement from Cuba: running agents; bugging adversary legations; spreading propaganda through journalists on the CIA payroll, Catholic organizations, labor unions, and student groups; and directly influencing the government (through, for instance, Velasco's nephew, a CIA agent who became minister of the treasury). He greeted the news that the agency's campaign had resulted in the ouster of the United States' biggest enemy in the Velasco administration, ten days after Agee got to Quito, with the exclamation: "Araujo's out!" The aftermath of rioting and tear gas he described with cold objectivity.[18] He exulted in agency-orchestrated arrests of Argentine-trained communist guerrillas that CIA agents had identified. "The guerrilla arrests are headlines this morning!"[19]

By June 1961, Velasco had prevailed on Cuba to withdraw its ambassador from Quito. He announced a moderate doctrine of cooperative liberalism, denouncing communism and championing representative democracy. But he remained mercurial and difficult to control, and in November the military dislodged him and installed his vice president, Carlos Julio Arosemena Monroy, as president. He was not the ideal choice from the United States' standpoint, as he too championed the Cuban Revolution and was a heavy drinker. But the CIA did manage to orchestrate the congressional election of a malleable, anticommunist vice president, Reinaldo Varea, though he was subject to protracted impeachment proceedings over an arms-sale scandal. The CIA hammered the new government's ongoing refusal to break with Cuba, which became a consuming national issue, and it helped conservative elements paralyze Ecuador's congress. By April 1962, Arosemena's government was teetering and he was compelled to reconstitute his cabinet substantially with anticommunist ministers, who voted unanimously to sever ties with Cuba. And in fact, Cuba was training and bankrolling Ecuadoran guerrillas and developing a strong network of pro-Cuban organizations in Ecuador.

Agee, for his part, ran two key agents, both members of the anticommunist Social Christian movement. Through one, a retired army captain, Agee organized about ten "militant action squads," including a bomb unit, to violently disrupt meetings and small demonstrations. Through the other, a charismatic and politically ambitious lawyer, he pulled together five units to keep tabs on suspected subversives. He also oversaw electronic surveillance operations against several suspected high-value agents of Cuba and liaised with government officials on how to deal with them. In particular, when José Marfa Roura, leader of a pro-Castro group, was arrested at the airport returning from China with $25,000, Agee suggested leaking the bogus story he was also carrying Che Guevara's "secret plan" for guerrilla warfare there and elsewhere in South America. This disinformation made "supersensational" headlines and Roura was detained.[20] Agee also helped manufacture an incriminating document that was placed inside an empty toothpaste tube and planted in the luggage of Antonio Benitez Flores, another pro-Castro figure, by police upon his return from Cuba. Flores was forced to go into hiding.

The Ecuadoran government, at the CIA's behest, formally banned all travel to Cuba. Publicity about the cases threw the communist movement in Ecuador into some disarray, but it also evidenced the government's weakness. In July 1963, a four-man military junta staged a successful and bloodless coup against Arosemena, quickly outlawing communism, imposing censorship, establishing a curfew, and canceling elections scheduled for 1964. To the CIA, the junta was "a favourable, if transitory, solution to the instability and danger of insurgency that were blocking development."[21] With the advent of the junta, agency liaison with high-level Ecuadoran officials and penetration of the Ecuadoran security forces became more systematic, the government's CIA-assisted counterinsurgency program more robust. The junta would rule until March 1966.

Having received his second in-country promotion, Agee regarded his first assignment, which roughly coincided with Kennedy's thousand days in office, as a successful effort to inoculate Ecuador against leftist influences that had also set him on the path of an estimable CIA career. Indeed, the celebrated left-wing journalist and *Ramparts* editor Warren Hinckle reckoned that covert agency tactics in Latin America "reached an apotheosis in Ecuador, where the

CIA owned as so much Tupperware government wheels, heads of political parties, leading editors and army officers, labor and student leaders, and even the country's vice-president."[22] This was the dispensation of which Agee was so proud. At the end of his Quito tour, he harbored qualified optimism about what the station accomplished in supplanting an elected government the agency considered dysfunctional with a CIA-indoctrinated military junta: "Now, at last, these [political] reforms can be imposed by decree and it seems certain that the order imposed by the junta will speed economic growth." These read like the words of a true believer.[23]

The CIA's approach in Ecuador during the early and mid-sixties proved to be quite a durable blueprint: it kept the people powerless. In her eye-opening 1977 book *Cry of the People*—chronicling, among other things, the way in which the CIA had worked nefariously through a cynical, blinkered, corrupt, and conservative Catholic Church to advance American geopolitical interests—Penny Lernoux noted that Ecuador was a "backward banana republic until the 1972 oil boom"; that it was "still the politically most retarded country of South America, with no more than 100,000 of its people able to distinguish between a conservative and a communist"; and that it was therefore "relatively easy for the educated elite to make and break governments, often with the United States' support."[24]

Agee conducted himself like an efficient technician. He facilitated the interrogation of Ecuadoran political prisoners by specially trained US Special Forces personnel brought in from the US Army's counterinsurgency school in the Panama Canal Zone; he wound up relationships with agents prior to his reassignment in the manner of any dutiful American careerist. He cultivated a kind of blithe coldheartedness, using his own dog, Lanita, to test out a tranquilizer for immobilizing any guard dogs at the Czech legation—which the CIA had targeted for a bug—rendering his pet comatose and joking that he'd send the agency's Technical Services Division a bill if she died.[25] As he said in recalling his attitude during this stretch, "The best part of being a CIA officer is that you never get bored for long."[26]

The darker side of the United States' containment strategy, however, also began to catch light. The first sign, perhaps, had occurred close to Agee's home state of Florida, with the abortive, US-orchestrated Bay of Pigs invasion of Cuba in April 1961. Privy to some details of the operation from classified cables, he seemed skeptical of its overall advisability, noting that it gave left-wing groups "all the excuse they need for another round of window-breaking" and that even conservative Latin Americans objected to it because "they just hate U.S. intervention more than they hate communism." Once it became clear that the invasion had been a failure, he grasped its flattening effect on agency morale. "I have never seen him so glum," said Agee of his station chief, likening the debacle to "losing a game you never even considered losing."[27] It also upset some of the CIA rank and file. One rough contemporary of Agee, a former special-operations soldier who had been directly involved in the invasion, left the agency utterly disillusioned by the "destruction" of what he'd "helped to build," by "the betrayal of the exiles," and by "peers and supervisors . . . who did not possess the courage to object," himself writing a plaintive, self-regarding book about the experience.[28]

Kennedy's fallibility, which he publicly owned, was revealed, and it may have opened Agee's mind to the possibility that the CIA's obsession with Castro might, at least when it drove the United States to undemocratic extremes, be counterproductive. The Cuban missile crisis in October 1962, during which Kennedy stared down Soviet leader Nikita Khrushchev and compelled him to remove nuclear weapons from Cuba, burnished his reputation for steely and sophisticated executive discretion. But the CIA's performance was spotty before though not during the crisis, which, as Richard Immerman notes, constituted "something of a prologue for the Company's fall from grace."[29] Subsequent American or US-sanctioned interventions would have bolstered this view. The November 1963 coup in South Vietnam, occurring toward the end of Agee's time in Quito, was especially conspicuous. That August, the US State Department had cabled Henry Cabot Lodge, the American ambassador to South Vietnam, that US policy was not to stand in the way of the removal of South Vietnamese President Ngo Dinh Diem, whose rule had become untethered from political reality and correspondingly unstable. The CIA had communicated this position to South Vietnamese army officers that American officials knew were planning a coup. On November 2, 1963, about three weeks before Kennedy was assassinated, the army officers arrested Diem and his brother, executing them a day later.

In November 1963, Agee subscribed to the aggressive economic cooperation and democratic reform agenda of the Alliance for Progress initiative, and he appeared to be something close to a New Frontier idealist. To many of that orientation, the president's death signaled uncertainty about presidential decision-making. Moreover, those inside the intelligence community, even at stations far from Southeast Asia or Langley, were likely to have heard rumblings about the US political leadership's tendentious distortions of intelligence from the August 1964 Gulf of Tonkin incident forward. And some might have lost faith in the integrity of the CIA and its supervisors at headquarters. By his own lights, Agee grew to regard US containment policy—which undergirded all US foreign policy in this era—as, at the very least, paranoid. Vietnam was both a symptom of this phenomenon and, as it evolved into a quagmire and a rallying point for revolutionaries, an exacerbating factor. The war marked a generational shift in political attitude in many American families, including CIA ones: Desmond FitzGerald's daughter Frances would write a seminal Pulitzer Prize-winning book, *Fire in the Lake*, highly critical of US intervention in Vietnam.[30] But the war's fraudulence and corrosiveness would take years to fully register with Agee, as it would with much of the American people.

FEAR AND LOATHING

Like most mid-twentieth-century Americans, Agee the novice intelligence professional would have uncritically accepted the Monroe Doctrine, which in 1823 established the United States' resistance to further European colonialism in North and South America, and over 125 years had evolved into a standing assertion of hemispheric American hegemony. Early in his CIA career, while the Bay of Pigs might have driven home to him American neuralgia about Fidel Castro, the Cuban missile crisis scarcely a year later might have made it seem justified. Certainly Agee was still sufficiently enamored with the CIA mission and lifestyle to soldier on with enthusiasm. Along with most of his contemporaries, Agee had grown up assuming that the United States was, if not infallible, more sound, politically and geopolitically, than any other country. Reinforced by indoctrination, peer pressure, fraternal elitism, institutional support, and professional insularity, this preconception supported his outlook. Frank Snepp, another well-known ex-CIA critic who did not go nearly as far as Agee, observed that the 1960s were "not just the years of rage, but the heyday of James Bond, before all of the anti-CIA exposés, when spying was still seen as romantic. It was easy to believe that you were doing God's work by joining up and staying in."[31]

Working in the CIA's Clandestine Service, however, also made Agee privy to many of the practical impurities of the United States' putatively noble Cold War policy of containment. In time, the grinding toll of the Vietnam War rendered any doubts that his inside view engendered more susceptible to intensification, while the civil rights movement would have shaken any pat assumptions of undiluted American rectitude. In addition, circumstances in Ecuador challenged Agee's pride in his Catholic background. He had insisted on a Catholic wedding, impelling his fiancée Janet, a Congregationalist, not to marry in her hometown of Pontiac, Michigan, and he took pride in his first son's baptism at a Catholic church in Ecuador when he was but ten weeks old.[32] In 1967, he would consult a priest in connection with his separation from Janet.[33] All in all, he had a distinctly Catholic sensibility.

Eisenhower regarded religious life and values as formidable aspects of US power and had featured "the religious factor" in his approach to foreign policy. Among other things, it lent American democracy a degree of ideological depth and cohesion comparable to that of Soviet communism. But his primary vehicle was a highly ecumenical public-private partnership, spearheaded by Edward Elson, Ike's minister at the National Presbyterian Church, and so not intensely Catholic. In the mid-1950s, the greatly respected Admiral Arthur Radford, whom Eisenhower had appointed chairman of the Joint Chiefs of Staff, proposed the idealistic "Militant Liberty" plan for situating religion and individual freedom at the center of an expeditionary, whole-of-government US foreign policy. The goal was to mobilize religious forces worldwide, both countering the Soviets' "militant communism" and revitalizing essentially Western cultural values. At the CIA, however, Frank Wisner, deputy director for plans, sent Allen Dulles an incisively detailed memorandum roundly dismissing Militant Liberty as simplistic, parochially myopic, and ultimately "untenable." According to this memo, the concept's central notion of the "sensitive, individual conscience" reflected "a protestant evangelical emphasis which has had considerable influence in our part of the New World, but is meaningless if not repugnant in, for instance, the webs society of Japan, or in those vast areas influenced by Buddhism and Mohammedanism." Dulles formally rejected the plan, noting in a letter to Radford that many foreigners would "deeply resent" the "implication that our particular formulations of 'liberty' constituted universal values."[34]

For the agency, then, religion was not exempt from political manipulation; it remained no more and no less than an expedient tool. Certainly by the time Agee was working in the field as a case officer, the CIA viewed Catholicism and other religions in thoroughly instrumental terms. However devious, this disposition was a logical extension of Donovan's appreciation of religion's political power. As a fledgling case officer on the verge of his first field assignment, Agee might have taken some muted tribal pride in Eisenhower's having given Notre Dame's commencement speech and received an honorary degree in June 1960, with Cardinal Montini—who would become Pope Paul VI—and Tom Dooley on the podium. But he would not have known that Dooley's ostensibly pious good works, and what he wrote about them, were stage-managed by the CIA.[35] And while JFK's presidency was a watershed for civic Catholicism, as a liberal hawk Kennedy tended to cordon off his faith from his policies. By the same token, the CIA's overarching requirement of ethical flexibility might not have been compatible with a good Catholic's tendencies toward a binary conception of right and wrong, a distaste for violence, and charitableness toward the less fortunate.

In Latin America, of course, the CIA had politically weaponized Catholicism. The church had opposed communism since the Russian Revolution and Lenin's establishment of the Third Communist International (Comintern) in 1919. When the Cold War arose, the United States had a ready ally that spanned the region.[36] In Ecuador as in most other Latin American countries, the CIA mobilized the Catholic Church, the hierarchy of which was conservative there, against Cuba- and Soviet-backed communists. It was an element of US strategy explicitly endorsed and mandated by senior officials in the Kennedy administration.[37] This made practical sense, as Ecuador's rural poor—those most susceptible to socialist revolution— were intensely religious Catholics, marching en masse on Good Friday despite heavy rain, as Agee pointedly observed.[38]

He initially admired the anticommunist writings and orations of the country's eighty-nine-year-old Cardinal Carlos Maria Javier de la Torre and the sympathy the cardinal attracted from "the poor and illiterate" to the detriment of the left-leaning president.[39] He was a CIA asset. Aurelio Dávila Cajas, a leader of Ecuador's Conservative Party, president of the Chamber of Deputies, and a CIA agent, had encouraged the cardinal to promulgate this rhetoric, and Dávila countered leftist backlash by channeling CIA money to local church groups and media to mount a public campaign supporting de la Torre. Dávila also arranged for a Catholic youth organization to protest the 1961 visit of a Soviet delegation exploring possible banana purchases with the Ecuadoran government. But while Dávila was a highly useful asset, in contrast the cardinal's "inflammatory, alarmist, almost hysterical" rhetoric came to discomfit Agee. In one anti-Cuban pastoral composed at the agency's behest, urging all Ecuadoran Catholics to take ominously unspecified action against communism, the cleric indulged in a rant "so emotional" as to be "counter-productive," prompting the agency to disseminate an unattributed fly sheet criticizing his remarks through Catholic university students.[40]

Several months later, the lethally manipulative conduct of an elderly priest outraged Agee. In a rural Indian village, a doctor, nurse, and social worker from a United Nations–supported mission entered the local Catholic church only to encounter increasingly frenzied hostility from villagers who believed they were communist. Frightened, the mission workers first took refuge in the church's vestry. When the villagers pursued them, they begged the priest to confirm that they were not communists, but he declined and left the premises. The villagers set upon the three, beating the doctor and social worker to death and severely injuring the nurse. It turned out the priest himself had told the villagers that the mission team was communist.[41] Agee, in recounting this tale, registered his dismay at how the CIA's political inducements had distorted and deracinated Catholic discourse and behavior in Ecuador.

By the time he had moved on from Ecuador to Uruguay, Agee's marriage was shaky. Tension had arisen between Philip and Janet over her insular complacency and his extroverted restlessness. She was unable or unwilling to learn Spanish, which confined her to relationships with other English-speakers, and immersed herself in bridge games with other American wives, during which they kvetched about their husbands. She had no interest in local politics. He enjoyed socializing—it was part of his job—and especially playing golf. The birth of a second son, Christopher, in February 1964, while the Agees were in Florida between overseas assignments, buoyed the relationship for a while.[42] In Montevideo, though, the marriage completely deteriorated: "no common interests except the children, no conversation, increasing resentment at being trapped in loneliness." He described it as "a hellish situation."[43]

Agee's grim disposition initially impelled him to reach for political content, while the state of his marriage rendered him more vulnerable to outside influences—especially those channeled through women—in Montevideo, which he considered "a marvellous city."[44] Politically, Latin America was accommodating, and Uruguay, its smallest country, had a uniquely liberal and egalitarian heritage among Latin American states. In the late nineteenth and early twentieth centuries, the development of Montevideo as a commercial port produced a healthy middle class and with it a budding democracy and the world's first welfare state. Divorce was legalized and the death penalty was banned, workers' rights were legislated, and free secondary education was established. State monopolies were created to administer basic services, such as electricity.[45]

Although economic struggles and political tension during the Depression led to five years of authoritarian rule, democracy was peacefully reinstated in 1938. State-led industrialization and protectionism, however, were vulnerabilities. Public employment became a tool for encouraging political compliance, without commensurate increases in economic output. When world demand for Uruguayan wool and agricultural products collapsed in the 1950s, economic growth and living standards declined, inflation increased, and strikes and student protests became endemic. In the early 1960s, a Guevarist urban guerrilla movement that would come to be known as the Tupac Amaru Revolutionary Movement—named for a revolutionary who had led an indigenous insurrection against Peru in 1780, and colloquially called the Tupamaros—emerged, initially robbing banks and small businesses and distributing the proceeds to the poor and later lethally targeting soldiers and policemen.[46]

When he first arrived there, however, Agee understood Uruguay as a salutary special case. "Indeed," he observed, "Uruguay is the exception to most of the generalities about Latin America, with its surface appearance of an integrated society organized around a modern, benevolent welfare state. Here there is no marginalized Indian mass bogged down in terrible poverty, no natural geographic contradictions between coastal plantations and sierra farming, no continuum of crises and political instabilities, no illiterate masses, no militarism, no inordinate birth-rate." He remained a CIA man in operational outlook: "In Uruguay I immediately perceive many of the benefits that I hope will derive from the junta's reform programme in Ecuador."[47] Uruguay had not been considered a dire CIA priority. E. Howard Hunt, who had the dubious distinction of helping to orchestrate both the Bay of Pigs invasion and later the Watergate break-in, had been a station chief there until 1960, in his only command assignment. According to Hinckle:

Hunt seems to have spent much of his time in Montevideo riding the cocktail circuit in a CIA Cadillac and cranking out the espionage dime novels that provided him with a sizable supplemental income. Early in 1960 he was notified that he was being routinely transferred back to Washington. Reluctant to give up the good life, he told the incoming Uruguayan president, Benito Nardone, that he, Howard Hunt, was indispensable to equitable relations between the two countries and urged him to urge Eisenhower during a forthcoming state visit to leave Hunt in Montevideo. To Ike's utter surprise, Nardone did just that. Eisenhower's military mind was affronted by such a deviation from channels. He told the U.S. ambassador that he had no intention of interfering with the CIA's staffing policies, and who was this fellow Hunt anyway?[48]

Agee was at least prepared to take his new posting more seriously than Hunt apparently had. He had been well briefed on and fully grasped the technocratic reasons for the increasing brittleness of Uruguay's polity, identifying "the dilution of Uruguayan political power" as an especially acute problem.[49] But Uruguay was not Ecuador. The cracks in its political armature were opening slowly, and the Montevideo station, lean but efficient with many agents in place, was managing them quite handily.

After April 1964, the station devoted considerable resources to collecting intelligence on Brazilians following deposed left-wing president João Belchior Marques Goulart into exile in Uruguay. It also spread propaganda in favor of Brazil's new military government, as it and CIA headquarters were worried about insurgency and a counter-coup there. The Uruguayan government's unexpected vote in September 1964 in favor of the Organization of American States' resolution imposing sanctions on Cuba over its meddling in Venezuela indicated that the agency's influence operations in Uruguay were robust and effective.[50] The vote did, however, touch off two days of violent confrontations between pro-Cuban demonstrators and police, student occupations of university and OAS buildings, and bombings and other attacks on several American businesses.

On top of this, the Tupac Amaru Revolutionary Movement—

described by Agee as "a small, activist revolutionary organization" and "the Sendic group," named after its leader, Marxist lawyer and labor leader Raul Sendic—had just started writing the "Tupamaros" nom de guerre at the sites of robberies and bombings, including one at the commercial offices of the Brazilian Embassy. [51] The outfit thus appeared to be gaining operational momentum and political traction. In April 1965, the government took its first steps toward forcibly suppressing extreme left-wing resistance, enacting legislation granting ministers special emergency powers to limit public gatherings.

Agee himself was performing well. His first station chief considered him the only case officer who was doing a good job, and his successor increased Agee's responsibilities—notably for penetrating the Soviet and satellite legations.[52] But Agee also experienced one of the most unsettling experiences a case officer can have: an attempted recruitment of a defector that goes bad. The man in question was an antsy Cuban code clerk who ended up getting caught, implicitly co-opted by the threat of harm to his family, and, despite strong agency efforts to intercede, escorted back to Cuba, where he was probably tried and sentenced to several years at a prison farm.[53] It was at about this point, it seems, that Agee began to question his vocation seriously.

An external prompt was the United States' military intervention in the Dominican Republic in April 1965. The Caribbean country, which shares the island of Hispaniola with Haiti, had effectively been a US client state since 1916, when Woodrow Wilson sent US Marines there to build infrastructure, establish nascent republican government, and impose order. The United States' principal legacy, however, was not democracy but militarism. Brutal right-wing General Rafael Léonidas Trujillo Molina used the American-created army to tyrannize the country from 1930 until dissident officers, with the CIA's complicity, assassinated him in 1961. Trujillo's state terrorism had become an embarrassment to the United States, and his successor, Juan Emilio Bosch Gaviño, was fairly elected. But Dominican clergy, businessmen, and military officers opposed his social democratic reforms and circulated rumors that he was a communist. Within seven months of his inauguration, a military junta overthrew him, installing a civilian figurehead president, Donald Reid Cabral, and securing American backing. The junta's rule was tenuous and embattled, and, a couple of years later, a group of constitutionalist army officers and civilian politicians sought to return Bosch to power. After their forces gained the upper hand against the junta in Santo Domingo, the capital city, the US embassy warned President Johnson that the island would become "another Cuba." After 1959, it was an immovable tenet of US policy that this not be allowed to happen.[54] Johnson deployed 23,000 US troops to the island on the pretext of protecting American civilians. They suppressed the revolt, which anonymous sources—echoed by Johnson—declared had involved "some fifty-eight communists." In 1966, Joaquin Balaguer, an anticommunist lawyer and Trujillo acolyte and front man, became president, defeating Bosch in a skewed election supervised by US Marines.[55]

Agee believed Bosch was not a hardcore communist, posed no real threat to American interests, and did not warrant the deployment of thousands of US soldiers and marines. "Why is it that the invasion seems so unjustifiable to me?" he asked himself that June, after the US military had begun to withdraw. But while Agee may offer a sardonically convincing rearview look at the United States' intervention in the Dominican Republic, he did not become conclusively skeptical about the strategic necessity of that operation as it was occurring or shortly thereafter. This Socratically neat paragraph indicates a very modulated viewpoint:

> It can't be that I'm against intervention as such, because everything I do is in one way or another intervention in the affairs of other countries. Partly, I suppose, it's the immense scale of the invasion that shocks. On the other hand, full-scale military invasion is the logical final step when all the other tools of counter-insurgency fail. The Santo Domingo station just didn't or couldn't keep the lid on. But what's really disturbing is that we've intervened on the wrong side. I just don't believe "fifty-eight trained communists" can take over a movement of thousands that includes experienced political leaders.

That's a pretext. The real reason must be opposition to Bosch by U.S. business with investments in the Dominican Republic. Surely these investments could have produced even while the land reform and other programmes moved ahead.[56]

The fact remains that while Agee placed considerable blame on the CIA station's operational failings, his thinking reflected wider cynicism about the United States' geopolitical outlook and methods. He was losing the idealistic hope that America's technocratic means of securing pro-American political alignments—republican governments, free markets, sound macroeconomics—would be conducive to better governance. He had himself reflecting in September 1965:

The more I think about the Dominican invasion the more I wonder whether the politicians in Washington really want to see reforms in Latin America. Maybe participation by the communists wouldn't be such a bad thing because that way they could be controlled better. But to think that fifty-eight trained communists participating in a popular movement for liberal reform can take control is to show so little confidence in reform itself. The worst of this is that the more we work to build up the security forces like the police and military, particularly the intelligence services, the less urgency, it seems, attaches to the reforms. What's the benefit in eliminating subversion if the injustices continue? I don't think the Alliance for Progress is working, and I think I may not have chosen the right career after all.[57]

In December 1965, an episode that involved and disturbed Agee far more directly took place in Montevideo. Agee and John Horton, the CIA station chief, were visiting Colonel Ventura Rodriguez, the Montevideo chief of police, and Roberto Ramirez, the head of the paramilitary force, to share and discuss a fabricated CIA intelligence report that would justify a break between Uruguay and the Soviet Union over Soviet intrigue in Uruguayan labor unrest. As the police chief listened to a soccer game on his portable transistor radio, Agee heard screams from a cell above the chief's office. The screams were those of Oscar Bonaudi, the leader of a Communist Party of Uruguay "self-defense squad," whose name Agee had supplied to Rodriguez. Like many Latin American security forces, the Montevideo police favored what they called a *picana* (Spanish for "goad")—a hand-cranked electric generator customarily attached to a suspect's genitals. A descendant of the cattle prod and forerunner of the Taser, the device administered shocks at high voltage but low current so as to minimize the chance of fatality and prolong the duration and frequency of effective torture. Agee recalled: "As Rodriguez read the report, I began to hear a strange low sound which, as it gradually became louder, I recognized as the moan of a human voice. I thought it might be a street vendor trying to sell something, until Rodriguez told Ramirez to turn up the radio. The moaning grew in intensity, turning into screams, while several more times Rodriguez told Ramirez to turn up the soccer game. By then I knew we were listening to someone being tortured in the rooms next to the AVENGEFUL listening post above Rodriguez's office."[58]

AVENGEFUL was a long-standing CIA wiretapping operation run through the Montevideo Police Department, targeting primarily Soviet and Cuban personnel, which helped cement the relationship between the two organizations. But some two months earlier Agee had learned that Juan José Braga, the Deputy Chief of Investigations, had ordered the brutal interrogation of Julio Arizaga, a left-wing activist believed to have knowledge about terrorist organizations. Braga had been especially intent on getting information about the Tupamaros, about whom little was then known, and exasperated over his inability to preempt their bombings.[59] So Arizaga was tortured, and this incident gave Agee pause. Still, in light of the AVENGEFUL tradition of cooperation, Agee had overcome new reservations about providing names to the department— including Bonaudi's. But overhearing his savage interrogation, said Agee, "made me feel terrified and helpless. All I wanted to do was get away from the voice and away from police headquarters. Why didn't Horton or I say anything to Rodriguez? We just sat there embarrassed and shocked. I'm going to be hearing that voice for a long time."[60]

In fact, CIA officers and other American "public safety advisers" were critical players in the development of Uruguay's paramilitary police and military organizations in the 1960s and 1970s, which fielded death squads to deal with left-wing subversives. The Americans furnished assistance far more extensive than the mere provision of suspects' names, including four-week courses of instruction in bomb design, weapons operation, and assassination provided in training facilities located in Texas or in the Panama Canal Zone.[61] Uruguayan officials so trained monitored and persecuted liberal Catholics as well as pursuing groups like the Tupamaro guerrillas with extreme prejudice.[62] The targeted groups responded in kind. Eventually supported by Cuba in various ways, their most notable operation was the 1970 kidnapping and execution of Dan Mitrione, a former FBI agent operating under the auspices of the US Agency for International Development's Office of Public Safety, and responsible for liaising with the local police and teaching them "the art of mass repression and torture" in coordination with the CIA.[63] During Agee's tenure in Montevideo, the Tupamaros had not yet graduated to lethal violence. But he did have security liaison duties related to the ones Mitrione would later assume, and the work they involved affected him.

The Bonaudi episode, in particular, appears to have been a pivotal moment in Philip Agee's conversion from a promising CIA case officer to a questioning dissident. At that point, in late 1965, most Americans had not yet twigged to the folly of US intervention in Vietnam or the ruthlessness of American support for free markets and illiberal regimes in the Western Hemisphere. As a CIA officer, however, Agee was coming to appreciate how the Vietnam War was galvanizing the Left worldwide. Back in April, the Tupamaros had bombed the Montevideo offices of the Bayer Company, leaving a note protesting US intervention in Vietnam.[64] The Battle of the Ia Drang Valley, the first major force-on-force battle between regular American and North Vietnamese troops, in which more than 300 GIs were killed over four days, had occurred in November; it marked the beginning of the United States' immersion in Vietnam.[65] Liberal Catholics had been questioning American intrigue in Vietnam for over a decade, and pacifism was infiltrating the mainstream church. These factors may have combined to liberate his emotional response to the Bonaudi interrogation. In any case, effectively witnessing torture induced him to change his operational conduct. After finding out that Bonaudi had been worked over for three days—without breaking—Agee resolved not to feed names to the police as long as Braga remained on the job.[66]

Less portentously, he also allowed acute irritation to surface over the arrogant remove and preconceptions of John Horton, who had been a first-generation CIA case officer and was now his station chief. Horton took over the station from Ned Holman, whom Agee disliked and regarded as oblivious, lazy, and vindictive, even though Holman evidently thought highly of Agee. Initially, Agee found Horton to be a breath of fresh air: "very approachable, good sense of humour, very anglophile."[67] Later, pondering futile CIA efforts to get the Montevideo police chief who had replaced Rodriguez to set up an autonomous intelligence unit, Agee seemed to regard Horton's old-world preening as merely fatuous: "Our efforts to convince Colonel Ubach to establish an intelligence division on a par with, or apart from, the ordinary Criminal Investigations Division haven't been successful. Horton, however, is determined to turn police intelligence into a British-style 'special branch' like the one he dealt with in Hong Kong. I'm not sure whether he thinks this is needed because it will work better or because it's the British way—he seems even more anglophile than before: country walks, bird-watching, tennis, tea-time and quantities of well-worn tweeds that he wears in the hottest weather."[68] Kim Philby had likened CIA officers to the "upper class wine-drinkers" of his own MI6, as distinct from the "earthier beer-drinking types" of the FBI and the MI5.[69] But Agee was, or at least saw himself as, something in between the two types, and closer to the latter.

Granted, these self-admissions still reflected a highly qualified moral dispensation: tentative, prudent, and safe. Agee noted that at the time, while he "would have liked" to discuss "matters of principle related to counter-insurgency" with agency superiors, "serious questioning of principles could imply ideological weakening and a whole train of problems with polygraphs, security clearance, career, personal security. For all of us the discussions remain at the level of irony." The thought had occurred to him that "[i]f we in the CIA . . . seek to strengthen this and other similarly clique-serving governments only because they are anticommunists, then we're reduced to promoting one type of injustice in order to avoid another."[70] But he kept it to himself for prudential reasons. Agee continued, for the time being, to value his career over ethical purity and to tolerate the CIA's standing ends-over-means institutional compromises, settling for sarcasm in private. Agee reflected with disdain on the Brazilian ambassador's assurances to Horton that Brazil would intervene should Uruguay appear vulnerable to communist subversion: "at least we won't have to send troops as we did with the Dominican Republic—the Brazilians will take care of those fifty-eight trained Uruguayan communists when the time comes."[71]

To use a term describing an exception to the law of evidence's exclusion of hearsay, Agee's candor about the lame fecklessness of his overall dispensation embodies a kind of "admission against interest"—the interest in this case being moral rather than legal liability—which militates in favor of its truthfulness. As Snepp would confirm: "That's how you begin making compromises in the CIA. If I hold my tongue today, I will pick up enough credit within the system to be able to tell the truth tomorrow. You keep postponing it."[72] Eventually, of course, Agee would stop demurring. But that was not only, or perhaps even mainly, because he reached a moral breaking point.

Whereas Agee claimed to have seen Ecuador in a positive light upon his departure, by the end of his tour in Montevideo Agee said he had seen Uruguay—once vaunted by liberals as "the model for enlightened democratic reforms"—as in fact "the model of corruption and incapacity" engineered by retrograde political factions.[73] Some CIA officers might have regarded that as a net win: better to have in place cynics whose politics can be bought than idealists whose politics are not for sale. Agee was uncertain. Yet despite his purportedly fading identification with the agency and its work, he still needed a job and knew espionage best.

By that point, Agee had decided to leave Janet, though the children and logistical circumstances kept them cohabiting for another year.[74] Meanwhile, Ned Holman, who had preceded Horton as Montevideo chief of station and was widely judged to have done a poor job, had targeted recriminations at case officers there by way of written evaluations to cover his own incompetence, although headquarters was reportedly aware of the circumstances and neutralized the reports with special memoranda to the personnel files.[75] Agee's sour domestic and professional circumstances opened him to a new and different worldview. While he refrained from ascribing strict cause and effect, he did connect the two phenomena: "Holman's attitude and my deteriorating domestic situation have caused some hardening, perhaps even embitterment, but the more I see of the [Uruguayan] government the more urgent become the questions of whether and why we support such things."[76]

While the Bonaudi incident had been an outright trauma, the less spectacularly dirty aspects of day-to-day spying too were getting to Agee. In April 1966, he oversaw an operation in which an elderly Yugoslavian defector was to try to recruit an employee of the Yugoslavian Embassy in Montevideo. The defector—whom the CIA was about to retire as an agent after years of service—had provided excellent intelligence and been sporadically successful as a recruiter. This time, however, after a promising initial approach, the attempted recruitment failed miserably, with the target leaving the spurned agent alone on the sidewalk. This agent was a dignified man, the former administrative chief of the Yugoslavian foreign ministry, but Agee now saw his reduction to "lurking in the streets" as "sad, almost pitiful." More soul-searching ensued. Headquarters told Agee that the agent was spent, which meant his salary would be terminated. He was a US citizen and would get Social Security benefits, but Agee surmised that his final years would be soul-crushing. "No wonder most defectors either become alcoholics or suffer mental illness or both," Agee reflected. "Once they've been milked for all they're worth to us they're thrown away like old rags."[77]

It was a disquisition worthy of Alec Lemas, the disaffected MI6 officer of John le Carré's *The Spy Who Came in from the Cold*. Agee, of course, identified most of the agents mentioned in *Inside the Company* by name, and he apparently failed to identify this gentleman only because he had forgotten his real name and cryptonym.[78] Yet, in the mid-1960s, he did inspire Agee's compassion despite being a witting tool of what Agee was coming to consider a cynical and immoral system. In time, Agee's position would harden.

RECKONING IN MEXICO CITY

When Agee returned to headquarters in September 1966, he was still concerned about his professional future at the CIA, ascertaining from his deputy division chief that despite heavy demand he would not be sent to Vietnam—that was for "expendables"—and from the Clandestine Services Career Panel that he had been accepted into the agency's generous retirement program.[79] He and Janet stopped living together in October 1966, Agee finding an apartment in the Washington area. That month he also tentatively decided to resign from the CIA. He planned to inform his superiors only that personal circumstances were driving this decision and that he would depart in due course when a suitable opportunity arose.[80] A notional, unsent resignation letter to Richard Helms, then director of central intelligence, stated that CIA operations merely advanced the United States' support for greedy elites and was incompatible with socialism, which was "the only real alternative to injustice in Latin America."[81] It did not mention the Bonaudi episode, which had occurred ten months prior, or other emotionally trying operational experiences. But it seems clear that they had gnawed away at his psychological shield and exposed his intellect to alien influences.

Still, Agee moved on dutifully to his next assignment in Mexico City, and in fact appeared to jettison his ethical qualms. As the posting loomed, he shelved his exit strategy—apparently owing to the juicy prospect of becoming the case officer assigned the cover job of US Olympic attaché for the 1968 summer games, which the Soviets were seeking to exploit heavily as a platform for recruitment. He regarded it as an "exciting job" insofar as it would afford him direct contact with communist counterparts, corresponding opportunities to develop better intelligence, and some distance from the quotidian activities of the station. He pushed aggressively for the assignment.[82] All the while, the agency manifested appreciation for Agee's abilities, sending him back to Montevideo station on temporary duty for two weeks to ensure President Johnson's security at the impending OAS Meeting of American Chiefs of State on April 12–14, 1967, in Punta del Este, a resort city on the Uruguayan coast about ninety miles from the capital. He did his job well and returned to the news that he had won the Mexico City assignment he coveted. This was a vote of confidence. On account of Mexico's size, strategic importance, and proximity to the United States, Mexico City station was the CIA's largest outpost in the Western Hemisphere and a hive of Soviet and satellite espionage activity.[83]

During the tenure of Mexican President Gustavo Diaz Ordaz, from 1964 to 1970, Mexico enjoyed healthy economic growth and largely harmonious relations with the United States. His party, the big-tent Institutional Party of Mexico (PRI), had exercised de facto one-party rule since the 1920s. Essentially centrist despite socialist origins, the party's economic model was state-orchestrated capitalism. It derived legitimacy from its legacy ownership of the 1910–20 Mexican Revolution and relative prosperity, retained power through patronage, and, under Diaz Ordaz, was on board with the United States' anticommunist agenda. While he publicly took a position of noninterference in Cuban affairs and asserted an independent foreign policy for domestic consumption, particularly the Left's, he discreetly cooperated with the CIA, brutally suppressing leftist agrarian activism and earning Washington's trust. Diaz Ordaz was at heart an inflexible authoritarian disposed, when push came to shove, to coercion rather than accommodation, the stick instead of the carrot. And, like most Cold War–era Latin American leaders, he subscribed to the antirevolutionary National Security Doctrine: in order to stave off leftist subversion and insurgency that would inevitably cause instability, an assertive and militaristic state was required.[84]

The general social and political conditions for a loss of faith in the CIA's mission, and America's more broadly, were getting riper. If the Johnson administration's overt military intervention in the Dominican Republic in April 1965 to prevent a suspected Cuba-engineered communist takeover spawned Agee's disapproval, US escalation in

Vietnam, in 1966–67, would have drawn the darkest and most visible line under the Kennedy administration and separated it from a less nimble or visionary Johnson team. It could not have escaped Agee's notice that none of the United States' NATO allies—not even France, Vietnam's former colonial steward—were lending it operational or even political support. While casual observers might have attributed this disinterest to lack of capacity, the participation of Australia, South Korea, and Thailand indicated that smaller nations could add effective operational contributions to the war effort, making the abstentions of larger allies more glaring.

Living and working in South America through 1965, Agee had been somewhat insulated from the simmering antiwar activism of college students and the blossoming of a larger counterculture fueled by that and civil rights protests. Being employed by the CIA, a cocoon of institutionalized patriotism, further shielded him. He could read the newspapers, but distance made the protests and social change seem, if not unreal, perhaps more provisional and aberrational than they actually were. As a case officer, however, Agee also had more direct, unmediated, and potent stimuli, seeing the victims of American intrigue firsthand and, as in the Bonaudi episode, sometimes even personally helping to arrange their suffering. Many were communists or something close, broadly aligned with Castro and the Soviets, and Agee's early Cold War mindset and CIA indoctrination initially inoculated him against overt sympathy with them. But he had a more adventurous and searching side that he not only enjoyed indulging as a matter of inclination but was also required to exercise as a matter of vocation. Eventually, he would connect the mass protests he read about in newspapers or saw in television news reports with his own experience, and they would resonate more intensely, conjuring his sympathy for the perceived victims of US policy.

Moreover, by the time Agee got to Mexico City, in July 1967, the antiwar movement had gone big and global. The Vietnam conflict became durable headline news that came to mobilize generational criticism of American foreign policy. Political dissidence, directed toward US military and civil rights policies, was becoming pervasive. Indeed, it would infiltrate the Olympic Games themselves when African American sprinters Tommie Smith and John Carlos, having just received gold and silver medals and standing on the podium, bowed their heads and raised black-gloved fists in the Black Power salute as "The Star-Spangled Banner" played. The CIA itself characterized protest against the war as "a world-wide phenomenon," and it was especially intense in Mexico, where groups combined their support for the Vietcong communist insurgents with insistence on domestic political reform.[85] War protest was also increasingly linked to a larger hemispheric leftward turn driven by a movement that was peculiarly salient in Latin America: Catholic liberation theology. The movement was all the more formidable insofar as "the power of the Church to sway Latin America is far greater than that of any government or political system."[86] As a Jesuit-schooled alumnus of Notre Dame, Agee would have been generally aware of these realities.

Liberal Catholic social teachings first emerged in the nineteenth century in response to the impact of the Industrial Revolution. The amassing of capital, the dehumanization of workers, and the social dislocation of populations all threatened the social order. In a definitive break with tradition, the church, which had theretofore thrown in its lot with governing elites, suddenly shifted to a defense of the working class. The principal vehicles of this viewpoint were two groundbreaking papal encyclicals: *Rerum Novarum* by Pope Leo XIII in 1891 and *Quadragesimo Anno* by Pope Pius XI in 1931. In essence, the two pronouncements defended the workers' right to strike and form unions, upheld their moral right to meaningful work and a living wage, and insisted that governments and societies work to achieve the common good and not merely the private good of industrialists.

Catholics, of course, had always accepted the centrality of obedience since theirs is an authoritative, hierarchical church where ethical and religious dictates come from the top down. At the same time, Catholic teachings have included a strong current of subjective conscience since Thomas Aquinas held forth in the thirteenth century. Although the bishops and most American Catholics opposed conscientious objector status during the Second World War, the extraordinary brutality of modern combat motivated dozens of Catholics to assert that status and an increasing number of Catholic scholars to argue that subjective conscience needed protection against a liberal democratic state that had become militaristic. During the Cold War, proponents of the Catholic doctrine of conscience and "self-sovereignty" maintained a strong and consistent voice, fully aware of the potential challenge it posed to national security, the rule of law, and indeed papal authority. The enduring controversy over the merits of the Vietnam War gave rise to the doctrine of "selective conscientious objection"—that is, a refusal to fight in an unjust war but not a just one. Mobilized through the New York–based Catholic Peace Fellowship, Catholic conscientious objectors increased exponentially from Second World War levels.[87]

The church also found itself in an awkwardly and dangerously paradoxical situation: large populations of Catholics in Eastern Europe were left with their bishops in prison and their priests on the run, walled off from the larger church and under the thumb of a dictatorial, atheistic power. In that situation, obedience would no longer serve them; in fact, disobedience was required if they wanted to be faithful. Theologians and church leaders accordingly began to unwrap the older tradition—namely, the belief that God speaks to the inner self of each believer and thus directly to the human conscience. It is this inner voice that the believer must honor. And if the inner voice is in conflict with some outer authority, then the believer is obliged to disobey that outer authority and be guided by conscience.

In this vein, from the mid-1950s, Dorothy Day—leader of the Catholic Worker Movement, an early advocate of conscientious objection, and a seminal Catholic pacifist—had mounted a steady challenge to the church's putative anticommunist militarism, epitomized by Tom Dooley, and her position developed traction as the Vietnam War raged. In 1954, she had written an article—published in the month that Dien Bien Phu fell to the Vietminh—decrying the United States' evolving penchant for imperial and colonial depredations with particular reference to France's excesses in Vietnam, invalidating a military solution there and exposing the spiritual faults of conventional anticommunism. Condemning "the Godlessness of our Western materialism," she concluded that the West must "recognize that it is not Christianity and freedom we are defending, but our possessions."[88] In turn, during the early 1960s, liberal pacifism started to percolate within mainstream Catholicism. The church, of course, called for the eventual abolition of nuclear weapons but provisionally accepted the morality of deterrence based on mutual assured destruction pending the feasibility of abolition, and most Catholics went along with this dispensation. But many were less comfortable with, and more exacting about, proxy wars and campaigns of covert influence and action. A new generation of liberal Catholic thinkers reinforced this anxiety. They included the American monk Thomas Merton; the Jesuit-raised democratic socialist Michael Harrington, self-described as "a pious apostate, an atheist shocked by the faithlessness of the believers, a fellow traveler of moderate Catholicism";[89] and the brothers Daniel and Philip Berrigan, respectively a Jesuit priest and a Josephite priest, both iconic antiwar activists.

The brutal persecution of Buddhists by South Vietnamese President Diem, a purportedly devout Catholic, galled some of these thinkers. More general opposition based on just war theory as well as unalloyed pacifism burgeoned as the United States' military involvement escalated and casualties multiplied, yielding various acts of civil disobedience. Catholic demonstrations took a shocking turn in November 1965 when seminarian Roger Allen LaPorte immolated himself in front of the United Nations building in New York— probably in emulation of the Vietnamese monk Thich Quang Duc, whose martyred incineration an Associated Press photograph had recently publicized.

Bolstering the attitude of dissent and agitation was the social liberalism of Pope John XXIII and of Vatican II. The church added peace and economic development to the Catholic agenda by way of *Pacem in Terris* by Pope John XXIII in 1963 and *The Constitution of the Church and the Modern World* promulgated by the Second Vatican Council in 1965, and then through Pope Paul VI's *Popularum Progresso* in 1967. In these documents, the church again rose to defend the powerless victims of war and economic oppression from the developed world. The latter two were published when Agee was coming to terms with his work in the CIA. More acutely, in Latin America radical priests had harnessed liberation theology in response to its widespread poverty and exclusionary politics. The most influential among them was the Peruvian Dominican priest Gustavo Gutiérrez (as of 2020, the John Cardinal O'Hara Endowed Professor of Theology at Notre Dame), who believed that the church should advance social and political revolution. Liberation theology interpreted Christianity in general and Catholicism in particular as a pacifist religion of the poor, and its Latin American adherents considered the Catholic Church hierarchy in South America part of the privileged class structure that had oppressed indigenous populations from Pizarro's conquest of the Incas onward.[90] Thus, liberation theology was immensely disruptive to the established Cold War order in providing religious sanction for the mobilization of the impoverished, whom US-backed counterinsurgency efforts in the Western Hemisphere and Kennedy's Alliance for Progress may have intended to help but had actually disempowered.

The revolutionary flavor of liberation theology found some reinforcement in dependency theory, articulated by Argentine economist Raul Prebisch, whereby developing nations of the Southern Hemisphere had been made economically reliant on industrialized ones of the North to buy their raw materials but systemically denied the added value of manufactured products and rendered ever poorer by having to purchase them—a kind of geopolitical gaslighting. The Alliance for Progress was intended in part to address this structural inequality through direct foreign investment. But its inadequacies had become apparent by the mid-1960s and given rise to the conviction among many impoverished Latin Americans and their supporters that their own governments were complicit in their suffering, intensifying revolutionary impulses.[91] Writing in 1971, Gutiérrez, who did recognize the risks of extreme polemicization and radicalization, put it this way:

Among more alert groups today, what we have called a new awareness of Latin American reality is making headway. They believe that there can be authentic development for Latin America only if there is liberation from the domination exercised by the great capitalist countries, and especially by the most powerful, the United States of America. This liberation also implies a confrontation with these groups' natural allies, their compatriots who control the national power structure. It is becoming more evident that Latin American peoples will not emerge from their present status except by means of a profound transformation, *a social revolution*, which will radically and qualitatively change the conditions in which they now live. The oppressed sectors within each country are becoming aware—slowly, it is true—of their class interests and of the painful road which must be followed to accomplish the breakup of the status quo.[92]

National Security Doctrine was, to put it mildly, incompatible with liberation theology and dependency theory. Although evangelical Protestantism would arguably become a stronger force for radical change in Latin America, liberation theology as well as dependency theory had taken hold in Mexico in the late 1960s.[93] As a rule, at that point Latin American rulers met the protesters fueled by these sets of ideas with brute force.[94] Diaz Ordaz was no exception.

This sociopolitical backdrop was a fertile one for Agee's disaffection. He had helped conceive of the Olympics cover slot that he was now filling, and the station chief and his fellow case officers all saw its remoteness from normal embassy functions as a promising means of minimizing suspicions that he was CIA and enriching recruitment possibilities. Agee was a free agent personally as well as operationally. With Janet back in Washington, in autumn 1967 he became romantically involved with a left-leaning American woman on the Olympic Organizing Committee who had relinquished her US citizenship. He gave her the pseudonym "Muriel" in *On the Run*, but her real name was Susan Torres de Espinda.[95] He introduced her to his children as "Susannah Jones."[96] Among other things, she aired to him her belief that the CIA had been involved in the killing of Che Guevara—he had just been shot dead by a Bolivian soldier in October 1967—whom she had admired.

In undertaking this relationship, it was as though Agee, girded by new love or at least consuming infatuation, were pushing himself to make the move he had long contemplated but repeatedly deferred. In June 1968, after a senior case officer had informed him that the agency was pleased with his work and intended to promote him, Agee told the case officer that he planned to resign, remarry, and stay in Mexico. Shortly thereafter, he affirmed these intentions to Winston Scott, the long-serving station chief, and followed up the two conversations with a memorandum—citing only personal reasons—to headquarters. "The sense of relief is very strong now that I have formally announced my intention to resign," he reflected. "Perhaps I should have done this on returning from Montevideo, because I have felt very strained beneath the surface since coming to Mexico." His divorce had become acrimonious, and Janet had threatened to expose him as a CIA officer to strengthen her hand on child custody arrangements.[97] By then, however, his prospective resignation had diminished her leverage.

The Olympics were to be held from October 12 to October 27. The Mexican government had mounted an immense financial and practical effort to make the event shine, and Diaz Ordaz was determined to present to the world a peaceful and orderly venue. During the summer, as the games approached, social and political protest spearheaded by students over economic inequality and authoritarian government swelled. Throughout Latin America, right-wing governments, usually supported by the CIA, had co-opted the Catholic Church, further stimulating dissenters who drew on, among other things, liberation theology.

On July 26, the recognized anniversary of the Cuban Revolution, a protest against the Mexican government in Mexico City led to outright rioting and police repression. Police occupied buildings of the National Autonomous University of Mexico (UNAM) in Mexico City, and the wave spread to the university towns of Villahermosa and Jalapa. Over the course of a week, eight students were killed, 400 injured, and over 1,000 arrested. On August 1, the rector of UNAM led a peaceful march, 50,000 strong, in Mexico City. Although a strike committee broadly influenced by the National Liberation Movement, the National Center of Democratic Students, and the Communist Party of Mexico provided rhetorical impetus, the protests themselves were largely spontaneous, and focused on the PRI's monopoly on political power and devotion to a privileged elite. The protesters demanded the resignation of the police chiefs, the disbanding of the riot police, the repeal of nebulous criminal prohibitions against "social dissolution," and compensation for the wounded and families of the dead. Later they insisted on the release of political prisoners. The government refused, claiming falsely that foreign agitators were behind the unrest and denying, preposterously, that there were any political prisoners in Mexico.[98]

After a couple of weeks of relative calm, some 200,000 demonstrators gathered to protest the cost of the Olympics—about $175 million. Fearing a mass effort to preempt the games, Diaz Ordaz announced he would use the military to ensure they were held. As students blanketed communities to explain their position, thousands of troops in tanks and armored cars seized UNAM on the pretext that was being used for political rather than educational purposes. Over the next week, another ten to twenty students were killed and over a hundred wounded in riots throughout the Mexico City. The Tlatelolco section of town, about a mile-and-a-half north of the city's main square, became the focal point of protest activity. It is the site of Aztec ruins, the Plaza of the Three Cultures notionally celebrating national solidarity, and one of the main vocational schools of the National Polytechnic Institute, after UNAM Mexico's most esteemed university. Government troops had also occupied that school. On October 2, in the early evening, about 3,000 students, parents, teachers, workers, and peasants gathered in the plaza to march in protest of this action. Taking note of the 1,000 troops in armored vehicles and machine-gun-mounted jeeps that had massed along the route, the planners called off the march but the rally continued, peacefully, in place. The troops nonetheless surrounded the plaza and opened fire, unleashing 15,000 rounds in several hours. The exact number killed remains uncertain, as some bodies mysteriously disappeared, but it was between 150 and 400. The following day, the International Olympic Committee convened a secret emergency meeting on whether to cancel the games, deciding not to do so by the margin of a single vote.[99]

Scott, though skeptical of Diaz Ordaz's capacity to deliberate prudently under pressure, had unquestioningly accepted the information that Mexican military officers and civilian officials had funneled to the agency. He filed a report, later proven false but passed to the White House, that cited only eight dead students and credited classified sources claiming that the protesters had been armed and had initiated the hostilities. He adamantly characterized the unrest preceding the military onslaught as a "carefully planned" left-wing provocation, when in fact it was a largely undirected reaction to government authoritarianism. It later became clear that the Mexican military's chief of staff, under orders from Diaz Ordaz to quell mass disturbances to project the image of a squared-away Mexico, had deployed ten soldiers on the top floor of a building overlooking the demonstration and ordered them to surreptitiously fire on the crowd to provoke a reaction.[100]

The Tlatelolco massacre was one of the most savage instances of government repression during the Cold War. But it was also a watershed for democratic political activism in Mexico, unequivocally incriminating the PRI, divorcing it from the Mexican Revolution, "puncturing the myth of consensual order," alienating the middle class, and galvanizing the protest movement.[101] Even though Diaz Ordaz shouldered all of the blame for the massacre at Tlatelolco, Luis Echeverria Alvarez, Diaz Ordaz's successor, was undoubtedly complicit in the bloodbath as then interior minister. As president, he felt compelled to pledge the "democratic opening" of Mexico in domestic affairs, overtly defend Castro's government in Cuba, explicitly embrace dependency theory, and adopt South-centric *tercermundismo*—Third-Worldism—in international affairs.[102] While most adherents of liberation theology did not expressly advocate violence, some did declare that Marxism could be consistent with Christianity and explicitly endorsed revolution.[103] After Tlatelolco, some radical Mexican priests proclaimed that the PRI was exploiting the Mexican people and called for its violent overthrow.[104]

Thus, for Agee, the Tlatelolco massacre was a perfect storm of confirmation—of American overreach, of the bankruptcy of the National Security Doctrine, of dependency theory, of liberation theology. If there was a point of no return for him, that event—not the US intervention in the Dominican Republic, not the Bonaudi interrogation, not some slowly coalescing epiphany about the CIA's failure to present a better way of life to Latin Americans than its communist adversaries did—was it. By October 28, 1968, Agee had adopted what appeared to be irreversibly anti-CIA convictions: "The difficult admission is that I became the servant of the capitalism I rejected. I became one of its secret policemen. The CIA, after all, is nothing more than the secret police of American capitalism, plugging up leaks in the political dam night and day so that shareholders of U.S. companies operating in poor countries can continue enjoying the rip-off. The key to CIA success is the 2 or 3 percent of the population in poor countries that get most of the cream."[105]

This echoes the overarching explanation he provides in the introduction to *Inside the Company*: "After twelve years in the agency," he wrote, "I finally understood how much suffering it was causing, that millions of people all over the world had been killed or had had their lives destroyed by the CIA and the institutions it supports."[106] He would maintain and reiterate these sentiments once he had established himself as an unprecedented CIA turncoat, years after he left the agency, sometimes wedding them to an antielitist strain rooted in his Catholic background.[107] But in late 1968, he had not yet decided to become a crusading outlier. He seemed more inclined to go quietly, cut his losses, and keep his philosophical grievances to himself, like most disenchanted CIA officers.

One has to take the realistic view: in order to fulfil responsibilities you have to compromise with the system knowing full well that the system doesn't work for everybody. This means everybody has to get what he can within decency's limits—which can be stretched when needed to assure a little more security. What I have to do now is get mine, inside the system, and forget I ever worked for the CIA. No, there's no use trying to change the system. What happened at the

Plaza of the Three Cultures is happening all over the world to people trying to change the system. Life is too short and has too many delights that might be missed. At thirty-three I've got half a lifetime to enjoy them.[108]

That they had crystallized so neatly on the eve of his departure from the CIA, however, still doesn't quite scan. His resignation letter, dated and effective November 22, 1968, was self-consciously if not obsequiously respectful, expressing "high esteem" for his colleagues, stating his strong belief that "their influence and example has been of real and lasting importance" to him and his hope that he would "maintain their friendship . . . during the years to come," and attributing his departure to his "personal circumstances incompatible at this time with the best interests of the Agency," clearly alluding to his separation and custody travails.[109] On the same day, he signed his termination Secrecy Agreement, by which he reiterated the written promise he had made at the outset of his CIA career never to divulge official secrets.[110] It seems doubtful that the resignation letter was merely disingenuous. If at that point he had firmly decided to inflict maximal damage on CIA operations and the conduct of US foreign policy, he would have been sorely tempted to forgo resignation and stay in the CIA as a mole. He does not remotely suggest that he entertained such a possibility. Accordingly, his explanation for the discrepancy between the respectful words he used in resigning from the CIA in 1968 and his subsequent active hostility toward agency activities several years later as merely prudential seems insincere.[111]

In Latin America during the 1950s and 1960s, the agency was supporting more brutal regimes than elsewhere, and Castro's Cuba was a uniquely sharp irritant that drove the United States to do over-the-top things in the hemisphere. But if those circumstances made Agee especially susceptible to disillusionment, there were also countervailing factors. He admitted that, after a dozen years with the agency, his jaundiced eye may have made it all the harder for him to reverse or moderate his stance. Cynicism is a hard habit to break, even in the light of the Bonaudi and Tlatelolco incidents. In 1969, when he finally left the agency, many were still inclined to rationalize the support for right-wing dictators in Latin America, along with détente and even the Vietnam War, as elements of the kind of strategic realism that Henry Kissinger would soon advocate, dignify, and popularize. And he acknowledged his own residual ambivalence, noting, however ruefully, that "old loyalties die hard."[112] He and Susan went their separate ways for nonpolitical reasons; he never did tell her who his actual employer was.

It clearly took time for Agee's certitude about turning toward radical ideology to solidify. His impulse to leave the agency does appear to have been primarily moral, but the behavior it immediately prompted was withdrawal rather than crusade. At the same time, he continued to feed his incipient radical appetite in his choices of left-leaning women while also seeking a way to succeed with distinction. In this quality he was something of what the British call a Jack-the-lad—one eager and determined to rise above his station, out to willfully exceed what others expect of him, intent on showing them up by flaunting his audacity, and confident that his special qualities exempt him from the normal rules. Glenn Carle noted that these kinds of sentiments are common among case officers and often impel their decisions to enter a profession that allows— indeed, requires—them to break the rules. "People usually become spies because their ego is very important. They may feel unrecognized or superior to others, and [as a spy] they're freed from conventional obligations. This is the positive interpretation. Agee had the arrogance of feeling superior."[113]

His father had been a highly successful businessman and an Eisenhower conservative. Agee chose to enter the CIA in part because such a life—especially if handed down to him by his father— struck him as ungratifyingly banal as well as unearned. The case officer's vocation turned out to be unfulfilling to him as well. But it's unlikely that it was just the unsavory subordination of means to ends that so bothered Agee about that life. His personality subsumed an overweening extrovertedness that professional secrecy and discretion probably could not have indefinitely accommodated even without the moral snares. The mid-to-late Cold War state of the world was complicit. The United States of the early 1970s, after Agee had finally left the CIA, was in many ways a burnt-out place. In the previous decade, as the government stumbled into Vietnam and tarried on civil rights, its arrogance and naiveté had energized a generation. The youth mobilization had been effective—yielding the Civil Rights Act of 1964, LBJ's stand-down in 1968, and finally the Paris Accords in 1973—but the process had been one of grinding attrition rather than sparkling triumph. The collective psychological result was not elation but exhaustion, and it did not sustain idealism.

3

The Consolidation of Dissidence

Agee's professional dissatisfaction grew during the most verdant period of American political protest, between 1965 and 1968, when student demonstrations against Vietnam and civil rights agitation were at their peak. Yet he largely missed it. Woodstock, the symbolic zenith of 1960s American idealism, took place mid-August 1969, shortly after Agee had left the CIA. But it was already dissipating. The Manson murders, one of the two episodes taken to mark the spiritual end of the sixties, actually occurred a week before Woodstock, and the other, the concert at Altamont, the following December. At the time, of course, they were not perceived with such momentous gloom. There would still be some politically powerful conflagrations, such as the Ohio National Guard's opening fire on student antiwar demonstrators at Kent State University in May 1970, killing four and wounding nine, but such events were more sobering than inspiring. Nixon's decade had begun in earnest.

Notwithstanding his unpropitious timing, Agee's resignation had been overdetermined by a diminished sense of geopolitical urgency and efficacy, agency conduct in which he was complicit that he found morally repugnant, marital discord, and the romance of dramatic dissent encouraged by women. At the same time, he had not yet manifested a personal need for a more celebrated form of distinction than the clandestine life of a case officer allowed. His personality did not seem to be quite that of a conspiratorial glad-hander, eager and embracing. Early in his transition from secretive spy to proactive dissenter, he chose discretion rather than publicity. Then he changed directions and became a public revolutionary. If he had been trying on this life merely for material gain or reputational aggrandizement, there were less disruptive avenues that would have enabled him to stay in the United States. He might have avoided the wrath of the US intelligence and law-enforcement communities as well as the intense scrutiny of their European counterparts. He chose a relatively hard way.

Yet there remains considerable doubt about Agee's change in political sensibility circa 1968–69 due to his disinclination to voice complaints about the agency in particular or US policy in general. In his foreword to Kim Philby's 1968 autobiography *My Silent War*, Philby's friend and fellow MI6 alumnus Graham Greene famously noted of the British mole: "The end, of course, in his eyes, is held to justify the means, but this is a view taken, perhaps less openly, by most men involved in politics, if we are to judge them by their ac-tions, whether the politician be a Disraeli or a Wilson. 'He betrayed his country'—yes, perhaps he did, but who among us has not com-mitted treason to something or someone more important than a country?"[1] The "something," a sympathetic Greene went on to ob-serve, can be a faith like Catholicism or an ideology like commu-nism, both of which preoccupied Greene himself. While Agee even-tually came around to something close to the latter, perhaps with the aid of the former, it took him a while. In the first instance he had a moral reaction to CIA machinations that did not immediately subtend an alternative political system or philosophy. Though thus unmoored, Agee may well have found strength in his religion that enabled him to progress as a dissident, as opposed to stagnating as a disaffected CIA case officer and nothing more, as well as to tolerate the civil limbo that he visited on himself.

His first impulse was not to write an earthshaking, combative, and treacherous CIA tell-all memoir. In fact, he stayed in Mexico

City doing other things for almost two years after he left the CIA.[2] He initially hoped to leverage some commercial connections in Mexico he had developed in connection with the 1968 Summer Olympics into a lucrative sports development program for Mexican youth—a notably apolitical venture. His designs were serious, as he had worked up a formal proposal casting himself as executive director, but he maintained official secrecy, describing himself as "Assistant Olympic Attaché of the U.S. embassy in Mexico, who is resigning from the U.S. Foreign Service in November 1968."[3] While he tried to develop that venture, he started and ran a mirror sales business for about a year, borrowing over $7,000 from his father. There was something almost comically confounding, and rather meta, about a disillusioned CIA case officer peddling a product that could enable people to either look at themselves or deflect attention to other things. The choice may have reflected Agee's confusion and ambivalence about leaving the agency. In any case, Agee was out of his vocational depth and also depressed by the collapse of his plans to marry the American woman he had fallen for. Neither the sports enterprise nor the mirror business panned out.[4] Although his vocational gifts for deception may have remained intact, evidently he still was no salesman.

Even after the business efforts collapsed, Agee was not ready to resort to the blockbuster political exposé. Instead he hoped to work toward a graduate degree in political science and international relations at the National Autonomous University of Mexico, then return to the United States to teach on the strength of a commissioned, straightforward, aboveboard book, albeit a very critical one, on the CIA. He pulled together an outline and a proposal for the book project in roughly six months but was unable to get a contract. The four editors he consulted in New York, he said, wanted "a sensationalist exposé approach—divorced from the more difficult political and economic realities that give the [intelligence] operations meaning."[5] So entrepreneurship had been his first choice as a retirement plan, writing a vanilla critique of US intelligence practices his second.

At this point, it's worth pausing to consider the literary nature of *Inside the Company* and the degree—probably quite modest—to which it might distort or occlude the picture of Agee's actual state of mind. On this score, the book is without doubt the most probative source, but it remains a highly imperfect one. Although Agee formally presents much of the narrative as an extemporaneous diary, it is in fact a largely retrospective—and therefore artificial—reconstruction of the real-time evolution of his thinking. A perceptive CIA analyst wrote in a book review:

> Agee publishes what appear to be chronological diary entries which describe his operations and their progress, other station operations, and new operational initiatives as they developed. However, whatever factual information may have been contained in his actual diary, the entries now have been expanded to include the historical, political and economic contexts of his operations as he now views those contexts since leaving the Agency. Thus, what we have in this book is not a diary of the period, but an account of that period interpreted after four years of subsequent research, and evaluated by very different ideas and attitudes than those he held at the time. Agee makes no attempt to conceal his methods of composition, but what he presents in the form and rhetoric of his reconstructed recollections is a "diary" that sounds more authoritative, comprehensive, and intelligible than any diary actually kept by a professional in similar circumstances could possibly have been.[6]

Agee's process couldn't help but be teleologically bent, informed by the fait accompli of the writer's attitude and beliefs at the time of writing and vulnerable to the temptation of reinvention. To an extent, that is true of all memoirs and autobiographies, and makes their authors inherently unreliable narrators. But Agee's very compulsion to make his case for an authentic ideological conversion warrants an especially high degree of vigilance and scrutiny. While he never tried to hide this fact, he also indulged in hindsight, self-justification, and some obfuscation. If the book is largely earnest, it is also tendentious and inevitably, in places, disingenuous.

From *Inside the Company*, it appears that a combination of abject post-CIA professional frustration and failure, on one hand, and ideological education, on the other, had driven him to the radical option. Under a diary entry headed "Mexico City—January 1971," he wrote: "I have decided now to name all the names and organizations connected with CIA operations and to reconstruct as accurately as possible the events in which I participated. No more hiding behind theory and hypothetical cases to protect the tools of CIA adventures."[7] Late passages in the book, such as this one, reflected Agee's thinking close to the time he was actually writing the book and would have been less amenable to invention than those corresponding to earlier periods. In any case, it seems safe to say that had any of Agee's politically tamer enterprises been a success, he might well have turned out like many an unsung retired CIA officer: cynical and disenchanted but content to keep his demons private.

Agee spent the last half of 1971 mainly in Cuba, traveling on a visa obtained in Montreal.[8] He was conducting "research" for the book in an arrangement facilitated by French publisher François Maspero, who had published Che Guevara's Bolivian diary, expressed an interest in Agee's memoir, and may well have been an agent of influence for Cuban intelligence.[9] Agee rather archly recounted the trip in the book itself, casting his jaunt to the island as a substantively logical means of finding "information needed to reconstruct . . . events" given that "for security reasons anywhere in the U.S. would be unwise," as well as an opportunity "to see first hand what the Cuban Revolution has meant to the people."[10] He does specifically note topics on which Cuban archives might have held useful material, such as a report on the Alliance for Progress and a Cuban position paper on the United Nations Economic Commission for Latin America.[11] But there were certainly other places he could have found such material besides the United States and Cuba, and his use of the passive voice or pronouns devoid of referents to obscure the identity or affiliation of precisely who in Cuba facilitated his visit is conspicuous. He is somewhat more candid in his 1987 book *On the Run*—the second memoir, detailing his life following the publication of *Inside the Company*—merely stressing that he resisted being treated as a defector and did not submit to debriefings on CIA operations or personnel and acknowledging the administrative assistance of the Communist

Party of Cuba and the Cuban Foreign Ministry.[12] Some of Agee's defenders elide his detour to Cuba in their accounts of his life. His son Chris omits it altogether.[13] Philip Agee Jr. torpidly states that "the only associations my father mentioned with the Cuban government were with the Cuban Institute for Friendship with the Peoples, news organizations such as Prensa Latina and Radio Havana Cuba, and, when he started his travel agency, the Ministry of Tourism and Ministry of Foreign Investment and Economic Cooperation."[14] Kaeten Mistry, in his admirably researched and cogently argued 2019 article in the *Journal of American History*, glosses over the point.[15]

Fidel Castro, a fiercely grandiose figure, was always determined that Cuba should operate substantially without Soviet constraints. Former Cuban Dirección de Inteligencia (DGI) officer Orlando Castro Hidalgo noted that "when one dances with the bear, one notices that the embrace grows tighter. Castro chafed in the embrace and tried to maintain his independence."[16] To a greater or lesser degree, of course, the KGB trained and funded the DGI for the duration of Castro's regime.[17] And Cuba could not survive economically against the American embargo without the Soviet Union's subsidies and goods, and especially its oil. But in the middle years of the Cold War, when military brinkmanship was one of that conflict's main idioms, Cuba's geographic proximity to the United States was even more valuable to the Soviet Union than Moscow's money and oil was to Havana and afforded Castro considerable leverage. Within the DGI, there was a fairly strong pro-Kremlin faction, but it was unable to prevail overall. The upshot was that the DGI was able to operate with substantial independence from the KGB.

While the Soviet stand-down in the Cuban missile crisis in 1962 may have marginally diminished Cuba's immediate strategic importance to Moscow, the immense political influence and prestige that Castro enjoyed among communist revolutionary movements in Latin America largely sustained Cuba's—and the DGI's—freedom of action through most of the 1960s. Indeed, Castro upon occasion would publicly criticize the Soviets' lack of support for direct subversion and guerrilla warfare and their softer, less aggressive political approach.[18] Internally, Cuban disdain could be even more sweeping and presumptuous—extending, for example, to the Soviets' perceived dearth of assistance to the Vietcong. At one point, Castro planned to bring this up at a proposed conference of nonaligned nations but shelved the idea when Moscow became more accommodating.[19]

Until the late 1960s, the Soviets allowed the DGI to pursue Castro's dramatic and overtly disruptive Guevarist designs of armed communist struggle in the Western Hemisphere. But after over a decade of trying, it became clear that the program wasn't working. No Latin American country became communist, and by the early 1970s two—Chile and Uruguay, where Agee had done his transformative second tour—would in fact fall to right-wing coups. Furthermore, Cuba's economic needs, especially for fuel, were burgeoning. In a secret deal, in exchange for more assistance, Castro would end his freewheeling criticism of Soviet policy and Cuba would follow Soviet guidelines for not only its management of domestic economic affairs but also its formulation and execution of foreign policy. Additionally, Moscow would insert some 5,000 Soviet personnel into the full range of Cuban government agencies. In particular, KGB people interacted more closely with the DGI as liaison officers, and DGI operations became more closely coordinated with the KGB's. The Soviet Union also comprehensively reequipped Cuba's military forces, instrumentalizing them in Angola and elsewhere and increasing Cuba's overall dependency. According to Hidalgo, the DGI "virtually became an arm of Soviet intelligence."

By 1970, Cuban officials appeared obeisant toward the Soviets.[20] After the failure of Castro's unrealistically ambitious plan for a ten-million-ton sugar crop that year, Cuba's economic situation became still more dire and called for even more generous Soviet material assistance. As a result, Havana was compelled to cut another Faustian bargain with Moscow, whereby a co-opted Castro had to both join hands with established communist parties to which he had once condescended and also dial back active support for the Guevarist movements in Latin America committed to armed revolution that he had previously elevated.[21] The undoubted presence of KGB liaison officers in DGI headquarters in Cuba strongly suggests that the KGB was aware of Agee's "research" stint in Cuba in 1971, though it remains uncertain whether the Soviet agency influenced the Cubans' decision to allow him in.[22]

Here Agee was clearly crossing the giddy line, at least half-consciously diminishing his options for crossing back to the other side. "I would be fearful of going to Cuba for several reasons: my past work against Cuba and communism, possible Soviet pressures, my reluctance to engage in sessions for counter-intelligence ploys, problems with the CIA afterwards. Mostly, I suppose, I am fearful that if the CIA learned that I had gone to Cuba they would begin a campaign to denigrate me as a traitor."[23] Obviously Agee was well aware that in traveling to Cuba he would be making himself a rich target for exploitation by adversary intelligence agencies. In the very next paragraph of *Inside the Company*, he makes it clear that even if they did not explicitly court him, he intended to use information gleaned in Cuba to benefit CIA opponents: "in Havana I could arrange to get information on the CIA to interested Latin American revolutionary organizations through their representatives — efficiently and securely."[24] It remains obscure precisely what book research there was to be done in Cuba that he had not done or could not have accomplished elsewhere: in substance, *Inside the Company* largely reflects widely reported and analyzed current events and Agee's own direct experience and inside knowledge. Notwithstanding his tortured circumspection and willful agnosticism on the page, he knew that in going to Cuba for no legitimate reason that bore scrutiny, he was confirming the agency's worst fears.

One estimable history of the CIA published in 1986, while providing what for that time was an unusually objective and dispassionate account of Agee's actions, still presumed that "Agee's sympathy with Marxist ideals was exploited by Cuban agents, who persuaded him to name everyone he knew in the CIA and associated with the CIA."[25] In *On the Run*, Agee conceded that some of the bureaucrats who minded him "had to be" intelligence or security officers, though he claimed not to know for sure — having orchestrated, presumably, plausible deniability.

Furthermore, Agee admitted to having written while in Cuba a memorandum on how the CIA might seek to subvert the socialist government of Chilean President Salvador Allende, and to giving the document to one of his Cuban handlers to provide to that government if Havana saw fit to do so.[26] The CIA had worked to deprive Allende, a Marxist politician, of the Chilean presidency throughout the 1960s, and Agee himself had been involved in its efforts to funnel cash to Allende's opponents—which he then merely considered a "nuisance assignment"—while posted to Uruguay in 1964.[27] With KGB support, Allende had been elected in August 1970 and taken office the following November, embarking on an ambitious but, in time, economically fraught and politically divisive path of nationalization, redistribution, and social reform. In 1971, Allende reestablished Chile's diplomatic relations with Cuba, rejecting the OAS's prohibition on such relations. He broadly supported Latin American revolution in line with Castro, who then aligned himself with Allende and called Allende's election "the most important event after the Cuban revolution in Latin America." But dysfunctional public policy, burgeoning anti-Marxist militancy and intimidation, the Left's countermobilization, and reactionary military repression whipsawed the Allende government, and the CIA and its clients preyed on the government's weakness. During Allende's tenure, the military put down at least five coup attempts.

With the approval of Secretary of State Henry Kissinger, the CIA supported a successful coup led by General Agusto Pinochet Ugarte on September 11, 1973—a singularly traumatic moment for Chile. Financing was provided by the International Telephone & Telegraph Corporation, which had extensive interests there. As the Chilean Air Force strafed and bombed the presidential palace in Santiago, Allende died from a gunshot, by either suicide or assassination. The coup marked the culmination of years of covert US support for authoritarian right-wing regimes committed to the suppression of popular left-wing political movements. Pinochet's military regime ruled Chile for the next seventeen years, killing and deporting several thousand political opponents and torturing over 30,000. In the historical record, the 1973 overthrow of Allende's government came to epitomize American overreaching in the name of the Monroe Doctrine and the dark dimension of Kissingerian realism.[28]

There is no available evidence that Havana ever shared Agee's wisdom with Allende's government. Cuban officials seemed to consider Agee's most valuable potential contribution to be the publication of the book he was researching and writing; passing Agee's information would have posed a risk to that outcome.[29] As it happened, Agee himself behaved recklessly and tipped his hand to the CIA. In November 1971, toward the end of that long visit, he sent a letter to the editor of *Marcha*, an influential, leftist Uruguayan weekly newspaper, and the paper duly published it. Identifying himself as a former CIA officer, Agee warned of CIA interference in upcoming elections and announced his intention to write an exposé. A CIA memo to the file indicates that the *Marcha* letter was the first indication it had of Agee's "change of heart," and that the agency's prior understanding was that he had been led to resign over a "personal crisis" precipitated by his separation from Janet—namely, that his overseas employment put him at odds with court-ordered child custody arrangements and a government salary would not support two households.[30] The Cubans truncated Agee's research sojourn, leaving him in a state of emotional and political suspense. He believed his hosts lacked confidence in the prospective book's ideological content, but they might have been more unhappy that Agee had unnecessarily called attention to himself and his activities in the letter to the editor.

WATCHED IN PARIS

In December 1971, after his stay in Cuba, Agee went to Paris with a wishful eye to attenuating CIA scrutiny. In *Inside the Company*, he himself judged the *Marcha* letter a tactical mistake insofar as it clued the agency to his radical designs, which could have jeopardized the book's publication. The CIA Operations Directorate then located him through the French intelligence services and dispatched Keith Gardiner, an old agency colleague and friend of Agee, to ferret out his rationale for publishing the letter to *Marcha*, to determine what he planned to disclose about CIA operations, and to pressure him to reconsider. Gardiner turned up at Agee's Paris hotel room shortly after Christmas, and Agee agreed to talk with him over dinner at a nearby café. Gardiner suggested that the Soviets were lashed up with Agee's French publisher. Agee did not feel close kinship with Gardiner—he would later portray him disparagingly in a *Playboy* interview as "a Harvard type"[31]—and declined to discuss the substance of the book. But, to get the agency off his back and ensure the publication, he comprehensively lied. He told Gardiner that he had completed a long draft of the book when he was only about a third done, and he said that he did not plan to divulge any secrets or damaging material and would submit the manuscript to the CIA for vetting—when in fact he had decided almost a year earlier to spill everything and evade the agency.[32] Dissembling under considerable duress to a CIA case officer, Agee ratcheted up his commitment to dissidence.

Journalist David Corn, in his 1994 book *Blond Ghost*, noted that Agee had earnestly told Gardiner that he was not the same person Gardiner had known at the agency and that he now thought its activities were simply wrong. Gardiner registered parochial puzzlement over Agee's jettisoning a career in which he had, in Gardiner's estimation, "done quite well."[33] As if to rub salt in the wound, Agee briefly returned to Cuba in May 1972 "for discussions on research left from last year, and on additional needs that have arisen since"[34]— nebulous phraseology that suggests something more substantive and operational, possibly including money, than innocent academic matters.

Despite his determination to make his book a blockbuster, however, by August the small advance he had received from the French publisher had run out and the Cubans had cooled on the project. He was broke, depressed, and nervous. Holed up in Paris, he regarded himself as effectively stateless and closely watched. "Events in the past three months have taken unfavorable turns, and I am fearful that the CIA is now closing in. My money has run out and I am living on small donations from friends, street surveillance has forced me to live in hiding, research still pending in Cuba was canceled, I still cannot find the information I need, and people who have befriended me and on whom I am depending show frequent signs of being infiltrators."[35]

His suspicions proved correct. The agency ran an operation against Agee over the course of about three months, from August through October 1972, using agents he knew as Sal Ferrera, a purported left-wing journalist, and Leslie Donegan, a friend of Ferrera who was supposedly a Venezuelan heiress and a University of Geneva graduate student.* They befriended Agee, gleaned information about his book project, and gave him money to support the effort. In desperate gratitude, and perhaps to some extent because he was smitten with Donegan, he allowed them to see his manuscript despite his suspicions. It became clear that they constituted a kind of modified "honey trap" when he discovered that the typewriter Donegan had lent him was implanted with a tracking device and a bug, and determined that Donegan's real name was Janet Strickland.[36] After he found the electronics, they tried in vain to coax him to come to Spain. He believed they were setting him up to be imprisoned, harmed, or possibly killed with the facilitation of Francisco Franco's right-wing, fascist government, with which the United States maintained a Cold War alliance of convenience to ensure military basing

---

* Ferrera was in fact a seasoned and high-achieving operative, recruited out of Loyola University in Chicago, for a domestic espionage program known as MH/CHAOS that targeted American citizens worldwide from 1967 to 1974. Before decamping to Paris, he had provided the agency with intelligence on left-wing organizations and publications in several American cities—mainly Chicago, but also Baltimore, Berkeley, Boston, New York, and Washington, DC. After the Agee operation, Ferrera returned to Chicago, changed his name to Allen Vincent Carter, and relocated to Costa Mesa, the Orange County suburb of Los Angeles, where the genuine leftist journalist Angus Mackenzie tracked him down. Ferrera aka Carter denied ever working for the CIA and claimed to be employed by a start-up travel company. When Mackenzie produced copies of informant reports that Ferrera had sent to CIA headquarters, obtained via a FOIA request, Ferrera gave him the finger and slammed the door. Angus Mackenzie, *Secrets: The CIA's War at Home* (Berkeley: University of California Press, 1997), 33–39, 55–57. See also Frank G. Rafalko, *MH/CHAOS: The CIA's Campaign Against the Radical New Left and the Black Panthers* (Annapolis, MD: Naval Institute Press, 2011).

access, among other things.[37] Although the operation was blown, Donegan had provided the agency with a copy of Agee's draft manuscript by October 1972, well before the publication of *Inside the Company* in 1975.

The book would not be redacted, and it disclosed the names and true status of over 400 CIA officers, collaborators, agents, informants, and fronts, both incidentally in the narrative and systematically in an appendix. The publication of the book, said an internal CIA reviewer, "will affect the CIA as a severe body blow does any living organ: some parts will be affected more than others, but the health of the whole is bound to suffer. A considerable number of CIA personnel must be diverted from their normal duties to undertake the meticulous and time-consuming task of repairing the damage done to its Latin American program, and to see what can be done to help those injured by the author's revelations." Further, the book gave communists and the extreme Left "specific knowledge of the CIA's Latin American operations and insight into CIA modus operandi in order to permit them to counter U.S. and particular CIA actions."[38]

In April 1968, Winston Scott, the Mexico City station chief, had told Agee that headquarters had confirmed that Agee was to receive another promotion, his fifth in eight years. But Agee's supervisors had also been aware of his marital and custody problems, and they made it clear he would have to clean them up to keep his employment secure.[39] In addition, his last evaluation was negative, stating that his work "was definitely less than satisfactory" and reflected "little or no effort to fulfill his obligations to the organization," Mexico City Station having reported that he had done "practically nothing of value."[40] The truth was he had been troubled and distracted, and some degree of corporate vindictiveness was unsurprising. A psychological assessment prepared in 1959–60, before Agee undertook his first field assignment, had concluded that "the chances of his remaining with the Agency on a career basis are poor."[41] Still employed in 1968, he had probably exceeded the psychiatrists' expectations.

Now agency psychiatrists did some retrospective concocting.

Their new narrative purported to illuminate innate and far deeper problems with Agee. The psychiatrists cast his disloyalty as the natural product of a deeply flawed personality and suggested that Agee's CIA supervisors had detected his professional liabilities before he left the agency. At the same time, the agency's reaction evinced more embarrassment than alarm and indulged an inclination to have it both ways. Agee was characterized, paradoxically, as both aberrational and predictable. Official documents that Agee later obtained via the Freedom of Information Act (FOIA) registered the CIA's shock, dismay, and by implication surprise over Agee's conduct. "PBFA is the first employee in the Central Intelligence Agency's history who has taken a public position in actual opposition to the Agency," said one. It went on to casually distort the facts of his departure, acknowledging his ability but suggesting that he was effectively fired rather than leaving voluntarily: "Agee was considered a competent officer and there were no indicators of disaffection at the time he was asked to resign."[42] In another document, supervisory officers rued that "whatever his motives and however he came to acquire them, Agee is the only officer in the 27-year history of the CIA's Clandestine Service to abrogate his oath of secrecy and his sense of loyalty to the agency and his comrades."[43]

Stupefaction gave way to vindictiveness, as the agency planted ex post facto smears in Agee's record. One memorandum to the file, entitled "CIRCUMSTANCES LEADING UP TO RESIGNATION," was especially self-serving and tendentious in its condemnation. It stated that a CIA security report said Agee was a "steady churchgoer" but added that "he always displayed considerable feelings of superiority over both his parents and talked of them with scorn, indifference, and detachment."[44] Another 1972 CIA assessment, comically indiscriminate and scattershot, harped on the egomania theme, saying that he was "an individual who was especially driven to achieve success and recognition, who had overblown estimates of his own worth, and saw himself as superior to other individuals" and one with "a need to blame others for his lack of success," attributing his purported ideological conversion to midlife crisis, a "Messiah complex," and "opportunism," possibly tinged with suicidal and "psychotic" tendencies.[45] This retrospective appraisal was supposed to be based primarily on observations made for the CIA's evaluation of Agee for suitability as a career case officer early in his tenure at the agency. Yet some of those very observations had been seen as consistent with his exceptional academic record, a high US Air Force Officers Candidate School rank (third in his class), and superior CIA active-duty performance evaluations.[46]

Agency counterintelligence officers were somewhat less condemnatory and more candid than the psychiatrists. A substantially redacted "talking paper" on the draft of *Inside the Company*, prepared by the chief of counterintelligence for the director of central intelligence to use in conjunction with charts in discussing the Agee case at the White House, reiterated that Agee was considered a competent officer and had not manifested disenchantment.[47] Echoing that view, another post-resignation analysis noted that "there is not the slightest bit of information" to explain Agee's turn, and that he was "politically conservative, quite content with the construction and make-up of American society, and wedded to the existing system." Thus, according to the agency, his break did "not appear to come about through a deep-seated, honest conviction to right the wrongs of American foreign policy," and he seemed in his role as a political crusader merely to be meeting his own "ego satisfying demands."[48] In other words, the CIA was ostensibly writing off Agee as some kind of black swan it could not have anticipated.

Unpacked, this looked like rather artless bureaucratic asscovering. The CIA's notion that Agee's protestations of philosophical conversion were merely a facade for venality, lust, drunkenness, or emotional breakdown that he conjured after his personal and professional life had fallen apart was wildly inconsistent with Agee's true biographical profile: that of a rather square young man, moderate in his habits, who married his college sweetheart and had never strayed far from the political or social center. He had hardly been the libertine beatnik-in-waiting that the agency tried to describe.

In May 1972, Ted Shackley—the titular "Blond Ghost" of Corn's book—was fresh from service in Laos and in Vietnam, where he had been chief of station, and returned to Langley to take over the

Western Hemisphere Division. He was assigned to control the damage anticipated from Agee's disclosures in the draft manuscript. In Shackley's judgment, as chronicled by Corn and others, Agee's prospective revelations required the wholesale dismantling of intelligence networks throughout the Western Hemisphere—a draconian measure that was highly controversial within the agency but nonetheless authorized.[49] "The purpose," as John Prados put it, "was to realign operations and terminate anything that Philip Agee knew about," which meant "pensioning off agents and shutting down projects."[50] This was a function of the agency's institutional conservatism rather than a reaction to any particular instances of personal misfortune to officers or agents, or to any specific intelligence failures. As Corn noted in 2016, "in the CIA in general—and this is a principle of most intelligence services—if someone could have been blown, you assume that they were blown."[51] Shackley was also trying to stave off a deeper congressional investigation of CIA activities in Chile, including its collaboration with ITT to thwart Allende, and dire characterizations of Agee's internal beleaguerment in Latin America might have been useful in blunting Congress's investigation of the CIA.

Given the agency's fears that Agee would make unprecedentedly damaging disclosures about its operations, it is likely that some CIA officials contemplated killing him. But there is no substantiated public evidence of any full-blooded plan to do so. The decision-makers probably balked at arranging Agee's death for prudential rather than moral reasons: he was an obvious target, the CIA would have been the obvious culprit, and the blowback of even unproven accusations could have been devastating—all the more so given the withering congressional scrutiny the agency had come under. There are, however, some highly inferential indications in heavily redacted, declassified cables that there might once have been an inchoate plan to assassinate Agee. Melvin Wulf, Agee's lawyer, took the view that the US attorney general's decision across several administrations not to prosecute Agee suggested that the CIA "had other plans for him."[52] The Civil Rights Division of the Justice Department, showing no deference to the front office, launched a criminal investigation of the

CIA for potential civil rights violations against Agee in the late 1970s. Drew Days, the head of the Civil Rights Division, later at Yale Law School, indicated in a transmittal memorandum dated January 16, 1978, that he sent a substantive memo to the attorney general "about whether to prosecute CIA officials for civil rights violations against Philip Agee." "We don't know specifically what they [the agency] were planning to do, except we've always theorized that if the Civil Rights Division was undertaking a criminal investigation of the CIA, it must have been a planned assassination," Wulf said in 2016. "But that's just speculation."[53] In any case, it seems likely that the agency contemplated endangering his physical safety and mental stability.

If in late 1972 Agee was paranoid, he was objectively so. The agency did not regard him as a loopy renegade but rather as the "leader of an anti-U.S. government radical conspiracy seeking to destroy the Central Intelligence Agency by exposing its personnel abroad in the media."[54] Stateside, a CIA assistant general counsel confronted Agee's father about his son's dangerous conduct, handing him copies of his secrecy agreement and the Supreme Court's decision in *United States v. Marchetti* upholding CIA prepublication review of writings by ex-officers and prohibiting their disclosure of classified information. The agency also pressured Janet Agee to refuse Philip visits with their sons, and the Internal Revenue Service audited the senior Agee.[55]

The agency had run the Ferrera/Donegan operation against Agee for about three months before he figured it out in October 1972. At this point, Philip Jr., almost eleven, was living in Falls Church, Virginia, with his mother. He sent Agee a short note in care of Sal Ferrera apprising Agee that "a man from the government came to talk to Mom about you, but she did not say anything except your address. What they told her is that they wanted to pay you money to stop and that they would offer you another job (the job I'm not certain about)."[56] Assuming the government official was from the CIA and actually did say the agency would give Agee a job, the overture would have been a mere ploy for locating Agee and impeding his activities: on Agee's Request for Personnel Action for his resig-

also intensified his revolutionary convictions. In fall 1974, when Agee, his sons, and Seixas were staying in Cornwall, the agency appears to have made another effort to ascertain just what he was going to disclose, this one rather pathetic. Robert Deindorfer, ostensibly a freelance journalist, had by letter requested an interview. Agee complied, inviting Deindorfer to Cornwall, where he and his family were staying. Deindorfer was a buffoon and an ignoramus, causing his hosts to snicker. Suspecting he was either an awkward plant or an officious spy buff, Agee gave him nothing substantive.*

Perhaps Deindorfer's ineptitude emboldened Agee. In England, his notions of being an ideological maverick—and a man who many would consider a traitor—certainly hardened into a standing commitment. Despite evidence of the CIA's ongoing surveillance, Agee insouciantly displayed his disloyalty to the agency, visiting Cuba

* Several years later, Agee noticed that Deindorfer's letters to him shared spacing idiosyncrasies and a phrasing tic—the expression "hitting the spacebar"—with portions of a letter to CIA press spokesman Angus Thurber, from which the writer's name was redacted, provided by the CIA in response to Agee's FOIA request. The letter to Thurber indicated that its author had "spent a couple of hours with your rogue agent Philip Agee." The CIA probably checked out Deindorfer. Agee's FOIA-obtained files also contained a copy of the frontispiece and title page of a book entitled *Secret Service: Thirty-Three Centuries of Espionage*, published by Hawthorn Books and written by Richard Wilmer Rowan with Robert G. Deindorfer, and a copy of Deindorfer's entry in *Contemporary Authors*; Agee Papers, box 5, folders 11 and 30. Deindorfer had plainly penned the letter to Thurber. It remains unclear whether the CIA affirmatively enlisted Deindorfer as an agent or merely received a smarmy overture from him before or after he had acted on his own, as a fatuous wannabe agent. Philip Agee, "A Friendly Interview," undated draft; Agee Papers, box 17, folder 32. Ken Lawrence, a friend of Agee's, tracked down four books Deindorfer had written or cowritten, confirming that he was a minor published writer who dabbled in intelligence. Lawrence thought Deindorfer's biographical information from *Contemporary Authors 1974* looked "spooky"—e.g., he was a Peace Corps consultant in 1961–65 and had traveled a great deal, spending eighteen months in Africa. Letter to Agee from Ken Lawrence, dated January 8, 1981; Agee Papers, box 2, folder 41. Agee and Lawrence concluded that Deindorfer was a CIA agent, and Lawrence proposed a *Covert Action Information Bulletin* article arguing as much. Note to Agee from Lawrence on Delta Airlines notepad paper, undated; Agee Papers, box 2, folder 44. The inference was defensible but not definitive; the article was drafted but never appeared in print. Philip Agee, "A Friendly Interview," undated draft; Agee Papers, box 17, folder 32.

twice in 1974 under the pointedly lame alias "Philip Franklin," which included two of his four given names.[61]

In late May 1974 Agee submitted the final draft of *Inside the Company* to Penguin. Meanwhile, CIA transgressions were reaching the public and placing the agency under pressure to avoid any unnecessary disclosures. Ex-CIA officers and agents had been involved in the Watergate burglary that ultimately resulted in Nixon's resignation in August 1974. In fall 1974, journalist Seymour Hersh detailed shocking CIA excesses.[62] Having completed his manuscript in this atmosphere, Agee was vacationing with Seixas and his sons in Cornwall and eschewing newspapers and television when Victor Marchetti sent him a telegram. Agee had exchanged letters with Marchetti, a former senior CIA analyst, and read galleys of his *The CIA and the Cult of Intelligence*, the first big agency exposé, which was due out later that summer. Marchetti warned Agee that the CIA might have been trying to prevent Agee's book from being published and advised him talk to Larry Stern, a sympathetic *Washington Post* journalist who had heard about the book.[63] Earlier in the week, on the Fourth of July, the *New York Times* had published an article by John Crewdson that did not name Agee but channeled the CIA's assessment of him as a "drunken and despondent" intelligence officer who spilled on agency operations to a KGB officer in Latin America.[64] Agee called his father, who said the *Tampa Times* had carried a substantively similar story by Michael Sniffen from the Associated Press, and that Stern had named him in a *Washington Post* story that day. A *Daily Telegraph* journalist turned up unannounced at the cottage Agee had rented hoping—in vain—for an interview.

The storyline for public consumption was that Agee had fabricated much of the substance of his account and was forced to resign on account of heavy drinking, laziness, chronic indebtedness, womanizing, and the distractions of divorce and custody proceedings. These public attacks on his character reflected a concerted retrospective effort engineered by senior US officials to falsely discredit Agee as an outright defector.[65] They echoed an inside brief, the basis for which consisted of CIA memoranda sent by cable or pouch to stations for discreet dissemination, eventually furnished in response to Agee's FOIA request. One described Agee as "egotistical," "shallow," with "no political convictions," "always borrowing money," "constantly involved in extramarital affairs," and having "a consummate preoccupation with sex."[66] Another memo referred to him as an "obsessed skirt chaser."[67] Agee saw no option but to counter CIA disinformation publicly.

He contacted Stern and said he'd talk to him. Stern arrived in Cornwall a couple of days later. Agee corrected a number of gross deceptions in the earlier stories and related his personal account of gradual disaffection. Although he refused to let Stern see the book manuscript, back in Washington the reporter managed to get hold of a copy; he could have spirited a finished one from Penguin, Agee's UK publisher, or from the (London) *Sunday Times*, which was serializing the book. Barraged over the next couple of weeks with additional requests for comments from other journalists — radio and television as well as print — Agee provided them. The *New York Times* and the *Washington Post*, among other news outlets, published denials that he was a KGB agent, citing both Agee and "official sources."[68]

When Marchetti arrived in London the following September for the UK release of his own book, he told Agee that the CIA had importuned him to steal a copy of the finished manuscript. At that point, the agency almost certainly had a copy, as xeroxed versions of the typescript were already circulating underground. Agee inferred that the CIA was just trying to drive a wedge between him and Marchetti. And it pissed him off. The CIA's anticipatory attempt to taint Agee also convinced him that relentless exposure was his best means of defense against the agency — personally as well as politically — and removed any residual discretion he might have had about disclosing CIA operations. At this point, Agee — now staying mainly in Cambridge, the lively chattering-class home to one of the UK's two leading universities — did not merely welcome the attention of the press; he courted it. In early October, he pulled together a press conference at the Old Bell Tavern on Fleet Street, announcing a campaign to expose CIA officers wherever they were operating and to have the CIA abolished. He promulgated the names of thirty-seven CIA case officers and administrative employees at the agency's Mexico City station. If anyone in the know had had any doubts about Agee's resolve, those doubts now evaporated.[69]

Any other result would have been improbable. Having advanced his revolutionary status by writing *Inside the Company* and publishing the names of CIA officers and assets, he had left himself few options other than staying the course of radical dissent or reversing that course in a mortifying retreat. In the language of gambling psychology, he was in the "realm of losses."[70] (A similar concept is the "sacrifice trap.") He had little more to lose with further recklessness. That is, he had already forsaken so much—family, security, career—that he felt increasingly compelled to go all in or those sacrifices would have been for nothing. And if there was no turning back, the risks of doubling down—a statistically prudent strategy in its original blackjack application though not in popular colloquial usage—on his audaciously antagonistic behavior seemed, however perversely, all the lower. Agee would have regarded himself as having lost a great deal, such that merely staying in the game—that is, continuing to challenge the CIA and what it stood for—constituted a show of commitment and defiance that compensated for his sacrifices.

RADICALISM UNLEASHED

Inside the Company dropped in the UK in January 1975. It was published at a moment when "secret intelligence" had become "the main item on the American political agenda."[71] Watergate had conditioned Congress to clean up government. In January 1975, Hersh's revelations prompted the Senate to establish the Select Committee to Study Governmental Operations with Respect to Intelligence Activities, chaired by Senator Frank Church, a Democrat from Idaho. Known as the Church Committee, it opened unprecedentedly revelatory investigations into CIA operations, including extensive domestic surveillance, assassination attempts, and covert subversion efforts—the so-called "family jewels." Soon 1975 would become known as the "Year of Intelligence."

Reaching back two decades, the Church Committee explored and exposed CIA excesses, including attempts to assassinate foreign leaders—some successful, some not—such as Patrice Lumumba of the Congo, Rafael Trujillo of the Dominican Republic, the Diem brothers of South Vietnam, and General René Schneider of Chile as well as Fidel Castro. At the same time, at the hands of Kissinger and others attempting to grapple with the gathering forces of economic globalization and political destabilization that were disturbing the postwar international order that the United States led, US foreign policy was becoming more pragmatic and nuanced and less susceptible to euphemism and romantic simplification.[72] These developments afforded Agee a kind of political cover—he was now broadly in line with disruptive trends rather than merely bucking a reticent status quo—and endowed him with both new confidence in the rightness of naming CIA names and optimism about his own place in history. In May 1975, as Agee anticipated Stonehill's US release of *Inside the Company*, he reflected:

> After a year of increasing doubt whether this diary would ever be published in the U.S. the way now looks clear. Had not Rep. Michael Harrington and Seymour Hersh and others made startling revelations in the year past, the political climate might not have permitted publication in the U.S. even now. . . . Yet in the end it is the CIA that gives way as its very institutional survival is brought into question. We already know enough of what the CIA does to resolve to oppose it. The CIA is one of the great forces in promoting political repression in countries with minority regimes that serve a privileged and powerful elite. One way to neutralize the CIA's support to repression is to expose its officers so that their presence in foreign countries becomes untenable. Already significant revelations have begun and I will continue to assist those who are interested in identifying and exposing CIA people in their countries.[73]

The book helped galvanize the Church Committee investigations that yielded legislation and executive orders that many national security professionals argue emasculated the CIA for a generation or more. But the US government was determined to maintain a facade of institutional cool.

In an internal review of Agee's book, the FBI in January 1975 noted "slanted revelations" that were "bound to have numerous repercussions around the world," but the review otherwise eschewed ad hominem attacks and was generally objective, professional, and matter-of-fact.[74] Similarly, a United States Information Agency assessment was purposeful in focusing on elements that cast doubt on Agee's credibility but also remained objective and professional.[75] Confidential cables dated July 1974, following the first wave of reporting about the forthcoming book, and January 1975, following its release, from Kissinger to the US Embassy in The Hague stated that US officials should say "No Comment" to press and public inquiries regarding Agee and *Inside the Company* and, if pressed, that a point-by-point refutation would be endless and fruitless.[76]

The subtext, however, was panic. The strong implication of this cable's omission of any direct denial is that most or much of what Agee disclosed was true. Opinions of diplomatic staff about Agee appear to have been widely varied. Some piled on him, probably taking their cue—as many did and still do—from CIA officers on station at the embassy. One dismissive and insulting review authored by "G. F." in the March 1975 issue of *Free Labour World*—a publication of the International Confederation of Free Trade Unions (ICFTU), which Agee and others characterized as a CIA front—questioned Agee's status as an ex-CIA case officer.[77] Others stuck to diplomatically relevant facts, reporting host-country concern about political fallout—in particular, that Agee was giving momentum to left-wing movements.[78]

The book drew international interest—especially that of the left-wing intelligentsia. Future Nobel laureate for literature Gabriel García Márquez published an interview in Spanish with Agee to coincide with *Inside the Company*'s UK release.[79] The two met in London on that occasion, and a few months later García Márquez invited Agee to testify before the International War Crimes Tribunal on political repression in Latin America. The tribunal was sponsored by the Bertrand Russell Foundation and organized by the French existentialist philosopher Jean-Paul Sartre, who in turn published an article of Agee's in his journal *Les Temps Modernes*. Agee also penned the preface to a British edition of the 1976 report of the Pike Committee—the Church Committee's counterpart in the House of Representatives—which was highly critical of the CIA's illegal activities and the Ford administration's withholding of information about them. Harcourt Brace Jovanovich sought a blurb from Agee for *Heartland*, a book by left-wing comedian Mort Sahl.[80] Opinion in popular media was generally more candid and shrill than the government was. On a Washington, DC, radio program, former senior CIA operations officer Harry Rositzke noted that in revealing the names of CIA agents that Agee himself had run, he had committed a transgression that "even Kim Philby" had not.[81]

It's possible the agency would have resisted actively persecuting Agee in favor of merely monitoring him and seeking to control him through discreet forms of pressure had Agee simply kept a low profile, sequestered himself in an office in front of an (unbugged) typewriter, and declined to court journalists and activists. This he did not do. In April 1975, an interview of Agee, in Russian, appeared in a Moscow-based Soviet magazine.[82] The US government had intimidated American publishers, and Agee had been able to get a contract only with a small, eccentric one—Stonehill—for an advance of only $12,000. That amount, given Agee's unprecedented revelations, bordered on derisory.

By the time *Inside the Company* was published in the United States, in June 1975, the book had been a sensational international news story for six months. García Márquez followed up his initial support with an English-language review in the *New York Review of Books* in August.[83] Energized by his celebrity, Agee was now past discouragement or hesitation. His supporters saw him as a principled revolutionary, his detractors as a self-glorifying traitor. For any CIA officer to have produced *Inside the Company* was surprising if not shocking, and most serious reviewers took its substantive arguments against CIA operations seriously.[84] But the book itself—susceptible as any autobiographical account is to twenty-twenty hindsight and sanitizing self-justification—doesn't clearly account for how he acquired his convictions or why he sustained them. As Richard R. Lingeman noted in the *New York Times* in an otherwise positive review, "as an account of Mr. Agee's conversion 'Inside the Company' falls rather flat; deep introspection is lacking, and the convert seems to have made a rather abrupt flip-flop from amoral CIA technician to knee-jerk Marxist-Leninist."[85] Certainly it is credible that Agee had increasingly acute moral objections to CIA machinations in the service of violent repression, triggered by the Bonaudi incident. That and the Tlatelolco affair did appear to plant in Agee durable skepticism about the effectiveness of the CIA's liaison relationships in spreading American principles and values, and that, for him, that skepticism invalidated transitory moral compromises in perpetrating bad acts for the greater good.[86] In subsequent reflections about and discussions of his reasons for writing the book, he dismissed cost-benefit calculations with respect to publicly naming CIA officers and agents. He also described Seixas's experience of being tortured by the Brazilian security services as catalytic to his decision to write *Inside the Company* and, implicitly, dedicate his life to undermining the CIA.[87] But, measured against both his offense to his country and his personal sacrifice, this is thin explanatory gruel. His deeper motivations did remain opaque. His primary psychological dispensation was simply to proffer his public defiance of norms as inferential evidence of the authenticity and integrity of his motivations: if I'm doing this, I must have good reason.

And what he was doing became increasingly provocative. That August, Agee went to Moscow for ten days, purportedly to discuss publication of the Russian edition of the book. At the very least, this was a rude taunt. Moreover, he kept naming names. He published an "Open Letter to the Portuguese People" in which he named eight CIA officers stationed in Portugal. In winter 1975, *CounterSpy* ran an article Agee wrote entitled "Exposing the CIA" accompanied by two photographs of Sidney Bearman, the agency's senior liaison officer at its London station.[88] The public revelation of CIA staff stationed in London prompted British authorities to assign special protective details to guard their homes. Shortly thereafter, Bearman left the agency after a twenty-five-year career. Right-of-center newspapers credited Agee with "triggering the current exposure of CIA agents around the world."[89] He was also getting traction with the northeast liberal cognoscenti in the United States. Garry Wills, for example, channeled a key Agee message: "It is silly to talk about making the president control the CIA. It is his means of *escaping control*." He added that "the mere existence of the CIA tempts a president to evade the constitution."[90]

Agee himself conceded that he'd had Cuban assistance with research for *Inside the Company* and that he had three meetings at the Cuban embassy in London in 1975 regarding the translation of the book into Spanish. *Pravda* ran an article explaining his motivations.[91] In July 1976, he visited Moscow for a week when the Russian version of *Inside the Company* came out.[92] He also publicly acknowledged three meetings at the Russian embassy in London, but said his travel to Moscow had been merely for publicity in connection with the publication of the book.[93] Among most Western government officials, and especially intelligence officers, this would have been very cold comfort. The tightened relationship between the KGB and the DGI extended to the DGI's overseas operations. In the early 1970s, the prevailing presumption among Western governments was that the KGB maintained close oversight of DGI operations in Europe.[94] If the DGI kept contact with Agee while he was living in the United Kingdom—as it appeared to do—chances are that the KGB at least knew about it if it did not actually control the relationship. From a counterintelligence standpoint, the fact that US intelligence agencies chronically underestimated the DGI may have afforded the Cuban agency operational advantages, especially in areas in which the KGB was also present and active and thus absorbed the attention and resources of American intelligence.[95]

In September 1976 came one of Agee's most audacious moves, and it rendered almost irrelevant any finely parsed, exculpatory niceties about his connections with adversary intelligence agencies. At the invitation of the Jamaica Council for Human Rights, a legal civil rights organization, he made a one-week visit to Jamaica and released a list of nine alleged CIA officers—including the station chief, Norman M. Descoteaux—and seven alleged agents, amid standing left-wing government suspicions that the United States was trying to destabilize it. His objective was to shore up election support for incumbent socialist Prime Minister Michael Manley, who enjoyed Cuban support and faced American and British opposition. If the US government had entertained any doubts about the depth or resiliency of Agee's conversion, the in-your-face brazenness of his trip to Jamaica would have dispelled them. In publicly tagging embassy staff as CIA officers, Agee did not send newspapers a list or name names to a reporter in a dark bar. Instead, he held a press conference at the Social Action Centre in St. Andrew Parish, north of Kingston.

He aimed to strip the agency bare. First, Agee identified the embassy attaché as the CIA station chief; his wife as his secretary; the embassy second secretary as deputy station chief; the consular officer, third secretary, and vice consul as CIA operations officers; and three other embassy personnel as CIA telecommunications officers and a CIA secretary. Next, he provided their names, addresses, and telephone numbers. Then he speculated that an embassy drug enforcement officer and the embassy's first secretary were also likely to be CIA, as those were routine covers. To lend credibility to his claims, Agee added that while he was a case officer in Guayaquil, Ecuador, he had in fact worked with the attaché and two of the other alleged CIA officers. He also noted that they had taken up their positions at the embassy during the previous year "prior to the initiation of violence"—clearly though not explicitly to establish a causal link. He wasn't finished. He went on to point out that the CIA station in Kingston had increased its contingent of case officers from three to five, which represented "a very significant build-up." Gilding the lily, Agee noted that the embassy first secretary had been expelled from Sierra Leone for interference in its internal affairs. He also explained how to figure out who on a list of US mission personnel was CIA. The *Daily Gleaner* and the *Daily News*—then the two most widely read and circulated papers in Jamaica—ran front-page stories on the press conference.[96]

Agee's time in Jamaica scored massive international press coverage and caused deep consternation and embarrassment in the US and UK governments.[97] Britain had ruled Jamaica for over 300 years before independence in 1962, the Caribbean island nation remained part of the British Commonwealth, and it was in the United States' geopolitical backyard. Manley, the prime minister, was a socialist who had become close to the Castro government. In a long cable to the US State Department on September 28, 1976, Embassy Kingston construed Agee's visit as part of a "carefully orchestrated campaign" by Manley to demonstrate American intent to destabilize Jamaica and thus cast blame on the United States in general—and the CIA in particular—for Jamaica's social and economic woes so as to ensure his victory in upcoming parliamentary elections. Embassy staff were worried that Manley would publicly request "clarifications and explanations" about the people on "Agee's list" in order to embarrass Washington, or declare some of them personae non gratae and expel them for CIA activities. In an even more dire scenario, radical left-wing groups would latch onto Agee's revelations as a *cause célèbre* and incite "violent action directed at U.S. employees or citizens." After presenting several possible responses that would register American dissatisfaction with Manley's perceived instrumentalization of Agee, embassy staff recommended that the US ambassador be discreetly recalled for "consultations" in connection with a "review of U.S./Jamaica bilateral relations."[98]

Despite US hostility toward Agee himself and denials of the substance of his disclosures, *Inside the Company* was more than a blockbuster book. It caused diplomatic ructions, particularly in Latin America but also in Europe. Beyond that, its publication had psychologically liberated Agee to expose—and thus sabotage—CIA operations on an active and ongoing basis. Agee's residence in England was obviously straining the special relationship that the UK and the United States embraced, and which the UK especially valued.

PERSONAE NON GRATAE

Agee wasn't the only American irritant to the Western intelligence community living in the UK. Freelance journalist Mark Hosenball published "The Eavesdroppers," an exposé of the electronic surveillance capabilities and operations of Government Communications Headquarters (GCHQ)—the UK counterpart of the United States'

National Security Agency—in a magazine called *Time Out* (unrelated to the cultural events magazine now published in several cities) in May 1976. He then started writing for the *Evening Standard*, a widely read national newspaper. He had contributed material to *Counter-Spy*, which set as its mission the exposure of CIA operations and activities, but he was not as closely associated with it as Agee, who was listed as Associate Editor of the December 1976 issue. In the spring 1976 issue, Agee was accorded "special thanks" and included on the magazine's advisory board along with David Dellinger, Mark Lane, Victor Marchetti, the eccentric former chief of special operations for the Joint Chiefs of Staff L. Fletcher Prouty, and other prominent critics of the CIA, while Hosenball was listed as a "contributor" in one issue.[99] If Agee was proud of the acknowledgment, it angered Hosenball. But the perceived mutual connection to the anti-intelligence press gave the appearance of a concerted journalistic besiegement of the US and UK intelligence communities.

The UK was under pressure from the US government for allowing Agee to utilize the United Kingdom as a platform for publicly attacking US policy and impeding US intelligence operations. The British government also needed American support for a crucial International Monetary Fund loan. Then as now, most British officials saw the special relationship as the factor most responsible for Britain's remaining a great power and first among equals in Europe. It was not terribly surprising that the UK government sought to deport Agee and Hosenball. On November 15, 1976, the Cambridge police served Agee with a letter from the UK Home Office stating that his application for a twelve-month extension of his stay in the UK would be refused and that he would be ordered deported. The stated reason was as follows: "The Secretary of State has considered information that Mr. Agee: (a) has maintained regular contacts harmful to the security of the United Kingdom with foreign intelligence officers, (b) has been and continues to be involved in disseminating information harmful to the security of the United Kingdom, and (c) has aided and counseled others in obtaining information for publication harmful to the security of the United Kingdom." Accordingly, said the note, his departure "would be conducive to the public good as being in the interest of national security." Hosenball received a substantively similar notice on the same day.[100] Since they were both writing on intelligence matters, Hosenball had met Agee in due course and spoken casually him between 1974 and 1976, but he did not know Agee well and generally considered him a risk-courting grandstander who indiscreetly embraced "radical chic" and was not to be trusted. Overall, Hosenball found Agee too comprehensively inimical to US interests for his taste. There are no indications in the Agee Papers or any other open-source material of any friendship or sustained personal or professional connection between the two men.

Agee surmised, and he was probably correct, that the Jamaica episode was the clincher that led to his deportation.[101] Hosenball in fact shared the British authorities' suspicions that Agee was lashed up with foreign intelligence agencies—in particular, the DGI—and was leery of him partly on that basis. Nevertheless, suspicions also arose that they had been working together. The British government prosecuted their cases together, which drew the ire of the British Left. In defending his right to stay in the UK, Agee captivated and mobilized a substantial portion of the British public. American diplomats speculated that discord over the Agee-Hosenball action could have an impact on domestic affairs in the UK—in particular, the disposition of a bill for nationalization of the shipbuilding and aircraft industries. The broader worry was that the British Labour Party would withdraw support from the UK government due to perceptions that the UK had colluded with the United States to have Agee deported.[102]

Agee and Hosenball were entitled to submit the Home Office's decision to an "independent advisory panel," held in closed session, that would counsel the home secretary on a nonbinding and nonappealable basis as to whether to proceed with deportation. They were not permitted counsel but could themselves present evidence and witnesses. Agee decided to take this opportunity and hired Larry Grant—a British law professor who ran a law clinic that took unusual, politically significant cases—to advise him. Grant, in turn, recruited a team of three progressive barristers. Agee also brought in other legal talent. He had initially contacted Melvin Wulf over a year earlier in connection with the CIA's interference with visitation arrangements for his sons he had made with his estranged wife Janet. Wulf, having represented Marchetti and his coauthor John Marks regarding their book, was handling a number of matters in the United States arising from the publication of *Inside the Company*. Wulf had been national legal director of the American Civil Liberties Union and was credited with transforming it from a demure amicus-filing organization into one that aggressively initiated and defended lawsuits. Now he was in private practice in New York, and Agee persuaded him and Ramsey Clark, the progressive former US attorney general, to join his legal team and testify on his behalf. Agee himself assumed an active—not to say hyperactive—role in his own defense. Starting on November 29, the day he notified the Home Office that he would avail himself of the advisory panel, Agee held frequent press briefings over the course of the proceeding. He helped his legal team compose abundantly supported statements for submission to the panel. And he used the process not only as a means of staying in the UK but equally as a platform for his political arguments against the CIA.

The gravamen of Agee's case was the UK government's refusal to inform him of the precise nature of the grievances against him other than his presence being harmful to British national security and his maintaining contacts with foreign agents of unspecified origin.[103] He also objected that he was not afforded due process of law owing to the absence of authentic fact-finding procedures and impermissibility of any appeal. Despite the UK government's obscurantism, though, the basic reasons for the US government's unhappiness with its ally were obvious: the UK was hosting a flagrant traitor who was seriously impeding CIA operations. The British government, as a former colonial power with residual interests in Jamaica and also the United States' closest European ally, would have reflexively aligned itself with US preferences. And to any reasonably knowledgeable observer, the government's case was hardly devoid of substance. The "List of Questions . . . Put to Philip Agee by the Advisory Board," for example, was an astute document, lodging strong inferences that he'd had some consistent and possibly systematic outside support after he left the CIA.[104]

In the defense statement he submitted in January 1977, responding to allegations that he'd had contact with Cuban and Soviet intelligence officers in the UK, Agee merely said that the Cubans were cultural attachés and the Soviets journalists and publishing people connected with the Russian release of *Inside the Company*.[105] This proffer would likely have been unsatisfactory to British authorities, who would have been well aware that Cubans and Soviets would use such designations as covers. But Agee was aiming at a broader popular audience less familiar with the wiles of espionage. With the statement he submitted (along with twenty-seven other attachments) confessional articles that he had earlier published in *Esquire* and *CounterSpy*.[106] Press coverage of the Agee and Hosenball cases and their activities in the UK was extensive and obsessive, comprising hundreds of news stories between November 1976 and December 1977.

The London-based Agee-Hosenball Defence Committee, organized by their friends and colleagues, would raise £4,101.21 by early March 1977.[107] While not a huge amount, it would have defrayed a nontrivial portion of their legal fees and signified appreciable public awareness and support. The committee also anchored a very active, high-profile defense of their position, generating significant public backing in spite of the government's imperiously opaque insistence on deporting Agee, which in turn rendered his plight itself headline news. The committee orchestrated public rallies, staged demonstrations at the Home Office, and picketed the US embassy and the homes of CIA officers. A petition to the UK government protesting the deportation order against Agee and Hosenball drew several hundred signatures, perhaps as many as a thousand.[108] Another signed public appeal presented directly to the US ambassador called for the removal of American intelligence personnel from the US embassy. Agee spoke at a "CIA teach-in" at the London School of Economics. At a 20,000-strong antiracism demonstration organized in Hyde Park by the Trades Union Council and the Labour Party—then in power under Prime Minister James Callaghan—groups among the crowd displayed banners and placards opposing the deportations and chanted slogans to the same effect. Public pledges of support in one form or another emerged from a transnational array of luminaries. They included, in addition to early backers like García Márquez and Sartre, Joan Baez, Simone de Beauvoir, the filmmaker Costa-Gavras, Jane Fonda, Nobel Peace laureate Sean MacBride, Ralph Miliband, Philip Noel-Baker, and Marxist historian Eric Hobsbawm.[109] Well-known French and Greek socialists also weighed in. In a letter to the *Times* of London, historian E. P. Thompson condemned CIA interference in other countries and scorned the UK media's "pusillanimity" in sparsely covering it.[110]

Several prominent Labour members of parliament took an intense interest in Agee's cause, and most of the party—150 MPs signed motions of protest—supported it. There was strong backing for Agee and Hosenball from the National Lawyers Guild (US) and from the National Union of Journalists (UK), of which they were members, while the PEN World Association of Writers offered rhetorical and political support.[111] Concerned Americans Abroad (a London-based group started in 1968) publicly took up his cause, pressing the US Embassy to help American nationals, albeit fruitlessly: US Embassy London officials displayed studied indifference, noting that there was no legal basis for US intercession on Agee's behalf.[112] This position, while disingenuously presented as blandly neutral, would undoubtedly have been influenced by the CIA's highly negative view of Agee.

In a nomination and statement, the University of Dundee Students Association proposed Agee as a rector of the university, in the hope that Agee would ultimately defeat the deportation effort.[113] On February 4, 1977, Wulf, Clark, and former senior US Defense Department official Morton Halperin made impassioned statements on Agee's behalf at Central Hall, Westminster.[114] Three days later, Clark sent to UK Home Secretary Merlyn Rees a soaring four-page testimonial to Agee.[115]

The British Left's passion and defiance in Agee's favor was to some extent an organic and spontaneous product of long-standing biases against the security state. But Agee's energetic self-promotion maximized active and vehement popular support for his position. American pressure on the British government, however, was determinative. Despite Agee's substantive and procedural arguments and his appreciable public and political support, the UK Home Office announced its intention to deport him and Hosenball and delivered them formal notices of deportation in late February 1977. The two writers spoke briefly the day after the notices of deportation had been served but never thereafter.

The stated basis for Agee's expulsion closely tracked the rationale stated in the November letter: that he had "maintained regular contacts . . . with foreign intelligence officers" and engaged in unspecified acts "prejudicial to the safety of the servants of the Crown." Clark likened the British tribunal to a "star chamber."[116] More whimsically but perhaps with greater popular oomph, chess champion Bobby Fischer's sixty-three-year-old mother, Regina Wender Fischer, protested Agee and Hosenball's expulsion by sleeping rough in front of Whitehall and fasting for ten days. She was arrested and briefly jailed for blocking the sidewalk, but she returned.[117] The House of Commons moved to adjourn the deportations. In debate, Conservative MP Jonathan Aitken said: "We should be under no illusions that the procedure adopted by the Home Secretary in the Agee and Hosenball cases has made Britain something of a laughingstock in other democratic countries. To set up a procedure where charges are unknown, no evidence is taken, no representation is allowed, and no result is given is worthy of a Kafka novel or of *Alice in Wonderland*."[118] In response to accusations that the UK government was kowtowing to the Americans, Rees offered perfunctory reassurances that the decision had been made solely in the UK's interest and not after consultations with any agencies of the US government, including the CIA—as if Downing Street regarded the two criteria as mutually exclusive—and proclaimed that Agee and Hosenball's expulsions were a matter of security rather than politics. In a last-ditch effort, Agee sent letters to thirty-five UK MPs requesting their support.[119] But once the decision was made, British support for Agee yielded diminishing political returns and dissipated quickly. Further association with him was an unnecessary liability. Ten MPs who tried to help Agee in the deportation case sent him letters of regret stating that they were sorry that they could not attend his farewell party.[120]

Agee decamped to Edinburgh in hopes that his lawyers could find a loophole in Scottish law that would permit him to stay in Scotland, and Hosenball challenged the panel procedure all the way up to the House of Lords, but neither effort bore fruit. Agee and Hosenball were finally ordered to leave the UK in June 1977. Louis Wolf, coeditor of the *Covert Action Information Bulletin*, had his leave to reenter the UK canceled due to his active association with Agee.[121] While Agee would be unable to gain comparable grassroots backing elsewhere in Europe, the political disruption caused by the UK deportation proceeding no doubt helped discourage other host governments from accommodating Agee. After his defeat in the UK, he tried to gain legal residence in the Netherlands. There too he picked his fights in full view. In summer 1977, he published a jaunty article in a radical British magazine called *The Leveller* about his anti-CIA conduct, which the Dutch government said constituted a breach of its condition for Agee's staying in the country—namely, that he engage in no activity endangering public order or national security.[122] The Hague threw him out. Though Agee mustered some public sympathy in France, the French government would not allow him to stay there.[123] Neither would Belgium or Italy. Western Europe, of course, was still the West, and its governments were inclined to bow to American pressure.

In March 1978, however, just before his expulsion from the Netherlands, Agee married Giselle Roberge (born Gysele Ingool), the American daughter of Therese Roberge, the French-Canadian expat who had assisted him with his manuscript in Paris. A justice of the peace performed the ceremony in Amsterdam, alongside a punk rock band.[124] He was forty-three, she was twenty-nine. Giselle was by trade a ballerina, raised in New York, with an impressive résumé of her own: Fiorello H. La Guardia Performing Arts High School, Balanchine School of American Ballet, New York City Ballet for eight years, and American Ballet Theater for two years, before she got an offer to dance in Europe. When they met she lived in Hamburg and was with the Hamburg Ballet, which was on tour and performing in Paris. Her life was not politics, but she was the one who suggested they wed, and the proposal assuredly did have a political dimension: as a legal foreign resident of West Germany, she was entitled by local Hamburg law to cohabit with a spouse. Under West Germany's federalist scheme of government, primary jurisdiction over Agee's residency status lay with Hamburg rather than Bonn. To the consternation of US officials, their counterparts in Bonn lodged their intention to acquiesce in Agee's residency in West Germany quietly and without public fanfare since the local authorities of Hamburg had resolved to take no further action.[125] He got his residence permit along with an official document that afforded him limited scope for travel within Europe.

West Germany's strategic, political, and sociological circumstances were not entirely uncongenial to Agee. After the Second World War, unlike the UK, France, and European states that had opposed Germany, West Germany had evolved only fitfully and uncertainly as a fully committed Western European security partner and NATO ally, and the comprehensive cooperation of its security institutions with the CIA could not be taken for granted.[126] Furthermore, Willy Brandt as chancellor had inaugurated *Ostpolitik*—literally, "eastern policy"—in 1969, and his successors Helmut Schmidt and Helmut Kohl carried it forward with an eye to achieving *Wandel durch Annäherung*: change through rapprochement. The idea was for West Germany to ease tensions and insinuate political influence with its eastern neighbors in the Soviet bloc by recognizing their frontiers and thickening contact, communications, and commerce with their citizens. By thus forging a degree of sociocultural interaction and economic interdependence without disavowing its Western alliances or validating postwar Soviet hegemony in Eastern Europe, West German leaders hoped to overcome the Yalta dispensation and peacefully reaffirm the basic unity of the German nation.[127] The policy ultimately contributed to the United States' and Western Europe's Cold War victory.[128] In the 1970s, it afforded Bonn nuanced distance from Washington, London, and Paris, while West Germany's geopolitical centrality gave it some additional leeway. These factors appeared to make the German government less obeisant to the United States (and the CIA) and more inclined to host Agee and leave him relatively unmolested.[129]

The fact remained that in defending his right to stay in Britain, Agee captivated and mobilized a large portion of the British and broader European public. His unabashed courtship of political celebrity was perhaps naive in light of the US government's Cold War clout in Europe, and made it more difficult for him to find a stable home there. But once he did, Europe proved to be an energizing host. As he got used to life as a paradoxically public fugitive, Agee rounded on the idea that regular publicity about even his most egregious depredations on the United States' or his hosts' national security could at least protect him against government action so grossly nefarious as to imperil his life. Furthermore, the wholesale US-led Allied triumph in the Second World War had produced in the United States an overweening sense of superiority that stretched and distorted the "American exceptionalism" that arose at the nation's founding, while the tense inconclusiveness of the Cold War that followed had given rise to contrapuntal American paranoia. Together these nerve-racking attitudes nourished an oppositionist transatlantic Left, which, despite the stateside enervation of the New Left by the early 1970s, drew strength from the US Congress's castigation and punishment of an elitist and unaccountable CIA and from disruptive European political trends that were just gathering momentum at the time. These forces drove Agee's ideological maturation and then sustained his political resoluteness.

4

Indefinite Limbo

In *Inside the Company*, Agee presented his day-to-day life as a CIA case officer in Quito, Montevideo, and Mexico City, working to roll back Cuban and Soviet influence. Interstitially, he recorded the particular incidents and broader evolution of his vocation, which he said led to his conversion from establishmentarian to political dissident and moved him to quit as a matter of conscience. Intelligence professionals like Miles Copeland, a former CIA station chief in Cairo, reviewing the book in the London-based *Spectator*, acknowledged that Agee's depiction of his quotidian existence was authentic and thorough.[1] A CIA reviewer in its in-house journal *Studies in Intelligence*, classified SECRET but obtained unredacted by John Marks (Marchetti's coauthor) via a FOIA request and sent to Agee, also recognized Agee's "accurate descriptions of each Station's operations under identifying cryptonyms" and added that his "description of the Clandestine Service's modus operandi is valid outside Latin America."[2] In recruiting case officers for the Career Trainee Program in the 1980s, and probably later, the CIA itself included *Inside the Company* on its list of recommended reading materials as an accurate and detailed account of the a CIA case officer's daily toil.

If Agee's transgressions had stopped with those sorts of relatively mundane laydowns of CIA activity, he might have escaped a degree of notoriety that limited his freedom and then nestled into a manageable niche, the way two other aggrieved former CIA officers who published unvetted books—Snepp and Stockwell—subsequently did. But of course those recollections were not the most extraordinary aspects of *Inside the Company*. It was the exposure of CIA officers and assets that made the book so uniquely treacherous. While this enterprise rallied the Left against the CIA, it also mobilized the CIA and other US agencies against Agee. Documents Agee and his lawyers uncovered by way of a large and arduously litigated FOIA request suggested that the agency had engaged in "illegal acts"— probably including the Ferrara/Donegan operation—in its efforts to thwart his attempts to undermine CIA missions.[3] The CIA did not press for his prosecution in the United States, probably for fear of disclosing sources and methods in general and in particular being compelled to reveal the details of those efforts, which were redacted in Agee's FOIA trawl, and exposing itself to federal tort claims or possibly even criminal charges by Agee. But there is little doubt that the agency enlisted the help of host-country security services to shadow Agee in Europe and ultimately have him deported.[4]

Agee, for his part, egged them on even after his expulsion from the United Kingdom and four other European countries. After he had inaugurated his public assault on the agency with *Inside the Company*, he became involved, as an advisory board member and contributor, with the Washington-based *CounterSpy*, which had started in 1973. In the January 1975 issue, the magazine published a list of over a hundred CIA station chiefs along with an article Agee wrote justifying their exposure. In 1978, Agee disengaged from *Counter-Spy* and cofounded the *Covert Action Information Bulletin*. He and five colleagues rolled out the maiden issue at a press conference at the Hotel Havana Libre the day before the Eleventh World Festival of Youth and Students that summer. The issue included an article by Agee articulating the rationale for publicly identifying CIA operatives and announcing the status and name of incoming CIA Jamaica Station Chief Dean J. Almy Jr.[5] The *Bulletin* continued to be published regularly, and ultimately disclosed some 2,000 CIA officers, agents, and other assets. Also in 1978, Agee and Louis Wolf composed *Dirty Work—The CIA in Western Europe*, which included a 392-page "Who's Who" of over 700 CIA officers and agents in Europe. He supplied the introduction to *Dirty Work 2: The CIA in Africa*, which exposed agency officers and assets on that continent. From the 1980s onward, Agee made a second career of openly commiserating and sometimes collaborating with leftist governments targeted by the CIA.

BLOOD ON HIS HANDS?

Inside the Company cost Agee his professional standing as an intelligence officer, but that is a sacrifice he consciously and willingly made. Other possible costs were more insidious and potentially more profound. In particular, assuming that Agee's motivation was in part religious, as it appeared to be, it is worth asking whether he might have subverted his own principles—that is, whether he sinned. The most obvious sin would have been that of killing, in contravention of the fifth commandment. He was concerned and quietly troubled about this possibility. He accumulated a large sheaf of clippings discussing the damage his disclosures did to CIA operations, including the lethal kind.[6] He was also compulsive about explaining and exculpating himself, contending from the time he made the initial disclosures in *Inside the Company* that his intention was not to bring harm to intelligence officers or agents. And he downplayed the lethality of the spy game in general, minimizing his own anxiety about being killed by the CIA even when in the UK, and about possible CIA–MI6 collusion to thwart the writing and publication of *Inside the Company*.

Agee's revelations probably did not, in fact, cause physical harm to any CIA officers or agents, though this assessment is inferential. In a March 1975 letter to Director of Central Intelligence William Colby, Attorney General Edward H. Levi contemplated "substantial sums . . . spent to re-assign Agency personnel and perform other administrative actions as a result of Agee's breach of his secrecy agreement" as potentially recoverable in a US government lawsuit against Agee. But Levi advised against bringing such a suit on the ground that winning it would require disclosing still more secrets about CIA operations. He also noted that prior publication of *Inside the Company* in the United Kingdom made the case for the "irreparable harm" required for injunctive relief dubious.[7] Levi mentioned no instances of harm or death to CIA officers or agents incident to the book's publication, which might have strengthened the case of irreparable harm. This omission suggests that the CIA did not disclose any such instances to the Justice Department—a strong indication that none had occurred. Over time, the received understanding was essentially that Agee's disclosures were largely accurate, and that "[t]he repeated publishing of operatives' identities around the world by former CIA officer Philip Agee and others has crippled recruitment overseas and damaged relations with foreign intelligence services."[8]

At least one unsubstantiated argument that Agee's disclosures were lethal has arisen. Writing in 2010 less than a year before his death, Murray Seeger, who in 1975 became the *LA Times*'s correspondent for West Germany and the eastern bloc after three years in Moscow, reported that a CIA source in Bonn had told him that Agee had blown a large network of pro-Western Polish agents. While the contact did not provide details, Seeger assumed that Agee's listing of a Mexico City–based agent of Polish extraction code-named BESABER (Agee had forgotten his real name) targeted against potential Polish assets had prompted Soviet intelligence services to notionally connect BESABER to Jerzy Pawlowski, a Polish fencer who won a gold medal at the Mexico City Olympics. The inference is loose, if not fanciful, but not completely devoid of credibility. In 1975, Pawlowski, then a lieutenant colonel in the Polish army, was arrested for espionage in Poland, and *Pravda* reported that a Western spy was executed in the Soviet Union. Seeger's CIA contact tersely informed him that the dots were connected, and reflected Agee's work. Seeger's editors at the *LA Times* killed the story he wrote about these episodes—he believed because the CIA pressured them to do so (probably to avoid further exposure of the agency's operations), and Agee, who threatened to sue Seeger, claimed because the story was inadequately sourced and attempted CIA propaganda.[9]

A Polish military tribunal found Pawlowski guilty of espionage and sentenced him to twenty-five years in prison, indicating that he was spared the death penalty urged by the Soviets because he admitted his crimes, revealed details of his activities, and named his operational contacts. Were Agee's exposure of BESABER directly connected to Pawlowski's arrest, of course, his close brush with execution—and lucky avoidance of it—would prove that Agee's disclosures imperiled lives. And if the execution of the spy in the Soviet Union had resulted from Pawlowski's confessions, that too would be on Agee. But no publicly available sources have confirmed Seeger's speculations.

Still, one durable myth is that Agee facilitated the assassination of CIA Athens Station Chief Richard Welch, some nine months after the date of Levi's letter, by the terrorist November 17 Organization. Whether they killed him on account of US activities in Latin America—he had been station chief in Lima, Peru—or American support for Lebanese Phalangists, US opposition to Greek Cypriot militants, or some other reason remains obscure.[10] And Welch appeared to have been exposed by means other than Philip Agee. His name appeared nowhere in *Inside the Company*. It did appear in the 1969 and 1973 State Department Biographic Register, and his status as a CIA officer could easily have been determined by reference to John Marks's notoriously cheeky article "How to Spot a Spook," which ran in the November 1974 issue of the *Washington Monthly*. *CounterSpy* had used the methods described in that article to ascertain the names of the station chiefs published in the January 1975 issue. The list included Welch, but as a CIA officer in Lima—his previous posting. The issue featured an article by Agee, but it was entirely separate. In November 1975, the *Athens News* named ten CIA officers in Greece, including Welch. The next month, Welch was executed outside his house with a pistol, in front of his wife and driver, as the couple returned from a Christmas party. In a February 1976 letter to the editor of the *Washington Post*, Agee repudiated allegations that his disclosures caused Welch's death.[11]

David Atlee Phillips, former CIA chief of operations for the Western Hemisphere, retired in part so he could confront Agee publicly with the agency's blessing. Phillips initially intimated that Agee had directly precipitated Welch's murder.[12] The campaign lost steam, and Phillips was reduced to snide, ad hominem attacks.[13] Two years after Welch's death, former CIA Director William Colby admitted to the *Los Angeles Times* that Welch had "accepted bad cover" by living in the same house as his predecessor, whom the assassins had stalked, and making only perfunctory efforts to hide his identity.[14] Colby seemed to be conceding that Welch's death was proximately attributable to CIA complacency and lax operational security. Twelve years after his inaugural accusation, while branding Agee a "moral primitive," Phillips would concede that there was no direct link between Agee's disclosures of the names of agency officials and assets and Richard Welch's assassination in Greece.[15]

Agee, however, was the avatar of CIA exposure, and *Inside the Company* was its most iconic and jarring instrument. His vocational credibility, international fame, and temperamental relentlessness far exceeded those of any other practitioner. His revelations started the trend of revealing agency operations, and his actions more than anyone else's were perpetuating it. They intensified the close congressional attention that Watergate had triggered to the US intelligence community, culminating in the publication of the Church Committee Report in April 1976. For the beleaguered CIA's staunchest and most powerful defenders, Agee was the highest-value target. Colby's successor, George H. W. Bush, zoned in on him. In a November 1976 briefing to President-elect Jimmy Carter, Bush noted that Agee had foreign intelligence contacts, was being expelled from the United Kingdom, and was "something much more sinister" than "a disenchanted former CIA employee who wanted to clean up the Agency."[16]

The Ford administration regarded the Welch assassination, though tragic, as a fortuitous distraction from the fresh Church Committee investigations. It took the opportunity to dramatize the way in which public disclosures about the agency's clandestine presence could compromise its operations and put American intelligence officers at risk; and it used the event to prop up the CIA's public image and reverse the momentum of the Church Committee in reining in the agency.[17] So the White House treated Welch as a fallen hero, politicizing his death to lionize the CIA. An Air Force honor guard greeted the plane carrying his coffin back to Andrews Air Force Base. Against precedent, Welch, a civilian intelligence officer, was buried at Arlington National Cemetery. President Ford himself personally escorted Welch's wife at the interment. The administration's official public consternation also blunted Agee's arguments for exposing CIA officers by implying that—no matter what its source—exposure led to their deaths. Shortly after Welch's incongruously celebrated funeral, CBS reporter Daniel Schorr began quoting juicy tidbits from a leaked copy of Representative Otis Pike's Report of the House Select Committee on Intelligence. Conservatives suggested that congressional investigations, by fixing a spotlight on the agency, had put a target on Welch's back, and further that Congress could not be trusted with classified information. Senator Church felt compelled to endorse criminal penalties against anyone who identified intelligence officers or assets. If Agee had once seemed a conscientious maverick to some, he now looked more like a treasonous felon.[18]

The myth of Agee's complicity in Welch's death appears to have endured. In 1975 Gary Hart was a young US senator keenly interested in American foreign policy and sensitive to CIA excesses, sitting on the Senate Intelligence Oversight Committee. Decades later he remembered Agee only as the man whose "disclosures led, directly or indirectly, to the assassination of Richard Welch."[19] Within the agency, the lethality of Agee's actions, though unsubstantiated at best and most likely false, remains a teachable moment. Vertically as well as horizontally, the CIA is a remarkably tight-knit organization. Contemporaries don't disagree much on crucial internal issues, and maximally negative views of turncoats tend to be passed on from one generation of intelligence officers to the next. One retired CIA case officer harbored vicarious contempt for Agee in part because his father—also an agency officer—had been a close friend of Welch.

Barbara Bush took her cue from her husband when she wrote in her memoir that Agee was responsible for Welch's death. Agee sued her for libel, reaching a settlement that compelled her retraction of that statement in subsequent editions of the book.[20] Even after that settlement, in his keynote address at the 1999 Texas A&M University intelligence conference, an unrepentant George H. W. Bush lumped Welch together with those Agee did expose in his book, tendentiously proclaiming, in dismissing the merits of Agee's lawsuit, that "he bears a moral responsibility for the lives lost in the wake of" those revelations.[21] David Atlee Phillips was Glenn Carle's recruiter. Despite the older man's eventual grudging admission of Agee's technical innocence in the Welch case, Carle has stuck with the view that Agee remained substantially guilty for his death by virtue of increasing the awareness of the CIA's opponents to its foreign presence, educating them about how to uncover it and encouraging them to do so. And in April 2017, Mike Pompeo, then the agency's new director, who is not an intelligence professional, adopted the same view after only a couple of months at his post.[22] He opened his first public speech as CIA director with this anecdote:

> So I thought I'd start today by telling you a story about a bright, well-educated young man. He was described as industrious, intelligent, and likeable, if inclined towards a little impulsiveness and impatience. At some point, he became disillusioned with intelligence work, and angry with his government. He left the government and decided to devote himself to what he regarded as public advocacy: exposing the intelligence officers and operations that he had sworn to keep secret. He appealed to agency employees to send him leads, tips, suggestions. He wrote in a widely-circulated bulletin, "We are particularly anxious to receive—and anonymously, if you desire—copies of U.S. diplomatic lists and U.S. embassy staff." . . . That man was Philip Agee.

Pompeo went on to say, falsely, that Agee had helped found the magazine *CounterSpy* and that it had outed Welch as CIA station chief in Athens, insinuating that Agee was partially responsible.

Nevertheless, Agee's disclosures no doubt impeded careers and impaired livelihoods.* In a 2017 book, for example, Eva Dillon noted that Agee's naming of her father, Paul Dillon—a case officer who was handling Dmitri Fedorovich Polyakov, an important Soviet double agent—as a CIA officer effectively ended Dillon's career in the field. Polyakov was outed to the Soviets by Aldrich Ames and executed in 1988.[23] Agee's revelations easily could have resulted in the assassination of a CIA officer, and it is arguably a matter of luck that they didn't. Agee undoubtedly knew about the Tupamaros' kidnapping and execution of American security adviser Dan Mitrione in Uruguay in 1970.[†] Yet Agee never mentioned this story in print. It's difficult to counter the judgment that, from a moral point of view, Mitrione's murder should have given Agee pause about naming names five years later. Richard Kinsman, a case officer stationed in Jamaica whose status was revealed by Agee collaborator Louis

* There are open-source rumors that MI6 alleged in a secret report that Agee's revelations might have been a factor in the execution of two of its agents in Poland. See Christopher Moran, *Company Confessions: Secrets, Memoirs, and the CIA* (New York: Thomas Dunne, 2015), 137. There appears to be no public elaboration of this claim, though it may involve the nexus between Agee and Jerzy Pawlowski inferred by Murray Seeger. See Murray Seeger, "Agee's Archive: The Truth Unredacted?," *Washington Decoded*, November 11, 2010, https://www.washington decoded.com/site/2010/11/agee.html.

[†] When Agee was a member of the *Covert Action Information Bulletin*'s board of advisors, the magazine published a statement it made before the House of Representatives' Permanent Select Committee on Intelligence as well as an exchange of questions and answers between members of the committee and the magazine's spokespersons. The latter indicated that they were well aware of Mitrione and his fate. See "Statement of *CAIB* before House Committee, Jan. 31, 1980," *Covert Action Information Bulletin* no. 8 (March–April 1980): 16. Although Ellen Ray, William Schaap, and Louis Wolf represented the magazine, the statement specifically noted that Agee was a contributor. From these circumstances, there's a strong inference that Agee too knew Mitrione's story. Moreover, it beggars belief that Agee, who stayed vigorously abreast of events in the intelligence world, would not have known about that story within a short time after it was publicly reported in August 1970. See, e.g., "Kidnapped U.S. Official Found Slain in Uruguay," *New York Times*, August 11, 1970, 1. Furthermore, the celebrated Greek-French film director Costa-Gavras, who publicly supported Agee, dramatized the Mitrione episode in his controversial 1972 movie *State of Siege*.

Wolf in July 1980, presumably with Agee's guidance, had to be reassigned when locals took potshots at his house.[24] Agee was fully aware of the incident.[25]

Others were inconvenienced in less momentous ways. According to Walter McIntosh, a retired case officer with no sympathy for Agee, a friend and former case officer traveling in China was interrogated for a day in a local police station because her name had appeared in *Inside the Company*, which the police officers showed her.[26] More broadly, in a January 3, 1976, memorandum to President Gerald Ford, Bush—then director of central intelligence—noted that "there is an increasing problem in providing decent cover" for CIA officers overseas.[27] Bush mentioned Welch in this context, but given the staying power of the agency's institutional loathing for Agee, if there had been any classified evidence that his disclosures had resulted in harm to case officers or agents, the agency probably would have revealed it to the president. Yet there is no open-source evidence of any such thing. CIA officials state generally that Agee's disclosures of the names of CIA officers and assets damaged CIA operations but offer no substantive detail.

Even if the agency had chosen not to pursue legal action against Agee or make public what damage his revelations did to CIA operations for national security reasons, presumably at least some of the officers and assets themselves (especially if retired), not to mention the survivors of any killed, would have tried to sue Agee for an intentional tort or wrongful death. None did. Indeed, while CIA officials contemplated recommending to the Welch family that it consider such a lawsuit, they did so only from a cynical, box-ticking standpoint, noting that "anyone can sue anyone for anything" in the United States and concluding that "the suit would be dismissed."[28] Victor Marchetti, the disaffected CIA officer who unlike Agee submitted his book to CIA vetting, indicated that the CIA had "reluctantly confirmed" in secret testimony before a congressional committee that Agee did not endanger lives by naming names.[29] Melvin Wulf, who represented Agee against the CIA, "didn't have any second thoughts" about his naming names. "It didn't offend me. Of all the people who were exposed, not one of them was hurt. What it did was fuck up the whole Agency body of activity."[30]

What seemed to rankle CIA officials most was not that Agee amounted to a murderer but rather that he was a public pest they couldn't effectively swat. In an affidavit filed in January 1980 by Stansfield Turner, then director of central intelligence, in opposition to Agee's FOIA complaint, none of the reasons he gives for why Agee's ongoing disclosures would have resulted in irreparable damage to national security include injury or death of a CIA or other US employee or asset; rather, Turner's focus was on Agee's impairing CIA operations.[31] The agency went to the mat, defending the classification of TOP SECRET for all of the documents he sought and asserting that their disclosure would seriously damage national security. Agee's legal team characterized all CIA affidavits supporting its withholding of the documents as nonsubstantive boilerplate. His was still a nuisance suit, the government's argument continued, designed to distract and harass the CIA, as it required agency personnel, who then lacked sophisticated computerized search capabilities, to comb through tens of thousands of documents. In his order dated October 2, 1980, Judge Gerhard Gesell of the US District Court for the District of Columbia denied Agee's FOIA requests for all but five (all of them letters from members of Congress) of 8,175 CIA documents pertaining to him, to which the CIA had completely denied Agee access. Agee's requests cost the CIA $325,000 in man-hours and $70,000 worth of computer time, according to then-Director of Central Intelligence William Casey. Similarly, Bob Woodward's book cited an estimate that processing Agee's FOIA requests had cost $300,000.[32] The CIA eventually agreed to release portions of 524 (redacted) documents of the over 8,000 requested. Its claim that the FOIA had let Agee pry secrets from its files was manifestly untrue.[33]

The district court's ruling included an injunction requiring Agee to submit to the agency everything he wrote about intelligence prior to publication for vetting in line with his secrecy agreement with the CIA, subject to its redaction. This effectively precluded him from publicly naming names of intelligence officers or agents from October 2, 1980, forward.[34] Despite this prospective prohibition, it was not clear that Agee had committed a crime. Impeding CIA plans and operations rather than telling secrets about their substance was Agee's primary intention, and that made it difficult for the Justice Department to charge him with a crime under the Espionage Act. While the act criminalized the disclosure of secret information, it was unclear that the mere names of officers, agents, and other assets so qualified. Within two years, Congress would make such disclosures criminal by passing the Intelligence Identities Protection Act of 1982—sometimes called "the Anti-Agee Act"—but of course it could not constitutionally be applied retrospectively.

Agee's circumspection in this regard bore on how he felt about treason. To him it was still a kind of secular sin, acutely so during the Cold War, and he was reluctant to acknowledge that what he did was anything so terrible as all that. While he could not help but recognize that he had violated his official oath, this was at best a venial transgression redeemed by the greater good of stopping the CIA from doing what he considered overridingly evil. Of the officers and assets he exposed, Agee stressed to one journalist, "the purpose is not to get them killed. The purpose is to force them to go back home so that through constant changes of personnel their effectiveness will be reduced."[35] The logic of this claim is credible. If Agee had wanted to place CIA assets at maximal risk over the longest possible period of time, he would have fed their identities to foreign intelligence agencies gradually to facilitate their discreet neutralization in one way or another. That is what Aldrich Ames did in passing intelligence on CIA assets in the Soviet bloc in the 1980s and 1990s and what Jerry Chun Shing Lee apparently did in divulging the agency's assets in China to Chinese intelligence in the late 2000s and early 2010s.[36]

Physical as well as professional jeopardy was an integral element of his rationale, however, in that it would further goad the CIA into withdrawing exposed personnel, who would then be unable to execute CIA operations. In this calculation there was a clear if implicit element of end-justifies-means expediency, which at least tactically put Agee on the same footing as the CIA itself. His default rejoinder was that his strategic end—undermining repressive regimes—was morally superior and secured him the high ground. This too was ironically CIA-esque. In an early interview with *The Real Paper*, Boston's alternative newspaper, Agee justified naming names on two basic grounds: (1) to lend credibility to the narrative accounts of CIA activities that he provided; and (2) to devalue those exposed as operational CIA assets so as to impede the agency's activities and effectiveness.[37] The CIA, specifically Ted Shackley and his team, assessed that he had been substantially successful in advancing the second goal, and the agency admitted as much publicly.[38]

Agee later submitted to several tougher interviews on the propriety of naming names. His argument essentially devolved to the characterization of the CIA as a criminal enterprise and its officers and agents therefore as criminals, and he implicitly acknowledged that while it was not his specific intent to endanger them, his revelations probably would do so. To his mind, though, this would merely increase their motivation to quit the spying game or at least the agency's compulsion to withdraw them from the field, which of course was his intent. The *Playboy* interview was especially probing and frank.

PLAYBOY: Many people agree with your aims but disagree strongly with your methods. They say that by revealing the names of CIA agents and exposing CIA procedures your book jeopardizes U.S. security. What is your answer to that?

AGEE: I think it's a little late in the day to pretend that what I've written puts the country in any danger. What I've written puts the CIA in danger. The CIA claims that secrecy is necessary to hide what it is doing from the enemies of the United States. I claim that the real reason for secrecy is to hide what the CIA is doing from the American people and from the people victimized by the CIA.

PLAYBOY: But many people who dislike the CIA as much as you do have charged that by revealing the names and functions of individual officers and agents of the CIA, you have endangered the lives of your former colleagues, many of whom you yourself induced to become employees of The Company. Your accusers ask: Wasn't it unnecessary, wasn't it immoral, wasn't it, in fact, a crime to reveal those names?

AGEE: Absolutely not. Those people talk about the CIA as if it were an international charity of some sort and about me as if I'd done something horrible to a lot of decent, well-meaning Y.M.C.A. leaders. In fact, the CIA, in my opinion, is a criminal organization at least as nefarious as the Mafia and much, much more powerful. Even more than the Vietnam war, the CIA represents the destruction of our national ideals on the pretext of saving them. What you've got to understand is that in revealing the names of CIA operatives, I am revealing the names of people engaged in criminal activities. These people live by breaking the law. Every day of the week, CIA men break the laws of the countries they're stationed in. I don't know any country in which bugging or intercepting mail or bribing public officials is legal.

At the same time, it's nonsense to say that by exposing the CIA officers and agents I knew, I have endangered their lives. I have exposed some to problems, but The Company can solve those problems for the indigenous agents in Latin America. As for the Company officers I've named, well, they can stay in Langley if they want to be safe.[39]

In a candid *Newsweek* interview, Agee said, "I really don't care too much about the element of vulnerability. The people who are really vulnerable are the people who are being murdered" by those the CIA supports and keeps in power.[40] He was parsing his rationale awfully finely: he didn't intend to harm any of the people he exposed, but he didn't care whether they were vulnerable.

Agee's unpublished paper "Why the CIA Should Be Exposed" (circa 1976) is key to understanding his more considered justification for naming names. The basis of Agee's argument was the absence of political will in the United States to bar the CIA from implementing covert action operations at the behest of the president.

"Plenty is known about what the CIA does," he wrote. "The next task is to discover who does it." He lodged assurances that "no violence or death is intended in these continuing exposures, only a disruption of a Station's operations by continued and untimely transfers of personnel back to Headquarters in Langley, Virginia." Finally, he suggested that in principle his disclosures were not unpatriotic or, therefore, treasonous. "We must recognize that the CIA's propping up of regimes that serve privileged, minority interests is doing more to turn people away from the U.S. than anything the KGB could ever concoct."[41]

Implicit in that statement was a cryptopatriotic premise: that there were aspects of the United States that really ought to attract people. Agee was not altogether anti-American, even if he wrote *Inside the Company* "as a contribution to socialist revolution." He saw plenty of merit in the liberal ideals that had blossomed in the 1960s with the triumphs of the civil rights movement, stunted though they turned out to be by his lights. This mindset certainly registered with his sons and his friends. Philip Jr. remarks:

> For those who knew him personally—especially those in the family—he never ceased to express and practice a lifelong patriotic commitment to the American people. What some Americans fail to understand is that his ideological shift was a way to maintain his idealism about the great values of the American tradition. He preferred to insist, for example, on real prosperity and real justice as an expected result of the Alliance for Progress, rather than to be satisfied when the initiative turned more into a public relations success than anything else. He refused to take the road others take in which they settle into a cynical realism that allows the nation to become as immoral as the enemies we claim to differ with.[42]

Indeed, Agee did not condemn the American system altogether, but primarily its foreign policy. It was on that basis that he felt he deserved wider acceptance among Americans—not just by the radical Left—and sought it.

For Agee, the conflicts and fragility of the sixties generation, along with the Catholic sensibility that the CIA as an institution was inclined to discount, made the giddy line all the giddier. He was well-bred but not inbred—establishment but not Ivy League, select but not Skull and Bones, an upwardly mobile ecumenical Catholic and not a patrician. He was, therefore, especially susceptible both to the vaunted promise of the American Dream and to extreme disillusionment when he apprehended its betrayal. He lived in a time bracketed by the promise and its breach. The period from his early youth in the forties to his resignation from the CIA in 1969 began with World War II and ended with the worst days of the Vietnam War (as well as the election of Richard M. Nixon as president), thus linking the zenith and the nadir of America's strategic self-image.

His new vocation, then, was to trumpet its vices and preclude the repetition of its transgressions, and to do so publicly. Many in the Catholic Worker Movement, including Dorothy Day, were conflicted about the efficacy of nonviolent public protest. Both she and Thomas Merton also feared that taking it up a notch, to the destruction of property, risked setting the perpetrators on a slippery slope to violence against fellow human beings.[43] Agee might once have shared this ambivalence. But the Vietnam War had afforded demonstrative resistance inexorable momentum. And Catholics had staged two of the most audacious displays. In October 1967, Philip Berrigan, a World War II combat veteran and then a Josephist priest, and three other Catholic activists broke into the Baltimore Custom House and poured blood on draft records. In May 1968, while he was out on bail for that incident, Berrigan, his brother Daniel—a Jesuit priest—and seven fellow Catholic protesters entered the Selective Service System office in Catonsville, Maryland, during working hours, restraining a clerk who tried to stop them. They gathered draft files into wire bins, took them out to the parking lot, poured their own blood on them, doused them with homemade napalm, and set them on fire, destroying some 378 files.[44] Then they prayed and waited to be arrested.[45] The symbolism was clear: napalm—jellied gasoline—

was a ghastly weapon of choice for US forces in Vietnam. The so-called Catonsville Nine's lawyer was the flamboyant and provocative William Kunstler, and their trial in Baltimore—they were all found guilty of destruction of federal property, destruction of draft records, and interference with the Selective Service Act of 1967—was a national spectacle. Kunstler's next major political trial, that of the Chicago Seven in 1969–70, would be an even bigger one.

By then, Agee had resigned from the CIA. Students were protesting against allowing CIA recruiters as well as Dow Chemical (which manufactured napalm) on the Notre Dame campus. The Catholic Workers would add tax resistance by way of self-imposed poverty to their political toolkit, and their resistance to the war and its dispensations endured through the Paris Peace Accords of 1973 and Vietnam's fraught reunification in 1975.[46] Agee did not identify himself as a distinctively Catholic dissident, in the vein of, say, the Berrigan brothers. When a friend of his indicated an interest in writing a story about him for the *National Catholic Reporter*, noting that "there should be a Catholic story in there somewhere," Agee failed to follow up.[47] But when consulted about a Greens-sponsored conference styled as a "Nuremberg tribunal" on moral aspects of nuclear weapons, he did advise a German colleague to invite "a leading member of the Catholic Bishops Conference to speak about the current debate on moral aspects of nuclear weapons."[48] Attending the conference in 1983, Agee sat next to Philip Berrigan.[49] Clearly he believed that Catholics in particular had a strong, positive, and public role to play in global politics.

US officials did not see any faith or piety in Agee's turn and his activities. When they didn't attribute his actions to libidinousness or drunkenness, they specified venality as a motive. An undated and heavily redacted CIA assessment declared that a "factor influencing Agee was his conviction that he was wasting his talents on the Agency and could become wealthy through the assistance of many well-off Mexicans he had met though his work"; it also noted, with a whiff of disdain, that "Agee's grandiose schemes for making money in Mexico did not bear fruit."[50] Those schemes—sports development and selling mirrors—were hardly grandiose. A July 1974 cable to the

FBI director from the FBI legal attaché in Mexico City indicated that Fulton Freeman, ex-US ambassador to Mexico, said in an *Excelsior* interview that Agee was writing *Inside the Company* only for financial gain, and several negative articles about Agee cited financial motivations.[51] But his US advance for *Inside the Company* from Stonehill Publishing Company in 1975 was only $12,000, while the advance for *On the Run* a decade later from Lyle Stuart, Inc., was initially a mere $20,000, and even that was later reduced to $15,000 plus $5,000 for a shorter book to be titled "The CIA for Beginners: 100 Questions."[52] His annual CIA salary at the time of his resignation was $13,392.[53]

Inside the Company, of course, was translated into twenty-seven languages, and Agee collected a considerable amount in royalties from sales that exceeded the advance. But a large proportion of that was used for legal fees to fight deportation, pursue his FOIA requests, and other legal matters. Melvin Wulf, the lawyer to whom Agee would owe the most, commented that "he was always broke."[54] He did have a working wife, was decently paid for teaching university courses, and in time made appreciable amounts from lecture tours. Furthermore, in 1992, another disaffected former CIA officer indicated to the FBI that Agee had told him that he was being paid $20,000 a year by Cuban intelligence.[55] But whatever streams of income Agee had did not make him rich.

Michael Opperskalski, a left-wing German journalist since 1982 and the editor of the singularly provocative Cologne-based magazine *Geheim (Secret)*, which he started in 1985, became a friend and colleague of Agee's shortly after he moved to West Germany and "saw him regularly." He testified to Agee's challenges of subsistence. "Don't think that every day he was on the run, that every day he gave a lecture," commented Opperskalski. "He was also struggling for a living. If he hadn't had his wife, who was a very prominent artist, he would have had problems just getting daily bread and butter."[56]

Agee's earlier failure to pique publishers' interest in a more conventional CIA history had informed his segue to an outright exposé. But the fact was that he had other more conventional post-government employment options—security consultancies or think-tanks, for example—that would have been more assuredly remunerative and less stressful than freelance writing that flayed CIA operations and personnel. His invoices and financial statements reflect a financially strained existence that he was willing to endure to pursue that vocation.[57] He did need moral support, though, and he got it from a range of sources.

Agee was the first to acknowledge, more readily than he might have wished in retrospect, that women often afforded him affirmation. In *On the Run*, Agee recalled rhetorically asking himself at a public speaking engagement in 1983 why he left the CIA, then responding, "I fell in love with a woman who thought Che Guevara was the most wonderful man in the world."[58] That would have been Susan Torres de Espinda, the sophisticated American divorcée from New York living in Mexico City whom he had wanted to marry. If his affection for her had intensified his chagrin in hiding his real employment behind his State Department cover, her angry conviction that the CIA was complicit in Che's death in October 1967 had hastened his resignation. Even thereafter, he did not detail his CIA past, but they drifted apart and she broke off their relationship anyway.[59] Next, in an apparently short relationship, came a Spanish artist he dubbed Veronica (also a pseudonym) who he said urged on his writing.

In 1972, while in Paris, he met Seixas. She had been a student revolutionary in Brazil starting in 1968, wounded by the Brazilian secret police in an early 1970 gunfight in which a friend of hers had been killed, then imprisoned and tortured by Brazilian authorities, which the CIA supported.[60] According to journalist A. J. Langguth, the torture she endured was extraordinarily brutal: she was stripped naked, beaten with rubber truncheons and bare-knuckled fists, whipped, and sexually abused, shocked with electrodes attached inside her vagina.[61] She and Agee started living together in the UK in 1973. Langguth perceptively connects Seixas to Mitrione, noting that he had advised Brazilian police for the US government from 1960 until 1967—well after the April 1964 coup that transformed Brazil from a democracy into the military dictatorship under which Seixas was arrested and abused.[62]

Superficially, this itinerant romantic history squares with the dire assessment of Agee's character that the CIA cultivated after it learned of his plans to expose agency operations and assets. Agee may have had a wandering eye that might have produced some awkward moments at embassy cocktail parties while he was a case officer—especially after he and Janet had become estranged. But Agee also seemed to settle down as his post-CIA life became more resolute. Moreover, Seixas was a living reminder both of the Bonaudi incident and of Mitrione's activities and death, suggesting a connection considerably deeper and more complex than a garden-variety romantic attraction.

Yet the libertine storyline is durable and represents the widely held view among other intelligence officers of all vintages and among many historians. Hardwired to accept sometimes unsavory means for patriotic ends, they are inclined to dismiss the idea that psychological turmoil might have emanated in part from Agee's moral qualms about his work for the CIA, and they credit the CIA's retrospective characterization of Agee as a priapic egomaniac.[63] The CIA's propaganda worked because it confirmed preexisting biases. The fact that over time Agee's commitment to exposing the CIA waxed rather than waned suggests that his stated motives were not merely circumstantial rationalizations. And there is evidence, eventually provided by the CIA itself in response to Agee's FOIA request, that at least some agency officials regarded the party-line portrayal as at best an oversimplification. One speculated that Agee might be conflicted, possibly suicidal, and itchy. "In general," the officer wrote in an internal memo, "it is my impression that Subject is waiting with some relish to do battle, and that the more actively we confront him, the more counter productive it is likely to be."[64] The FBI, which has lead responsibility for domestic counterintelligence and counterespionage operations, was also inclined to let presumptively sleeping dogs lie, and, while remaining alert to Agee's activities, did not undertake an active investigation in the mid-1970s.[65]

Certainly the CIA underestimated Agee's capacity to find a delicate sufficiency of stability amid turmoil. Agee and Seixas were together for four years, starting in 1973. During this tumultuous and, for Agee, traumatic period, she was an unstinting companion,

standing by him as he endeavored obsessively to expose CIA officers and agents and contain the efforts of the agency to discomfit
him; she helped shepherd his children through four of the countries that would expel him. But she and a wrung-out Agee parted
precipitously—though apparently amicably—in 1977. Her very sto-
icism made Agee feel compelled to carry forward what may have
been a quite tentative ideological agenda. "Angela never badgered
or pushed me to accept this or that," he explained. "But she was
so supportive that the effect was the same: like a huge conscience
casting a long and constant shadow."[66] Agee would admit openly
that his renunciation of the CIA was the result of "many factors"
that included compelling females—"disillusionment with my work,
the breakup of my marriage, another woman I met with left-wing
opinions. Women have often influenced me at crucial times of my
life. From a tiny opening, there was a progression. My head literally
opened up."[67] But such candor is well short of a concession that he
was putty in their hands. Datebooks indicate that Agee and Seixas
were physically together only sporadically in 1975–77, suggesting
that the attraction may have been increasingly ideological as opposed to physical.[68]

Furthermore, his separation from Seixas seemed to reflect Agee's
determination to consolidate and stabilize his new identity as a
career dissident. After she left, he reflected, "I just felt I could no
longer allow the anti-CIA struggle to be my whole world. From now
on, I decided, I would work a reasonable day, then shut the door of
my office and live my life."[69] Agee doggedly countered his phobias:
his compulsion was not to flee the source of his anxiety but rather
to revisit and conquer it, even though this confrontational course
sometimes turned him into "an emotional basket case."[70] He wasn't
quitting, just pacing himself.

Like Agee, Giselle Roberge was raised a Catholic but had not remained actively religious. Despite her relative youth, she was hardnosed and practical. It was she who suggested that they wed, and
convenience was a central and unabashed motivation: she noted
that marriage was a solution to Agee's legal residency challenges
since she was legally entitled to cohabit with a spouse as a legal

foreign resident of West Germany.[71] That said, she would not have made the proposal absent a strong foundation of affection. Though politically sympathetic and "a good listener," she was more passively accommodating than actively inspiring of his dissident impulses, essentially looking the other way. "We didn't talk so much about my work and problems as about the books she was reading, the ballets she was dancing, the movies we'd seen or just plain trivia," recalled Agee.[72] Opperskalski confirmed this picture and stressed her dedication to Agee: "She was very loyal to him—very loyal. Any other woman under those circumstances of pressure would have gone; she didn't. But she knew very little about what he was doing. That would have created unnecessary problems."[73] Based on her own experience, Giselle rated the amoral horndog portrayal as "nonsense."[74] His fidelity and respect for their relationship enabled her to provide basic emotional compatibility and domestic and legal stability.

DOMESTICATION, RETALIATION, RETRENCHMENT

Philip and Giselle's twenty-nine-year marriage would involve long periods of separation owing to divergent professional activities—for example, she took a six-month ballet-teaching course at the Hartford School of Ballet in Hartford, Connecticut, while Agee undertook long lecture tours in the United States and protest stints in Latin America.[75] But there is no substantial reason to doubt his fondness for Giselle. The frequency of her name in his datebooks indicated an intense courtship. In early 1978 he was still winding up the relationship with Seixas as he developed the one with Giselle, as Giselle herself acknowledged (the two women never met).[76] He became a "ballet groupie."[77] In this capacity, his references to her occasionally impart irrepressibly effusive emotion that is atypical for him— for instance, "Giselle's big day! All day, all year!" with respect to the opening of a ballet in which she was performing.[78] In any case, their romantic arc suggests that, in the end, Agee did not need or want either a demure hausfrau or an actively sympathetic and partisan muse to sustain his political mission. In times of extreme instability and stress, he had sought and welcomed such galvanizing personalities. But now he wanted a lively, extroverted domestic companion, and that's what he got.

In leafy Hamburg, Agee and Roberge lived in cozy apartments with insular courtyards. One of their later street addresses—Rehm Strasse 18B—had a Sherlock Holmesean feel of cheerful intrigue. Agee adopted a high bohemian lifestyle, modest, cautious, and agreeably domestic. He loved to cook; paella, lamb, and ratatouille were his specialties. He liked to sing, especially in the kitchen, and noodled on the piano, having taken lessons as a kid. He was fairly handy, putting up shelves and making pillows. He was also an antiques aficionado, and he enjoyed buying them sight unseen on the basis of magazine advertisements, using his mother-in-law as a proxy. Giselle adored cats; Agee didn't initially, having grown up with a dog, but he got used to them.[79] He drove a Volvo, occasionally caught a play (*Ain't Misbehavin'*) or a concert (The Moody Blues and Ray Charles), played a little tennis, and later did Pilates.[80] He took standing security precautions, but they appeared light and somewhat erratic. For instance, he subscribed to some periodicals under the name "Mr. G. Roberge" or "P. A. Roberge," but some others he received under his own name. If he detected human surveillance, he drew on his professional tradecraft to evade it. Outwardly, he seemed to be having his cake and eating it too: to be living the romantic life of an exiled man of conscience, an expatriate dancer by his side, right under the noses of the governments he had, directly or indirectly, assailed.

His comfortable roost in West Germany was the product of two factors peculiar to that country. One was its unexceptionably strict adherence to the law—in Agee's case, the right of a legal resident to live with her spouse—which prevailed despite pressure from the CIA to expel him and a degree of uneasiness about letting him stay on the part of the West German intelligence services. The other was a more nuanced approach to intelligence, less reflexive than that of the United States or the United Kingdom, whereby hosting suspicious characters was considered a means of keeping watch over them and, if necessary, constraining them.[81] Certainly the CIA and other friendly agencies kept a close eye on Agee and were not averse to jamming him in various ways. On the day of their wedding in Amsterdam, after they'd celebrated with a champagne breakfast, Giselle had to fly back to West Germany to rejoin the Hamburg Ballet. West German officers stopped her at the airport immigration gate and interrogated her about Agee's whereabouts and when he was coming to West Germany; they also strip-searched her. Later, at Hamburg Airport, the immigration officer processing Giselle called another officer over to his desk, pointed to her theatrically, and said, "Look—the wife." [82]

Even so, Agee got comfortable enough living in West Germany that he soon overreached. Shortly after Iranian students loyal to the Ayatollah Ruhollah Khomeini ousted the shah of Iran and took fifty-two US government employees hostage at the US Embassy compound in November 1979, several journalists sent Agee copies of classified US documents that the students had captured and disseminated, seeking his assessment. The documents were damning enough: they included false identity papers for CIA officers, instructions for their use, and personnel files indicating the officers' real identities. [83]* Given the damage already done, a grand bargain occurred to Agee whereby the United States could secure the release of the hostages—some of whom were the CIA officers identified in the documents—by offering the Iranians all of the CIA's files on its operations going back to the coup against Iranian Prime Minister Mohammed Mossadegh in 1953 and before. In that case, he reasoned, the CIA and the United States as institutions rather than the individuals being held would be put on trial. He communicated the idea to Irish Nobel Peace laureate Sean MacBride, who had offered to mediate a solution to the crisis, and to the Iranian consulate in

---

* The Agee Papers include some of the documents sent to him, such as a draft fitness report of a US defense attaché officer stationed in Tehran; commercial documents relating to the shipment of film and spare parts to the United States from Iran; and items regarding the shipment of spare parts for the Iranian Air Force to Iran from the United States. They do not include the more sensitive documents involving the identities and covers of CIA personnel that Agee described in *On the Run*. See Agee Papers, box 10, folder 15; box 14, folder 1; box 15, folder 8. This suggests that the CIA and other agencies probably confiscated the documents in 2009.

Hamburg. He received no direct response. Instead, a sensationally reported story emerged in the *New York Post* saying that the Iranians wanted an anti-imperialist, anti-Zionist American on a judging tribunal for the hostages, and that Philip Agee fit the profile and was at the top of the list, burying in the fourth paragraph the fact that "it was not known whether Agee agreed." The story also recycled the Welch smear. Initially the headline tagged Agee a "traitor," though in later editions that word was replaced by "defector."[84] In fact, Agee had not remotely agreed to function as a judge and had stated publicly that he would not visit Iran until the hostages were released. Subsequently, he telephoned the Iranians holding the hostages directly and told them of his files-for-hostages notion. They seemed receptive.

The FBI had actively resumed investigating Agee in 1978 and continued into 1979. On December 23 of that year—a few days after the *New York Post* article appeared, and one day after Agee had phoned the Iranians—the State Department made Agee's residency in West Germany all the more important by revoking his American passport.[85] Official notification of this action came by way of a knock on the Agees' door by an official from the US consulate in Hamburg. The deputy director of the CIA had assessed that Agee's ability to travel internationally on his US passport "greatly enhances his potential to disrupt and damage American foreign policy and national security interests." The sequencing indicated two things, one practical and the other political. First, the Agees' home phone must have been tapped.[86] Second, in the US government's eyes, Agee's communicating privately with the Iranians, whatever the specific substance of the exchange, constituted a new level of meddling that couldn't go unanswered. The CIA, Justice Department, and State Department had judged the passport revocation the best way of inhibiting this degree of interference, given the agency's disinclination to prosecute him for fear of being compelled to reveal operational secrets or to take extralegal efforts to stifle him.

For the US government to revoke the passport of an American citizen, however, was an extremely rare measure, constitutionally difficult to defend. Agee and his lawyer, Melvin Wulf, took the case to the

US Supreme Court, which upheld the government's action in *Haig v. Agee* (1981) in a seven-to-two decision, with the invariably liberal Justices William Brennan and Thurgood Marshall dissenting.[87] This politically charged decision not only upheld the appeals court order reversing the district court's reinstatement of Agee's passport but also reversed *Kent v. Dulles*, the Supreme Court's own 1958 case invalidating the State Department's revocation of artist Rockwell Kent's passport, which the government had premised on Kent's being a communist activist. Writing for the court, Chief Justice Warren Burger stated that "restricting Agee's foreign travel, although perhaps not certain to prevent all of Agee's harmful activities, is the only avenue open to the government to limit these activities."[88] Thirty-five years after *Haig v. Agee* was decided, Wulf recalled: "I had argued seven or eight cases before the Supreme Court before that, and I had always had a very nice reception and was thought to be quite professional in my presentation. But they ripped into me, and it was perfectly clear that they couldn't get Agee, so they were going to get his lawyer. It was very hard going. They surprised me with their aggressive approach."[89]

Following the revocation of his passport, the West German government appeared to contemplate deporting Agee, and he had to stand down on any Iran initiative in order to safeguard his legal residency status.[90] He had not had in mind dooming the hostages to prison or worse in Iran but rather envisaged a heroic role, in which he would save them, albeit by blaming US policy and the institutions that implemented it for Iran's troubles and eliciting Iran's mercy for the individuals that those institutions might have seduced by manipulative patriotism. He made his disposition clear in a letter that he titled "Gut Feelings," sent to the *New York Times* in response to a discursive *Times* editorial. The piece had cast the files-for-hostages proposal as "offensive" if "not a crime," noted that Agee had "brought discredit on those who want to expose C.I.A. misdeeds . . . for the worthy purpose of bringing intelligence agencies within the rule of law," and lamented the Supreme Court's decision in the *Haig v. Agee* passport case even though Agee did not fall into "a better class of victim."[91] In its entirety, the letter read:

Contrary to the advice in the *Times* editorial of Jan. 7 about me, we must *not* put gut feelings aside because such feelings clearly dominate the Tehran Embassy crisis. It is the hatred and fear of clandestine intervention by the CIA and of its support for repressive regimes like the Shah's that motivates the student captors.

Under Secretary of State Newsom's affidavit explaining Secretary Vance's revocation of my passport rightly attributes these gut feelings abroad to increasing awareness of the CIA's operations. Yet to focus attention only on me ignores the role of the *Times* itself and many others of the "better class of victim," who have increased public knowledge of the CIA's harmful clandestine activities.

Compared with my limited contributions to the huge body of knowledge about the CIA made public in recent years, the *Times*'s own contribution has been immense—including individuals' names—from its 1967 series on CIA fronts and finance conduits, to publication of the Pentagon Papers in 1971, to its series on media operations in 1977. And *Times* reporters had no inhibitions in taking many names and leads from me among others.

Many others have contributed to the gut feelings abroad about the CIA. Former employees through books, the U.S. Congress through official investigations, and the world communication media by putting the word about.

The gut feelings of hostility produced by the revelations are, I believe, wholly justified and are sure to continue, so long as U.S. Presidents, through the CIA, engage in covert actions.

In accusing me of bringing "discredit" to others (presumably including the *Times*) who want to bring intelligence agencies within the rule of law, the *Times* failed to see that the real discredit lies with the failure of the Carter administration to do just that—to produce appropriate charter legislation.

My idea of the exchange of the CIA's files on Iranian operations for the 50 Americans remains a good one, I believe. To obtain release of the 50 people *and* make public the files would help the Iranian case for the return of the Shah; it would unveil for us another valuable and instructive phase of contemporary American military history; and it might revive worthy efforts to control the CIA. Publication of the files would also show why the Americans now held in Tehran are paying the price for what hundreds, probably thousands, of other Americans did there for 30 years.

Should the CIA's Iran files ever become available, would the *Times* find them, like the Pentagon Papers, "fit to print"? I've a gut feeling it would.[92]

This was vintage Agee hedging: arrogant yet beseeching, snide but still earnest, closing on a note of mildly endearing wit. The *Times* did not publish the letter.

It may have been true that the Carter administration assimilated the rising critiques of the CIA and US policy in Latin America and elsewhere, fueled in part by Agee's work. Among other things, Carter appointed the aggressively reformist Admiral Stansfield Turner director of central intelligence and orchestrated the prospective forfeiture of the Panama Canal on the last day of the twentieth century, signaling a more relaxed application of the Monroe Doctrine. But popular and praetorian openness to questioning the CIA was winding down, and in any case fell far short of embracing and lionizing a man who had exposed CIA assets. The tension between Agee's Western cultural sensibilities and anti-American actions and ideology had left him in a state of indefinite limbo. He continued to antagonize US authorities in ways that guaranteed his effective statelessness. This tilt, perhaps, is the best evidence of the ultimate genuineness of Agee's convictions.

Yet Agee could not help but feel "American." He continued to seek to vote in the United States, applying to the state of Virginia for an absentee ballot.[93] He considered relinquishing his American citizenship to emblematize his opposition to US policies, but ultimately decided that doing so would diminish the credibility of his criticisms.[94] He unambiguously chose to remain in the West. Wulf stayed in touch with the Justice Department and periodically confirmed its provisional forbearance from prosecution—clearly the US government continued to consider a public trial a toxic can of worms—and Agee was able return to the United States with some frequency, applying and paying fees for identity cards and registration from the US Foreign Service for each individual trip. And he relentlessly pursued the reinstatement of his US passport.[95] Even Paul Robeson, the great black singer and activist and an open supporter of the Soviet Union, whose passport was confiscated in the overtly racist 1950s, eventually got his back. That Agee was never successful in reclaiming his despite repeated attempts is both a measure of the United States government's immovable hostility toward him and his resistance to it as an American. In a way, his post-CIA existence was giddy in perpetuity.

When Opperskalski encountered Agee, "it was like a James Bond movie, running around to different places and trying for two or three hours to get rid of people who were following him, not only CIA guys but also West Germans."[96] To Giselle's knowledge no officer from the CIA or any other intelligence agency had ever approached her; "what was I going to teach them about—a grand jeté?" But she learned from a friend who was the underdirector of the Zürich Ballet and wanted to hire her that she had been passed over for the job because of the director's view that Agee was "a communist spy." She recalled that she "hadn't seen Phil cry much in my life, but that night he cried."[97]

At the same time, Agee's mobility within Europe was greater than he might have expected at the height of his immigration travails, thanks to authorized German travel documentation. By 1986, Giselle had stopped dancing on stage and become credentialed as a ballet instructor. She was hired by a small company in Ulm, West Germany—about halfway between Munich and Stuttgart—where she and Agee went to live. After eight months, the National Ballet of Spain recruited her. They lived in Madrid until 1991, though the Spanish authorities would not grant Agee a legal residency permit and merely turned a blind eye to his lack of one. The Agees then returned to Hamburg and she to the Hamburg Ballet.

His ex-wife Janet, who lived in Falls Church, Virginia, had retained primary custody of their children, Philip Jr. and Christopher. Agee invariably remembered their birthdays—October 12 and February 28, respectively.[98] After the initial flare-ups over custody while he was still in the CIA, Agee's relationship with Janet appeared to be distant but civil, and it was largely limited to telephone conversations about the boys' upbringing and support.[99] They met infrequently, and during the rare times that they did, very briefly.[100] Philip Jr. lived with Agee and Giselle in Hamburg for a year, attending the International School there. Philip Jr. then left to attend New York University, transferring to and finishing college at Columbia. Christopher then stayed with them for four years, also attending the International School. Later, with both parents' agreement, Christopher went to live in Brooklyn with Dale and Corinne Wiehoff, two activist friends of Agee, who helped pay for his schooling.[101]

Christopher had his troubles—including colitis, some fairly typical teenage disaffection with school, misadventures with alcohol, and a despondent stint as a taxi driver—and for a time did not answer Agee's letters.[102] But he completed his bachelor's at Hunter College, majoring in history, and got a master's degree in sociology at the New School. Christopher has taught as an adjunct at several New York area institutions, including Borough of Manhattan Community College, Hofstra University, and State University of New York at Farmingdale. Philip Jr. never fell out with his father, and he became a computer programmer. Both sons have lived in New York City for most of their lives, latterly in Greenwich Village. Perhaps most gratifyingly to Agee, the two sons adopted their father's far-left liberal politics. Philip Jr. wrote for and was a coeditor of *Campus Watch*.[103] He spearheaded an effort to popularize and disseminate a DIY handbook for student organizers for resisting CIA recruitment efforts on college campuses in the late 1980s with Agee's endorsement and support.[104] Christopher is the editor and publisher of *Covert Action Magazine*, a direct descendant of *Covert Action Information Bulletin* and *Covert Action Quarterly*, with which his father was closely affiliated. Both sons consider their father a fiercely independent political hero and reject any notion that he actively worked with or was manipulated by Cuban or Soviet intelligence.[105]

Likewise, Agee's own father Bill and stepmother Nancy—Agee's mother Helen died in late 1969 of pneumonia following a car accident—were loath to disavow or alienate him, even though his father initially had had serious reservations about Agee's turn. In addition to lending him over $7000 for his failed business ventures in Mexico, the elder Agee referred his son to a Chicago lawyer, John J. Casey, in 1979, at the height of his notoriety.[106] The Agees were reticent with the CIA assistant general counsel when he discussed Agee's activities with them at their home, and they took pains not to prejudge him or sell him out.[107] They visited Agee and Giselle in Hamburg for ten days in 1980.[108] Agee called his father on his eightieth birthday.[109] "He loved his father, and they were very close," recalled Giselle in 2016. "Nancy was wonderful. Bill was a charmer." In time, Bill became so supportive of Agee's position that he brought several Tampa television journalists to Hamburg to interview Agee and compose a program about him. The Tampa television station they worked for refused to air it. When Agee and Giselle later went to Tampa to visit his parents, the older couple escorted them unself-consciously around Central and South Florida, to Disneyworld and Key West. Agee's books were on the coffee table. "Bill was proud of his son," Giselle said.[110] Bill Agee died at age eighty-five in 1994. Notified by Agee's older sister, Barbara Agee Steelman, Agee and Giselle attended his funeral in Tampa. He was too upset to deliver a eulogy.[111]

Given the circumstances Agee had brought upon himself, he enjoyed familial good fortune. But he scarcely rested on his laurels, and he did not seem to blanch much once he had settled in Hamburg. He liaised with radical journalists and continued to write anti-CIA articles for left-wing magazines. To be sure, he strained, sometimes rather conspicuously, for money through aggressive litigation and acrimonious bargaining for writing fees. But he spent far more time — blocking out entire days for correspondence — providing substantive help and encouragement, gratis, to a motley series of activists, graduate students, and writers. Most of them were unknown cold contacts, unlikely to reciprocate. His only prerequisite seemed to be a modicum of political sympathy.[112] Naturally he granted interviews for magazine articles, as publicity was a form of political sustenance for him.[113] But, out of public view, he helped doctoral candidates with their theses and college students with senior projects, advised a playwright on a book on politics and theater, and informed Douglas Valentine's book on the CIA's Phoenix Program in Vietnam—providing, among other things, the name of ex-military intelligence officer K. Barton Osborn—which was highly critical of the CIA.[114] According to Giselle Roberge Agee, he just felt "compelled" to respond, perhaps gratified not to be isolated.

Agee was assiduously courteous about answering mail. It included somewhat frivolous inquiries. One woman, Giselle recalled, said in a letter that she wrote to him while in the toilet on the theory that the metal stall doors would jam the devices that were trying to "zap" her. He answered her, too.[115] A New York City chiropractor, Rose Smart, wanted some expert advice on bugs and telephone interference, and he directed her to the Center for Constitutional Rights.[116] More substantively, Agee reached out to Mr. and Mrs. Edward Horman in connection with the acclaimed Costa-Gavras film *Missing* regarding background on relevant CIA practices.[117] (The film famously chronicled the death of the Hormans' son Christopher at the hands of the Chilean security forces following the 1973 CIA-backed coup against Allende.)

Naturally Agee also came up with a few ancillary, highly speculative ways to try to cash in on his notoriety. Almost inevitably, he wanted to write a screenplay for a feature film based on *Inside the Company*.[118] He tried to promote the book as a dramatic project to the director Oliver Stone and the producer Jon Peters, though both declined.[119] He later worked as a technical consultant for *Mission: Impossible*. All told, his efforts in the film trade ultimately didn't yield much more than three documentaries: PBS's three-hour *On Company Business* (1980), in which he, Victor Marchetti, and John Stockwell appeared and on which Agee was a special consultant; TBS's *Secrets of the CIA* (1998); and the independently produced *One Man's Story: Philip Agee, Cuba, and the CIA* (2008). They received little attention. Producer Jamie Otis, who had made *Secrets of the CIA* with support from noted director Richard Linklater, did offer Agee a $1.00 token option for a film version of his life story, but the picture never materialized.[120] And he continued to glom status via epistolary dalliances with liberal luminaries like Irish Nobel Peace laureate Sean MacBride, who wrote a preface for *Dirty Work 2*, and leftist historian Howard Zinn, who contributed an article to the *Covert Action Infor-*

mation Bulletin.[121] Agee was susceptible to flattery and gratified by attention—especially positive, but negative as well. But he was not indiscriminate. He declined, for example, to provide Irish playwright Stephen Elliott Wilmer with input for a play about him, and Wilmer decided not to write it.[122]

Agee maintained relationships with some fellow dissidents who had served in the US government, while others sought to distance themselves from him due to his wholesale rejection of the American system and his willingness to imperil intelligence officers, agents, and operations. Marchetti and Frank Snepp publicly condemned him on that basis.[123] He considered Snepp "hostile" and "right wing," and never reached out to him.[124] Certain journalists took pains to distinguish the likes of Agee from Marchetti and his ilk. In particular, Jonathan Kwitny of the *Wall Street Journal*, then WNYC, and later Gannett, rated Agee's accounts of CIA activity and practices in *Inside the Company* accurate and CIA covert action inimical to American interests.[125] But Kwitny considered Agee abjectly unpatriotic. At a 1988 bookstore appearance in Berkeley, California, Kwitny said: "Unlike the other best-known CIA renegade, Philip Agee, Marchetti has clearly spoken out from a desire to help, not hurt, the country." Kwitny also reportedly noted that Agee had blackened the names of all other insider critics of the CIA because they were now lumped together with Agee "the traitor."[126] But Agee and Daniel Ellsberg, the former Defense Department official who turned the top secret Pentagon Papers over to the *New York Times* and the *Washington Post*, were friends. They met in Madrid in December 1981, and Agee stayed with Ellsberg and his wife in California during a lecture tour in the late 1980s, visiting a nude beach in the bargain ("when in Rome . . . ," he commented to his wife in recounting the story).[127]

Stockwell was not publicly critical of Agee. Like Agee, he believed the CIA was incompatible with a free society (he considered the agency the "secret police") and a "great negative influence on U.S. national security." He and Agee were friends, and Stockwell stayed with the Agees in Hamburg. Unlike Agee, though, he tended to regard the agency as more incompetent than malevolent. They maintained a fairly close personal friendship, meeting in Europe occasionally, speaking quite frequently on the telephone, and lecturing together in the United States on Agee's book tour for *On the Run*.[128] They also promoted each other's respective protest efforts. Agee, for instance, in 1985 extolled the virtues of Stockwell and his book on US intervention in Angola to Petra Kelly, the prominent Green Party activist and member of the West German Bundestag, and on his behalf asked her how to generate German interest in Stockwell's annual "Pantex Pilgrimage" in Amarillo, Texas, protesting nuclear weapons at the Pantex bomb assembly plant.[129] He and Stockwell along with fellow soured ex-spies Philip Roettinger and David MacMichael in 1987 announced the establishment of the Center for the Study of Covert Action in Elgin, Texas, to serve as a "watering hole" for disillusioned CIA officers who want to help end US overseas intervention.[130] Stockwell didn't harbor the ideological animosity toward the agency that Agee did, and thought he had gone too far in blowing covers, but he appreciated the logic of Agee's actions given his viewpoint. He also admired Agee's pluck and moxie, while looking askance at Snepp's incessant public complaining about the government's confiscation of his book income owing to Snepp's failure to submit his book for CIA vetting. "Agee doesn't whine and cry about his situation the way Snepp does," said Stockwell.[131] That sentiment might have looked charitable after the 1987 release of *On the Run*, which could be interpreted as one big *cri de coeur*.

Agee was similarly close to Ralph McGehee, the fellow Notre Dame alumnus and former CIA case officer who had written *Deadly Deceits*, another memoir that was highly critical of the CIA, though it was vetted and did not disclose classified information. They wrote frequently, coordinated legal tactics, and worked together with a computer expert named Daniel Brandt to compile a database (and eventually a website) of public information on matters relating to the CIA and its activities, known as CIABASE.[132] Their correspondence indicates considerable intellectual kinship, though not the same degree of ideological fervor on McGehee's part. McGehee too was aware of and worried about CIA surveillance, and he speculated to Agee that the agency might try to kidnap Agee.[133] But since the public appetite for disaffected spy stories was inevitably limited, relationships among the spies got testy. Agee, McGehee, and Stock-well were all involved in an organization called the Association of National Security Alumni (ANSECA) but they were at odds about a range of issues and very competitive. "Egos, egos, egos, egos," commented Louis Wolf.[134]

Agee's habits and lifestyle cut against the greed, profligacy, or other ulterior motivation that the agency sought to conjure, while his persistent activism put the lie to agency judgments that he lacked durable political convictions. He appeared to figure out that to sustain his high political profile, he required a stable emotional base. He found it with Giselle in Hamburg. Despite being effectively a self-employed freelancer, Agee maintained a high-tempo schedule devoted to telling his story and advancing left-wing causes without seriously neglecting his wife or two sons, which a large number of datebook entries (maybe a third) concern. He often made fifteen to twenty substantive telephone calls per day.[135] He did not mute his politics, maintaining an advisory relationship with Jusso, the youth branch of the Social Democratic Party of Germany.[136]

Despite the unavoidable urge to keep looking behind his back, Agee kept his sense of humor and *joie de vivre*. In an "Open Letter" to Admiral Stansfield Turner, he dubbed the then-director of central intelligence "Admirable Stan Turner" and generally demonstrated caustic humor and unrelenting sarcasm.[137] He cowrote a mordantly funny fictional piece for the men's magazine *Oui* imagining strategic conversations circa 1975–76 among the CIA inspector general, deputy director of operations, and director of management and services.[138] And there's a goofy photograph of Agee holding a copy of *Inside the Company* under his nose, mocking stealth, in the Boulder-based *Garage Dibune* in connection with a supportive column written by University of Colorado (Boulder) associate professor Rolf Kjolseth.[139] Holding forth with passionate audacity about the CIA and its iniquity seemed to be what Agee really wanted to do in life.

5

Agee and the Transatlantic Left

Agee had initially tendered an aboveboard insider's point-of-view history of the CIA to American publishers but got no takers. Disappointed, he resolved to up the ante by getting cozy with the Cubans and exposing CIA operations and assets. His hope may have been that a robust American Left would embrace him as its own. It was too late. By the time he had broken free of the CIA and consolidated his choice to radicalize, the moment of the American counterculture's peak receptivity to a regular guy's crossing over from the establishment had passed. Agee had found his radical sensibility, but the fierce and euphoric idealism that had arisen in the 1960s was giving way to doubt and paranoia, a kind of creeping corporate co-optation, and, ultimately, downbeat social lassitude and introverted resignation. The antiestablishment impulse had been largely domesticated.

The American New Left's apotheosis occurred when Agee was still an employee of the CIA. At the 1968 Democratic National Convention in Chicago, the substantially nonviolent Students for a Democratic Society (SDS) joined professional revolutionaries like Yippie leader Abbie Hoffman and Black Panther chairman Bobby Seale and provoked a Chicago police force, clad in riot gear and primed for violence by the reactionary (if Democratic) Mayor Richard J. Daley, into cracking their skulls on national television. Large-scale riots and arrests occurred, culminating in the trial of the Chicago Seven. Although this was a signature event in the history of the American Left, it amounted to a coda rather than a crescendo. Drawn from college campuses, most of the rank and file had depleted their idealism or simply lost their nerve. The US protest movement shrank and went into hiding, commanded by a few maximalists epitomized by the Weather Underground.

The SDS was composed mainly of middle-class whites inspired to bolt their comfort zone by the Vietnam War and the plight of African Americans. That kind of demographic grouping as well as the SDS's predilection toward structure and community organization might have been an apt home for someone like Philip Agee. But the persistence of the Vietnam War and the unenforceability of the civil rights and antidiscrimination laws had repudiated the group's founding notion of nonviolent change from within (if only just within) the American system of government, and the latter had prompted the expansion of the movement as a whole to include blacks.[1] These evolutionary factors, both equitable and inevitable, splintered the SDS and weakened the movement's sense of purpose. By 1969, the cohesive activism of the New Left was giving way to the demonstrative withdrawal inherent in the lifestyle of the counterculture as the primary engine of protest in the United States.[2] This moved radical American politics farther away from its Marxist roots. As John Patrick Diggins put it in 1973:

> The counterculture was not the affirmation of Marxism but its repudiation. The affluent children of technology represented a challenge not only to capitalism but to the basic philosophical and political assumptions of historical Marxism: the validity of material reality, the imperative of organized, collective action, and the inalienable quality of work as the highest source of life's meaning and value. Countercultural radicalism moved far beyond New Left radicalism, for it sought a new consciousness not so much to realize as to obliterate the Western industrial idea of consciousness.[3]

The New Left and counterculturalism faded to a vestigial point in the early 1970s. The counterculture became an expression more of complacency than of confrontation. It may have looked attractive to a blossoming idealist like Agee from the near distance, but it was a bit of a drag once he got there—an insular refuge, perhaps, but hardly a redoubt from which to attack or defend. For diehards still seeking to do battle, there was a more dangerous alternative. The SDS yielded to the Black Panthers and the Weather Underground, which both resorted to outright political violence. Their conduct was on the order of the Provisional Irish Republican Army, the Red Brigades, and Euskadi ta Askatasuna (ETA), but did not acquire such a high degree of political traction. The Weathermen usurped the SDS and went underground; they planned a nationwide recruitment drive targeting the working class and undertook a campaign of street violence known as "Days of Rage" for October 1969.[4] Soon thereafter they simply abolished the SDS. When three members accidentally blew themselves up when a nail bomb detonated prematurely in a Greenwich Village townhouse in March 1970, though, the Weathermen looked inept and spent if also dangerous. Jesuit priest Daniel Berrigan—veritable New Left nobility—helped convince the Weathermen to end their violent campaign, at their invitation penning a letter of advice in early 1970 admonishing that "[n]o principle is worth the sacrifice of a single human being," that "the revolution will be no better and no more truthful and no more populist and no more attractive than those who brought it into being," and that left-wing activists should start thinking of the radical underground not as "temporary, exotic, abnormal" but rather as "an entirely self-sufficient, mobile, internal revival community" and "a definition of our future."[5]

From that point, the Weathermen and cognate groups were struggling against the tide. Between the 1969 Days of Rage and its attack on a San Francisco federal building in March 1974, the Weather Underground was essentially dormant, the end of the Vietnam War having spelled its demise in the popular imagination. Its resurgence in the mid-1970s momentarily lent strength to and drew it from black and Puerto Rican nationalist movements, until its official self-renunciation occurred in late 1976. As Bryan Burrough notes, "there remained a ragged core of armed radicals who refused to surrender their dreams."[6] Although 1981 would be left-wing urban guerrillas' most lethal year thanks to a few Black Panther and Weather Underground holdouts—ten of them perpetrated the notorious Brink's robbery that October in Nanuet, New York, killing a guard and two policemen—the spike was an aberration. The violent fringe's reemergence in the 1970s flattened and diluted the richer and more credible legacy of their 1960s nonviolent forebears.[7] They were seen as desperate players hanging onto a failed agenda; they had not registered the overall deflation and malaise of the ensuing decade.

For that, the presidential election of 1972, which featured the humiliation of an unabashedly liberal, antiwar Democratic candidate, George McGovern, set the tone. Watergate did confirm some of the Left's fiercest points. But the very egregiousness of the Nixon administration's conduct produced comprehensive public outrage that required mainstream politicians to mount an effective bipartisan response that reformed US institutions, or at least appeared to do so. It pacified the Left and exposed its lack of depth. Unlike the Old Left of the 1930s, which had embraced Marxism and harnessed American labor to expand unions and empower workers, neither the New Left nor the radical underground had gained the following of the American working class, whose patriotic anticommunism and anti-intellectualism trumped any appeal that a truly radical ideology might have held. More than anything else, the inability of the New Left to enlist labor in its cause made it strategically weak and tenuous.[8] It was why, for all his optimism, Herbert Marcuse—the New Left's prime intellectual and philosophical patron—did not believe genuine revolution could take hold in the United States.[9]

He turned out to be correct. The malignant self-deception revealed by the Pentagon Papers, released in protest by Ellsberg, produced mainly fatigue and cynicism, and the morbid procrastination of the Paris Peace Talks merely amplified those dispositions. As early as 1973, American prisoners of war in Vietnam having just been released, CBS president William Paley, who had been sympathetic with the New Left, postponed the airing of a televised version of

Vietnam veteran David Rabe's Tony-award winning play *Sticks and Bones*—about a wounded soldier whose romance with a Vietnamese woman moves his parents to induce his suicide—until "things have calmed down."[10] If there was a chance that the sixties generation would rediscover and renew its founding verve, Watergate seemed to extinguish it. While historians still argue about when the sixties as a sociopolitical phenomenon really ended, few would put the date later than 1974, when Richard Nixon resigned under the pressure of inevitable impeachment.[11] There was a sense that white Europeans and Americans were no longer dominating world affairs anyway, and that others were best suited to advance new interests.[12]

To a considerable degree, mainstream America, including some right-of-center, assimilated the cultural markers of the radical left— long hair, beads, and recreational drugs.[13] But at least insofar as the sixties generation was driven by politically awakened white Americans, many were humbled and enervated, as well as sapped latterly by the economic bane of stagflation.[14] The liberal consensus was certainly diminished. The stereotypical view is that only the most extreme elements of the protest contingent stuck it out—that as most erstwhile campus radicals neared their forties, they settled for wife-swapping, pills, and a little weed in the comfort of suburbia in lieu of taking it to the streets and getting arrested as an expression of their discontent. Two leading chronicles of the epoch—Lawrence Kasdan's 1983 film *The Big Chill* and Rick Moody's 1994 novel *The Ice Storm*—reference lower temperatures. *The Limey* (1999), Steven Soderbergh's masterful revenge flick, nails the shattered dream of the California counterculture. Peter Fonda's Terry Valentine—a vain and aging record producer turned cynical drug financier stalked by Terence Stamp's baleful Cockney ex-con Wilson for killing his daughter—says dismissively of the sixties: "It was just '66 and early '67. That's all there was." Even in a more thoughtful moment, his take is that they were ephemeral: "Did you ever dream about a place you never really recall being to before? A place that maybe only exists in your imagination? Some place far away, half remembered when you wake up. When you were there, though, you knew the language. You knew your way around. That was the sixties."

If this portrayal resonantly provides the big picture, it misses a few subtler details. American liberalism, though not the extreme Left, remained quite vigorous in the 1970s, propelling the feminist, environmental, and human-rights movements, among others.[15] Those who had mobilized against the Vietnam War drew some satisfaction from having belatedly won the argument that the war had been wrong, and most did enter a long latency period, tilting toward middle age and sequestered in academia or seduced by commerce. Thomas Borstelmann has observed that "beyond resentment and ironic detachment was a broader tendency to turn inward from public to private life, to focus on one's self rather than the corrupt or unknowable larger world."[16] Over the course of the decade popular culture would expose the deep wounds of Vietnam in books like Robert Stone's *Dog Soldiers* and John del Vecchio's *The 13th Valley* and movies like *Apocalypse Now*, *Coming Home*, and *The Deer Hunter*. But in the grand scheme, these amounted more to retrospective consolation than to prospective exhortation. In the United States, the dominant political voice of "the long 1970s"—which broadly saw human rights and social welfare give way to individual rights and neoliberalism as central concerns of government, despite strong criticisms of American institutions that included the CIA and its partial disempowerment at the hands of the Church Committee—was that of the formerly silent majority that had fueled the rise of Nixon.[17] It condemned any disloyalty toward the world's exceptional nation. Near the end of the decade, that majority would crystallize into what conservatives since the 1960s had been aspirationally calling the New Right and elect Ronald Reagan president.[18] Following a dialectical pattern, Reagan's policies would reawaken the American Left, which would become more inviting for Agee and more hospitable to him.

For now, though, he needed active, not receding, support. He would not find it in the United States. The Johnson and Nixon administrations, to be sure, had rated the New Left a serious threat, such that the intelligence community had routinely instrumentalized the Internal Revenue Service's Special Services Staff to investigate and harass people and organizations on a secret watch list. They included Joan Baez, Jimmy Breslin, James Brown, Sammy

Davis Jr., Jesse Jackson, Coretta Scott King, Norman Mailer, Shirley MacLaine, the American Civil Liberties Union, the National Association for the Advancement of Colored People, *Playboy* magazine, *Rolling Stone*, and hundreds more.[19] But Nixon's forced resignation, the Church Committee and the CIA's "time of troubles," Carter's expiatory musings—these phenomena appeared to satisfy and tame the radical impulse. The net result, until the rise of Reagan conservatism, was the tranquilization of American civic life.[20]

Though the United States in the early 1970s might have been a fertile plain for Agee's debut as a public radical, and his revelations reinforced the American institutional response in the middle of the decade, by 1977 it was no country for him. Politically, *Saturday Night Live* was about as risqué as mainstream culture got, and Agee stood little chance of being a guest host. In recognizing the relative dormancy of leftist radicalism in the United States and seeking out and nurturing a discreet, informal, and durable transatlantic network of support, Agee seemed to hew especially to the last prescription in Berrigan's letter to the Weathermen, apprehending the radical underground as a permanent community with a shifting geographical center.

EUROPE'S POLITICAL HOSPITALITY

During Europe's long and eventful 1970s, its polities were to a significant extent responding to their own domestic and regional politics.[21] From Agee's personal and instrumental perspective, however, they usefully counterbalanced the United States' rightward bend. He saw the European continent through an America-centric lens. As far back as 1971, as he contemplated writing a CIA exposé, committed himself to antagonizing the agency by going to Cuba, and then headed for Paris, Agee sensed that for a minatory brand of dissent, the fresher, more febrile, more embracing locale was Europe.

Europe displaced the United States as the epicenter of Western political dissent in the 1970s. Its populations had watched with interest and trepidation the tumult of the early to mid-1960s in the United States, but for the most part Europeans stayed quiescent until the end of the decade, manifesting what Tony Judt called "carefree opti-mism" rather than intense radicalism.[22] In May 1968, French stu-dents, directly emulating their American counterparts by protesting university and broader class repression, triggered nationwide dem-onstrations and strikes that brought the French economy to a virtual standstill for two weeks. Irish republicans and Basque nationalists drew on the US civil rights protests to mobilize movements in North-ern Ireland and Spain, respectively, that soon became armed insur-gencies. In 1970, far-left students founded the Baader-Meinhof Gang in West Germany and the Red Brigades in Italy. Each group launched lethal terrorist operations aimed at creating a revolutionary state over the course of several years. Against a transnational political backdrop that included several active, left-leaning ethnonationalist or ideological terrorist movements, Agee might have calculated that a disaffected CIA officer should be able to speak out without jeop-ardizing his freedom or safety. He would discover that this outlook, while unduly optimistic, was right enough.

Beneath the liberal West German overlay of *Ostpolitik* on the more rigid and dominant great power relations in northern and central Europe, radical political change that jibed with Agee's own acquired and still developing disposition was occurring country by country in Mediterranean Europe. This generally salutary political backdrop eventually overrode any depressive effect that Agee's serial expul-sions from five European countries might have had. In his depor-tation battle in the UK, especially, he had confirmed the standing support of the European Left and at least the ongoing interest of its counterparts in the United States. Europe, in short, provided him in-spiration.

For bashing the CIA in particular, of course, the mid-1970s were a glorious time on both sides of the Atlantic. In the larger context of European perceptions, Agee's expulsions probably made him look, on balance, less villainous than noble in Europe. Much of the agency activity that piqued the Church Committee's interest—and opprobrium—involved Latin America, and it caught light in a more politically combustible Europe that, post-Vietnam, had seen its doubts about the prudence and propriety of America's strategic behavior confirmed. The revelations included the 1973 US-assisted coup against Allende in Chile, installing Pinochet as president, and the Argentine military junta's "dirty war" against left-wing Peronist guerrillas that the United States had strongly supported. Since Agee had served exclusively in Latin America and implemented US policy there, the news from Washington lent him gravitas and credibility in Europe.

Senator Church himself had characterized US intelligence agencies as "rogue elephants," and he and some congressmen—in particular, Senator Daniel Patrick Moynihan (D-NY)—seemed inclined to dismantle them. In the end they were constrained from doing so, but they certainly clipped the agencies' wings, establishing permanent congressional oversight by way of a standing US Senate Select Committee on Intelligence and conditioning the executive branch to curtail licentious CIA behavior. President Gerald Ford issued an executive order strengthening government supervision of the intelligence community and prohibiting any US government employee from engaging in political assassination or conspiring to do so. His successor, Jimmy Carter, enhanced that executive order and appointed a director of central intelligence, Admiral Stansfield Turner, who was determined to cleanse the CIA's reputation for nefariousness despite fears from his predecessors, William Colby and George H. W. Bush, and others that he would eviscerate the agency. In 1975, the agency publicly acknowledged that it had used unwitting humans to test the effects of LSD, and that one of them—a CIA bacteriologist named Frank Olson—had committed suicide in 1953 by hurling himself out of the window of a New York hotel.*

Coming to his epiphany just as the American Left wearied, Agee did not want to withdraw to the woods as those presumptively sympathetic with him had done stateside. Neither did he care to disavow socialism. His view had been informed by the struggle of landless

---

* Eric Olson, Frank's son, believes the CIA planted the inculpatory evidence of Frank's LSD-induced suicide in order to conceal and preempt the real story: that Frank Olson had suspected the United States of using biological weapons in Korea, and the agency murdered him to shut him up. The younger Olson's pursuit of proof of this story is chronicled in Errol Morris's 2017 docudrama series *Wormwood*.

peasants against aggrandizing elites and valorized by heroic figures like Castro and Guevara. Groups that had failed to enamor Americans of these classes and personages would not have galvanized him—at least not in his formative state circa 1975. And Agee was not prepared to align himself with resolutely underground groups of more desperate and cynical designs. Social democracy in Western Europe, at least compared to the United States, was well integrated with the working class and had not lost touch with its socialist roots.

Furthermore, the European Left wasn't depleted in the early seventies. In some ways, it was just gathering steam. France and the United Kingdom, though warrior nations, had opted out of the Vietnam War. While that may have deprived European youth of the motive force that its American counterpart had enjoyed in the previous decade, it also relieved it of the opportunity to exhaust itself. Social democracy was a reality in most Western European countries, and they had relatively small nonwhite minorities, so civil rights protests hadn't come into play, either, except in compartmentalized causes like republicanism in Northern Ireland and Basque separatism in Spain, which merely drew some inspiration from America's black leaders. That is not to say that the European Left had been stagnant in the sixties; it was in fact intensely engaged but at the level of philosophical ideas rather than civic action.

As Judt has demonstrated, the postwar period in Europe really extended a full forty-five years after World War II, until the Soviet Union collapsed.[23] Roughly midway through the coextensive Cold War, when Agee came to Europe to work on *Inside the Company*, leftists were busy trying to distill lessons of World War II for the disconcertingly strange era of potentially suicidal confrontation that it had produced. Without a hot war to distract them to street protest and civil disobedience—the post-colonial French-Algerian War had ended in 1962—they had been free to ponder modern strife writ large, now with the added nuclear threat to mankind itself. What they developed in cafés and bookstores for handling these lofty yet vital challenges was the philosophy of existentialism. Sarah Bakewell has observed that "a popularised brand of existentialism fed into the growing counterculture." Thus "they adopted the double

Sartrean commitment: to personal freedom, and to political activism."[24] Idealism found actualization, not merely in set-piece protests but also in day-to-day affairs, as when antiapartheid dockworkers in the Netherlands refused to unload South African ships. This was meat and drink for the new Philip Agee.

So too was Europe's political dynamism. Cultivating dissidence would have been harder on a continent in which radicalism was submerged, enfeebled, or nonexistent. Whereas 1960s left-wing idealism had atrophied into wistful cynicism in the United States, with its remaining zealots increasingly underground and violent, Europe had become a vortex of conspicuous political upheaval that tended to reinforce dissidence. Radical change that jibed with Agee's own acquired and still developing disposition was occurring country by country in southern Europe—in particular, in Greece, Portugal, and Spain. "All three countries," noted Tony Judt, "were governed in the early 1970s by authoritarian rulers of a species more familiar in Latin America than Western Europe; the political transformations of the post-war decades seemed largely to have passed them by."[25]

In Greece, a militaristic, royalist, and resolutely anticommunist government had enjoyed NATO's material and political support until insular economic policies and a rash attempt to annex Cyprus lost it public favor. Antonio Salazar's thirty-eight-year corporatist and authoritarian stewardship of Portugal had enforced a retrogressive brand of stability, but the inept and desperate tenure of his handpicked successor Marcello Caetano, exacerbated by the collapse of Portugal's colonial rule in Africa, gave way to a popular military junta keen on democratization, decolonization, and economic reform, and ultimately to Mario Soares's waveringly socialist agenda. Francisco Franco's forbidding thirty-year dictatorship, and with it the most abject tremors of the Spanish Civil War, came to an end with his death in 1975, whereupon surprisingly enlightened inside technocrats managed a swift and effective transition to a federal parliamentary monarchy.[26]

As fossilized right-wing regimes in these countries gave way to more democratic and socialist ones, the corresponding leftward dynamics would have recalled Agee's encounters with Latin American opposition movements. But these were successful and inspiring where those he had witnessed earlier had been largely fruitless and dispiriting. He took note in his datebook of the November 1975 coup in Portugal by procommunist forces (they would soon yield to more moderate elements who restored the democratic framework established in April 1974), and Seixas went to Lisbon a couple of days later.[27] He was writing an article on Portugal's long political transformation in summer 1976.[28] *Inside the Company* also received considerable attention in Portugal, and his exposure of CIA officers, agents, and assets in particular had a major media impact there. US diplomats in Lisbon were worried that Agee was giving momentum to left-wing movements in the Western Hemisphere.[29] He also penned a rather long article entitled "The 'American Factor' in Greece" in 1977 in which he caustically and indignantly named names of sixty-four purported CIA officers and agents there—a particularly obnoxious and antagonistic act in the wake of Welch's assassination.[30]

That year, Penny Lernoux published the groundbreaking *Cry of the People*, illuminating the CIA's ruthless instrumentalization of the Catholic Church and generously citing *Inside the Company*.[31] Like Agee, Lernoux was a Catholic and had been a presumptive US government Cold Warrior, having worked as a staff writer for the US Information Agency in Brazil and Colombia from 1961 to 1964. While in those countries, however, what she saw as US-supported economic exploitation, class inequality, and military repression, often facilitated by a co-opted Catholic Church, impelled her to embrace liberation theology and to leave government, eventually writing for the *National Catholic Reporter* and the *Nation*. Her book's publication came during a period of conspicuous dynamism in Latin American politics. The Argentine military junta institutionalized its dirty war, Pinochet consolidated right-wing rule in Chile, and Venezuela was becoming a petrostate; at the same time, Brazil started to "decompress" its military dictatorship, the Shining Path began to infiltrate Peruvian civil society, and the Sandinistas gained critical traction in Nicaragua.

These changes marked a shift in global relations. In 1969, Henry

Kissinger himself had burdened Gabriel Valdes, then visiting the United States as Chile's foreign minister under Allende, with a flatteningly condescending view of Latin America's historical irrelevance: "You come here speaking of Latin America, but that is not important. Nothing important ever came from the South. History has never been produced in the South. The axis of history starts in Moscow, goes to Bonn, crosses over to Washington, and then goes to Tokyo. What happens in the South is of no importance."[32] Now positioned less than three hundred miles from Bonn, Agee seemed determined to prove Kissinger wrong. Kissinger was about to become Agee's inadvertent muse.

As Latin America acquired greater international resonance, even within the Western European social democratic disposition, there was room to behold Cuba as the aspirational exemplar of "socialism with a human face," as posited by the New Left in the United States, in contradistinction to the fallen totalitarian socialism of Eastern Europe.[33] In witnessing the institutionalized demonization of Fidel Castro in the CIA's efforts in Latin America in the 1950s and 1969s, and concluding that the agency was the American president's dedicated mercenary force for capitalist imperialism, Agee had internalized the New Left's romantic embrace of Cuba and Castro. While in England promoting *Inside the Company*, Agee publicly admitted that he had had Cuban assistance with research for the book and that he'd had three meetings at the Cuban embassy in London in 1975 regarding the translation of the book into Spanish.[34] The admission may have been arch, but he didn't seem to care. Yet Agee was also loath to disavow his independence and impartiality. For example, while in a letter to the *Washington Post* he refrained from objecting to columnist Jack Anderson's representation that Agee did not deny or care about being in the company of Cuban intelligence officers or agents in London or Paris, he did cite other "serious inaccuracies" in the column and denied Cuban influence with respect to *Inside the Company* or his actions.[35]

The tainted status of the CIA in the 1970s was not lost on European audiences, most of which were already opposed to US foreign policy over Vietnam. It's true that the US government was able to prevail on most European governments to deny Agee residence. But those governments also would have noticed that, even though the Justice Department clearly had a colorable case for treason, the United States had not charged Agee with any crime and therefore could not urge his detention or extradition.[36] Despite this formal position, the US government continued to hang the possibility of indictment over Agee like a sword of Damocles. In March 1981, his lawyer, Melvin Wulf, warned Agee not to return to the United States as he would face subpoenas, arrests, and indictments—"even more so now under the reactionary, cold-war, bellicose Reagan administration"—amplifying advice given in a letter ten months earlier.[37] Wulf's instincts were sound. In September 1982, Director of Central Intelligence William Casey urged Attorney General William French Smith to prosecute Agee for violating the injunction issued by Judge Gesell.[38]

Not all of the reasons for the Justice Department's initial forbearance, however provisional, were terribly opaque. The Church Committee had sensitized the US government to public scrutiny of CIA operations, and the CIA knew Agee would, in defending himself, seek a public trial. Agee was often mentioned in post–Church Committee articles discussing the perceived damage done to the CIA and its overall diminishment, and the agency was quite conscious of it.[39] Given the agency's now proven proclivity for lethal expediency, some intelligence officers might have been inclined to kill Agee. In David Corn's view, there would have been "discombobulation" within the agency when senior officials discovered that he was going to reveal "sacrosanct stuff" like the names of agents and former comrades. "I'm sure there were considerations of how they could totally neutralize him. Knowing people who were working in the agency at that point, I'm sure there were several who said, let's just take him out, one way or the other. But obviously they didn't. This shows that sometimes the darker conspiracies that people have about the CIA are more cinematic than accurate."[40]

Agee's very celebrity as a tell-all ex-CIA activist and author would only have invited more suspicions of renegade agency behavior, so that celebrity to an extent served as insurance against assassination.

That said, the West German government did not embrace Agee in a way that showcased any defiance or disdain of American authorities. In fact, it kept close tabs on him and no doubt provided information about him to the CIA. But tolerating his presence as long as he didn't engage in outright espionage was in line with its less confrontational approach to the Cold War. Agee's legal residency in West Germany would turn out to be durable, lasting as it did for thirty years.

THE DARKER SIDE

As systemic and legitimate political protest and change swept across southern Europe in the 1970s, kindred but darker leftward political impulses were also at work. Dangerous radicalism was certainly in the air. Airline hijackings and kidnappings became part of the normal European as well as Middle Eastern landscape.[41] Several violent insurgencies in Europe were gathering steam as the once latent "pathologies" of the 1970s broke out. Though mostly small in scope, they smothered the blitheness of 1960s Europe that Judt had identified and "contributed to the widespread atmosphere of unease."[42] Underneath the roiling political surface, pro-Soviet intelligence agencies sought to exploit the accommodating approach that some Western European governments—in particular, West Germany by way of *Ostpolitik*—had adopted vis-à-vis the Soviet Union, while pro-Western intelligence organizations tried to hedge against that dispensation. Agee appears to have found this layered byplay stimulating rather than intimidating.

Sustained and focused insurgencies based on long-standing, barely latent grievances also lent weight to the sense of unfinished political business in Europe. The Provisional IRA lashed out against Northern Ireland's Protestant majority, which had marginalized Catholics there since the inception of the British province in 1922, as well as their sovereign British protectors. Although a Catholic civil rights movement stimulated in part by the American one had established a voice there, the IRA took the position that only the ejection of British troops and Northern Ireland's unification with the

Irish Republic could adequately protect Catholics, and it set to attacking security forces, economic targets, and, at least at first, Protestant civilians. The other major ethnonationalist push came from ETA, which sought to separate the Basque region from Spain and used methods similar to the IRA's to achieve its goals. The Marxist-inspired Baader-Meinhof Gang—dubbed the Red Army Fraktion (RAF) by leaders Andreas Baader and Ulrike Meinhof themselves and fed mainly by universities—tried to radicalize Germany through terrorist attacks and political assassinations. The Red Brigades, in Italy, had a similar provenance and ideology and used comparable tactics but were more broadly based and killed more people.[43] Right-wing neo-Nazi groups also arose in West Germany, one of them killing thirteen people and injuring 220 in bombing Munich's *Oktoberfest* in 1980. The West German organizations, both Left and Right, were strategically and methodologically incoherent and failed to disrupt Germany's civic life, invalidate its national institutions, or destabilize the federal republic. The government's response—excluding those from the far ends of the political spectrum from government employment—was relatively tame and produced no appreciable backlash in a population predisposed to moderation, conformity, and order. But the Baader-Meinhof contingent did draw on the ideological sympathies of intellectuals and academics.[44] These were Agee's natural interlocutors.

The conduct of the headlining ethnonationalist and left-wing ideological terrorist groups of the day was often heinous. The West German Left probably assisted Palestinian terrorists in their murder of eleven Israeli athletes in September 1972 at the Munich Olympics, and it was the two West German operators—not the two Arab ones—that singled out Jewish passengers for execution on the Air France flight that they hijacked to Entebbe in June 1976.[45] In the Kingsmill massacre in 1976, IRA gunmen selected ten Protestants from a busload of construction workers and shot them dead, sparing the Catholic laborers.[46] In 1973, ETA killed Spanish Prime Minister Luis Carrero Blanco as well as his driver and bodyguard, blowing up his car as he returned from Mass. In 1977, the RAF abducted and murdered Hans Martin Schleyer, chairman of Daimler-Benz and president of the West German Federation of Industries, and killed Siegfried Buback, the West German attorney general, and Jurgen Ponto, head of Dresdner Bank. In 1978, the Red Brigades kidnapped Italian Prime Minister Aldo Moro and, after holding him for fifty-five days, killed him.

Dissident activists like Agee could opt to support nonviolent organizations with the same political goals as the terrorist groups, like the Social Democratic and Labour Party in Northern Ireland and the Basque Nationalist Party in Spain, and draw little opprobrium from the political middle. But each of the violent groups also had a delicate sufficiency of popular local support. Some, like the Red Brigades, cribbed from the playbooks of left-wing Latin American urban guerrilla movements that resisted the kinds of right-wing governments the CIA supported and Agee had come to loathe, and might have tweaked a romantic nerve in him.[47] In addition, substantive policies had superseded political allegiances as the drivers of European political discourse, leaving the field considerably more open to outside participants.[48]

Certainly the atmosphere of kinetic dissent, open to one and all, in Europe kept Agee motivated. Yet he still sought a voice primarily among Americans who had a finite capacity for criticizing their own institutions and had tired of it. In 1980, the three-hour PBS documentary *On Company Business*—which featured Agee, Marchetti, and Stockwell, and for which Agee had been a special consultant—garnered generally dismissive reviews.[49] By 1981, when the Supreme Court affirmed the State Department's decision to revoke Agee's passport, a mainstream American consensus had formed that Agee was simply a bad actor who had spitefully imperiled decent American civil servants. The *New York Times* said he was "contagious," like a virus, and supported a congressional prohibition against disclosing the identities of CIA personnel that extended beyond those who signed the secrecy oath. Agee himself was well aware of these sentiments.[50] He needed Europe more than ever, and it would accommodate him.

If the late 1970s were the headiest days of the RAF, the IRA, ETA, and the Red Brigades, by the early 1980s Carlos the Jackal and Abu

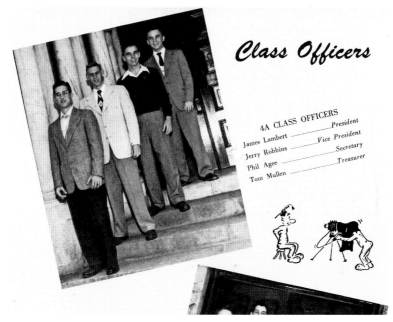

FIGURE 1. From Philip Agee's high school yearbook.

FIGURE 2. Angela Camargo Seixas, Philip Agee Jr., Christopher Agee, and Philip Agee in London, at a protest against his and Mark Hosenball's deportation from the United Kingdom; January 1977. Keystone Press/Alamy Stock Photo.

FIGURE 3. Philip Agee and Giselle Roberge Agee at their wedding in Amsterdam; March 15, 1978.

FIGURE 4. Philip Agee and Giselle Roberge Agee sailing on the North Sea; summer 1985.

FIGURE 5. Philip Agee and Giselle Roberge Agee at their apartment in Madrid; summer 1991.

FIGURE 6. Agee holding forth at the Hotel Nacional de Cuba in Havana; July 2004. Sven Creutzmann/Mambo Photo/Getty Images.

Nidal further charged the European zeitgeist. They were globetrotting, transactional terrorists with a distinct preference for Europe as both a target and a staging ground. Both, and especially the reputedly priapic Carlos, had a swashbuckling air that somehow leavened their ruthless brutality.[51] Born Ilich Ramirez Sanchez in Venezuela, Carlos styled himself an "international revolutionary," sported a Che Guevara-style beret, and eased gracefully from one terrorist outfit to another. He was a masterful self-promoter—a kind of terrorist-concierge-cum-hit-man.[52] He recruited substantial operational support in West Germany from the Revolutionary Cells, a loose umbrella organization subsuming independent groups that denounced the influence of American multinational corporations and on occasion firebombed their offices in West German cities.[53] Inspired by Guevara and at times supported by the Cuban DGI, Carlos made his reputation by leading the siege of an Organization of Petroleum Exporting Countries (OPEC) conference in Vienna in December 1975 in which he, with five Revolutionary Cell accomplices, killed three people, held sixty-two oil ministers hostage, coerced the Austrian government into broadcasting Palestinian demands, and secured a DC-9 to escape to Algiers, only to resurface in central Europe.[54] At one time or another, he provided weapons or other operational assistance to Palestinian groups and to most of the major ethnonationalist and ideological terrorist groups based in Europe.

From detailed intelligence on Carlos's movements, the CIA had concluded that the governments of Bulgaria, Czechoslovakia, East Germany, Hungary, and Romania were providing him sanctuary. From the US government's standpoint, Carlos was emblematic of the Soviet bloc's sponsorship of international terrorism. Both the CIA and MI6, however, decided not to try to kill or capture the Jackal for fear of raising East–West tensions to a level that he did not merit. But the State Department did exert diplomatic pressure on Eastern European governments, and by the mid-1980s they had closed off his access to their respective territories.[55] He was temperamentally disposed to the derring-do life of the fugitive and was not inclined to sequester himself in the Middle East or North Africa. He preferred Europe. Carlos married Magdalena Kopp, a diffident

Frankfurt-based member of the Revolutionary Cells on whom he had a svengali-like effect. While the terrorist methodology would not have appealed to Agee, Carlos's anti-Western and anticapitalist motivation, Cuban bona fides, and West German connection would have chimed with Agee's wholesale rejection of the American project, his notion that the CIA was in essence a bizarrely Cuba-obsessed capitalist instrument deployed by the president to benefit elites, and his choice of host in exile. He might also have drawn inspiration from Carlos's defiant, catch-me-if-you can attitude.

Abu Nidal, a maximalist Palestinian militant and the most violent opponent of Yasser Arafat's early-1970s pragmatism vis-à-vis Israel, was arguably an even nastier piece of work than Carlos. He decisively preferred bold international terrorism to local guerrilla war and political negotiation as a means of advancing the Palestinian cause. Nidal's first terrorist act, which he planned and supervised from Baghdad, was the seizure of the Saudi embassy in Paris on September 5, 1973. Agee was in London at the time, having left Paris a short while earlier. Five armed Palestinians took thirteen people hostage and vowed to detonate the building unless the Jordanian government released Abu Dawud, the notorious dissident commander of Arafat's Fatah forces in Jordan rumored to have been involved in the attack on the Israeli Olympic athletes in Munich exactly a year earlier.

While Saddam Hussein saw his sponsorship of the Abu Nidal Organization as a means of elevating Iraq as the most assertive champion of Arab nationalism, Patrick Seale has noted that Nidal's "vanity would not allow him completely to be anyone's agent."[56] Between 1974 and 2002, he would base his operations in Iraq, Syria, Libya, and again Iraq, where he was killed or committed suicide under suspicion of spying. His most spectacular operations in Europe were the attacks on the El Al ticket counters at the Rome and Vienna airports in December 1985, killing twenty and wounding 138 all told—though his team's July 1988 attack on the Greek cruise ship *City of Poros*, in which nine passengers died and eighty were hurt, was also flagrant in its senselessness, given that Greece was especially sympathetic with the Palestinian cause.[57] Like Carlos, Nidal cultivated tactical relationships with Eastern European intelligence agencies, including those of Poland and East Germany. He offered them exemptions from terrorist operations in exchange for sanctuary, which included safe houses and arms deals involving eastern bloc weapons, and in order to undermine their relationships with Arafat's mainstream Palestine Liberation Organization. In the early 1980s, Abu Nidal lived mainly in Warsaw, Vienna, Zurich, and Berlin, trading arms, laundering money, and acquiring assets.

AGEE'S DEFT CALIBRATIONS

Europe, then, was a dense and motley battleground in the 1970s. The Provisional IRA mounted an armed challenge to the British state to unite Northern Ireland with the Irish Republic, ETA sought to force the Spanish government to yield a separate Basque state, and the RAF and Red Brigades terrorized West Germany and Italy respectively in hopes of stimulating wider left-wing uprisings against systems they considered invidiously bourgeois. Most of these were durable organizations: the IRA, ETA, and the Red Brigades were cranking up armed campaigns that would persist for more than twenty-five years. On top of their efforts against particular states, there was a colorful transnational dimension. Swashbuckling, peripatetic terrorists-for-hire like Carlos the Jackal and Abu Nidal treated the European continent as a staging area for Middle East operations. Menacingly romantic, they sharpened the point with airline hijackings and the odd siege in a European capital, raising the pitch and tempo of Europe's already ominous mood music.

Compared to them, Agee was lawful and civilized. The resilience, proximity, and increasing familiarity of these movements and figures might have made him feel more at home—certainly less alien—as an antiestablishment voice. At the same time, he would have felt less conspicuous than violent extremists, so they provided him with partial political cover: by comparison, he was preferable. Agee could occupy the space between strictly legal, nonviolent protesters and violent terrorists in the narrative of European radicalism. Here too Agee straddled a giddy line. His liminal niche enabled him to enjoy a notional association with dangerous players without subjecting him to criminal penalties. That he could thus have his cake and eat it probably helped sustain his political disaffection.

Agee did, of course, selectively court the kind of notoriety that would antagonize law enforcement and intelligence agencies and intensify their conviction that he was an enemy agent. Perhaps the most flagrant instance was the 1976 appearance in Jamaica to expose CIA officers stationed there and influence the election, while he was still living in England. After he had been expelled from five European countries and conclusively lost his US passport, he had to be more careful about placing his West German residency at risk. In the early 1980s, he did travel to Grenada on a Grenadan passport he had personally obtained from its Marxist-Leninist prime minister Maurice Bishop, who would be executed by a right-wing military junta shortly before the US invasion in 1983. He also went to Nicaragua to engage in pro-Sandinista protest activities on a Nicaraguan passport. Overall, though, Agee had self-preservationist discipline. After the district court had issued its October 1980 injunction requiring him to clear all of his published work with the CIA, he invariably did so, and the agency had few major qualms with anything he wrote. With respect to articles, Agee and his lawyers "followed that to the letter, and they [the CIA] never deleted anything," recalled Melvin Wulf.[58]

Well after *Inside the Company* was published, there had been public outrage and corresponding pressure on the Justice Department to prosecute Agee as he continued to expose CIA officers, assets, and operations in *CounterSpy*, the *Covert Action Information Bulletin*, and *Dirty Work: The CIA in Western Europe*. One British journalist, Robert Moss, characterized the *Covert Action Information Bulletin* as "offering assassination lists for left-wing extremists."[59] Shortly thereafter, Agee elected to have his name excluded from *Dirty Work 2: The CIA in Africa* and changed his designation on the *Covert Action Information Bulletin* masthead from "editor" to "editorial advisor" to avoid jeopardizing his residence permit in West Germany.[60] Of course, by the time the injunction was issued, in 1980, Agee had already done his most direct damage by revealing the most sensitive information he had learned as an intelligence officer. That helps explain the agency's relative permissiveness, though it invariably took the maximum thirty days for review just to annoy him.

He became a less edgy journalist and writer, and he ceased contributing to publications that risked offending and mobilizing law enforcement or intelligence agencies. A late 1980 piece titled "Destabilization in Jamaica" was the first article Agee was required by the injunction to submit to the CIA for redaction. Agee complied, and he had composed the piece carefully; the CIA required no deletions or changes.[61] He did push his boundaries with the CIA a little by refraining from submitting oral presentations for its review. "We were never sure about whether we should submit speeches or not, and we never did and never had any problem," Wulf said.[62] To an extent, he had been normalized. He calibrated his conduct in ways that would allow him a measure of security and freedom from harassment.

If he had vaulted to the status of traitor prior to the district court's issuance of the vetting order, he arguably backpedaled to that of mere dissenter once constrained. Indeed, some of his natural sympathizers have edited out Agee's exposure of officers and agents in their assessments of the man. Philip Agee Jr. reflects that "because of the agency's generally insular ethos," Agee's CIA colleagues "were incapable of questioning the larger ideological context." By 1969, Agee had become "curious enough . . . to make contacts outside the Agency with artists, writers, and academics who introduced him to critical interpretations of American policy from the perspective of intellectuals close to their own ground zero where covert actions were occurring. As he drifted away from the intelligence world he embraced the antiwar movement and began what would become many long-standing collaborations with Americans living abroad and at home—patriotic Americans who saw themselves exercising their civil right to dissent and who believed that a fully informed public would spur government efforts to abolish covert actions."[63]

However bowdlerized that account may be, Agee was nothing like an IRA volunteer or an ETA militant, a Black Panther or a Weatherman, or even a fugitive Abbie Hoffman. Once he settled into post–*Inside the Company* life, Agee was closer to a Green Ulster Protestant or a confrontational observer-chronicler in the mode of James Baldwin. Kevin McGrady, an IRA volunteer, apparently provided Agee with his "Written Statement After Caution," taken at Castlereagh Police Station in Belfast in January 1982, in which McGrady admitted to participating in lethal IRA operations—probably in the hope that Agee would take up IRA grievances against Northern Irish authorities and the British state.[64] Agee did not.

But Agee flirted with nastier pieces of work. While he did not openly court the RAF or any of the other violent insurgent groups operating in Europe, he was reflexively sympathetic with them and condemnatory of the governments they opposed. When he settled with Giselle in Hamburg in 1976–77, the RAF was peaking. This was the period during which they killed the West German attorney general, the chairman of Daimler-Benz, and the head of Dresdner Bank. But the group flamed out, as Meinhof was found dead in her prison cell in May 1976, Baader and cofounder Gudrun Ensslin in theirs in October 1977. Agee had offered and planned to testify for Meinhof, but she died before he and other former intelligence officers he had organized could do so. He took the conspiratorial view that she had been murdered, against the official line that she had committed suicide.[65] More broadly, probably in the late 1970s, he drafted a query for an article prospectively titled "The Trial of the Red Army Fraction [*sic*]: Modern Democracy, German Style," that would showcase the West German government's treatment of the RAF as an example of unfair suppression of left-wing views, which Agee viewed as systemic.[66] The CIA, for its part, appeared to place the Baader-Meinhof contingent and Agee in the same broad category of anti-US irritants. In Grenada, CIA officers detained Regina Fuchs, a West German nurse whom Agee had endorsed to work there, and interrogated her about terrorist contacts in West Germany, including the Baader-Meinhof Gang and the RAF, and asked whether she knew Agee.[67]

Agee had himself to blame for his forced exile. But far from alienating him further from the American polity, distance made it all the more important to him. Transatlantic synergies played a significant role in Agee's rise and sustenance. Europe did offer Agee a richer environment for political activism. On a deep emotional level, though, he was always working his way back to Cuba and trying to impede the CIA en route to reconditioning the American geopolitical mindset. More practically, the United States' had been the first mover in terms of postwar political radicalization. The United States still offered a ready left-of-center infrastructure, however depleted, for establishing and burnishing a compelling public image. Among the most important components of that infrastructure were America's alternative media—except for a few larger outfits with beveled countercultural sensibilities, mainly seat-of-the-pants publications started to service political and intellectual niches. Agee endeavored to use them.

In the early 1960s, the New Left flagged the moral and strategic dubiousness of the Vietnam War, but it needed to explain the conflict's roots, illuminate the machinery of war, and tease out the implications of the United States' immersion to intellectually consolidate its position. Furthermore, traditional American liberalism did not accommodate the full range of views on the war. In particular, since liberal hawks supported and arguably deepened US involvement in Vietnam, mainstream liberal outlets like the *New York Times* did not, in the early days, before the likes of David Halberstam and Neil Sheehan began to speak their minds, remotely oppose the war. There was an acute demand for more open-minded platforms. As the war escalated, so did the fortunes of the alternative magazines that advanced viewpoints that were, for the time being, well out on the fringe.

Among the most audacious and effective was *Ramparts*, which swaggering editor Warren Hinckle transformed from a Catholic intellectual journal into a muckraking vehicle of exposé. His article

"The 'Vietnam Lobby'" in the July 1965 issue was a watershed. It revealed that far from merely reacting emergently to communist depredations on a putatively democratic partner, as advertised, the United States had been introduced to South Vietnamese President Ngo Din Diem in the 1950s by Cardinal Francis Spellman, who had groomed him in a New York seminary and cultivated his official backing.[68] Appearing less than a year later, in February 1966, was Sergeant Donald Duncan's piece on US military conduct in Vietnam. Duncan was a decorated ex-Army Special Forces soldier who had recently served in Vietnam, which meant the story could not be dismissed as an indulgent lefty rant. He detailed the American military's torture and murder of captured Vietcong, mass saturation bombing, illegal assassination plots, and racist attitudes toward both black Americans and South Vietnamese—phenomena that would suffuse popular perceptions of the war.[69] Owing to this piece and other *Ramparts* articles of its vintage—exposing a Michigan State University–run technical assistance program for South Vietnam as a CIA front (April 1966), condemning the use of napalm (August 1966), and depicting war-caused injuries to Vietnamese children (January 1967)—the magazine's influence and visibility peaked, its circulation reaching nearly 250,000 in 1968.

Agee was an admirer of Hinckle and strongly recommended *The Fish Is Red*, Hinckle's book on CIA operations against Cuba, to acquaintances.[70] By the late 1960s, however, the war had spawned dozens of kindred magazines. The violence of the 1968 Democratic Convention in Chicago, widely perceived to have been incited by antiwar protesters, afforded the prowar political mainstream the upper hand and culminated in the migration of the Left underground, where it developed a more extremist and violent countenance and, inevitably, lost popular support. In fact, *Ramparts'* cripplingly expensive coverage of the convention triggered its decline, which coincided with the retreat of the American Left overall. The magazine, thus diminished, published fitfully and ended its operations in 1975. Even so, a number of the little magazines had consolidated reader bases and generated sufficient revenue to continue even as their initial readership drifted into relatively calm middle age. An alternative press appeared important to a healthy counterculture and conducive to the positive outlook of its members. As David Armstrong has put it: "Without media of their own to convey messages that radicals and dissidents themselves select and shape, activists become isolated and weak. If activists supply alternative media with a constituency, alternative media supply activists with a sense of identity and collective purpose. There is a symbiosis between alternative media and alternative culture—an exchange of vital energy that is critical to the health of both."[71]

Yet because the alternative media were generally far to the left of center, government efforts to muzzle them drew few major objections or protests. This, and the inducement of a gentler brand of journalism's greater marketability and profit, took the starch out of underground reporting.[72] By 1973 or so, the soft-core pornography magazines *Playboy* and *Penthouse* had supplanted expressly agitating protest publications. *Playboy*'s main claim to seriousness was its monthly interview, which earned a reputation for unexpected and sometimes politically consequential candor—most notably, when then-candidate Jimmy Carter admitted that he "looked on a lot of women with lust" and had "committed adultery in [his] heart many times."[73] These were at bottom bourgeois magazines that, on account of their sexually risqué and presumptively hip and liberated visions of the ideal lifestyle, tended merely to encourage armchair readers (or spectators) to consider themselves edgy and thus were able to masquerade as alternative. *Esquire*, without pictures of naked women but suffused with a kind of Rat Pack attitude, constituted an even tamer incarnation of the phenomenon.

The overt objectification of women always made the genuineness of these magazines' purportedly progressive mission rather dubious. Associated impulses were sublimated into and domesticated by libertine underground comics such as those Robert Crumb drew, insular newspaper weeklies like Boston's *Phoenix* and *The Real Paper* and Chicago's *Reader*, and purist lifestyle publications like the *Whole Earth Catalog* and *High Times*.[74] Even *Rolling Stone*, which started as a genuinely alternative magazine, evolved into a mainstream publication dedicated to normalizing rock music and its cultural warp.[75]

National Lampoon, however irreverent and provocative, was mainly a market for professional funny guys. *Ramparts* alumni decamped to magazines like *Mother Jones* and the *Nation*, which continued to question American policies sharply, and from a far-left perspective. But even those with residually activist sensibilities now tended to favor narrower identity politics—for instance, feminism and gay rights.

The alternative media had become small-bore and modest. It was more about the freedom to cope with extant problems as one saw fit than about the will to solve them. Armstrong, on drug use, puts it aptly: "Unlike the underground, the alternative media did not proselytize for drugs. The alternative media's tone was cooler, less certain. Sure, our constituents use dope, they seemed to say, but they used it to have a good time or just to get through the day, not to meet God or get His address."[76] On bigger political, social, and philosophical issues, such as the environment, alternative media were merely suggestive rather than stridently insistent. "The implicit message," Armstrong concludes, "was that the establishment is corrupt, and frequently ridiculous, but probably here to stay, and, while fundamental social change might be nice, actively advocating it is a bit like tilting at windmills."[77]

It was during this post-sixties period of the Left's retreat that Agee emerged from the CIA disdainful of the United States' durable and obsessive neuralgia about Cuba. The Church Committee's revelations—which included entanglements between the CIA's anti-Castro intrigues and Watergate, CIA-Mafia connections, exotic agency assassination attempts on Castro, and its malicious seeding of rainclouds over Cuba[78]—were earthshaking enough to overcome the cynicism that had sedated left-wing journalism in the early-to-mid-1970s. By the same token, though, they sucked a lot of the oxygen out of the room: there wasn't much capacity left in alternative writing for other outrages. The very extremeness of the Church Committee's trawl conspired with the new cynicism by effectively raising the bar for socially or politically actionable information from a single wayward case officer acting on his own. Considerations like these may have pushed Agee toward making more groundbreaking revelations than his predecessors had, and thus toward outing the case officers and agents. In his estimation, another book of narrow-gauged gripes against the agency wouldn't have been enough.

The diminished American market for truly revolutionary journalism was a plangent reality that clashed with Agee's rather shrill sense of urgency. Myriad politically forward "little magazines," even daily newspapers, would spring up in Europe in the 1970s and 1980s, when radicalism was ascending there as steeply as it was declining in the United States, and particularly in southern Europe, where left-wing tendencies were strongest. These included the daily *Lotta Continua* (The struggle continues) and *L'Unita* (Unity) in Italy; *Liberation*, an anticolonial monthly, *Morning Star*, and the Workers Socialist League's fortnightly *Socialist Press* in the UK; and *Geheim* and many monthly and weekly student publications in West Germany. Agee would occasionally write for foreign-language periodicals, submitting articles in English for translation. One was Greece's *Ethnos*, which crucially misconstrued Agee in a sloppy translation and helped sour him on the enterprise.[79] He also wrote articles for *Geheim*, translated into German by Opperskalski, whom he trusted; in turn Agee provided useful advice to him on the authenticity and credibility of information he was considering for publication in the magazine.[80] But Agee's favorite subject was the CIA, and he tended to spin his tale as ultimately a patriotic one. Though in exile, he rightly regarded his primary target audience as Americans. Accordingly, he did not aggressively court even English-language publications in Europe. His wheelhouse was the US market, and there he had little choice but to push his story on anyone who would take it.

He did manage to score the *Playboy* interview—certainly a major coup in those days—in August 1975, which roughly coincided with the US release of *Inside the Company*. And he wrote a piece for *Esquire*. This probably constituted the zenith of his journalistic endeavor. The article that he and Stephen Weissman published in *Oui* magazine, "CIA vs. USA—The Agency's Plot to Take Over America," was a notably jokey one conjuring a strategic dialogue among senior CIA officials. But *Oui* was the poor man's *Penthouse*, at least two steps down from *Playboy*. Moreover, Agee, like most with a political mission, preferred a standing bias in his favor. He couldn't rely on such magazines to stay in his corner. About three years after Agee's triumphant *Playboy* interview appeared, *Penthouse* ran a condescending interview with former senior CIA official Miles Copeland in which he disparaged Agee's self-made "martyr image."[81]

In spite of the Church Committee revelations and the American press's evolved criticism of the Vietnam War, mainstream reporters generally upheld the Cold War presumption in favor of national security, which cut against Agee. Consequently, his traction with them was always limited. In January 1976, *60 Minutes* aired an interview conducted by Morley Safer, a CBS journalist who had covered Vietnam and criticized the United States' involvement early and often, with David Atlee Phillips, the retired senior CIA officer whom the CIA had deployed to publicly discredit Agee, in which Phillips strongly suggested once again that Agee had caused Welch's death. Media critics ridiculed Safer's interview as a pro-CIA puff piece.[82] Correspondence and other materials indicate that Agee tried to use the implied threat of a libel action to cajole CBS into devoting a *60 Minutes* spot to a corrective interview with him at his residence in Cambridge, England. There then appeared to be a hiatus in discussions due to a perhaps too conveniently misaddressed CBS letter to Agee.[83] Negotiations resumed two years later, but by that time the issue was stale and no interview materialized.

Among general-interest alternative magazines, he never landed a piece in *Mother Jones* or in the increasingly expansive *Rolling Stone*, whose column inches on "national affairs" Hunter S. Thompson tended to saturate. For the *Nation* he managed only a review of a book on torture in the French-Algerian War, and that not until 1990.[84] Agee's most consequential work after *Inside the Company* ran in bespoke anti-CIA publications like *CounterSpy* and its successors *Covert Action Information Bulletin* and *Covert Action Quarterly*, from which the two *Dirty Work* books were fashioned. These publications were largely self-funded—themselves good examples of the "little magazine" phenomenon. Those who composed them were hounded by the CIA, and the publications atrophied as nervousness over CIA

excesses died down in the late 1970s and Reagan's conservative resurgence took hold. While mainstream news magazines like *Newsweek* and *Time* would periodically report on Agee's thoughts and activities, Agee himself never wrote for them. He tried to target the
holdouts from the idealistic 1960s underground who still wanted
to publish controversial material at the risk of discomfiting government scrutiny. In fact, the largest article advance he secured was
$4,000 from Larry Flynt's short-lived magazine *The Rebel*, for two
articles on Nicaragua and Grenada in the early 1980s. But it folded
before anything of Agee's appeared, and he never got paid.[85]

Defying these frustrations, Agee persisted in his transatlantic
vocation. He initiated an exchange of long letters with Weather
Underground insurgent Kathy Boudin while she was in jail in White
Plains, New York, awaiting trial for murder in the 1981 holdup of a
Brink's armored truck in Nyack, in which three people were killed.
This was another example of his discreet flirtation with the violent
fringe. A survivor of the 1970 Greenwich Village townhouse explosion and underground between 1970 and her arrest in 1981, Boudin would eventually plead guilty to one count of felony murder for
each victim and robbery and serve almost twenty years in Bedford
Hills Correctional Facility, becoming an adjunct professor of social
work at Columbia after her release in 2003. According to the letter,
he considered Boudin a kindred dissenter. In addition to expressing
general sympathy, Agee wrote about his own history and in particular his catalytic relationship with Angela Camargo Seixas, though he
did not explicitly name her. Thus, several years after their romantic
relationship was over, Agee continued to cast Seixas as a role model
and heroine.[86]

In a return letter, Boudin said that Agee was one of her "heroes."[87]
Notably, he did not personally know Boudin, and he seemed impelled to reach out to her simply on the basis of her left-wing celebrity and apparently strong political convictions. That they were both
upper-middle-class converts to left-wing radicalism—Boudin graduated from Bryn Mawr in 1965, and her father Leonard Boudin was
a renowned civil liberties lawyer and left-wing activist—may also
have been a factor. The upshot is that Agee felt he was part of a broad

if shallow transatlantic left-wing movement, and he appeared determined to be part of every conversation in that movement—even those with people who had committed violent and overtly illegal acts. At the same time, he did not have to share the public limelight in all instances; often private contact seemed to satisfy his need to affirm his status as a political player. In 1984 he also corresponded with David Truong (1945–2014), a Vietnamese antiwar protester convicted on espionage charges, who was then serving a sentence in Danbury Federal Prison.[88] Also in the 1980s, Agee met Weather Underground cofounder Bill Ayers while Ayers was in Havana with a group of students, having drinks with him for a couple of hours while sitting at the outside patio of a downtown hotel.[89]

Despite the dire result of his stab at mediating the Iranian hostage crisis—the revocation of his passport—Agee continued to undertake only slightly less flammable provocations. In 1982, he requested a visa to Iran, trumpeting his anti-CIA credentials, to research and discuss a possible television program based on the secret documents the Iranians recovered from the US Embassy in Tehran.[90] This gambit, especially coming so soon after the hostage crisis and the passport revocation, indicated Agee's willingness to taunt the CIA and perhaps a compulsion to one-up other disaffected CIA officers. Ultimately, though, Opperskalski convinced Agee that going to Iran was too risky. "I said don't go," Opperskalski remembered. "I said, 'Look, you don't know the country, you don't know the culture, you don't know the language, you know nothing. Unwittingly, you might be used by some forces that are not so positive.'"[91] Agee stayed in Hamburg.

If Agee had been uncertain about following the path of the career public dissident when he first landed in Paris in 1975, over the next few years he had made his commitment. In mid-1978, Victor Marchetti characterized Agee as "very much his own man and for all the deportations and media blasts, for all the Cuban connections and media smears, the evidence still suggests that he is the one thing the world of espionage can't handle: a self-motivated counterspy who goes his own way."[92] Five years later, in 1983, Petra Kelly invited him to participate in a Greens mock trial that cast the United States' use of nuclear weapons and Hitler's war crimes as moral equivalents. He accepted the invitation, and in the proceedings, seated next to Philip Berrigan, accused the United States of systematically protecting war criminals at the end of World War II.[93] The chutzpah and intellectual brinkmanship Agee displayed in this episode, as well as the files-for-hostages initiative, reinforced the image he wished to project of a resolutely independent activist driven by conscience and an unquenched thirst for a fight. It made his functional independence from the DGI and the KGB a somewhat more plausible proposition. The true picture is far murkier.

6

Uneasy Normalization

Back in the early 1970s, the CIA's leadership seemed incongruously unworried about the vertiginous lines case officers might walk. Due to James Angleton's paranoid overthinking, the CIA almost from its inception—and certainly after Philby's defection—had harbored a suspicion of defectors to the United States so extreme as to be counterproductive as well as an obsession with moles.[1] But the fervor with which first-generation case officers embraced the Cold War as a new and existential threat and the United States' postwar geopolitical primacy as a salutation of America's destiny also seemed to entrench the assumption that these factors would lose none of their inspirational potency. The pioneers had faith that the next generation would remain impervious to competing circumstantial and ideological influences.

The agency's institutional presumption had been that immersing intelligence officers in a mission aimed at safeguarding the United States would cement their instinctual loyalty with brotherhood, shared secret knowledge, and an ennobling appreciation for challenging duty. Little thought went to the other distinct possibility: that officers with an increasing awareness of American foibles might be less inclined toward moral relativism and exceptionalism. They than that of the first. Factors included stabilization of nuclear deterrence, the frustrations of Vietnam, and the establishment of détente, all of which informed, focused, and fueled Catholic liberation theology and pacifism. The Vietnam War, in particular, had palpably hurt CIA recruitment in the late 1960s and the early 1970s, as campuses increasingly barred CIA recruiters and the end of the draft stanched the flow of ROTC personnel into the agency.[5] The cultural tension and "credibility gap" that engulfed the CIA in the 1970s further eroded its appeal to liberal prospects, while its disempowerment under Ford and Carter would have made it less sexy to conservative ones. After several other disillusioned intelligence officers like Snepp, Stockwell, and McGehee followed Agee in airing withering criticisms of the agency and US policy—Vietnam in particular and covert action generally—CIA management finally became genuinely worried that Agee's conduct had set it up for a generation of case officers who would lack the talent, determination, and commitment of their predecessors.[6]

Agee's vocational frustrations notwithstanding, through the process of publishing his views he did consolidate his status as a crusading writer of conscience, in it for the long haul. He also gained and valued respect within the academy. London School of Economics professor Adam Roberts cited *Inside the Company* to bolster the case for abolishing the CIA in a peer-reviewed article that also drew heavily on the findings of the Church Committee.[7] Agee thereby migrated from a disposition of comprehensive besiegement to one of world citizenship in which he could explain away his nominal disloyalty as an anachronistic artifact of the obsolete Westphalian array of competitive states that he now rejected. The primary structural support for this view was the transatlantic Left, which Agee was always able to access in smaller ways for moral backing and sometimes able to marshal in big ways that, accidentally or intentionally, perpetuated his notoriety.

Through the late 1970s, Agee had continued to argue in print that his working against the CIA was not treasonous and that his exposing CIA officers was not intended to jeopardize their lives by enabling their assassination.[8] His correspondence with Louis Wolf,

might in fact become less tolerant of the ethically slippery r
and practices of espionage in a way that might alienate the
the agency in particular and, more rarely, from the Americ
ect as a whole. While Agee's motivations were complex, he
to have been especially open to this risk. The very belated
the agency's recognition that it was salient helps explain tl
durable loathing for him.

More substantively, Agee prompted concern in intelliger
cials that he would be part of a trend. The author of a 1972
had declared that "the CIA is confident that he will be the
its turncoats.[2] But if Agee was officially cast as an aberratio
visceral level "the Agee disclosures were painful because the
at the time, the most open and damaging and ideological,"
Walter Pincus, who covered the Agee story and for decades re
on intelligence for the *Washington Post*. "He was also of a ne
eration and created a new kind of fear that you could not trus
comers who may disagree with policy." The CIA was worri
added, "about the transition to younger people."[3] The Agee
dent alerted them that the loyalty and commitment of other se
generation CIA case officers could be quite brittle.

This is not to deny the idiosyncratic aspects of Agee's tu
subsequent years, he said he was sheepish about the Che Gu
remark as well as the rather pat suggestion that a bland coı
ment to humanitarian principles and a preciously political lo
fair made him do what he did. The arduous pace of his trans
overall, and especially the agonizing reticence he manifested a
leaving the agency during his final posting in Mexico City, stre
suggest that his conversion was psychologically byzantine and |
ably quite opaque even to Agee himself. In a 1987 article in a
fessional intelligence journal, Winn Taplin, a former CIA ofi
offered the sensible view that Agee's conversion was a complic
and gradual combination of ideology, post-CIA financial failure,
self-importance.[4]

In the event, Agee was perhaps as much a harbinger as an a
ration. The loyalty and compliance of the CIA's second genera
would turn out to be considerably more susceptible to challe

one of the most zealously anti-CIA editors of the *Covert Action Information Bulletin* and the *Dirty Work* books, was intensive between 1977 and 1982, and he coordinated legal tactics with Ralph McGehee with respect to their publications.[9] His voice, though, was largely redundant at this point. Although the CIA's rootedness in establishmentarian elitism did afford it a degree of insulation that sustained it, the late 1970s were barren years for the agency. At the same time, the very exposure and weakening of the CIA that Agee had helped nurture produced a backlash in Ronald Reagan's administration.

The Reagan Doctrine, formulated early in his first administration, was to abandon détente, move beyond containment, and repel Soviet geopolitical aggression by providing aid to anticommunist resistance movements.[10] William Casey—Reagan's old-school, ex-OSS director of central intelligence—rescued the agency from besiegement by way of this self-conscious reassertion of American primacy. Yet, as Daniel T. Rodgers sees, "Reagan was a more cautious Cold Warrior than his pre-Vietnam predecessors had been. He preferred surrogates—*contras* in Nicaragua, Jonas Savimbi's UNITA rebels in Angola, the anti-Soviet *mujahideen* in Afghanistan—to direct military intervention."[11] This only meant more work for the CIA, and Casey was willing not merely to support resistance movements but also to create them.[12] Furthermore, Casey's focus was on operations in Latin America, which the administration regarded as geopolitically vital: if the United States could not dominate in its own hemisphere, it would lose credibility and influence elsewhere.[13] Since Agee had spent his CIA career there, this development catered to his particular expertise and preoccupations. And energized agency operations afforded its critics a prominent new target. The CIA's revitalization meant Agee's as well.

REINVIGORATION—AND CAUTION

In July 1979, the socialist Sandinista National Liberation Front (FSLN) had overthrown the right-wing regime of Anastasio Somoza Debayle after a guerrilla war in which 30,000 to 50,000 Nicaraguans had died, entering the capital city of Managua in force and establishing a new government that embraced political pluralism, a mixed economy, and a nonaligned foreign policy. Somoza, a long-time American proxy, had been a brutal dictator, typically fascist and corrupt. Enamored of America's post–Church Committee self-cleansing, Carter disowned Somoza. At the same time, he disfavored a Sandinista takeover and sought a more moderate opposition as a third way. But Nicaragua's neighbors—Costa Rica, Panama, Mexico, and Venezuela—all now tilted left, and the OAS rejected the United States' proposal of joint intervention in Nicaragua through an Inter-American Peace Force. The Carter administration then supported a CIA initiative to back more moderate elements of the new government.[14]

The Sandinistas, through European affiliates, actively encouraged Agee to undertake political activity that catered to their interests and even pushed him to uncover and expose US intelligence assets in Nicaragua.[15] In October 1979, he published "The CIA's Blueprint for Nicaragua" in the *Covert Action Information Bulletin*. On the basis of his experience as a CIA case officer and using open-source reports, Agee speculated that the CIA was preparing contingency plans for clandestine intervention in Nicaragua designed to split the Sandinista leadership, project an inflammatory international anticommunist cause, and isolate leading radicals by tarring them as Cuban and Soviet allies. Among the tools of anti-Sandinista subversion that Agee arrayed were strikes to impede reconstruction, the withholding of foreign aid, media propaganda operations harping on the need for free and fair elections and the guerrilla forces' return to barracks, covert funding for right-wing political parties and candidates, and support for armed counterrevolutionary groups.[16]

A few months later, he published an article on the Jamaican elections in the *Free West Indian*, a Grenadan journal, impugning the Jamaican opposition party's alignment with the United States and (again) championing Jamaican Prime Minister Michael Manley, his socialist agenda, and his Cuban backers.[17] In 1981, Agee promulgated a detailed written assessment—later published through an affiliate of the *Covert Action Information Bulletin*—discrediting the State Department's unclassified "White Paper" on El Salvador, which purported to justify American support for its brutal right-wing regime.[18] In particular, over the course of twenty-seven pages, he concluded that there was no evidence that the Soviets significantly supported the Salvadoran guerrilla movement, contrary to the State Department's view, and that the White Paper incorporated falsified documents purportedly establishing Cuban arms supplies to that movement.[19] The effort was moderately successful, as lengthy articles in the *Wall Street Journal* and the *Washington Post* appeared to channel his analysis, though they cited different sources.[20] He had pointedly rejoined the fray in Latin America.

Initially, despite the CIA's efforts, the Sandinistas encountered little resistance in establishing dominant control. But Reagan regarded the US role in Latin America as a matter of not only reasserting the United States' hemispheric interests against the predatory Soviets and their Cuban proxy but also of "restoring American vigor" in the wake of Vietnam.[21] Already on the CIA's radar as a state successfully captured by the Soviets and the Cubans, Nicaragua became the linchpin of the Reagan administration's developing policy of rollback in the Western Hemisphere. During his presidency, the agency grew more enterprising and aggressive again, and it used all of the levers Agee had listed in the ways that he had predicted. They included covert backing for the right-wing Nicaraguan *contra*—that is, counterrevolutionary—rebels, who had decamped to Honduras after Somoza's ouster and drawn support from Argentina's military junta. Although Agee's prognostications were just informed common sense, the mere act of publishing them constituted a fairly brazen intervention in US foreign policy. Their broad accuracy only amplified his authoritativeness and credibility.

On the strength of his overt and participatory leftist tilt, Agee had obtained a Grenadan passport, personally arranged by Grenada's Marxist-Leninist prime minister, Maurice Bishop, a Castro protégé, in 1980. He visited Grenada frequently. In October 1982, he held a one-week training course there, lecturing on CIA operations in Latin America, its funding of covert operations, and how to identify CIA officers. Bishop was ousted and executed in October 1983 by hardliners who considered him insufficiently revolutionary, and the US invasion a few days later secured a right-wing government which perforce invalidated the passport. But the Sandinista government granted him a Nicaraguan passport to replace the Grenadan one. He traveled to Nicaragua several times between 1981 and 1984 to support the government and expose the *contras* and their CIA backing, first on the Grenadan passport and then on the Nicaraguan one. He remained active, confrontational, and unabashedly hands-on on this "solidarity circuit."

The Solidarity Movement, as it came to be called, consisted of a network of campaigns undertaken by Western European and American activists, journalists, filmmakers, labor organizations, religious groups, and scholars, provoked mainly by the United States' support for the *contras*. It was a major feature of the United States' cultural and political landscape in the 1980s, drawing in as active participants prominent Hollywood celebrities like Ed Asner and Oliver Stone, cultural critics such as Fredric Jameson, revisionist historians on the order of Gabriel Kolko and Walter LaFeber, and newspapers including the *Guardian* and the *Nation*.[22] They operated in the larger context of what Christian Smith calls a "participation revolution" whereby the American people and like-minded citizens of other countries asserted the right to directly shape US foreign policy.[23] As Jessica Stites Mor puts it, "longstanding leftist notions of anti-imperialism, pan-regionalism, solidarity, and social and economic justice found a way to compete with the powerful discursive frame of human rights and democracy whose tone was often set by the imperial ambitions of the United States, complicit nation states, and military regimes. Popular groups and literary figures reshaped notions of cosmopolitan ethics to include their own leftist critiques of capitalism, embracing the global as an arena of social responsibility while resisting the global as a preeminent source of authority over local markets and national interests."[24]

Even if the main locus of activity was the Americas, appreciable European diaspora and a robust infrastructure of left-wing protest organizations and publications led to substantial European involvement, propelled by the Sandinistas' electoral victory in 1979.[25] Indeed, Agee had helped seed the participation revolution a decade or so earlier from London and Hamburg: Belgian historian Kim Christiaens counts as a factor in the European mobilization "the appeal of the ideas propagated by the defected CIA agent [sic] Philip Agee, who presented Latin America and Western Europe as common victims of US imperialism and 'dirty' CIA involvement" in the 1970s."[26] Agee now found himself in a similar transnational vortex. From 1983, fueled by Nicaragua's increasing economic dependence on Europe due to US and World Bank boycotts, Swedish Prime Minister Olof Palme's diplomatic leadership in opposing US intervention, and the perception that Washington was marginalizing Europe in Cold War debates more broadly, local committees protesting American intrigue in Nicaragua burgeoned in Western Europe. The country that contained by far the most—400—was West Germany.[27]

In October 1983, at a solidarity conference in Managua, Agee gave a self-consciously incendiary speech. He identified the US ambassador in Managua as the CIA station chief and urged the exposure and harassment of CIA officers, exhorting Sandinista supporters to mount mass protests at US embassies and the homes of such officers, and even to seize or burn the US embassy in Managua. More broadly, he called for a continental front opposing the agency and offered his advice and participation in building and activating it. According to the Mexico City newspaper *Uno Mas Uno*, Agee stated that for each fallen Sandinista, two CIA agents "must fall." In general, these tactics mirrored those that left-wing, anti-American protesters had employed in Europe. US Vice President George H. W. Bush warned publicly that the United States would respond to any such action with force. According to news reports, Agee's speech prompted a formal evacuation alert, and Agee urged Nicaraguans to "meet violence with violence." This was a major provocation that exemplified Agee's radicalization and commitment to the global, left-wing anti-American cause, while circumventing the letter of the 1980 injunction (no writing was involved) but violating its intent. Bush characterized Agee as "turned," and US government agencies suspected him of prompting the public naming of thirteen other US officials in Nicaragua as spies. CIA analyst David MacMichael had recently left the agency in disgust, and he too publicly opposed the United States' Nicaragua policy.

The United States' covert activities in Nicaragua were outré even by early Cold War standards, ill-judged and poorly executed to the point of being inadvertently overt. Notwithstanding 1982 congressional legislation barring the United States from attempting to overthrow the Nicaraguan government, the United States continued to support the *contras*. This fact made the news that the CIA had written for the *contras* an eighty-nine-page manual titled "Psychological Operations in Guerrilla Warfare," revealed by the Associated Press in 1984, especially outrageous. Even more egregiously, the pamphlet seemed to incorporate terrorist as well as insurgency tactics and to recommend assassination in violation of an executive order—though the agency tried, unconvincingly, to explain away the suspect passages.[28] By early 1984, the agency was mining Nicaragua's harbors to prevent cargo vessels carrying imported arms, fuel, and other vital supplies from reaching the government. And the United States' efforts seemed ineffective relative to their alacrity, counteracted by more generous and operationally muscular Soviet and Cuban support for the government. That year, Agee joined other activists in Nicaragua on a Sandinista-controlled plantation to harvest coffee as part of a seasonal workforce in a show of solidarity against the *contras*, who were trying to infiltrate coffee farms.[29] His son Chris came to Nicaragua and participated in the coffee-production brigades.[30] Such tactics were right out of the Cuban and SDS playbooks. Agee received a formal testimonial from the FSLN for his "Solidarity with the Nicaraguan people and the Popular Sandinista Revolution."[31]

Agee's globetrotting 1980s itinerary seemed calculated to serially antagonize the American government elites and vested interests he had initially targeted. His position on the editorial board of the *Soberanta*—the Managua-based magazine of the Anti-Imperialist Tribunal of Our America, which had links to Castro and which the CIA considered a Cuban propaganda front—only further aggravated them. Presumably so did his extensive speaking tour beginning in March 1984 for the Maurice Bishop and October 19, 1983, Martyrs

Memorial Foundation, which included presentations in Luxembourg, Hamburg, Zurich, Brussels, Antwerp, The Hague, Amsterdam, Utrecht, Linz, Graz, Salzburg, Regensburg, Nuremburg, Freiburg, Munich, Copenhagen, Aarhus, Gothenburg, Oslo, Stockholm, Braunschweig, Münster, Osnabruck, and Helsinki.[32] But Agee had jumped on the right bandwagon and made himself relevant again, denting regional perceptions of the US policy. Moreover, the Sandinistas won by a landslide in the 1984 elections. Meanwhile, the disruption of a proxy civil war had produced economic dysfunction and repressive government policies in Nicaragua.[33]

The CIA under Reagan left a dubious legacy. Worse still, in June 1986, the International Court of Justice ruled that the United States' support for the *contras* and its mining of the harbors were violations of international law. Five months later, in November 1986, a Lebanese newspaper revealed the Iran-*contra* scandal, whereby Reagan's National Security Council staff had used the proceeds of secret and illegal arms sales to Iran to bankroll illegal aid to the *contras*. Agee appeared to be on the right side of history and, along with the rump American Left's selective mobilization and the administration's own maladroit lawlessness, had effectively contributed to the frustration of the Reagan administration's Central American policy.[34] Political vindication, of course, hardly exonerated him in the eyes of his detractors.

Agee recounted, in the January 1980 *Free West Indian* article, how vexing his life had been after leaving the CIA and moving to Europe, especially since his infamous 1976 trip to Jamaica, during which he spoke out against the CIA and fingered CIA officers. He "never considered betrayal of the millions of others who are working for socialism." Thus, he identified strongly enough as part of the international Left that his loyalties lay entirely with that movement and had expunged any guilt about his efforts to undermine the CIA and the United States more broadly. But he admitted feeling pressure to hang back from active political struggle.[35] Effectively barred since 1980 from disclosing CIA officers and secrets in writing, he refrained from doing so. Furthermore, his involvement with Michael Opperskalski's *Geheim* had caught the potentially troublesome attention of West Germany's mainstream Christian Democratic Union party in the 1980s, and Opperskalski counseled caution on Agee's part to ensure that his residence there would remain legal.[36] He considered mentioning the KGB in a book promotion but decided against it.[37] His own writing projects tended to be tame—for instance, an article for a book on Cuba on the assassination of a young Cuban-born activist in Puerto Rico, written for no fee, was an act of solidarity and friendship with the editor.[38]

Still, he remained drawn to controversial and disruptive issues in Europe. He had contact with several Basques, including employees of Radio Euskadi, which trumpeted the cause of Basque nationalism and separatism. His association with Opperskalski was insouciant. Like Agee, Opperskalski thrived on operating along the fluid boundary between underground advocacy of political violence and radical public rhetoric. He was close, for instance, to the armed wing of the African National Congress and entered South Africa illegally. His magazine *Geheim* was the subject of an indignant full-page feature in *Der Spiegel*—the most prominent German weekly news magazine then and now, based in Cologne—that mentioned *Geheim's* association with Agee, and Opperskalski himself became a target of surveillance by intelligence services.[39]

Nevertheless, concrete reasons did arise for Agee to avoid making himself too conspicuous. Active CIA monitoring had abated during that period, and Agee started to return to Cuba, visiting more frequently and staying for longer. Throughout the eighties, the CIA under Casey endeavored to "get the Philip Agees of the world," prompting the passage of the Intelligence Identities Protection Act of 1982—"the Anti-Agee Act"—which made publicly naming CIA employees or agents a criminal offense.* Agee was keenly aware of the

---

* From a liberal perspective, the law was an unfortunate by-product of Agee's acts of conscience. See, e.g., the editorial "Secrecy Is Not the Only Security," *New York Times*, July 7, 1981. Yet its most celebrated application damaged a conservative administration—that of George W. Bush—in the Iraq War drama over intelligence about Saddam Hussein's weapons of mass destruction. Seeking to punish former diplomat Joseph Wilson for publishing an op-ed doubting that Iraq had purchased uranium from Niger and to discourage the intelligence community from questioning the White House's rush to war, the Bush team leaked the fact that Wilson's

law and commented to a journalist: "I haven't named any names of CIA people since 1977."[40] He wrote a 1985 piece entitled "Uncloaking the CIA" that asserted the ongoing importance of exposing CIA officers, agents, and assets, pivoting mainly on Reagan's revitalization of the agency, but it went unpublished.[41] He seemed averse to even hinting at a violation of the 1980 injunction against such exposure or the Anti-Agee Act. He remained willing to consult respected journalists like Thomas Powers and scholars like Fred Ingall of Princeton's Institute for Advanced Study, whose prestige might burnish his own for posterity.[42] And he made gestures that would preserve his bona fides as a dissenter so long as they weren't too risky—for example, donating a dust jacket to a 1986 silent auction to raise funds for the Central American Resource Center, based in Minneapolis.[43] But these efforts were subject to his convenience and often merely decorative. Certainly he could no longer be considered even partially underground. Indeed, he retained a lecture agent, Sarah Becker, based in Florence, Massachusetts.[44]

Nevertheless, during this period Secretary of State George Shultz accused him, on the basis of CIA reports, of being a paid adviser of Cuba's intelligence service, training leftist Nicaraguan operatives, and trying to subvert the US invasion of Grenada. In fact, Agee had been in Nicaragua for about three weeks, at the end of 1983 and the beginning of 1984, and had spent five weeks in Havana in 1984.[45] This part of his itinerary no doubt resharpened US government sensitivities.

Furthermore, he could not suppress his impulsive disdain for the US establishment, and at times he appeared to verge on violating the 1980 injunction. Purportedly based on an interview with Agee, an article published in the February 14, 1983, issue of the Danish Com-

wife, Valerie Plame Wilson, was a CIA officer, and conservative columnist Robert Novak—who, ironically, had been a fierce critic of Agee's—revealed her employment status. A federal investigation found that Bush administration officials had violated the Intelligence Identities Protection Act by exposing her as a CIA employee, and former vice-presidential aide I. Lewis "Scooter" Libby was convicted of related offenses. In 2012, ex-CIA analyst and case officer John Kiriakou became the first former intelligence officer to be convicted of violating the Intelligence Identities Protection Act.

munist Party newspaper *Land og Folk* identified an alleged CIA official in Denmark. When Agee was visiting Madrid in 1983, he made a television appearance in which he named a former CIA Madrid station chief and stated that that individual was now directing US policy in Central America. His October 1983 speech in Managua pushed the envelope even farther. In an interview published in the March 19, 1984, issue of the Belgian Communist Party newspaper *Drapeau Rouge*, Agee accused the CIA of backing Latin American death squads, attributing his purported knowledge to his own experience in supporting such activities while a CIA case officer. Agee identified the alleged location of CIA stations in Spain and claimed that the CIA founded Orbe, a Chilean news agency, in an interview published in the February 18, 1985, issue of the Spanish magazine *Tiempo*. Whether actually violations of the injunction, these instances antagonized the US government and doomed Agee's attempt to obtain a new American passport, which he undertook in Madrid in 1987. Judge Gesell, who had issued the original injunction, upheld the State Department's denial of Agee's passport application.[46]

Agee's emerging timidity may have had additional, less acute sources that took hold of his psyche only gradually. Olive branches from pre-CIA friends could have softened him a little. In 1982, Agee received a friendly letter from his high school friend Clyde Wells, who had become an editorial cartoonist for the *Augusta (GA) Herald*, asking whether he'd like to meet somewhere in Europe.[47] Certain incidents could have spooked and sobered him. Ricardo Morales, an anti-Castro Cuban CIA agent allegedly tasked to keep track of Agee, was murdered in Key Biscayne in 1983.[48] Agee's subject-matter interests also segued away from the main areas of aggravation between himself and the agency. In 1984, for instance, he began working with Greece-based documentarian Nabil Maleh on a series on terrorism.[49] In private correspondence, in which he would have been maximally candid, he expressed theretofore withheld charitableness toward former agency colleagues, describing former Montevideo CIA Station Chief John Horton—whom he had criticized in *Inside the Company*—as "a marvelous man, honest, decent and sensitive like you so rarely saw in the Company."[50] Day-to-day life could have gotten in the way, too: in March 1985 his mother-in-law was hit by a car and had to spend two months in the hospital.⁵¹

So when Ron Ridenour encountered Agee at this time, he found a hero in hibernation. Like Agee, Ridenour was a US Air Force veteran and a former adherent of the United States' Cold War anticommunist mission. Both of their fathers admired General Curtis Le May. As a young enlistee serving in Japan between the Korean and Vietnam Wars, though, Ridenour was brutally hazed by fellow Air Force personnel for socializing with black servicemen. This triggered a broader disenchantment with the United States. After his discharge in the mid-1960s, he went to college in California and got radicalized. Two mainstream newspapers fired him for too openly supporting left-wing causes and groups, including some extreme ones like the Black Panthers, in his spare time.* The *Riverside Press-Enterprise* let him go a day after two FBI agents informed the paper's management about his purportedly suspect activities. He moved on to underground publications like the *Los Angeles News Advocate*, the *Los Angeles Free Press*, and the *L.A. Vanguard*. As a journalist-protester, he was frequently jailed for short periods and served a four-and-a-half-month jail term for resisting arrest.

He read *Inside the Company* when it was first published, while working as a stringer for the *Washington Post*. "I fell in love with this man in a sense," he said of Agee in 2016. "He was righteous, he was a gutsy son of a bitch. He comes out and he supports socialist revolution. He wasn't just a whistleblower, he went far beyond that. He re-inspired me. I saw him as a hero who had everything going for him and turned his back on it."⁵² So inspired was Ridenour that he later published the names of those he thought were CIA case officers working in Havana, where he lived and worked in the 1980s. He also burned his US passport in front of television cameras there. In 2016, he was open about having cooperated with the Cuban government.

---

* This Ron Ridenour is not to be confused with Ronald Ridenhour (1946–98), the American soldier (later a journalist) who while serving in Vietnam gathered information about the 1968 My Lai massacre and brought it to the attention of senior US officials, spurring an investigation of the incident, which was eventually brought to light by journalist Seymour Hersh.

"I was sometimes asked my opinion on this or that, and would give it freely."

Starting in 1980, Ridenour based himself mainly in Denmark. Having initially decamped to Europe in pursuit of a woman, he eventually found, as Agee did, that, especially on nuclear and environmental issues, European left-wing groups were reinvigorating the grassroots radicalism that had originated in the United States in the 1960s but declined when groups like the Weather Underground "frightened off the working class" and "discredited" American radicalism.[53] Peace and solidarity protests endured in Europe through the 1980s and didn't die out until the Cold War ended. This factor induced him to stay in Denmark. Ridenour met Agee in Copenhagen in 1985, after a lecture Agee had given. Subsequently, they spoke on the phone about protest marches and the like but never saw each other again. Agee struck him then as a "reserved man." He was "a really solid radical and revolutionary" with whom Ridenour felt a "kinship," but he was also "cautious and disciplined. His military and CIA background probably had to do with that."[54] Agee enthusiastically blurbed Ridenour's book *Yankee Sandinistas*.[55] Ridenour personally believes that Agee was right to name CIA names and expose its operations, and that he probably never abjectly regretted it. "When you're in the Agee class, or [Chelsea] Manning or Snowden, and you're known and interviewed and your picture gets in the paper, that gives you animation, and courage to go on." But Agee did not strike him as a friendly, happy person. "I think he carried the burden of great conscience."[56]

It goes almost without saying that Agee was unable to shed that burden. In the mid-1980s, right-of-center journalists still enjoyed conjuring up episodic Agee connections to throw stink on left-of-center counterparts, as the *Washington Times*'s John Lofton did on Nicole Szulc; her father Tad Szulc, a high-profile *New York Times* journalist; and NBC, which was then Nicole's employer.[57] Although the CIA had guardedly cultivated a relationship with Tad Szulc on account of his knowledge and contacts, the agency and the FBI also harbored suspicions that Szulc, who had frequently tried to interview agency personnel in Latin America on false pretenses of having been "cleared" to do so and who broke the Bay of Pigs story for the *New York Times*, was an agent of the Soviet Union or Cuba or at least a willing propagandist on their behalf. A highly sensitive CIA source had also claimed that Nicole Szulc had worked with the DGI to try to expose the CIA in Cuba. In the acknowledgments section of *Inside the Company*, Agee had credited Nicole Szulc for having "obtained vital research materials in New York and Washington."[58] The CIA wondered whether Tad Szulc had helped his daughter with the research for Agee's book.[59] So Lofton hyped the highly circumstantial link between Agee and NBC through Nicole.

The agency itself, at least at the operational level, was getting over Philip Agee. Agee submitted an article on Nicaragua titled "Subversion Failed, Nicaragua Reunited" to the CIA for review in 1983. Had the agency really wanted to jam him, its lawyers could have censored it. But they had no security objections. Neither did they hesitate to clear his "Uncloaking the CIA (1907–84)" or "Foreword for Publication of the CIA's Psychological Operations in Guerrilla Warfare and the Freedom Fighter's Manual."[60] Agee's clout with publishers was also diminished. When various foreign-language presses published the CIA Psy Ops Manual in Europe, and Viking did so in the United States, Agee wanted to publish it with his own foreword through Zed Books in the United Kingdom. But they felt the Viking effort (which included a foreword by a *Washington Post* reporter) preempted an effective launch on Zed's part.[61]

In his direct dealings with publishers, he started to get a little lazy and to rest on his reputation. In 1983, the infamous *Hustler* publisher Larry Flynt had just started *The Rebel*, based in Los Angeles, with an eye to publishing serious journalism, and planned to subsidize it with revenues from his more lucrative pornographic magazines. Agee contacted Marc Cooper, the senior editor, and asked whether he would be interested in publishing articles on Nicaragua and Grenada. Cooper himself knew a great deal about Nicaragua, having been there several times and written about it, and the US invasion of Grenada had just occurred. The pitch was especially appealing because Cooper was familiar with Agee by reputation and was politically sympathetic with him, and because Agee said he was traveling to the two subject countries anyway on other business and would not require *The Rebel* to cover expenses.[62] Cooper commissioned Agee to write two 4,000-word articles—one on Grenada and another on Nicaragua—for $2,000 per article, with CIA approval. Agee submitted longer pieces and requested $5,000 for both.[63]

In 2016, Cooper sourly recalled his association with Agee, which was limited to telephone conversations, characterizing the experience as "negative" and "distasteful" despite his political sympathy with Agee. "He was really a great disappointment. These stories were very much in the news, and he promised a lot of access to the Nicaraguan leadership, which was not hard to get. These were really easy stories for him, but he delivered junk. He delivered long, polemical pieces. We didn't necessarily object to the politics, but there was no reporting that I could detect. He was extremely aggressive and arrogant with us, and his lawyer [Melvin Wulf] was even worse. Not only did the articles come in too long but they wanted more money." The magazine declined to publish either piece and was willing to pay Agee only a fractional kill fee. After producing only about eleven issues, Flynt Publications had to shutter *The Rebel* in February 1984 without paying him a nickel. "I wasn't misty-eyed about Agee going into this, but I can't stress enough that it was really a negative experience because it felt fraudulent, to be frank," Cooper said. "What he wrote was a very long opinion piece that you could have written from your desk in Oklahoma."[64] Even so, Agee importuned Kim Fellner, executive director of the National Writers Union, to pursue his case against Flynt Publications for fees owed him by the then-defunct magazine.[65]

By now immersed in his own legend and a tad grandiose, Agee had begun to dine out on his past notoriety rather than to replicate it—a disposition that resonated in his 1987 memoir *On the Run*, which recounted US efforts to thwart the release of *Inside the Company* and to discredit and harass him. A certain lassitude and lack of follow-through on Agee's part had arisen in other areas of his professional life as well. Agee's papers do not contain copies of any personal letters that he wrote in 1986, which suggests that he declined to answer personal correspondence that year. The CIA and FBI probably did confiscate some of Agee's letters, both sent and received—his datebooks indicate that during this period he exchanged mail with John Stockwell, which would have interested the government—but it's not likely that they would have seized all of his letters for a single year.[66]

The more probable explanation is that his conscientiousness about being a political interlocutor was flagging. He had developed an armchair interest in Australia and New Zealand's domestic affairs, and his contacts included Murray Horton, who was secretary of a nongovernmental organization called the Campaign against Foreign Control in New Zealand, based in Christchurch. Horton suspected that the CIA was involved in advancing better-than-market loans to officials of the Maori Affairs Department of the New Zealand Labor government of Prime Minister David Lange. The transactions were linked to a Hawaiian native rights group that the CIA had penetrated. Ex-Australian minister Clyde Cameron believed that the CIA was similarly seeking to disrupt the Australian Labor government of Prime Minister Gough Whitlam.[67] Agee shared Horton's suspicions. With his encouragement, the Campaign against Foreign Control in New Zealand arranged for Agee a paid and sponsored trip to New Zealand and a speaking tour there. To Horton's considerable annoyance, however, Agee summarily canceled the trip.[68] He seemed enervated. Potential libel problems with On the Run cropped up, perhaps further subduing him.[69]

SETTLING

One probative indicator of Agee's mindset in the mid-1980s comes from his interview with Frank Deese, whom Tri-Star Pictures had retained to write and direct a film about the life of a CIA case officer, from college recruitment to field operations.* CIA public rela-

* Deese did in fact write the film, which had the working title "The Company Man," and its development went fairly far. Tri-Star enlisted Kevin Reynolds, then an up-and-comer, to direct the film. When the Berlin Wall fell and the Soviet Union collapsed, however, the studio killed the project. But Hollywood did not appear to completely bypass Agee. In 1980, AVCO Embassy Pictures released Hopscotch, an action comedy starring Walter Matthau as Miles Kendig, a disgruntled former CIA

tions were unwilling to assist Deese—they wouldn't even tell him "the color of the linoleum at Langley"—so he went directly to Agee, initially contacting him by telephone. Tri-Star hired Agee at $100 an hour to act as a consultant on the movie.[70] An intent Deese, who was only twenty-five at the time and somewhat "nervous" about talking to someone who was likely being watched by several intelligence services, spent two days with him in early April 1986 at a house in Ulm, West Germany, a small, scenic city on the Danube near the western foothills of the Alps, where Albert Einstein was born.[71] The Agees were living there while Giselle completed a stint with the city ballet.

On their first encounter, "he invited me in, introduced me to his wife, sat me down, and I was like, wow, this guy is so nice, he's really making me feel at ease," Deese recalled in 2016. "Then he said, 'Let's take a look at the contract.' That was when I saw his paranoid streak." It wasn't that Agee thought Deese was an agency plant, though; his worry was that he would somehow lose control of his personal story to Tri-Star and Deese. "I don't know if he was on the spectrum or had a condition, because when he looked at the contract, he snapped into a different mental mode. I was like, what happened to the guy who was pouring my tea?"[72] Deese assured him that he and Tri-Star wanted only to gain background on the CIA's recruitment and training process for purposes of composing a wholly fictitious story. Still, Deese had to confirm as much with Tri-Star and secure an amendment to the contract before Agee would proceed. Deese himself wrote down Agee's requirements, phoned Tri-Star legal in Los Angeles to get approval for the exact language, typed up the amendment on a German typewriter, and to obtain the required signature mailed it global express to the Tri-Star lawyer, who signed the document and overnighted it back to Deese. He then paid Agee with travelers' checks, sitting at a table and countersigning over $2,000 worth in

---

case officer intent on publishing a comprehensive exposé whom the agency unsuccessfully tries to thwart. While the film was based on Brian Garfield's novel of the same name, and Kendig's grievances involved the agency's general incompetence and its mistreatment of him in particular rather any ideological conversion, the similarities between its plot and Agee's story are palpable.

$100 denominations in front of him.[73] Once they had all those pre-liminaries squared away, he was "generous and thoughtful" about all and sundry, from recruitment to training to field work.[74]

In their extended, freewheeling conversation, Agee displayed dis-ciplined circumspection in registering his political views, though Deese detected in him a strain of apologism with respect to the KGB and the DGI, about which he declined to say anything negative.[75] In-triguingly, Agee also proved an enthusiastic raconteur about trade-craft—cryptonyms, secret writing, "flaps and seals," bugs, concealed cameras, microdots, surveillance, losing a tail—and the intelligence world overall. He clinically went through various niceties, such as the distinction between official cover (for which a case officer is merely cast as a State Department or Pentagon employee) and non-official cover (for which the officer poses as a private-sector person unconnected with any government). Agee also manifested a fairly detached awareness of the generational challenge that the CIA was facing—and knew it was facing—in the 1960s.

> There was a problem of attrition, because so many of the people
> whom they recruited in the 50s were at a young age, like 21 or 22,
> getting their bachelor's, they didn't really know what they wanted to
> do. Through the course of the two-year training program, there were
> resignations of four, five, six, ten people. Some might stay in for one
> tour abroad and then they would resign. So the attrition was pretty
> high. And when you get into the 60s and the activism on the campus
> and the civil rights movement, and especially with the anti-war move-
> ment, I noticed that the people—and I'm talking now about when I
> went back to Washington for about six months, eight months in '66–
> '67. And there I noticed that—and I talked to people about this, too—
> that the people were being recruited were to a much lesser degree
> recruited out of universities when they were getting their bachelor
> degree. They were older people. I noticed quite a few who had served
> in Vietnam in the military. Through their service with the military,
> they had some connection with the CIA in Vietnam. Because of course
> the CIA was very active in Vietnam. There was a spotting and assess-
> ment program going on in Vietnam by the CIA of military people who

were working with them for possible recruitment into the CIA. For example, one person who came and worked at a desk next to me had been a Marine officer in Vietnam. He had gone through university, he had then gone into the Marine Corps, maybe he was ROTC, I can't remember, but then he'd been recruited to come into the CIA, and he was like 35. The idea then was that first they would avoid recruiting people who were so young they didn't really know what they wanted to do. And then they'd spend all this money training them, and have this person resign or go into some other kind of work. There was another factor too, and that was with the problem of political alienation among young people during the 60s. There was one good way to assess them, and that the person's reaction to Vietnam. If you had a person who was all for the intervention in Vietnam, who worked in it, like the Marine officer I just mentioned, then it was pretty certain that that person was not going to have political problems with doing CIA work. It was more like parallel or continuation of what the person's been doing in Vietnam. And so the tendency in the 60s was to get older people and people whose political convictions were quite clear and defined over the Vietnam question.[76]

Yet despite this implicit recognition of tectonic political and cultural forces that arose in the 1960s, which helped explain and at least excused and arguably vindicated his own path, Agee romanticized his friend Ernie's politically muted but strangely fitful withdrawal from the intelligence field. Ernie had been an administrator at the Montevideo CIA station, and Agee thought he'd make a fine operations man and recruited Ernie himself. After six months or so at Camp Peary, Ernie was assigned to Bolivia as a case officer. There one of his principal agents was killed, apparently owing to his connection with the agency. Ernie became despondent. After he was transferred to Mexico, his wife, morally disenchanted with his work, separated from him. He chose to resign from the CIA and reconciled with his wife. They went back to California, where she became a college professor and he a landscape painter. The agency, however, eventually reenlisted him to act as liaison between friendly, talent-spotting professors and Langley. When his wife found out, she left him again. The agency changed his name and sent him to Portugal under nonofficial cover—he was a "NOC," pronounced "knock," in trade-speak—as, of all things, a painter.[77]

Agee's understanding was that during his eighteen months in Portugal in 1974–75, Ernie had handled the most important CIA penetration of the Armed Forces Movement (MFA), the procommunist cabal of junior Portuguese military officers who engineered the largely nonviolent "Carnation Revolution" military coup in April 1974—grateful citizens affixed carnations to the soldiers' uniforms and placed them in the muzzles of their guns—that ended the authoritarian right-wing regime that had ruled the country since 1933. The United States and its European allies were naturally uncomfortable with the MFA's ideology, and over a rocky two-year period supported moderate elements that eventually prevailed and ushered in stable democracy and swift decolonization. His work done, Ernie quit the CIA again, this time for good, reconciled with his wife one more time, and, in Agee's telling, disappeared into the mountains of Colorado.[78]

This, of course, was Agee's road not taken. In his conversation with Deese, he segues from his somewhat wistful reflections about it to a hardnosed acknowledgment that the agency had been "accurate" in judging that he "was not a good long-range prospect" because they didn't think he really knew what he wanted to do.[79] From there he moves on to the cheeky observation that the agency had failed to polygraph him over the entire course of his near-decade of fieldwork following training, which he had also noted in *Inside the Company*.[80] Especially given the assessment of Agee's tenuousness as an operations officer, overlooking routine polygraph examinations that might have revealed his ambivalence was an egregious and improbable error on the CIA's part. However comfortable it might have been for Agee to metaphorically evanesce into the Colorado Rockies, he seemed to be suggesting, his destiny must have been to do something more to thwart the agency.

Accordingly, he refocused on what he perceived as his mission. He remembered that his CIA indoctrination courses in the 1950s planted the notion that the Soviets, "in order to retain power internally had to continue to expand externally," which necessitated containment. A key corollary of this view was that the revolutions in Cuba and Nicaragua as well as Vietnam were all "creatures of the Soviet Union." If détente had relaxed this "right-wing interpretation of history," he said, the Reagan administration had revived and amplified it, most pointedly vis-à-vis Latin America.[81] This perception kept Agee running on at least a few cylinders. But his engagement was increasingly sporadic and selective. He focused predominantly on easy and relatively glamorous undertakings like book tours and eschewed substantively peripheral adventures like exposing CIA meddling in Australia and New Zealand. In the CIA, he told Deese, "you're always on the make. Constantly."[82] He had learned this occupational imperative well, and in fact had carried it over into his life as an anti-CIA activist.

After fifteen years, though, he was getting tired. Among the effects was a diminution of his sanctimoniousness. In his dialogue with Deese, there was little hint of wholesale distaste for CIA methods. He mentioned AVENGEFUL merely as an example of an operation for which he was responsible, making no note of the fact that it produced Bonaudi's brutal torture and sent him into slow-burning guilt and professional discomfort.[83] His talk about co-opting local telephone companies for wiretapping verged on boastful; he certainly manifested no shame.[84] He spoke nonchalantly, and crassly, of other nefarious aspects of the spy trade, such as considering a recruitment approach to a Russian diplomat he called Borizov whose wife was using her Saturday afternoons "to fuck the KGB [station] chief," which Agee knew because the station chief's "bed was bugged."[85]

Against Agee's public presentation of himself as a man of rediscovered rectitude, this kind of voyeurism and vulgarity was unexpected. Even his recollection of German intelligence's stealthily monitoring and opening his mail was dispassionate, shared for purposes of illustrating the use of a special scanner that illuminated writing through an envelope.[86] He spoke admiringly of Desmond FitzGerald, the legendary CIA deputy director for plans, referring to him as "Des" and remembering a direct encounter with him when FitzGerald visited the Montevideo station.[87] He fondly recounted the field exercises in Baltimore that he and fellow trainees engaged in out of Camp Peary. "Most of our nights were free. I think almost every night we went down to Baltimore Street to the strip joint."[88] From a calming distance, and perhaps exhaustion, it seemed his CIA life hadn't been so bad.

Even more explicitly, Agee was proud of the initial promise he had shown as a case officer, despite the agency's earlier assessment of his long-term unsuitability. Perhaps he was also looking to repudiate its retroactive character assassination. After finishing training at Camp Peary, prior to his first field assignment as a case officer, Agee worked on the Latin America desk at CIA headquarters in Langley. There he impressed the chief of the Venezuela desk, who had been chosen to become the station chief in Quito, Ecuador. He cut through red tape and got Agee his first assignment to that station, substantially sooner that any of Agee's classmates had been give their first postings. "I was very pleased," he admitted.[89] He also took pains to burnish his credentials as a high-performing operative, noting that

> throughout the sixties the problem that caused the most difficulties in the CIA was Vietnam, because the CIA was required to provide so many bodies for Vietnam—so many per month at one point—for some years. So that had to snatch people from different area divisions and put them on the road to Vietnam. The order from the president was that the best people had to be sent to Vietnam. But it turned out in practice that the worst people were sent . . . [b]ecause the division chiefs and the station chiefs didn't want their best people sent to Vietnam, they needed these people. When I went back to Washington in 1966, after six years in Latin America, I knew that our division had a quota to fill. . . . And I asked [the deputy division chief] what are my chances of being put on that list. . . . And he said, no you won't be sent, don't worry. We won't send you.[90]

Whether these remarks were merely self-serving or genuinely felt, for all his expressed disgust with the agency's mission and activities, Agee wanted Deese to register that he, Philip Agee, had been an elite case officer. Later that day, in brainstorming a movie plot, he alluded to his own psychological transformation when he imagined a CIA case officer under nonofficial cover who "would come to identify with the human factors in his environment, as opposed to the black-and-white anti-communism which he had been taught both before and after he went into the CIA. He would begin to develop a kind of crisis of conscience and an ideological crisis."[91] When pressed, he spoke of the case officer's occupational hazard of "falling in love" with an agent. "That's the expression," he elaborated. "And that can take many different forms. It doesn't [necessarily] mean man/woman or especially romantic. It means you fail to keep a certain emotional distance from the people you are working with, who are your agents. You have to control them, you have to be in a position to correct and criticize them. And this is all under the rubric of agent control. If you lose that sense of distance and begin to identify with the person, then your ability to handle the operation properly is compromised."[92]

This NOC, in Agee's movie scenario, would have shown great initial potential as a case officer before his humanization, whereupon he would pit himself against a more thoroughly immersed anticommunist CIA case officer insusceptible to enlightenment to undermine the recruitment of a fence-sitting target.[93] The NOC sounded an awful lot like a more valorized version of Agee himself. Still, Agee had no problem showing Deese some less than admirable carryover qualities. In particular, he seemed to relish the memory of the power a case officer brandishing a polygraph held over the prospective — and possibly desperate — agent who was about to be examined in a safe house. "The agent goes white and gets all nervous. And then you tell him it's ready right now, and then he starts shuffling and getting more nervous, and you ask him, you don't mind do you?"[94] Clinically he noted that the specter of periodic polygraph examinations was "a control and intimidating factor," and a "very good" one.[95] And while he allowed that "some case officers fought against using the polygraph because they were afraid it would spoil the rapport with certain agents," it was conspicuous that Agee — who was usually quick to stamp his ethical sensibility on a conversation — did not mention that he was one of them.[96] He acknowledged that "black-mail in intelligence is very bad motivation, because it's negative motivation," noting that "the CIA wants people to work for them who want to work for them, and not who are doing it because they are under duress."[97] Yet he himself urged blackmailing the KGB deputy station chief who was sleeping with the Russian diplomat's wife.

If there was something about the CIA's peremptory, smug swagger and manipulativeness that Agee found off-putting, he had also to some extent internalized it. When Deese took him and Giselle out to lunch, Agee peremptorily scolded Deese for overtipping.[98] Psychological coercion was never entirely alien to Agee, not before his ideological conversion or after it. Even seventeen years after he decided to leave the agency—supposedly on principle—he was proud of his own tradecraft and not especially shy about hiding his skilled deviousness. It's fair to say that he thought that his very talents as an intelligence officer could be effectively applied in besting the CIA. Agee certainly had not been reborn, innocent of darker vocational influences. He valued his own evolved stealth and he used it—not only to advance what he considered a righteous anti-CIA cause but also to disguise plain fatigue as earned ennoblement.

REHABILITATION

As late as February 1985, the US Attorney General was unwilling to give Agee assurances that he would not be subject to prosecution if he came to the United States, maintaining the same position asserted since 1977.[99] In January 1987, however, Melvin Wulf encouraged Agee, then in Madrid, to return to the United States to promote *On the Run*, assessing the likelihood of legal action as "pretty low."[100] The Justice Department, of course, had merely indicated that it would decline to indict or prosecute Agee for the time being; it did not concede that Agee had not violated federal espionage laws or that its forbearance was necessarily permanent. But perhaps Agee's tight compliance with the injunction against exposing CIA officers and assets had moved the Justice Department to ignore him. So Agee started to visit the States, initially flying to Canada and crossing the border by presenting his birth certificate and later being granted other special dispensations by US consulates in Europe on a trip-by-trip basis.[101] And in fact the Reagan administration took no action.

The book received obligatory praise from celebrity liberals like Ramsey Clark, Sean MacBride, and Gabriel García Márquez, and a strong review, though a fastidiously neutral and descriptive one, from the esteemed intelligence expert Thomas Powers in the *New York Times*.[102] Agee drew decent crowds in several book and lecture tours in 1987, 1988, and 1989.[103] The 1987 tour marked Agee's first time back in the United States since 1972 — some fifteen years. The publisher made a big push, with full-page ads in the *New York Times* and the *New York Review of Books* stating "PHILIP AGEE IS BACK."[104] His lectures had a confessional tone that was endearing to callow students seduced by the notion of a moral crusade against the CIA by a blooded spy. In one talk, he admitted that he had gone into the agency like "a lamb" and "a true believer."[105]

Agee certainly won over some skeptics. A note from Carleton College student Julie Oppenheimer said she had expected to "boo and hiss" at a traitor but now wanted to get involved in his cause after hearing his speech on Nicaragua at the Carleton chapel in summer 1988.[106] By then, however, he was largely preaching to the converted, especially liberal contingents on college campuses. The Progressive Student Organization, centered at the University of Minnesota in Minneapolis, was seeking to rebuild the student protest movement behind the impetus of Reagan administration policies. The group offered him a speaking honorarium of $200 to $500, plus travel expenses, for engagements at the University of Iowa, the University of Minnesota, the University of Wisconsin, the University of Chicago, the University of Illinois, and several East Coast colleges.[107] It arranged contracts for Agee lectures with eight schools — Trinity, Purdue, Illinois State University, Luther College, Northwestern, Ohio State, Fordham, and Bradley. The organization also set up paid talks at Vassar, SUNY, the University of Missouri, the University of Minnesota, Rutgers, the University of Illinois (Chicago) as well as Carleton.[108] His 1989 itinerary included three State University of New York (SUNY) campuses, Hamilton, Fordham, Elmira, Cornell, Carleton, the University of Michigan, Reed College, Northeastern University, the University of California at Santa Clara, and the College of New Paltz; he also spoke to the Democratic Socialists of North America.[109]

He spent large portions of 1987, 1988, and 1989 in the United States.[110] The highlight of his visits was surely his trip to Notre Dame in early March 1989. Agee's name had been dropped from the Notre Dame Class of 1956's "Class Notes" in *Notre Dame Magazine*, the quarterly alumni publication, when news of his turncoat status surfaced with the publication of *Inside the Company* in the mid-1970s. *Common Sense*, a left-of-center Notre Dame independent monthly newspaper, in February 1989 ran an article by Agee himself entitled "How to Become a Non-ND Alumnus."[111] But the practice of airbrushing Agee out of Notre Dame alumni affairs ended with the publication of the May 1988 issue of the magazine, which reproduced in "Class Notes" a supportive letter by classmate Mike Mooney from January 6, 1978. Inevitably, these rehabilitative successes produced some backlash. Prior to Agee's visit, another independent Notre Dame University newspaper published a hatchet job on him that included blame for the Welch assassination.[112] And Agee did retain written communications from Notre Dame classmates questioning his conduct and indeed his loyalty—for example, a handwritten note from "Hal" probably passed on to him from Mooney—and registering disdain and even violent impulses.

Despite these blips, his return to Notre Dame was a net gain. Agee addressed the student body on March 14 in a "packed house" per classmate Roger K. O'Reilly's April 17, 1989, letter to class secretary John Manion, a copy of which O'Reilly sent to Agee.[113] Other supportive Notre Dame alumni included David E. Collins and Henry S. Dixon, both of whom also wrote him letters.[114] The Class of 1956's Daniel Boland, who held a doctorate in theology and was a priest, seemed to capture a more nuanced judgment of Agee in a private letter to Michael Mooney, who shared it with Agee. Boland did note that Agee's actions might also have caused people to be killed, but he expressed agreement with Mooney's letter that the class's "praying" for Agee at its thirtieth reunion was condescending. Boland wrote: "If—as one might surmise—the reason was to pray for him because he had violated some norm of acceptable action, I would resent this as a judgment arrogantly made."[115] Agee seemed to value this normalization, qualified though it was, and took care to preserve his delicate political acceptability in the United States as well as the US government's benign neglect.

Agee did not, of course, completely disengage. He was hardwired to identify potential tools of CIA exploitation. Furthermore, the release of *On the Run* was topically fortuitous and, within limits, energizing. Agee was consistent and could at least feign humility, and his story had some residual oomph. It roughly coincided with a resurgence of American activism in opposition to US support for the right-wing *contras* against the Sandinistas, who had prevailed in elections in Nicaragua, and the revelation of the Reagan administration's clandestine and illegal sale of weapons to Iran in order to finance support for the *contras* that was not congressionally approved. The Progressive Student Organization, which more than any other advocacy group had helped Agee promote *On the Run*, focused explicitly on the "illegal and immoral war being waged on the people of Nicaragua by the government of the United States."

Yet many who might have thought Agee had some crucially valid points to make in 1975, when *Inside the Company* was published, seemed to feel he was past his sell-by date and was now milking what had become a permanent exile of essentially his own making. The tone of the reviews tended to be: "OK, but what did he expect?" Some regarded his persistence in the face of American politics and attitudes that had changed over the previous twenty years as "ludicrous."[116] Others detected smugness: he had perhaps become a legend in his own mind. Whether due to besiegement or arrogance, he could be fatuous, sophomoric, and egotistical, and these qualities were in evidence in *On the Run* when they had been far less pronounced in *Inside the Company*.

Notwithstanding the radical lurch his life took in the early 1970s, Agee had usually been more calculating than impetuous. And he might well have gauged that his moment of maximum impact had passed, and that it was time to relax. Over the course of the decade, Agee increasingly played it safe. When eccentric political groups like the Berkeley-based Anti-violent Continental Army contacted him, he apparently did not respond. Nor did he follow up on Nicaragua activist Elliot Cohen's suggestion, as a means of getting around the "Anti-Agee Act" criminalizing the public disclosure of the identities of intelligence officers, of going after only those officers whose identities were already publicly known, or publishing their names only in Nicaragua.[117] After his improbably civilized reception by campus audiences and especially Notre Dame alumni during the release of *On the Run*, and the US government's legal forbearance while he was in the United States, Agee might have felt compelled to preserve his marginal acceptability and his freedom of movement—to favor discretion over valor.

His more abject fear—that is, for his safety—never completely left him. In April 1988, he got a letter from a man asking why the CIA didn't just kill him.[118] He kept clippings about Brian Willson, who lost his legs in an act of civil disobedience against a US Navy shipment of arms to the Nicaraguan *contras* in September 1987.[119] And he also cubby-holed material on Jim Reed, who was murdered in Nashville in March 1987—some suspected by US-backed operatives for supporting the Sandinistas and other left-wing liberation movements.[120] Agee may have been a committed dissident, but he was not a martyr and did not consider himself one. He did not want to die or go to jail for his principles. In fact, he seemed to have wearied even of mental discomfort.

To be sure, Agee still gave thoughtful interviews attuned to radical sensibilities. But they tended to be more tempered, such as the one with a University of Michigan student-run newspaper in which he said he believed governments *should* have intelligence agencies to collect intelligence "to prevent war and to keep the peace" but "not to wage war against defenseless peasants in Central America, for instance."[121] A radio speech he made on covert action drew strong interest.[122] He had supplanted his messianic, narcissistic, and self-aggrandizing tendencies with a cooler, less egocentric persona conveying a less strident political message. In turn, he serviced the campus faithful in the ways of the anointed but now rather earnest old radical. In 1989, he wrote the foreword of the Bill of Rights Foundation's *CIA Off-Campus Handbook for Student Organizers*.[123] He endorsed Philip Agee Jr.'s effort, as coeditor of *Campus Watch*, to spearhead the popularization and dissemination of a DIY handbook for student organizers for resisting CIA recruitment efforts on college campuses.[124] He delivered a standardized speech to campus audiences during this period called "The CIA, Human Rights and American Democracy."[125] And he duly served on the Advisory Board of the Student Action Union, which was seeking to revive left-wing campus political activism.[126]

While these activities confirmed Agee's dissident standing, they were for the most part quite vanilla: symbolic and anodyne. By the late 1980s, he didn't feel he had to reestablish his bona fides. His reputation was insusceptible to amendment absent a complete renunciation of his turn, his historical credentials as a disaffected spy who leaped into either principled betrayal or reprehensible treason—depending on your point of view—firm and self-maintaining. But there wasn't much he could do to build on it either. In Agee's files is a framed cartoon dated October 22, 1989, by Tony Auth of the *Philadelphia Inquirer*, who had won the Pulitzer Prize in 1976. A trench-coated figure labeled "C.I.A." writes on a bathroom mirror: "Free Me So I Can Kill Again." The handwritten inscription reads: "For Philip Agee, with high esteem.—Tony Auth."[127] Agee had little left to prove to the audience that mattered to him. If he was exhausted at that point, though, he would prove to have at least one more surge of radical energy left.

7

Whipsawed, Stalked, Tired

Agee's activity in the seventies could be written off as impulsive but perishable idealism, but his persistent disparagement of the CIA some fifteen years after his decision to leave it demonstrated a durable commitment to principle and genuine political conversion. The eighties brought a measure of vindication for Agee, as *On the Run* seemed to suggest. At the same time, the book documented the costs of his decisions. He had disrupted the lives of his sons, who lived mainly with his ex-wife Janet and whose upbringing was bankrolled in part by friends from New York. He had stigmatized his parents and embittered Janet. Despite finding a modicum of happiness and security with Giselle in Hamburg, he was tense and insecure, his nerves shot.

True, he had escaped incarceration or worse, and by the latter part of the decade was able to travel to the United States, which he still considered his country, without fear of arrest even as he gave antigovernment speeches on college campuses and promoted a book that reiterated old criticisms of the US intelligence community and raised new ones. Among Notre Dame alumni, he had been partially rehabilitated: whereas most of his classmates had seen him as a repugnant traitor in the wake of *Inside the Company*, a fair number now embraced him as an embattled man of conscience. But European left-wing activism faded in 1990–91 as the Cold War ended. Francis Fukuyama had blithely posited that the demise of Soviet communism meant "the end of history" insofar as the victory of Western liberal democracy over Soviet communism marked the culmination of ideological, social, and cultural evolution.[1] The practical corollary was that protest was futile because now the United States was all-powerful and could do whatever it wanted.

FIERCE AMBIVALENCE

Agee remained generally unwelcome in his country, resigned himself to never being fully accepted and normalized there, and did not consider permanently relocating stateside. His remedy, as it had been since he had left the CIA, was to assert his ideological turn and write fiendishly—to double down rather than give in—subject to the not inconsiderable constraints of preserving his safe haven in West Germany and obeying the 1980 federal court injunction. In 1990, the Nicaraguan foreign ministry revoked his Nicaraguan passport. According to Agee, "when Violetta Chamorro [a centrist candidate] was elected president, she was desperate to have the Bush administration release the hundreds of millions of dollars they had promised in aid for relief and reconstruction. In order to release the aid, Bush made a series of demands and the revocation of my passport was one of them."[2] But Agee was then able to secure a German passport, facilitating a twenty-city tour of campuses and community groups organized by an outfit called Speak Out!, which then launched a campaign to have Agee's US passport reinstated. On Agee's behalf, Melvin Wulf wrote to *New York Times* columnist Anthony Lewis suggesting a column on the dubious constitutionality of the United States government's ongoing refusal to allow Agee a US passport, noting that for three-and-a-half years prior Agee had been allowed entry into the United States on a Nicaraguan passport.[3] But instead of placating the United States government to condition leniency, Agee published a philippic speech he had planned to give on the tour tearing down US policy throughout the Cold War.

He started with President George H. W. Bush's invasion of Panama and worked backward.[4] In December 1989, Bush had unilaterally dispatched roughly 22,000 American troops to oust Panamanian military dictator Manuel Noriega, declining to consult Congress in advance. Noriega had worked with the CIA and drawn US support as a resolutely anticommunist partner, helping the Reagan administration to support the contras and weaken the Sandinistas in Nicaragua. Though he exercised complete control over Panama from behind the scenes, in 1984 he decided to allow the country's first presidential election in sixteen years with an eye to presenting a democratic facade and blunting political criticism. Guillermo Endara, the opponent of the pro-Noriega candidate, won decisively, but Noriega nullified the result. He proceeded to turn his country into a narcostate and hedged against US disenchantment by accepting military aid from the Soviet Union, Cuba, and Libya. Now irretrievably corrupt and autocratic, he harassed American civilians and military personnel in Panama, and US officials feared that he was becoming too independent and potentially hostile. They were concerned for the US bases in the Canal Zone, and that he could render Panama an unreliable custodian of the Panama Canal, which the United States was to hand over to Panama by 2000.

Losing twenty-three of its own, the American force killed 500 to 1,000 Panamanian soldiers and several hundred civilians, installing Endara as president, arresting Noriega on drug-trafficking charges, and spiriting him back to the United States for trial and incarceration.[5] With no American lives at dire risk, Panama comprehensively undemocratic in any case, American strategic interests (including the Panama Canal) under no immediate threat, and the United States' stated concern for drug trafficking pretextual, the US operation was arguably an illegal exercise of US military power.[6] Noriega was an awkward case for Agee: while Agee abhorred US and CIA support for precisely that kind of brutal right-wing dictator, he also opposed US military intervention aimed at controlling the internal politics of Latin American countries. Agee ended up characterizing the American invasion in harsh geopolitical terms, as an attempt to "smash Panamanian nationalism for the foreseeable future." From there Agee's talk moved on to the Gulf War—in his view, Bush's "necessary crisis" for justifying the United States' "international mercenary army for hire."

Rhetorically, he continued to reject the American project wholesale. In speeches and radio spots on the Gulf crisis of 1990–91 and Cold War precedent, Agee reached back to the Constitutional Convention. In a draft speech, he characterized American foreign policy as an elitist exercise "to protect and increase . . . private wealth and other interests," citing the distinguished left-wing historian Howard Zinn. Agee demanded, on behalf of a notional global movement and using the first-person plural, "a new constitution, real democracy, with popular participation in decision-making."[7]

The CIA, the subject of his primal grievance, still consumed his writing life. His view, while still minatory, did not completely lack nuance or calibration. In fall 1990, he published "The CIA's Prospects in Eastern Europe" in the *Covert Action Information Bulletin* (renamed *Covert Action Quarterly* in 1993). He acknowledged that "1989 was quite likely a boom year for counterintelligence operations against Eastern European intelligence services" and mentioned corresponding "significant setbacks in Soviet intelligence capabilities." He added that "the U.S. has an interest in the stability of the USSR and even of the KGB."[8] During this period, Agee was working on "The CIA for Beginners: 100 Questions and Answers on What the CIA Does and Why," his draft for a book that was never published. The title made the project sound deceptively rudimentary, almost like a "For Dummies" book. In fact, the manuscript was quite detailed and sophisticated, carefully researched, and pitched at a well-educated audience engaged on world affairs. For instance, he conceded that the CIA had been quite good at *watching* the Soviets, and that CIA monitoring has played an important role in preventing war.

The central problem for him was the CIA's covert action against politically discordant governments and its aggressive support for brutal and unjust regimes as an "instrument of the President for applying U.S. foreign policy." For Agee, the CIA was "subtle confirmation of the 'open door' policies that go back over a hundred years and whose aim was to provide for penetration of foreign resources and markets by American companies." This activity has immense "human costs," he said. He also listed KGB penetrations of the CIA by John Paisley, Christopher Boyce, William Kampiles, David Barnett, and Edwin Moore, and, rather conventionally, counts the CIA's biggest counterintelligence success to have been the recruitment of Soviet military intelligence officer Oleg Penkovsky.[9] Penkovsky provided important information about the Soviet nuclear arsenal, missile fueling methodologies, and missile guidance systems as well as the deployment of Soviet missiles in Cuba.*

If executive coercion in the name of capitalism was Agee's main grievance with respect to the CIA, it always had a faith-based overlay. There is no direct evidence of precisely what Agee was reading as he contemplated breaking with and turning against the CIA, and he remained frustratingly opaque about his motivations for doing so—merely wondering, for instance, "whether the Jesuits had something to do with it" twenty years later.[10] But his loose fealty to his religion suggests that he kept up with developments in church teachings and the conduct of Catholic activists, and that he could well have found justification in them for his transformation. In Question 27 in "The CIA for Beginners: 100 Questions," Agee considered the extent to which the CIA worked through religious groups—especially the Catholic Church—and how that had spurred the march of liberation theology. He cited Lernoux's *Cry of the People* as a "superb account of the transformation of the Catholic Church in Latin America from an almost exclusive ally of the rich oligarchies to a major force for change, even revolution, on the continent."[11] That transformation mirrored Agee's own earlier shift, as a serious social-action Catholic, from a patriotic American fixer to revolutionary citizen of the world. His path evoked Robert Stone's prophetic 1981 novel *A Flag for Sunrise*, about CIA intrigue in a fictional Central American coun-

---

*This is the consensus view. Former MI5 scientific officer Peter Wright, however, celebratedly contended that Penkovsky was a double agent tasked with deceiving the West into believing that the Soviet nuclear weapons program was less advanced than it actually was. See Peter Wright with Paul Greengrass, *Spycatcher: A Candid Autobiography of a Senior Intelligence Officer* (New York: Viking, 1987).

try amalgamating El Salvador and Nicaragua. In that book, Tom Zecca, a CIA officer bragging drunkenly of having opted out of various wartime atrocities, says, "I don't claim virtue . . . I don't claim to be a kindly man. I claim to be capable of honor." Frank Holliwell, the anthropologist discreetly sent by a skeptical senior CIA officer, asks, "Do you expect to conduct your career in one American-sponsored shithole after another, partying with their ruling class, advising their conscripts on counterinsurgency and overseeing their armaments, and not compromising your oath or your honor? Because that sounds tricky to me."[12] These respective viewpoints resonate more deeply in Father Egan, a depleted alcoholic priest, and Sister Justin Feeney, a tragically idealistic young nun with whom Holliwell falls in love. Agee's worldview had moved decisively from Zecca's to Holliwell's.

Agee also observed that "the CIA worked to assist the right-wing opposition within the Catholic Church," noting the "battle against liberation theology" mounted in collaboration with the conservative, cult-like Opus Dei, the secret Catholic society.[13] He was in possession of a script by James Angleton on the CIA's covert "Gladio" campaign, which involved facilitating cooperation between the Mafia and the Catholic Church, and a sheaf of clippings about it.[14] At this stage, he had seen the emptiness of any inspiration he had drawn from Tom Dooley's apparent rectitude to join the agency. In an aside to the answer to Question 27, he quipped: "Who knows? Dooley may become the CIA's first known saint."[15] Agee's papers also indicate that he took an especially keen interest in a 1983 *Mother Jones* article by Martin A. Lee entitled "Their Will Be Done."[16] The piece chiefly theorized that by the 1970s the CIA had recognized a deepening split between traditional conservative elements of the Catholic Church and advocates of liberation theology inspired in part by Pope John XXIII's benevolent populism and resolved to mobilize the former against the latter. This strategy yielded, among other things, the election of the staunchly anticommunist Cardinal Karol Józef Wojtyła to the papacy as Pope John Paul II, whose political partisanship—especially on behalf of the right-wing elites in Central America that Agee loathed—only intensified the polarity within the church.[17]

Thus, Agee apprehended quite clearly a Cold War–era contest between positive and negative forces within the church and the implicit need to take sides. These forces had infiltrated ordinary Catholic families, in some cases ripping them apart. James Carroll, for instance, recounted in his 1996 memoir *An American Requiem* how his Catholic father had joined the FBI and later switched careers to Air Force intelligence. As a lieutenant general he was responsible for targeting Vietnam bombing strikes, prompting James to become a Catholic priest and a vociferous Vietnam war protester.[18]

In mentioning liberation theology, Agee also revealed his focus on a distinctly Latin American movement. Framed by the Peruvian priest Gustavo Guttiérez, *A Theology of Liberation* (1971) in turn influenced the Catholic Worker Movement. Insofar as the CIA sought to perpetuate privileged classes' oppression of indigenous populations in Latin America, from the vantage of contemporaneous Catholic intellectual discourse, it is easier to see why Agee did what he did. Giselle Roberge Agee—who also grew up Catholic—noted: "I think being raised a religious Catholic was part of what made him turn against the Agency and do what he thought was right. You're fed as a very young child this complete vision of right and wrong: there is no gray, there's black and white, you have to confess your sins. You come out of it with a feeling of guilt about everything you might have been able to do to make things better."[19]

Ideological justifications aside, most would still infer that Agee had a traitor's heart. Glenn Carle offered a hardnosed but certainly understandable interpretation of this pathway: "I think at the beginning he was just a whore. But I think he became sincere as time went on." Nevertheless, he continued, "he seems to be a pretty clear case of treason. The motivations you can argue about, and I'm sure they were contradictory and multiple. That's always the case in any operation initially. Things simplify when the consequences of one's acts become clearer; traitors then tend to dress up their conflicted behavior in clear principle."[20]

The section of the manuscript "The CIA for Beginners" on post-war and early Cold War history, while typically informed and considered, reads like Soviet apologism.[21] And in the 1990s, he started making frequent trips to the scene of his original sin: Cuba. He traveled from New York to Miami on March 13, 1990, then to Havana on March 14, staying until March 20, when he returned to Florida. The Havana trip is not noted on the dedicated datebook page for March 14. During the week he was in Havana, he made datebook entries only on March 16, and only as to matters unrelated to Cuba. This is somewhat conspicuous given Agee's habitually assiduous recordings during travel—sparer entries generally correspond to time at home in Europe or on vacation—and arguably raises suspicion about the nature of his activities.[22] In November 1990, Voice of America—which was then closely linked to the CIA[23]—canceled a broadcast involving Agee.[24]

Inside the Company naturally remained his touchstone, and the view of the agency set forth in the book and his subsequent years in the hinterlands certainly endured.[25] His regional preoccupation was, as it had been, the Western Hemisphere. In 1992, he penned a far-reaching lecture titled "After 50 Years: More of the Same" concerning mainly US policy in Latin America.[26] Agee would collect and file any clippings or other material on just about anything that cast aspersions on the CIA for any reason, from mind-control experiments to slipshod counterintelligence. He stayed fixated on the infiltration of the International Confederation of Free Trade Unions by the CIA or CIA assets, such as, in his view, the AFL-CIO.

He did endeavor to update his insights and render them currently relevant. His "Special Introduction" to the 1992 edition of the German version of *Inside the Company* addressed the post–Cold War fate of the international Left movement. He sees some vitality there in the form of wide acceptance of conspiracy theories like that evidenced by the Oliver Stone film *JFK*, which attributes the Kennedy assassination to the US government.[27] In this assessment, he turned an op-ed published on New Year's Eve 1991 by Senator Daniel Patrick Moynihan (D-NY) on its head. Moynihan had argued that *JFK* "is not parody, and it is not funny. It could spoil a generation of American politics just when sanity is returning. All of us in politics ought to see it. This is what citizens under 30 or 40 are going to be thinking soon."[28] Agee, in turn, had circled that passage exclusively in a clipping of the piece.[29] Although Agee might have broadly respected Moynihan—a major thorn in the CIA's side who believed the Cold War's end had rendered the CIA obsolete and favored its abolition—he did not share the New York Democrat's despair over the prospect of a cynical, paranoid Generation X; indeed, Agee seemed to welcome it.

He remained engaged outside the classroom—for example, advising a doctoral candidate on a dissertation on the CIA in 1990 and conferring with journalist David Corn about FOIA documents and furnishing some to him.[30] His quest for a voice in mainstream American magazines with a purported edge continued, as he attempted, for the most part unsuccessfully, to cultivate *Esquire*, *Penthouse*, *Playboy*, *Rolling Stone*, and *Vanity Fair*.[31] But his essential nourishment came from teaching international relations as an adjunct professor at Hamburg University, where lefty students knew who he was and what he had done, and he basked in the quiet adulation that they tended to accord him. Tim Rutten described him as "witty, cultivated and unpretentious in a haunted sort of way."[32] Opperskalski recalled Agee's "charisma," his ability to transfix people, and the confidence he inspired in the genuineness of his ideological conversion and "emotional" commitment to left-wing causes—that is, "the human factor." "He was a simple character. For example, when he was lecturing, at the end of the session, he was very happy. He liked to sit around having a beer or two or three into the night just talking to people, and sometimes he forgot that he had to take a train. He was really a nice guy."[33]

Agee was not an overly self-regarding or parochial teacher. He worked hard as a professor, drafting seminar lectures in English and translating them into German, though his facility in the language was limited.[34] He did not predominantly assign his own work or that of sympathetic colleagues, or unduly skew his syllabi toward espionage critiques or attacks on Cold War orthodoxies. Of course, he didn't ignore them either. With 1994–97 course notes on the CIA's postwar involvement in Greece, Agee listed a CIA paper entitled "Possible Consequences of Communist Control of Greece in the Absence of U.S. Counteraction," produced in 1948 and declassified in 1976.[35] Used as a reading assignment, this piece constituted an early articulation of the "domino theory." But overall, in choosing reading materials for his courses and seminars, Agee was eclectic and wide-ranging.

His seminar lectures were thorough and provocative, marked by sound if not terribly original synthesis. In one, for instance, he linked NSC-68—the pivotal 1950 National Security Council policy paper that effectively militarized the strategy of containment—with the Korean War and the limitations of rollback.[36] As Agee noted, following the postwar reduction in military spending, NSC-68 had recommended heavy increases in order to blunt Soviet expansion, but the prospect of a general war between the United States and the Soviet Union that could go nuclear always circumscribed how far either side could go militarily. This reality placed a premium on proxy contests and clandestine activity by intelligence agencies.

Agee also nursed a growing concern about burgeoning right-wing extremism prompted by the rise of neo-Nazi groups in Europe and militia groups in the United States, which he considered in part a product of CIA machinations. Germany was a focal point of a latent extreme Right, and Agee would have been sensitized to it.[37] He linked this new threat to old grievances in a 1993 seminar styled "The CIA, the Cold War, and Right-wing Extremism," which attracted over a hundred students—about twenty-five of them American—and which Agee offered through 1996 at the university.[38] In the unpublished "Thoughts on the New World Disorder," written in October 1993, he suggested that while other threats may have been nurtured by US policies (e.g., Islamic extremists arising out of the US-backed campaign against the Soviets in Afghanistan) and may serve as pretexts for US remilitarization, they could also have been real.[39] While there was some flailing and confusion on Agee's part, the ongoing ascent of the Far Right in Europe, the United States, and elsewhere make these particular points seem prescient.

In his courses, Agee stressed the American and Allied tolerance for and partial tactical embrace of ex-Nazis during postwar de-Nazification. He viewed the expedient instrumentalization of selected ex-Nazis regardless of what they had done during the war as formative with respect to the CIA and US government views on the practice of intelligence in general.[40] He gathered material for a book on Reinhard Gehlen, a former Nazi intelligence officer who cut a postwar deal with the United States.[41] He was also very interested in the Vatican's cynical assistance to Nazi fugitives, the principal figure being Archbishop Alois Hudal of Italy, who ran a seminary for German Catholic priests in Rome.[42] Vaulting forward in time, Agee held forth on the rise of the extremist Right, including the British National Party and France's National Front, in Europe in the 1980s and 1990s.[43] He compiled a fat file on the reemergence of fascism in Italy between 1993 and 1997.[44] His sheaf on the extreme Right in the United States and Canada in the 1990s was relatively thin—so indeed was the United States government's, and journalistic concern was perhaps correspondingly sparse[45]—but his lecture thereon was long.[46] Agee kept a self-annotated article on the Christian Identity Movement in the United States from 1995, suggesting that he was increasingly concerned about right-wing domestic terrorism in the United States in the wake of the Oklahoma City bombing.[47] In 1995, his request to Hamburg University for financial support for his Cold War/CIA seminar and related research and writing specified the ascendance of neo-Nazi, neofascist, and ultraright movements in Europe and the United States as a research topic.[48]

Agee also appeared to harbor some hope that the United States government would reform its espionage establishment of its own volition. He retained a copy of S. 126, 104th Congress, 1st Session, January 4, 1995: A Bill to unify the formulation and execution of United States diplomacy—"Abolition of the Central Intelligence Agency Act of 1995."[49] Introduced by Senator Moynihan, the bill would have transferred the functions of the CIA to the State Department on the grounds that during the Cold War the CIA had "undermined the State Department as the primary agency of the U.S. government in formulating and conducting foreign policy and providing information to the President concerning the state of world affairs."

Moynihan also proposed "The Disclosure of the Aggregate Intelligence Budget Act of 1995."[50] On balance, Agee remained intensely critical of American policies and institutions. But he did not appear to be a man who had even remotely abandoned genuine concern for his country or, for that matter, who comprehensively hated it.

In 1993, at age fifty-eight, Agee began to experience some health problems, and, not untypically, to entertain late-middle-age worries about his mortality. According to several datebook entries that year, he was monitoring his blood pressure, which was quite high— up to 164/99, stage 2 hypertension—but lower "after pill," indicating effective medication.[51] His steady following among countercultural loyalists and left-leaning students presumably offered comfort. Even at politically less forward Midwest universities, he got some love. There's a plaque of appreciation among his papers that reads:

TO PHILIP AGEE

~

WITH APPRECIATION FOR YOUR EFFORTS

ON BEHALF OF THE STUDENTS OF THE

INDIANA UNIVERSITY—PURDUE UNIVERSITY

THE OHIO STATE UNIVERSITY

STUDIENPROGRAM AN DER UNIVERSITAT HAMBURG

SPRING 1994

On campuses, carefully calibrated critiques of US policy sometimes won Agee favorable if temperate comment from leftish college publications.[52]

More broadly, though, the American Left, under Bill Clinton's leadership, was bending toward the center in a successful effort to claw back political influence from Reagan's constituency. One telling indicator was the effort to gain Senate confirmation of Morton Halperin—a distinguished foreign policy expert and former senior Defense Department and National Security Council official—as assistant secretary of defense for democracy and peacekeeping, for which Clinton had nominated him. On account of his left-leaning political views and activities, including his association with and defense of Agee, Halperin was forced to withdraw from consideration.

Perhaps as a kind of hedge against unrealistic expectations, Agee maintained a latent interest in CIA infiltration of ostensibly aboveboard enterprises and continued to support its exposure. He strongly suspected that the American University in Cairo was a CIA front. Christopher Thoron, its president from 1969 until his death in 1974, was a former Foreign Service officer and a confirmed CIA asset. Agee made handwritten notes listing nineteen suspected additional CIA assets at the university.[53] He also had materials on Jeffrey Schevitz, an American sociologist working at Germany's Nuclear Research Center in Karlsruhe who was arrested by German authorities on espionage charges in 1994 on the basis of uncovered Stasi documents.[54] Schevitz said he was actually working for the CIA as part of an elaborate intelligence operation, and he claimed to have been run by Shepard Stone, the former director of the Aspen Institute in Berlin, who had died in 1992. The Aspen Institute denied these allegations, while the State Department, the CIA, and German officials declined to comment.[55] Schevitz pressed unsuccessfully for CIA files that would exonerate him or at least verify his claims of CIA control. Agee contributed money toward Schevitz's $65,000 bail. In November 1995, a German court in Stuttgart convicted Schevitz of spying for East Germany.[56] Agee also gave $50 to the Abbie Hoffman Activist Foundation, with a personal note to the organization's president, Johanna Lawrenson, Hoffman's widow (Hoffman had committed suicide in 1989, at age 52).[57] And Agee supported the Association of National Security Alumni, formed in 1989 in part to stop US covert operations.[58]

All the same, Agee remained drawn to the United States, staying there for over seven months—January 1 through August 5—in 1994.[59] Consistent with that attraction, he did not give up on securing a durable and respectable American legacy—or, if that was not possible, on defending his name. His pursuit of vindication was alacritous. Agee was a ubiquitous and integral panelist in PBS's rollout of its 1994 documentary *The Cold War Remembered, Part 2:*

Historical Perspectives on the KGB. Quite typically, he took a very proactive—not to say pushy—approach to the task, voluntarily reorganizing the discussion outline and adding topics to it.[60] He also became more circumspect, at least in public, about his ideological beliefs. In "America's Continuing Cold War against Cuba," a paper or lecture composed in 1994, he wrote: "Eventually I came to support the Cubans because of their advances in education, health care, and other social programs that are outstanding in the Latin American context."[61] This is a heavily parsed, arguably disingenuous statement, given the likelihood that Agee was lashed up with Cuban intelligence from the early 1970s. Agee found himself whipsawed between the highly limited trajectory of any rehabilitation he might attain in the United States and the prospect of humble rustication as an expat.

A LITIGIOUS SPY

In times of existential uncertainty—which describes much of Agee's post-CIA life—Agee galvanized himself by aggressively challenging those who attacked him. Through Wulf, in September 1994, he filed a civil suit under the Federal Tort Claims Act against the US government, based on the CIA's alleged surveillance and harassment in 1970–74, mainly in the UK, to prevent him from finishing *Inside the Company.*[62] A year later, Agee brought a libel suit against Barbara Bush for channeling in a memoir her husband George H. W. Bush's accusation that Agee had caused CIA Athens Station Chief Richard Welch's death back in 1975.[63] Bush, of course, had been the director of central intelligence when Welch was murdered. For this case, Agee hired as his attorney Lynne Bernabei, a highly respected Washington lawyer who had established something of a specialty in representing whistleblowing US intelligence officers or contractors who had gotten "ground up" in one way or another.[64]

The soured CIA officers she had represented had far more finely parsed grievances than Agee's. In the early 1980s, for instance, Bernabei handled former official CIA historian Jack Pfeiffer's suit against the agency seeking disclosure, via the FOIA, of official historical accounts he had prepared revealing the internal cover-up of responsibility for the catastrophic 1961 Bay of Pigs invasion of Cuba. The legal effort was unsuccessful. In another case, an officer of the now-defunct Maryland National Bank had realized that covert accounts that the CIA had asked him to oversee were illegal money-laundering channels for the benefit of the Nicaraguan *contras* and Angolan rebels; he had demanded written authorization from the agency to protect himself legally. CIA harassment, including threats to his family, caused him to have a nervous breakdown, and Bernabei filed a lawsuit on his behalf against the CIA. A federal magistrate ruled that the case could not proceed due to the risk of exposing state secrets, and Bernabei's appeals failed.

While the federal judiciary used the state secrets doctrine widely to shut down lawsuits against US intelligence agencies during the Obama administration, they had rarely employed it before then. Yet fear of exposing such secrets was the implicit basis for the government's reluctance to criminally indict Agee in the first place. In Bernabei's view, the United States' forbearance from prosecuting Agee, keeping him out of the country by denying his passport, and enjoining further disclosures stifled and cauterized what otherwise would have been spirited public debate about CIA conduct. "There was a lot of sympathy—even within the Agency—for his point of view at the time."[65]

This is a credible if unusual assessment. Bernabei has a decidedly progressive point of view, but for her to have operated so successfully in Washington for decades, she'd have to have sound radar about submerged opinion. And indeed, the upright, principled CIA dissident had been lionized in popular movies like *Three Days of the Condor*, which appeared in 1976, only a year after *Inside the Company*, and starred the presumptively immaculate Robert Redford. But the US government's approach of tainting and isolating Agee had limited the political arc of that kind of portrayal, and the exposure, trial, and conviction of Aldrich Ames in the mid-1990s had squelched the popular cachet of the disaffected spy. The space between Agee's credibility and his iniquity was thus very narrow. But Bernabei judged that a lawsuit by Agee based on agency misrepresentations against a private citizen—here, Barbara Bush—might bear fruit if the relief requested were more palatable than CIA disclosures that might compromise its objective of keeping the lid on Agee's narrative.

Beyond that, Bernabei herself believed in Agee. He had convinced her that the agency had willfully libeled him with respect to Welch's assassination, and, via Morley Safer's *60 Minutes* segment and the government's denial of his passport such that he could not come to the United States to defend himself, railroaded him. Its aim was to salvage a "cheap and dirty cover story" that served to discredit Agee's disquieting revelations about CIA operations and obscure the CIA's heavy-handed conduct and careless security in Greece, which had made Welch vulnerable to assassination. Bernabei doubted Agee's revelations had resulted in harm to any CIA officers. "One, I don't think there were a lot of big surprises about who these people were; two, I don't think it caused any damage to anyone in particular, at least no proven damage. That's why [the CIA and its supporters] are hanging onto this Welch thing: they had to say somebody had gotten hurt because of the revelations, when in fact that couldn't be further from the truth." Finally, she found Agee personally prepossessing and philosophically and behaviorally integrated. "He was a very smart guy, very principled, and hardheaded." From her perspective, "he did the things he did, and he made his life more difficult than it had to be, because he really believed in what he was doing and wanted to undo the harm that he had done when he was working for the CIA."[66]

Bernabei saw his primary aim as setting the historical record straight—he was not responsible for Welch's death—and making it clear that the CIA's blaming him for it was designed to silence him and invalidate his claims about agency operations.[67] But it is clear that his litigation motives were also to an extent mercenary, even if, as she maintains, his desire for a financial payoff was "secondary."[68] This was understandable, given that he had no government pension or tenure at Hamburg University and earned only a modest amount of money from freelance writing and editing. He sought $6 million in damages in the tort action. In a January 1995 letter to a UK solicitor, Agee stated his desire to sue Barbara Bush for "financial damages as high as possible. In this regard, I've seen on the *New York Times* Bestseller list that [her] book was at least 16 weeks on the list, and I wonder if we could claim an amount equal to all her income from the book (even though most was undoubtedly earned in the U.S.) plus more money for the damage to my reputation." He also wanted a public retraction of the passage in question, a public apology, and withdrawal of the book from the market.[69] The federal tort claim was dismissed, which only made Agee more adamant about pressing the libel action. He made a press statement at the National Press Club when the suit was filed, with former CIA officer David McMichael, a whistleblowing client of Bernabei's, offering his own statement in support of Agee.[70] He enlisted the likes of British journalist Christopher Hitchens, a notoriously outspoken maverick who had advised Agee to sue Barbara Bush at the outset of the memoir's publication.[71] The Philip Agee Defense Fund was established for *Agee v. Bush*, and raised about $1,532, much of it from small donors. "Defense Fund," of course, was a bit of a misnomer since Agee, though defending himself against false claims, was not the defendant but rather the plaintiff in the lawsuit.[72]

As sympathetic as Bernabei may have been with Agee's plight, she was also a clear-eyed legal practitioner. Although Agee requested a contingency arrangement, her firm Bernabei & Katz represented him on the basis of hourly fees plus expenses.[73] She rendered measured and prudent legal advice, and she did not hold with using the courts for political crusades that were legally pointless. The First Amendment makes it extraordinarily difficult to make a case for libel in the United States, and Agee's status as a semipublic figure with an already tainted persona made a successful damages claim—which would have to prove loss of reputation—all the more improbable. The actual complaint in *Agee v. Bush* demanded not damages but wide injunctive relief, including an order that Barbara Bush cease and desist from making any future public comments that Agee caused Richard Welch's assassination or that his "book jeopardized the safety of CIA employees *in Europe*."[74] The emphasis is supplied, along with the observation that the geographic limitation of this request for relief to Europe suggests that Bernabei and Agee thought he would be on shakier ground in extending the implied claim that his disclosures had not jeopardized CIA employees elsewhere—in particular, Latin America—and intimated the inherent weaknesses of a case brought by a man many regarded as a traitor.

In March 1997, after a year-and-a-half of litigation, Bernabei suggested to Agee that they propose a modest settlement to Barbara Bush in return for an agreement that Agee would not sue outside the United States—in particular, in the United Kingdom, where it is far easier to win a libel action.[75] Ultimately, the parties merely agreed that Bush would remove the offending allegation from all subsequent editions of the memoir and issue an apology.* It's worth noting that no other public allegations surfaced that Agee's many actual and undisputed public disclosures of CIA officers or assets resulted in their death, injury, or other harm, and to ask why not. His revelations did, of course, crash intelligence networks, impede the careers of intelligence officers, and neutralize other spies. But if the CIA had had good evidence that Agee's disclosures had caused physical harm to officers or agents, it might have done more to bolster the Welch tale by at least discreetly leaking kindred results. Exposed Latin American agents, under the scrutiny of repressive national security apparatuses and lacking access to American protection or the US legal process, would have been especially vulnerable. Even if the agency had chosen not to pursue such claims or publicity to avoid revealing sources and methods in a public legal proceeding—the usual reason—presumably at least some of the officers and assets themselves, especially if retired, not to mention the survivors of any killed, would have tried to sue Agee for an intentional tort or wrongful death had an appreciable number of them been harmed by his disclosures.

---

*Agee also sued George Crile and Grove Atlantic for defamation because the Welch claim and the even more baseless contention that Agee exposed Gust Avrakotos, a CIA operative, appeared in Crile's book *Charlie Wilson's War: The Extraordinary Story of How the Wildest Man in Congress and a Rogue CIA Agent Changed the History of Our Times* (New York: Atlantic Monthly Press, 2003). A similar settlement was reached in 2004. See Agee Papers, box 7, folder 8.

Agee's primal sin—burning officers and agents—might have been forgotten had it not been for his ongoing taunts to the CIA through his dalliances with the Cuban DGI, and, at least by association, the KGB. One 1983 assessment settles on casting Agee as "an open ally of the KGB."[76] Such characterizations were useful to Agee: they copper-fastened the infamy and afforded him the kind of street-cred and danger quotient that ultimately secured his legacy as an authentic dissident. As far as Opperskalski—a highly partisan Agee supporter—is concerned, while Agee was "emotionally attached to the Cuban experiment" and "admired Cuba's resistance," the notion that he was closely run by even the DGI, let alone the KGB, is a "myth."[77] But suspicions have been understandably durable. Certainly Agee maintained his connections with Cuba fully aware that the CIA and the FBI would infer a relationship between him and the DGI and target him for surveillance and investigation.

It is practically undeniable that the DGI, Cuba's intelligence service, facilitated Agee's revelations by allowing him to work on *Inside the Company* for those several months in Havana, with access to documentary materials, in 1971. Agee also openly admitted to being in contact with Cuban embassy officials in London in the early to mid-1970s, without volunteering whether they were intelligence officers. The harder questions are whether Agee continued to maintain active contact with the DGI while in exile mainly in Hamburg, and, beyond that, whether the KGB insinuated itself into what would have begun as the DGI's play. The Cold War–era conceit was that the intelligence services of Soviet "satellites or surrogates" were "extensions (intimacy depending on the country) of Soviet state security."[78] But the relationship between the KGB and the DGI, at least, was more complicated, as the latter resisted subordination to the former despite its increasing material dependence on it.

The most comprehensive and objective unclassified source on the DGI is the book *Castro's Secrets*, by former CIA analyst Brian Latell. Latell quotes a retired CIA Cuba expert as casting the DGI as "the best intelligence service in the world." Glenn Carle, among other CIA veterans, agrees with that assessment.[79] Based on his own experience as an intelligence officer and interviews with several Cuban defectors—in particular, Florentino Aspillaga Lombard, the most highly decorated among them—Latell takes the view that a perennially underrated DGI outmaneuvered the CIA virtually from the time Castro took over in 1959 nearly until the end of the Cold War in 1987.[80]

He is confident that Agee did not work for the DGI before he left the CIA. He is equally confident that the DGI recruited Agee (along with former CIA officer Frank Terpil and another he does not name) after he left the agency, and that Agee shared secrets about CIA sources and methods, provided expert advice, and may have served as a spotter or bait in DGI operations against the CIA. Latell adds that the three worked for the DGI for "extended periods," and that Agee did "considerably more damage" than the unnamed defector, though it was he, not Agee, whom the DGI pampered with a deluxe guest villa. As for corroboration, Latell notes that Soviet defector Oleg Kalugin, a former KGB major general and counterintelligence chief, said that Agee approached the KGB in Mexico City in the early 1970s after leaving the CIA but was spurned as too risky a recruit; Agee then turned to the DGI. But Aspillaga gets the last word in Latell's account: Agee worked only for the Cubans, "never for the Soviets."[81]

The conventional wisdom within the US intelligence community, too, is that Agee was a Cuban asset but not directly a KGB one.[82] The FBI conducted at least three investigations of Agee's activities—one in 1978–79, in the wake of the publication of *Inside the Company*, and two in the early to mid-1990s. During this period, the US government was not formally hostile or especially vindictive toward Agee. For instance, while the State Department repeatedly denied his applications for a passport, it did grant him the official US identification card required for him to maintan his residency in West Germany (later Germany) and routinely extended him one-time authorizations for round trips between Europe and the United States.[83] Yet he had obtained a Cuban passport in October 1990, and in 1991 and

1992 apparently managed to travel on a bogus passport issued by the World Service Authority—a protest organization that advocated world citizenship and issued documents that were not considered valid by any government.[84] The increased frequency and duration of his visits to Cuba and a source's information that Agee wittingly worked for the DGI prompted the latter probes.[85] A source also raised concerns that Agee's lecture tours to US college campuses suggested that he was recruiting American students to work for Cuban intelligence, though it is not clear how seriously the FBI took those concerns.[86] In conjunction with the first of the two later investigations, the FBI issued a yearlong "lookout notice" (also known as a "stop") commencing on February 27, 1992 to the Immigration and Naturalization Service (INS) listing several known aliases and instructing the INS to obtain as much information as possible from Agee's passport or other documentation, to determine his destination in the United States and his port of entry and departure, and glean any other useful information, without detaining Agee or "causing undue delay or suspicion" even though the bureau understood that Agee might be traveling on a World Service Authority passport.[87] In early April 1992, a reliable source told the FBI that Agee would be flying from Hamburg to Miami on such a passport and later proceeding from Miami to Havana.[88]

The FBI learned from a human asset that Agee was "aware that DGI, section Q-13 operations against the CIA and FBI were being financed by the KGB." Section Q-13 is the DGI counterintelligence unit, working exclusively against the CIA and the FBI, that would have been primarily responsible for handling Agee. At the same time, the "asset stated that once Agee was recruited he let it be known that he did not want to work with the Russians."[89] At that point anyway, direct KGB collaboration appeared to be a red line that Agee would not cross. In the FBI's view, "Agee knew, however, that his work represented a joint DGI/KGB effort."[90] The FBI's New York field office, tasked because Agee usually entered the United States through New York and was using a New York apartment at 55 Cooper Street, had earlier linked him to an individual who had tendered a credit card traceable to the Cuban Mission of the United Nations and the DGI's former New York station chief. In December 1992, New York special agents, lightly undercover, monitored him giving a speech at the Movement for a People's Assembly about various CIA excesses, including alleged attempts to assassinate him.[91] The New York office concluded that "prosecution of Agee is still a viable alternative, with the cooperation of the CIA."

In the course of the investigation, the FBI also lodged worries, based on information given by a defector, that Agee was assisting the Puerto Rican terrorist group Ejercito Popular Boricua-Macheteros. While it did "not appear to New York . . . that much more about the CIA could be revealed by Agee than he has already revealed," the FBI's New York field office felt that "the absence of prosecutive action against Agee establishes a bad precedent" and registered its view that "Agee's activities are within the scope of prosecution for treason."[92] The Justice Department and the CIA, however, still showed no interest in prosecuting Agee, and the FBI closed the investigation in late 1993.[93]

Yet Agee kept coming up in the ordinary course of the FBI's counterintelligence business. In September 1994, the FBI's New York office opened a preliminary inquiry regarding Agee, based on the debriefing of Cuban defectors who claimed that a recent female defector had been a DGI officer and one of Agee's handlers.[94] Given the new information, the New York office was eager to pursue the investigation of Agee for espionage, and its request for a full investigation was granted in November 1994.[95] The CIA cooperated, but rather circumspectly; it had also been guarded in its liaison with the FBI in the 1980s—from which no investigation resulted—at least in part over concerns about protecting CIA agents' identities.[96] By August 1995, the investigation had progressed to the point where FBI New York was planning a sting operation against Agee.[97] While this apparently was never carried out, the bureau maintained an aggressive posture—for example, objecting in writing to the UK's readmitting Agee after he had been barred from the country for almost twenty years.[98]

In 1994, Kalugin had published a book in which he claimed that Agee had offered the KGB "reams of information on CIA operations" in Mexico City in 1973.[99] Kalugin's representations about Agee intrigued the FBI, which rated them "persuasive," obtained authorization to interview Kalugin, and did so.[100] The results of the interview remain classified, but by inference did not strengthen the case for treason against Agee sufficiently to convince the Justice Department and the CIA to move forward with prosecution. In November 1996, the FBI's New York office closed the renewed investigation, having been "unable to detect subject as being involved in any intelligence activities on behalf of any foreign intelligence service."[101]

In the larger context of Soviet-Cuban relations, it certainly makes sense that Agee was a witting DGI asset, but one who tacitly understood that the DGI and KGB often worked jointly while consciously spurning involvement with the KGB. On balance, it appears unlikely that Agee was tasked by the Soviets with his knowledge, but the available information does require careful parsing. There is no solid, publicly available evidence that the KGB cultivated and recruited him while he was a case officer, although that was reportedly a pet theory of the famously skeptical CIA counterintelligence chief James Angleton, whom Philby had deceived and rendered effectively paranoid. According to Edward Jay Epstein, Angleton believed Agee was recruited in Montevideo during his tour as a CIA case officer there from 1964 to 1966 by a Soviet KGB colonel named Semenov, who purportedly arranged Agee's handling by the DGI to afford the KGB "a modicum of distance."[102] But Agee had duly reported his contact with Semenov to his superiors and credibly explained it as standard spycraft.[103]

In 1999, however, long-serving KGB archivist Vasili Mitrokhin, who had defected to the United Kingdom in 1992, with Cambridge professor Christopher Andrew published *The Sword and the Shield: The Mitrokhin Archive and the Secret History of the KGB*. In the book, which distills the private notes on KGB files that Mitrokhin brought with him into narrative form, Andrew and Mitrokhin say that Agee was in fact a recruited Soviet agent, code-named PONT. Characterizing him as "the CIA's first defector" and quoting Kalugin, they indicate Soviet counterintelligence officers rejected Agee's offer of "reams of information about CIA operations" in Mexico City as a probable trap (a "dangle" in trade-speak) because it was "too good to be true." Then, claim Andrew and Mitrokhin, again citing Kalugin, Agee successfully peddled the information to Cuban intelligence.[104] Up to this point, their story jibes with Aspillaga's by way of Latell, and with Kalugin's. According to Murray Seeger, William Colby told him the same story in a 1974 interview on background, somewhat cryptically describing Agee as a "strange case."[105]

Andrew and Mitrokhin added that the DGI in turn shared Agee's intelligence with the KGB. According to KGB files, the two services together then, in effect, ran Agee, jointly preparing and vetting the text of *Inside the Company*. The temporal proximity of Agee's visits to the Cuban embassy in London and his trip to Moscow constitutes some circumstantial support for the proposition that the DGI and the KGB coordinated his handling. Opperskalski, for what it's worth, considers Mitrokhin, who died in 2004, a peddler of "disinformation" and "serious bullshit."[106] In any case, Mitrokhin and Andrew conceded that the KGB files from which their account was derived were "self-congratulatory" and that their representations were cast "doubtless with some exaggeration." And even those files, while describing Agee as an agent of the DGI and detailing his alleged collaboration with the KGB, did not explicitly characterize him as a KGB agent.[107] They did assert that while Agee was writing the book in the UK, the KGB maintained contact with him through a Russian reporter and prevailed upon him to remove all references to CIA penetration of Latin American communist parties.[108] In a subsequent book, though, they admitted that they neglected to get Agee to omit the names of several CIA assets listed in the notorious appendix—among them Mexican President Luis Echeverria Alvarez— whom the KGB was in fact trying to turn.[109] This rather flagrant error suggests that KGB oversight could not have been too tight or direct, if it existed at all.

In any case, Agee was not the most egregious of turncoats in the annals of US intelligence. Robert Hanssen, a senior FBI counterintelligence officer arrested in 2001, probably did the most harm, having sold thousands of classified documents to the Glavnoye Razvedyvatel'noye Upravleniye, or GRU, the Soviet/Russian military intelligence agency; the KGB; and its post-Soviet successor over the course of twenty-two years for roughly $1.4 million. Among CIA officers, the most damaging was Aldrich Ames. He was a true mole, and Agee's case warrants comparison to his. Ames was an erratic but ostensibly successful career CIA operations officer, but he was also a heavy drinker who'd undergone an expensive divorce and had an extremely extravagant second wife. Though miffed at what he considered inadequate promotion, Ames became a KGB agent for primarily mercenary reasons. He operated as an agent in place while working mainly in CIA counterintelligence from 1983 to 1994, when he was arrested following a long CIA and FBI investigation focused on his personal spending.[110]

Agee himself was keenly interested in Ames. Agee's papers contain copies of FBI search warrants for Ames's possessions and his public statement of April 29, 1994.[111] That statement included the following justification:

> First, I had come to dissent from the decades-long shift to the extreme right in our political spectrum and from our national security and foreign policies.
>
> Second, I had come to believe that the espionage business, as carried out by the CIA and a few other American agencies, was a self-serving sham, carried out by careerist bureaucrats who have managed to deceive several generations of American policymakers and the public about both the necessity and the value of their work.

While self-serving insofar as they seek to dignify Ames's treachery, these claims are also probably genuine given that, psychologically, he couldn't have done what he did had he not lost faith in the American project and the means of and rationale for defending it. Without doubt Agee would have validated Ames's contentions about the political shift and the CIA's dysfunctional nature. But he also would have sussed out that in Ames's case they served conveniently as cover for greed.

The price Ames extracted came to what the US agencies assessed was $2.5 million ($4.6 million according to the KGB) over the course of nine years, much of it spent while he was in the employ and under the scrutiny of the CIA. While working for the CIA, Ames tore down the CIA's Soviet-bloc network of agents by covertly passing their identities to the KGB. Some were executed. Agee did not appear at all affluent or even terribly comfortable financially while he was in the CIA or after he left. Indeed, if Agee's motives had been truly venal, he would have stayed in the agency, parceled out the names of CIA agents and fronts piecemeal and privately to Cuban or Soviet case officers, and exacted payment each time, as Ames did.[112] In fact, Agee enjoyed little if any net material gain from his turn, he waited until well after he had resigned to cross the giddy line, and it remains unlikely and certainly unproven that any of the agents he exposed were killed. The KGB's handling of Ames also suggests that, had it been deeply and directly involved in recruiting and running Agee before he left the CIA, it would have urged him to stay in place and thrown money at him.

Insofar as a juxtaposition of the two cases reflects less avarice and cynicism and more ideological purity on Agee's part, it helps explain why Agee refrained from stoking any inference of equivalency or even comparability between himself and Ames. Preserving the distinction, of course, was a pyrrhic victory: if Ames was the more squalid character for having only been in the treason business for the money, Agee was arguably the geopolitically more dangerous one for having been ideologically motivated in his treachery.

David Corn, for his part, has settled for agnosticism as to whether Agee was an agent of any foreign intelligence agency. Such a stance he finds analytically adequate, as it seems to him unnecessary to form a judgment one way or the other. The psychological, moral, and political reasons Agee himself offers

would be sufficient, in the course of human events, to motivate him to do what he did. I'm not saying that proves he wasn't an agent. But to me his story is perfectly believable. I'm not saying it's 100 percent accurate, but it's perfectly believable that he did what he did because of the reasons that he stated. To a degree, it doesn't really matter whether he was run by the Cubans or not. The only way it matters is that it gives them bragging rights; what he did was still the same. And even if he was being run by the Cubans, he was probably doing it for the same reasons that he has publicly stated. I don't think he did it because the Cubans gave him millions of dollars that we don't know about. He didn't follow the path of a Philby.[113]

Naturally the KGB exploited the sensational publication of *Inside the Company* in 1975—it became a bestseller—and rejoiced at the unprecedented degree of political embarrassment and operational compromise it visited on the CIA. And, as Andrew and Mitrokhin recount, the KGB may well have helped choreograph the establishment of the *Covert Action Information Bulletin*. But Agee himself emphatically dismissed as predictable disinformation allegations that he consciously collaborated with the KGB. Andrew and Mitrokhin also testify to the DGI's hemispheric operational independence from the KGB—noting, for instance, that "[i]n Latin America, the KGB found itself—somewhat to its irritation—being upstaged by its Cuban ally, the DGI."[114] In a 1999 conference styled "U.S. Intelligence and the End of the Cold War" at Texas A&M University, recounted in a transcript released by the CIA under FOIA, Paul Redmond, an ex-CIA station chief, remarked that the KGB had merely shown "support for the likes of Agee." Kalugin himself was in attendance, and he did not challenge Redmond's characterization. Furthermore, when asked by former CIA Director James Woolsey to expand on the CIA–KGB defector "scorecard," Kalugin specifically mentioned Ames, Harold Nicolson, and Edwin Moore, but not Agee.[115]

Agee evidently had to scramble perpetually for money—hence the multiplicity of book deals, some notional and redundant, and his willingness to publish in just about any periodical that would air his views. Material support from the KGB might have made this indiscriminateness unnecessary and enabled Agee to target more reputable outlets. But he did have an ongoing relationship with the DGI, stretching back to 1971. For much of its duration, the connection may have been logistically veiled and finessed, and operationally passive and even dormant, such that he did not actively work for the DGI. Even so, there is little room for doubt that the relationship was clear and witting, and that Agee, merely by virtue of settling in Cuba in the 1990s, took advantage of the bona fides he had earned long before.

BACK TO THE FRINGE

The Bush lawsuit appeared to have scant net effect on Agee's public reputation, and the FBI's stand-down likewise scarcely absolved him. The larger US intelligence community still nurtured the presumption that Agee was complicit in Welch's death and continued to work for the Cubans. But the legal contest did keep him in the news. All the while, Agee continued to cultivate a modest following among Hollywood liberals. He worked as a technical consultant for the Tom Cruise film *Mission: Impossible* in 1995.[116] He participated in a documentary film called *Under the Flag*, which arrayed the views of eight dissident former CIA officers—Verne Lyon, Marita Lorenz, David MacMichael, Phil Roettinger, Mary Embree, Diane Kuntz, Ralph McGehee, and Agee himself—and coexecutive-produced by Richard Linklater, who was becoming a celebrated A-list director. He and others hosted a fundraiser for the film in Beverly Hills in October 1996, to which Agee was invited.[117]

While Agee's concern about his image seemed to reflect a durable cultural affinity for the United States, whatever its faults, his competing hostility to US policy and affection for Cuba did not appear to diminish. At Hamburg University, he burnished his credibility and left-wing cachet by flaunting his opposition to official American conduct. In a seminar lecture entitled "Nationalism as a 'Communist Threat' and Military Dictatorship as a Solution: Iran, Guatemala, and Indonesia," Agee bragged that student militants had seized CIA documents during the 1979 takeover of the US embassy in Tehran as the shah was overthrown, reconstituted shredded documents, and published them, "over thirty volumes of which I have on my library shelves."[118] Among the documents were the US naval attaché's fitness evaluation and records relating to commercial shipments of goods, such as spare parts for the Iranian Air Force.[119] But Agee acknowledged the CIA's efficacy on its own terms. In the same lecture, he noted that the CIA "achieved notable successes" in replacing un-desired governments with more cooperative ones in the 1950s.[120]

Agee's files of open-source publications on Cuba—others with more sensitive material may have been seized by the CIA and FBI—include an August 1994 Inter Press Service (IPS) article focused on US economic and anti-immigration policy that contained heavy handwritten annotations and underlinings by Agee. Judging by their content, Agee could have been contemplating his own prospective travel business in Cuba. He highlighted licensing requirements, Guantanamo-based American activities, and the possibility of an end to the trade embargo.[121] Certainly he was feeling less shackled. With the Cold War over and past ructions smoothed over, Agee was allowed back into the UK in 1995 and returned there for a visit, dining with the Anglo-Pakistani international activist Tariq Ali and other *New Left Review* people. He also went to the House of Commons for a "welcome back."[122] A couple of years later, in May 1997, Agee would fax Robin Cook, the UK Foreign Secretary, whom he knew, to congratulate him on the Labour Party's victory in the general election and thank him for opposing Agee's deportation in 1977.[123] This qualified reentry into polite diplomatic society, however, did not blunt Agee's resentment toward the CIA or his disapproval of the agency. In his 1995 applica-tion to Hamburg University for research funding, he indicated that while the CIA had redacted relevant documents in responding to his FOIA request in the early 1980s, the documents nonetheless revealed that there was some kind of criminal government conspiracy against Agee, and that in the early 1990s two unconnected former CIA officers told him that this conspiracy involved a plot to assassinate him.[124] This might have been a ploy to win funding, as years earlier he had not stressed the personal physical threats he faced.

In "The CIA's War Against Ché Guevara," written in 1997, Agee said: "To those who say now that Ché was merely an adventurer, I say: consider how much he was feared by the CIA."[125] Agee might well have been alluding to his own status as someone the agency denigrated yet secretly feared. In any case, Guevara—and, by exten-sion, Cuba—remained central to Agee's self-image and his iden-tity as an effective and pertinent dissident. In the early 1990s, he wrote an introduction to an ultimately unpublished biography of Guevara. It is a first-person account, typical of Agee in its ostensible candor and consistent with his earlier accounts, and it sheds some additional light on the psychological pathway of Agee's ideological turn. More than twenty years on, he notes that he resigned from the agency even though he was in line for a promotion at Mexico City station. While he had then developed qualms about CIA activities, he says it was his (American) lover's disgust with them that was determinative in his decision to resign. But they did not stay together, and it was in the aftermath of their breakup that Agee developed the idea of writing the massive exposé that would become *Inside the Company*. The picture these circumstances suggests is that of a man who sacrificed a rising career for a relationship that ultimately didn't pan out, now needing and seeking independent justification for that sacrifice to afford it lasting personal legitimacy. Agee took special note of how much strength he had drawn from his solidarity with Che Guevara's supporters.[126]

More ominously, in October 1997, James Risen—then a reporter with the *Los Angeles Times*—published an article reporting CIA allegations that Agee acted as a field agent for Cuban intelligence in Mexico City in 1989. According to Risen's sources, Agee posed as a CIA Inspector General staffer at the CIA station there and attempted to get information from a female support employee; although she reported the contact and two operations officers tried to build a case against him, they neglected to involve the FBI and Agee was able to abort the effort before US agencies could develop sufficient evidence to have him apprehended and prosecuted. In their book about Aldrich Ames, Sandy Grimes and Jeanne Vertefeuille—two of the CIA counterintelligence officers who ferreted him out—confirmed that Agee had made this "false flag" approach, which was one of the episodes that had distracted CIA counterspies from the task of getting to the bottom of the agent attrition in the Soviet space ultimately traced to Ames's treachery. They added that Agee had shown the employee a fake letter from William Webster, then the director of central intelligence, requesting her cooperation, that he had said he was looking into the possible use of official agency pouches to smuggle narcotics, that the CIA employee had identified him from a photograph, and that the FBI had connected a contact address in New York that Agee had given her with a Cuban intelligence officer.[127]

In response to Risen's inquiries, Agee sent him a fax from Hamburg in which he denied he was a Cuban agent and offered theories as to why the CIA was disseminating such disinformation—mainly, he said, to compromise Agee's then-pending tort suit against the United States government for illegal acts to impede the publication of *Inside the Company*. Agee had been in Cuba in July 1997 for an international student festival, and he admitted his solidarity with the Cuban people and opposition to US policies with respect to Cuba.[128] In 2000, Pedro Riera Escalante, a disaffected former senior DGI officer then seeking asylum in Mexico, provided Mexican officials with a document detailing operations he had run over the previous thirty years. The Mexico City newspaper *Reforma* published excerpts from that document. They indicated that Riera had first handled Agee in 1973, as liaison between Agee and the Cuban Politburo. He had supposedly communicated the DGI's ideas about what Agee should write in *Inside the Company* and had thereafter worked with him on and off for years. Riera obtained useful phone numbers of CIA officials stationed in Mexico City from Agee, and he ran an operation code-named "Moncado" in which Agee had tried to recruit the CIA deputy station chief in Mexico City.[129] The episode reported by Risen would have been part of Moncado.

As a matter of common sense, however, Agee's denials seem credible: having proven his general utility to the Cubans for years while narrowly avoiding criminal liability, it would have been foolishly reckless for either Agee himself or any DGI handlers to have risked his incarceration or even his further exposure—and for a notorious CIA turncoat to pose as a senior CIA officer at the very station where he had resigned would have been a truly outsized gamble. It did not scan with Agee's demonstrated instinct for self-preservation and aptitude for pragmatic calibration. Furthermore, Riera's document, at least as it pertains to Agee, warrants considerable skepticism. Riera was desperate to get asylum and therefore motivated to provide striking intelligence. But he could have merely conjured the information in the document from accepted inferences and open-source material. That Agee had established links to Cuban intelligence while writing the book was obvious and had long been assumed; Agee had promulgated CIA telephone numbers in publicly available periodicals until legally barred from doing so in 1980; and Risen had made the alleged penetration of the Mexico City station public knowledge. Perhaps unsurprisingly, the Mexican government rejected Riera's application for asylum and deported him back to Cuba.

In any case, Agee's enthusiasm for intrigue would have been winding down. By the mid-1990s, Agee's datebook entries had become sparser and less frequent. They impart a sense of exhaustion. He had long experienced high blood pressure but was able to manage it with standard prescription medication. Over the course of 1997–98, Agee's doctor appointments and medicine purchases became more frequent. In February 1998, he was trying Zyban, a drug used to suppress the urge to smoke and, less commonly, to treat depression. Later that year, he was diagnosed with prostate cancer. He underwent treatment at UKE Orthoped Klinik in Hamburg and ultimately successful surgery and radiation at the University Medical Center Hamburg-Eppendorf—the teaching hospital of Hamburg University.[130] He also had a successful operation for an aneurysm.

In his 1999 datebook, however, there was a noticeable deterioration in his handwriting, which was customarily neat and elegant, and he lagged in delivering on standing projects. One was a point-of-view history of the Cold War. Earlier in the decade, Agee had prepared several undated chapter manuscripts, with supporting research materials, on big geopolitical and ideological Cold War issues—for example, "The Real Meaning of Containment," "Vietnam: Everything for a Lost Cause," and "Rollback, Not Just Containment."[131] Judging by the minimal degree of scrutiny it exercised after Agee began complying with Judge Gesell's injunction in the early 1980s, the CIA would not have censored such a manuscript much if it all. Yet Agee appeared to make no effort to sell the manuscript, and no book was ever published. Agee seemed to be running out of gas.

8

Posterity for a Traitor

Tired as he was, it was not Agee's wont to fade away too quietly. In fact, as the new millennium dawned, he seemed to recover some of his vigor and health. Official US passivity about his activities might have caused Agee to let down his guard: the FBI as of November 1996 had closed its investigations. Agee, in turn, made Cuba his main domicile and intensified those activities. He started an online travel agency, Cubalinda—"beautiful Cuba"—in Havana in 1999, having obtained his own domain and established an e-mail address (reservations@reservations.cubalinda). The business technically violated the long-standing US embargo of Cuba. To start up Cubalinda, he had no funds of his own on hand but rather withdrew $175,000 from a $600,000 trust set up by his father, Bill Agee, for distribution among Agee and his two sons.[1] Other notable American exiles in Cuba had received financial support from the Castro government.[2] Agee's succor to the regime—whether as a mere propagandist or as a recruited and managed agent—was more substantial than that of most of them. In all likelihood, Agee himself got at least a small stipend. Certainly he availed himself of Cuban sanctuary, and he did not bite the hand that fed him: he publicly extolled the Cuban model, including its health care system, high literacy, and ideal of social equality, while staying silent about its grinding poverty, lack of free speech, and martial governance.[3] To his idiosyncratic way of thinking, relocating to Cuba was perhaps a way of getting closer to his true homeland—the United States—while maintaining his revolutionary vocation.

He felt secure and comfortable enough to post several comments to an online message board for his 1958 Air Force Officer Candidate School graduating class. Gordon Brymer had registered some sympathy for him, remarking in November 1999 that he could "come incognito as Guest Speaker to the next reunion. Before one has any preconceived notions about Agee I suggest they read his works first."[4] In February 2000, another classmate, retired Air Force Colonel Edward Callicotte, "knowing that a particular government agency would like to get their hands on you," allowed that he found it improbable that "the real Phil Agee" would use his real name in an e-mail address. He therefore presented the suspicious interlocutor with an identity test based mainly on OCS experiences and Agee's personal background.

By any fair measure, Agee passed it. Having acknowledged, with perhaps wishful understatement, that some classmates "may disapprove" of the choices he'd made, he also provided Callicotte with an explanation for his openness about his location and activities. "Those guys you mentioned don't bother me a bit," he wrote. "I spent 25 years touring with a high profile including 10 doing hundreds of lectures at universities, churches, civic centers, etc. in the States. For many reasons they couldn't take action and they still can't." He was open about his son Chris's forthcoming visit to Cuba—he was sailing from Florida, and Agee was meeting him at Hemingway Marina—and even bold enough to promote the impending launch of Cubalinda: "We're going public on Wednesday with a press release so you may see something in the media there." He remained cheerfully defiant. "For all I know," he said in a subsequent post, "they'll indict me in Washington under the Trading With the Enemy Act."[5]

Within a year, journalists had gotten wind of his audacious rustication. Tracey Eaton of the *Dallas Morning News* tracked him down and wrote a profile, quoting him as saying: "It's been a life of turmoil in a way but one that's been very satisfying. Very reassuring."[6]

In 2001, he traveled more than he had in the previous couple of years, renewed his focus, and regained his neat handwriting. He and Giselle gradually moved their primary home to a Cuban apartment while retaining their flat in Hamburg and returning there periodically. He continued to defend the status he felt he had earned as a principled dissident as opposed to a sniveling traitor. In a letter to CNN dated December 2000, he confronted the network with respect to a broadcast erroneously claiming that he was responsible for Welch's death, and he demanded corrective action.[7] He had long harbored plans to relocate semipermanently to Cuba. However subdued he might have intended the move to be, it was inherently provocative for a notorious Cold War–era American turncoat to make it, and it was bound to attract the attention of the CIA as well as the press.

Yet his selective reputational rehabilitation among mainstream Americans continued: in March 2003 he hosted some faculty from the Massachusetts Institute of Technology's Sloan School of Management in Havana and received a plaque of appreciation.[8] Cubalinda also helped arrange visits to Cuba by Jerry Brown in 2000, when he was mayor of Oakland, and later by Jimmy Carter and other officials of the Carter Center, arguably in violation of US law.[9] Brown was apparently ignorant of Agee's background and was predictably maligned for making the trip itself as well as the connection with Agee.[10] It could not have been lost on either Carter or Agee that Agee's passport had been revoked during the Carter administration.

TWILIGHT MUSINGS

Agee had in mind a long retirement, and, however unrealistically, one in which he might finally be welcomed back to the United States without legal impediment or anxiety. By way of a letter dated June 13, 2005, to the US Interests Section, Consular Section, Citizenship Affairs, Embassy of Switzerland, in Havana, he again applied for a US passport on the grounds that "allegations made in *Haig v. Agee* do not now apply" and that his activities were no longer causing "serious damage to the national security and foreign policy of the United States." He stated candidly that he had lived at Rehm Strasse 18B,

22299 Hamburg, Germany, from 1978 to 2005; that he had shown proof of US citizenship to the US Consul General in Hamburg and registered therewith; that he was temporarily to reside in Havana until August 5, 2005; that his US passport was revoked in December 1979; and that the US Supreme Court had upheld that revocation in *Haig v. Agee* on June 29, 1981. He provided a telephone number in Hamburg and an e-mail address.[11]

That Agee would unabashedly flout US policy by living in Havana— temporarily or not—and request the restoration of his US passport meets the definition of chutzpah. It could not be mere obtuseness: it is not credible that he, having been well around the block with the US government at multiple levels, was simply naive about its institutional memory and vindictiveness. Most likely the US intelligence community was continuing to look at Agee as a possible Cuban or Soviet asset. Many of the pages of his 2001 datebook were removed, and his 2002, 2003, and 2005 datebooks are missing in their entirety, all apparently confiscated by the CIA and the FBI. They probably regarded the datebook entries as probative with respect to Agee's espionage activities. None of the 2004 datebook is missing, but the entries in it are extremely sparse.[12] Agee likely knew the passport request would be denied and was simply following his old stratagem of absorbing US bureaucratic resources in order to strain, in his own little way, their capacity.

From 2004 on, he and Giselle lived mainly in Cuba, at 159 Calle E, Esquina Linea, Vedado, on one of downtown Havana's main drags. Of the two, she spent more time in Hamburg, as she still had professional ballet commitments. His lifestyle was considerably more modest than the one he enjoyed in Hamburg. His apartment was a fourth-floor walk-up connected to the street by a dark stairwell with a rusty banister, the ancient elevator long kaput. It did include a study piled with material on international affairs and intelligence, most of which later made its way to the library at New York University. He drove a ten-year-old Russian Lada. Shopping at a local market, he stood in line with paper bags to buy vegetables along with his Cuban neighbors and requested no luxuries from outside visitors save for back issues of the *New Yorker*.[13] When Giselle had to return to Europe from Cuba to teach a course, she got Agee a kitten to keep him company. He was initially ambivalent, but by the time she returned two months later he had grown fond of the pet and rescued two more kittens from the streets of Havana, prompting a nearby family to dub him "Cat Man."[14]

The motivation for Agee's emigration certainly was not an improved quality of life; only political conviction and a desire for a legacy that squared with his actions could have driven him. When in Cuba, Agee did not blanch at taking public positions at odds with US policy. A paper he presented at a conference in Havana in October 2004 was titled "United States Policies for the Manipulation of Foreign Civil Societies as Applied in Cuba." It targeted mainly the National Endowment for Democracy (NED), the propaganda and inducement program rolled out during the Reagan administration.[15] Styled as a democracy promotion initiative, it had drawn bipartisan support (as a means of advancing rollback against the Soviets) and opposition (as a wasteful boondoggle). The program emphasized five activities: (1) leadership training; (2) education; (3) strengthening institutions of democracy; (4) conveying ideas and information; and (5) development of personal and institutional ties. Agee believed that the NED was ripe for CIA covert manipulation.[16] There he was in the early twenty-first century, as he had been in the 1970s: a leading heckler from a vituperative and improbably dedicated peanut gallery.

The previous August, he had traveled from Cuba to Venezuela, which since 1998 had been ruled by Hugo Chavez, the left-wing populist ideologically aligned with Fidel Castro and Sandinista leader Daniel Ortega.[17] He was apparently working on a book about the CIA's activities there.[18] During this period, Agee had no passport that either Cuban or Venezuelan consular authorities would have routinely honored, suggesting that the two governments facilitated such trips at a higher level. In May 2006, Agee contacted someone named "Ortega" and met this person in Caracas in July.[19] This might conceivably have been Daniel Ortega, who, as leader of the Sandinistas, had long been a socialist revolutionary, had led Nicaragua from 1979 to 1990, enjoyed Chavez's generous support, and would again be elected president of Nicaragua the following November. Agee had been backing a winner since the early 1980s.

Casually, at least, he continued to court radicalism and celebrity, his datebooks indicating appointments with John Pilger, the crusading lefty journalist from the UK, in 2006, and with Michael Winterbottom, the British film director, in 2007.[20] In Europe, Claudio Fava, a Sicilian member of the European Parliament, headed a commission that conducted an official Parliament-funded investigation of the CIA's extraordinary renditions—that is, transporting detained terrorist suspects for questioning in secret prisons in countries that afford them no civil rights protections—and issued a public report condemning the practice and calling for the closure of the interrogation and detention facility at the American military base at Guantanamo Bay, Cuba. In hearings leading up to the report's release, the commission promulgated detailed logs of hundreds of CIA rendition flights through European airspace, registration and other identifying information on twenty-five of the civilian airplanes that the CIA used, and the names of shell companies set up by the agency as cover for the renditions. The American conservative writer Kenneth Timmerman aptly called Fava "the ghost of Philip Agee," even if Agee wasn't dead yet.[21]

His bid for a US passport, unsurprisingly, met disappointment. On Groundhog Day, 2007, he received a letter from the Assistant Secretary of State for Consular Affairs denying the request based on the applicant's failure to carry burden of proof that the *Haig v. Agee* allegations—namely, damage to US national security and foreign policy—no longer applied and citing as support for this decision Agee's continued unauthorized dissemination of material related to the CIA.[22] This disposition seems at best ill-informed, probably disingenuous, and possibly vindictive: for over twenty-five years Agee had been substantially complying with Judge Gesell's order requiring him to vet published materials through the CIA.

The adverse news began what would be the last year of Agee's life. He was characteristically resilient and didn't let it get him down. Based firmly in Cuba, Agee spent significant portions of that year in Ireland, giving a well-publicized lecture titled "Blowing the Lid on the US War on Terror" over the course of a week in late March and early April at Queens University in Belfast, Trinity College in Dublin, and Galway Town Hall. Several years earlier, he had published an article impugning the CIA's orchestration of terrorism against Cuba.[23] Stateside, he had pushed for the release of the "Cuban Five," five Cuban intelligence agents arrested by US authorities in Miami in 1998. All had been convicted on espionage and related charges for activities aimed at undermining US-based terrorist operations against Cuba and sentenced to long prison terms. The entire judicial process was criticized as unfair by the United Nations Commission on Human Rights and Amnesty International. Agee's agitation had caught on with labor unions and human-rights groups and fueled the Five's legal appeals. In the lecture, his immediate aim was to illuminate the cover that the post-9/11 counterterrorism mobilization had afforded the United States in skirting civil liberties and thus to bring attention to injustices visited on the Cuban Five. He also wanted to promote *One Man's Story: Philip Agee, Cuba, and the CIA*, a short documentary about how US efforts to subvert the Cuban government had influenced his thinking and actions, coproduced by Bernie Dwyer, an Irish journalist and filmmaker who had also advocated the release of the Cuban Five.[24] Her film had been featured at the Havana Film Festival in December 2006.

Agee, though he had been buffeted by health problems, appeared to have no concrete notion that his life was drawing to a close. In January 2007, British journalist Duncan Campbell interviewed him in Hamburg and published a feature on him in the *Guardian*, recounting his life in the thirty-plus years since the publication of *Inside the Company* and affirming that the ideological shift that prompted it had held:

> If the CIA were hoping that age would mellow Agee, they were wrong. I had last seen him nearly 30 years ago at his farewell party in London as he said his reluctant goodbyes to what had become a large and vocal defence campaign. He wept on the ferry that took him away from Britain as he contemplated what the future might hold for him and his family, and you wondered how he would survive. But he re-

mains as committed as ever, and busy working on another book, this time about the CIA's activities in Venezuela over the years. "I never stopped what I started in London," he says, "and I don't expect to stop till I'm dead."[25]

A couple of months later, Agee himself published a passionate op-ed about Cuba, also in the *Guardian*. He argued that "the wave of progressive change sweeping Latin America and the Caribbean" was following Cuba's lead, noting that the United States and its allies had systematically punished Cuba for its political vision and defiance. He also celebrated Cuba's economic rebound, exemplary health care, and successful transnational literacy program, and he applauded both the Non-Aligned Movement's election of Cuba to lead it and the UN's consistent condemnation of the long-standing US embargo.[26]

A diary entry on the Fourth of July, 2007, indicates that he had some contact with Michael Scheuer, the ex-CIA officer who had run (and after 9/11 advised) the CIA Counterterrorism Center's Bin Laden Issue Station (aka "Alec Station") in charge of tracking Osama bin Laden.[27] Scheuer had written an initially anonymous book highly critical of US policy that the CIA had not authorized, resigned from the agency disaffected, and continued to malign US policy publicly.[28] To that very limited extent, they were kindred spirits. Scheuer's view, then crystallizing, was that US interventionism in the greater Middle East imperiled US national security.[29] This too would have attracted Agee. Even if he were unlikely to share Scheuer's policy prescriptions or increasingly right-wing ideology, Agee had never disavowed tactical alliances. In November, Agee traveled again to Dublin, when he did an interview with Pat Kenny, a leading current events analyst on Raidió Teilifís Éireann (RTE), Ireland's national radio station, and had meetings at Trinity College.[30]

Agee's last datebook entry, on December 15, 2007, was: EUR 442. DUE TO BARCLAY CARD.[31] Handwritten in frail block printing, it is rendered urgent by solid capitalization. For all the disruption and instability he visited on himself, his concern for keeping his credit card payments up to date seemed typical of his enduring middle-class sense of order and personal responsibility. Its banality and lack of portent also suggest that he did not expect to die so soon. Indeed, he had hopes of sailing trips in balmy Caribbean waters with Giselle and his sons.[32] On the same day that he recorded that last note to self, however, ulcers in Agee's intestines ruptured and he was hospitalized.[33] Four days later, Giselle flew from Hamburg to Havana, having planned to join him for the holidays, as usual, in any case. Once in Cuba, she spent every day at his bedside. After surgery, his doctors initially expected him to recover, and told her he would be home for Christmas. But another ulcer burst. He contracted peritonitis and had to remain in the hospital.[34]

Over a quarter-century earlier, the conservative columnist George F. Will, in a much-quoted line, had called Agee "a soiled bit of flotsam from the 60s."[35] This was a premature, incurious, and triumphalist view. Query who, in the end, had more influence. But Agee may well have felt that way lying on a gurney in a Havana hospital. On January 6, he signed a living will that Giselle had copied from his father Bill's; it included a do-not-resuscitate order. Assured that he was not in immediate danger, she went back to the apartment. Twelve hours later, the hospital called. Agee had died that morning, January 7, 2008. One of the last things he said to Giselle was: "No one can say I didn't make my contribution."[36]

Still, it must have been depressing for him to witness a second re-empowerment of the CIA, turbocharged by 9/11 and fears of jihadist infiltration, blessed by George W. Bush and his handlers to "rendition" and torture suspects and to call in drone strikes on terrorist targets, thus usurping a presumptively military function. Agee was candid and clear-eyed enough to have seen himself as merely an old pet for progressives: proven but taken for granted, and on the way out. Agee's late-life migration from his hedged redoubt in Germany to unequivocally enemy territory in Cuba brings to mind Lawrence Osborne's description of another distressed expatriate protagonist: "He had adapted to his own failure and turned it into a way of being happy."[37] Maybe his evolution from functionary patriot to revolutionary world citizen had been situational, but over time he had resolved to stop questioning that status and to find existential satisfaction in it while preserving his physical freedom and modest creature comfort. He lived on the giddy line. From a teleological perspective, winding up in Havana may be precisely the kind of thing that ought to have happened to a principled dissenter who still has to grow old and be human and die somewhere. There was some poetic justice in that fate.

Happy, on balance, he probably was, albeit conflicted. Philip Agee Jr. provides the sunny view: "my father never had any regrets and would on occasion marvel at all the things that happened. He never regretted leaving the Agency and telling the truth. My sense is that his departure allowed him to maintain the uncompromised social conscience he grew up with, which others lose through ideological rationalizations and denial. Throughout the years I think it was a never-ending source of relief for him—knowing that one has done the right thing and able to sleep at night with a clean conscience."[38]

On a practical level, Agee wasn't much of a provider and couldn't uphold his upper-middle-class bona fides. He left Giselle more than $50,000 in credit card debt from Cubalinda start-up costs that his trust distribution hadn't covered, and $20,000 in arrears on rent for the Havana apartment. Fortuitously, their German landlord, who had become a friend, left her their Hamburg apartment in his will.[39] As of 2016, though ailing, she still had to teach ballet to make ends meet. But the friends he made after he had left the agency and published *Inside the Company* were loyal, and he became a symbol of high defiance as much as low treachery.

On May 3, 2009, a memorial service for Agee, with about thirty people in attendance, was held at the Marjorie S. Deane Little Theater at the West Side YMCA on West 63rd Street in Manhattan, announced in the *New York Times* and the *Nation*.[40] Three Notre Dame alumni came, and the university sent a huge bouquet.[41] One rather pompous Agee detractor whined that a memorial service for a traitor "is now being held on the Upper West Side of Manhattan, with the commercial and ideological consent of one of the oldest liberal weeklies in America"—referring to the *Nation*—but otherwise outsiders took little notice.[42] Melvin Wulf, William Schaap, and Len Weinglass—all of them crusading lawyers—gave eulogies. Wulf decried the revocation of Agee's passport as bad law as well as personal hardship. But Wulf concluded: "In a way, though, Phil had the last laugh. He continued to travel the world for another twenty-six years on a variety of passports and travel documents issued to him by Nicaragua, Grenada and Germany, and he continued to effectively criticize the CIA and US foreign policy."[43]

So there was that. The dogged optimist in Agee resisted the idea of failure and conjured countervailing factors: the reckoning for the United States' post-9/11 excesses necessitated by their revelation, and the prospective opening of relations with Cuba after the Democrats reclaimed power. The investment in Cubalinda reflected his upbeat side, and it's not hard to imagine that he projected his own audacity as a vindicated ex-CIA man who lived out his days in Cuba as a prescient post-Castro entrepreneur and made a healthy living off Americans on tropical vacations. Though he died a year before Barack Obama took office and began to relax the United States' diplomatic and economic isolation of Cuba, Agee did recognize the promise Obama and like-minded Democrats held for easing the US economic blockade of Cuba and for hemispheric affairs in general.[44]

IN DEATH AS IN LIFE?

The presumption that the KGB ran Agee still has considerable currency among mainstream journalists. In a 2016 piece in the *Financial Times*, Sam Jones wrote that although "he said he was a whistleblower and became a feted figure of the left in the west," in fact "he was carefully directed by the KGB."[45] Almost inevitably, he was likened to Julian Assange, the thoroughly amoral purveyor of Wikileaks.[46] He probably would have had little time for Assange, but just as probably he'd have found a way to contact Snowden and commiserate.[47] When the Trump administration resolved to crack down on leakers by expanding the Intelligence Identities Protection Act, a number of journalists recycled versions of Agee's story, sometimes oversimplified and tendentious, as the source of their potential woes.[48] And Agee has continued to hover ominously over the US intelligence community. Its loathing for him remains deeply ingrained and undiluted. As of 2015, slide 26 of a PowerPoint presentation of the Office of the Director of National Intelligence's online training course for Unauthorized Disclosures of Classified Information, required for all federal employees handling such information, read as follows:

EXAMPLES OF DAMAGE FROM UNAUTHORIZED DISCLOSURE

Welch/Kinsman—Loss of Life

BACKGROUND: In 1969, Philip Agee, a former Case Officer, resigned from the CIA, moved out of the country, and began his campaign to weaken the CIA because of his ideological differences with the mission of the agency. As part of his campaign against the CIA, Agee was determined to expose CIA activity outside the U.S., including identifying CIA employees assigned overseas. An early 1975 edition of the magazine, *Counterspy*, published an article which included the following quote from Agee, "The most effective and important systematic attempts to combat the CIA that can be undertaken right now are, I think, the identification, exposure, and neutralization of its people working abroad." In the same issue of *Counterspy*, Richard Welch was identified as the CIA's Chief of Station (COS) in Greece. On November 25th, a Greek newspaper, the *Athens Daily*, also published Welch's identity. In 1980, the magazine, *Covert Action Bulletin*, also with reported affiliation to Philip Agee, revealed the identities of 15 CIA officials working in Jamaica.

RESULT: On December 24, 1975, just one month after the article was published in the *Athens Daily*, COS Richard Welch was assassinated outside of his home in Athens. In 1980, just two days after the *Covert Action Bulletin* article was published, an attempt was made on the life of Richard Kinsman, who had been identified as the COS in Jamaica. Agee ultimately settled in Cuba, where he ran a travel agency until his death. He never returned to the U.S. after he began disclosing information about the identities of CIA employees and their activities.

This account, of course, embeds the usual misleading information.

It might have pleased him, of course, that the US government apparently couldn't hang much more on him than a bogus connection to Welch's death and a flimsy one to the rather pathetic attack on Kinsman's house. And he would have found gratifying the increasing mainstream acceptance of the view that American exceptionalism has disguised a form of often abusive American imperialism as liberation—especially during the Cold War, and especially in Latin America.[49] This was essentially Agee's take fifty years ago, and he regarded the CIA as the United States' prime instrument of deception. He could find no political space for this position in the 1970s mainstream American Left and had to look toward the extreme, radical end of the spectrum, whence he sought and found some vindication for his views—notably in Nicaragua. Daniel Ortega's insidious transformation from a left-wing freedom fighter into the kind of repressive autocrat Agee once castigated would have deeply disappointed him. So would the ascension to the office of attorney general of William Barr, a retrogressively conservative Catholic affiliated with Opus Dei. But it is also possible Agee would have been heartened by the protests of many students and the disdain of liberal Catholics for Barr's vituperative October 2019 speech at Notre Dame, Agee's alma mater, against "militant secularists" and in support of near-absolute presidential power.[50]

And it is also defensible to see Agee as more profoundly prophetic. The United States supported illiberal, autocratic dictators throughout Latin America during the Cold War. When indigenous left-wing movements gained political purchase against them, it redoubled its efforts to suppress them through the CIA. Despite this systematic hostility to such movements, they enjoyed ascendancy in the early twentieth-first century, most conspicuously in Bolivia, Ecuador, and Peru as well as in Venezuela, albeit inauspiciously. While there has been some movement back toward the political center—in some cases, like Brazil's, to the Far Right—the interests of the indigenous poor are now more entrenched in Latin American politics than they were during the Cold War. Arguably that phenomenon led to the selection of the Catholic Church's first Latin American pope—Pope Francis, born Jorge Mario Bergoglio in Buenos Aires—who in turn has championed social justice and the eradication of poverty in the vein of liberation theology.

Agee would have taken solace in the new pope's election and coronation, and perhaps outright delight in seeing José Mujica, one of several Tupamaro guerrillas imprisoned and abused for twelve years, from 1973 to 1985, elected Uruguay's fortieth president in 2009, the year after Agee's death. Mujica served with distinction until 2015 as "the world's humblest head of state," continuing Uruguay's maturation into a healthy two-party democracy, donating 90 percent of his salary to charity, and raising and selling chrysanthemums in retirement.[51] Amplifying Agee's persistent opacity on the issue of lethal risk to CIA personnel, it remains unclear how or even if Agee might have qualified his praise for Mujica with condemnation of the Tupamaros' kidnapping and murder of US security adviser Dan Mitrione in Montevideo in 1970—only four years after Agee had served there as a case officer and performed similar security liaison duties.

The characterization of Agee as heedlessly treacherous—based on his naming of names and the Welch assassination—has not completely endured. In the character of Bill Adler, a fearless, swaggering ex-CIA man who has gone rogue, American novelist Marlon James memorialized Agee and his most intrepid moment in history in the novel A Brief History of Seven Killings, which won the Man Booker Prize in 2015. It's a highly innovative work—the narrative is dense, distributed across multiple points of view à la Faulkner, hyperkinetic and violent like James Ellroy's work—that provocatively interprets twenty-five jangled years of Jamaican sociopolitical history, from 1976 to 1991. In 1976, the sitting prime minister was Michael Manley, the socialist who had grown increasingly close to Cuba. His challenger was the US-supported, right-wing opposition candidate Edward Seaga, whom the Rastafarians called "CIA-ga."[52] In the book, as Agee in fact did, Adler has shown up in Jamaica in 1976 to help tilt elections in Manley's favor by naming CIA agents and officers and exposing the agency's influence operations and direct support for right-wing, anti-Manley elements. That support allegedly included weapons funneled to criminals who tried to kill "The Singer"—a messianically popular pro-Manley reggae musician based on Bob Marley, whom gunmen actually did try to assassinate in December 1976. Barry Diflorio, the novel's CIA station chief in Jamaica, is torn between grudging admiration and utter disdain for Adler. He remains unclear about Adler's political motivations but convinced of his moral ones.

> Bill Adler checked out of the Company in 1969 a very bitter customer. Maybe he was just a disgruntled left-wing commie, but tons of those are still in the Company. Sometimes the good ones are the worst, the mediocre ones are just civil servants with wire-tapping skills. But the good ones either become him or me. And he was sometimes very good. After he was done with Ecuador, a four-year job done with, dare I say it, *brio*, all I had to do was clean up the stray debris. Of course I'd much rather remind him of that lovely mess in Tlatelolco. The boss called me an innovator but I was just following the Adler rulebook. Ceiling mics, like the one he used in Montevideo. Either way he left the CIA in 1969 with a critical case of conscience and has been making trouble and endangering lives ever since.[53]

Clearly James had read up on Agee in some depth. In the novelist's relatively nuanced and impressively fact-based rendering, he initially correlates Welch's exposure as a CIA officer to the precedent Agee had established in *Inside the Company*, again suggesting what was in fact the case: CIA complacency might well have been a factor.

> Last year he dropped a book, not a very good one but there were explosions in it. We knew it was coming but let it go, thinking well, maybe a diversion with his out-of-date info would actually help us out there doing real work. Turns out his info was very nearly top-notch, and why wouldn't it be, come to think of it. He named names too. Inside the Company. Top brass didn't read it, but Miles Copeland did, another whiny faggot who used to run the Cairo office. He ordered the London office restructured from the ground up. Then Richard Welch got murdered in Athens by 17 November, a second-rate terrorist group

that we wouldn't have sent a candy-striper to monitor. Killed with his wife and driver too.[54]

Notwithstanding the recrudescence of the Welch connection and James's literary embroidery—Welch's wife and driver were in fact spared—Agee would have reveled in the credit Diflorio accords him for frustrating CIA operations in Jamaica: "the bastard did his damage." Never mind that Agee gave windy speeches "like his name was Castro or something" and wrote for magazines like *Penthouse*, which meant that "the conscience of America airbrushes pussy for a living."[55] Agee actually might have liked the novel's portrayal of him as a fearless bad-ass. Through James's deft authorial ventriloquism Agee was enabled, a good five years after his death, to defend himself against the Welch accusation as Adler, in a phone conversation with Diflorio:

—Hold the fucking line, you think I got the Welches killed?

—You and your little exposé, your little trashy novel.

—He's not in the fucking book, you idiot.

—Not like I'm ever gonna read it.

—Really? You think I'm to be blamed for Welch? I overestimated you, Barry. I thought the company trusted you with more info than you've clearly got. I must be talking to the wrong man.[56]

Yet even James—plainly a sympathizer—cannot resist imparting to Adler/Agee an aura of danger and intrigue and prurience, probably apocryphal, that he'll never be able to escape. Again from Diflorio's point of view:

Yes I can imagine why he would be here, even on his own. What I don't get is why he's making such a public spectacle of it—public for us, anyway, unlike Carlos the Jackal, who's been here too, laying low, rubbing his belly while whores suck him off. Those two have a history. I'm paid to know these things.[57]

Still, even as a novelist assigning Agee a pseudonym, James shows impressive fealty to history in absorbing that Agee's disclosures did not really kill Welch and that Nixon's (and Kissinger's) extravagant use of the CIA made all of its case officers, who were soft targets to begin with, more attractive and compelling ones. James has Diflorio in a more reflective and objective frame of mind three years on in the narrative, in 1979:

> Funny, when Bill Adler called me that time in '76 I blamed him for Richard Welch's death in Greece. Said some bullshit about him leaking the names of company people and jeopardizing their safety, but it was all bullshit. He knew and I knew it. I just had to say it. Fucking Nixon killed Richard Welch. Telling us to spread all sorts of shit in Greece that just blew up the war in Turkey over Cyprus. And then worse, letting all that crap get leaked. Next thing you know, Richard Welch and his poor wife—all killed. All fucking dead. Jesus Christ, a station chief.[58]

They have one more phone conversation initiated by Adler after his expulsion from the UK. "Come on Bill," says Diflorio, "As small as America's dick is, those limeys will stretch across the Atlantic to suck it." James had clearly absorbed the UK's obsequiousness toward the Bush administration during the invasion and occupation of Iraq, as well as the political subtext of Agee's expulsion from the UK almost forty years earlier. Following a long, angry, similarly obscene, ad hominem tit-for-tat, Diflorio suggests: "Tell Fidel you want an ocean view."[59] Until now, that sarcastic crack was the last substantive public word on Philip Agee. However loose his geopolitical analysis and however colorful his language, James got the US–UK special relationship and the CIA's standing attitude toward Agee dead right.

Literary immortalization as an antagonist's foil is a form of political and moral validation, and Agee has secured at least that much.

He stayed part of the espionage conversation for over thirty years after publishing *Inside the Company* on account of his intimate knowledge of the CIA's modus operandi and his unflagging insistence on its counterproductive amorality: despite the aspersions that the agency and others cast on his character and integrity, objective observers could never be sure that he was wrong on the merits. Len Weinglass, who represented the Cuban Five, met Agee toward the end of his life and was able to take his measure as an *éminence grise* of the dissident community. "It must have driven the CIA crazy," he reflected, "to try to attack the credibility of a man so eminently credible."[60] The CIA itself declined public comment on his death.[61]

For all his genuineness and his unstinting dedication to his cause, Agee behaved far more objectionably than necessary or proper to make his point. Most Americans would undoubtedly contend that his treason was more than just the "drop" that Rebecca West contemplated to keep good nations true to their foundational principles.[62] While originally writing mainly about British fascists who abetted Nazi Germany, in a later edition of her classic book *The Meaning of Treason*, she showed little mercy for Cold War–era turncoats. Paradoxically, though, Agee's point might not have been so catalytic or so durable had he not lodged it in the dramatic and consequential way that he did. And he probably would not have been compelled to perpetuate his lifelong campaign against the CIA had he not burned his bridges to the establishment so irreversibly, leaving himself no honorable option besides staying the course. He was perhaps as close to an embattled antihero as he was to an outright cad.

If Agee seemed like a wasting asset as the Cold War ended, it was only because the Clandestine Service was atrophying and the CIA itself becoming a less active player in the execution of US policy. Once 9/11 effectively reempowered the agency, and it went nefarious again with renditions, black sites, and torture, his mission again became relevant to upholding true American principles. Thanks to some extent to Agee and his followers, disclosures by guilt-ridden or merely conscientious spies were less likely to condemn them to iniquity than to earn them some qualified respectability. Whatever his precise motivations, the strain of Agee's grievance was one of the twentieth century's successful viruses: undeniably effective and impossible to kill.

Counterintelligence analysts use the mnemonic "MICE" to identify the basic motives for betrayal: money, ideology, compromise, and ego. As US intelligence agencies have increasingly employed second- and third-generation immigrants, competing nationalism has become another key factor.[63] On the surface, the MICE categories are objective and value-neutral, and such analysts are sophisticated enough to recognize that human behavior is complex and rarely driven by a single motive. But the very premise of the counterintelligence vocation—that someone seeking to damage vital national interests must be stopped—logically crowds out the plausibility of a valid motive, such as political justification. Nevertheless, it remains possible. However complex Agee's psychology and however questionable his actions might have been, he made a reasonably defensible and uniquely informed argument that American foreign policy was, against the received view of the United States' honor and nobility, in fact duplicitous and mercenary. As Christopher Moran notes, "Agee, in particular, showed that the engine of foreign policy was fuelled not by any devotion to morality or democratic values, but by a desire to make the world hospitable for globalisation, led by American multinational corporations. Renegades and whistleblowers also revealed the forgotten victims of US strategy abroad, such as the people who suffered under the authoritarian Shah of Iran, installed by the CIA (and MI6) in 1953. In sum, they held a mirror up to the face of the nation; few liked the reflection staring back."[64]

In a palpable way, Agee's life and story recast the conventional American sense of those periods. He was perhaps the only CIA officer who turned against the agency for reasons that were truly and deeply political. While Marchetti, Snepp, Stockwell, and others did have cognate experiences with the agency, Agee took his political commitments beyond narrow, circumscribed attacks on analytical misrepresentation and excessive secrecy into a lifelong political struggle with the agency that firmly allied him with the social movements of the global Left from the late sixties until his death. The wholesale condemnation of the American project is the one thing the CIA cannot tolerate. The resulting fury against Agee has lingered in intelligence historiography as well as in the agency itself, leaving him the caricature of a disaffected traitor or, at best, a demonized symbol. Perhaps now he appears a more substantial and full-blooded character than that.

Greg Grandin has pointed out that, although "on one level the Cold War was a struggle over mass utopias—ideological visions of how to organize society and its accoutrements—what gave that struggle its transcendental force was the politicization and internationalization of everyday life and familiar encounters."[65] Agee was the kind of public figure who, for better or worse, embodied exactly that in airing his grievances in Europe and taking them to Central America as part of the Solidarity Movement. In so doing, he helped demonstrate that, as Nick Witham has observed, "in order to be effective, peace activism needed to be fundamentally transnational in scope."[66] Beyond that lesson, the proposition—posed by the sheer durability and persistence of Agee's convictions—that an American traitor's conduct may be politically justified has become more salient since the end of the Cold War, perhaps because the geopolitical stakes have not seemed as high. Even Snepp, who has always taken pains to distinguish himself as a tortured patriot in contrast to Agee's abject "turncoat," conceded Agee's philosophical genuineness, in 1999 characterizing him as a Catholic who had experienced an "inversion of faith" and a "true believer."[67] Americans have taken a far more nuanced and sympathetic view of Edward Snowden than they did of Agee: in an August 2018 Rasmussen Report poll, while 29% considered Snowden a traitor and 14% regarded him as a hero, a large plurality—48%—saw him as a more complicated and ambivalent figure.[68]

The possibility of a principled and acceptable rejection of the US government seems to loom especially large in the age of Donald Trump. Trump's grim ascent would have appalled and depressed Agee all over again. Certainly he would have seen the Trump administration as confirmation that the entire US government (not just the CIA) was an agent of and a front for American corporate interests and capitalism, cloaked in toxic populist nativism. And he would have read the Trump administration's bureaucratic beleaguerment of the CIA as the systematic suppression of its only possible legitimate function: providing objective analyses of collected intelligence. It may be tempting to think that, in light of Trump's distrust of the CIA, Agee might have found himself rooting for his old agency and nemesis as the lesser of two evils. More likely, though, he would have considered his own comprehensive rejection of US policy and national security institutions as pyrrhically vindicated by Trump's transmogrification of American government and governance. So emboldened, he might have pointed out that the integrity and loyalty of an intelligence service ultimately depends on its officers' pride in and respect for the country they serve.

That pride and respect can survive, and have survived, episodic and even epochal lapses. In this respect, Agee was unusually thin-skinned. At the same time, his life itself exemplified the brittleness of the American vision. His detractors might say he just got mildly disenchanted with CIA work; tried to take the quiet, nontreasonous way out; got frustrated; was seduced by a couple of lefty women; felt the allure of dissident celebrity; and only then became a real dissenter. On the known facts, that's a gross oversimplification: Agee paid for his proclaimed beliefs with lifelong anxiety and displacement. But even if the more dismissive account of Agee's turn were accurate, the accidents and coincidences that produced Agee's turn wouldn't make it any less genuine or durable.

No president before Trump has assaulted the country's constitutional and ethical pillars so savagely or frontally. As he refused to recognize his loss to Joe Biden in the 2020 presidential election and sought to subvert American democracy altogether, ultimately inciting violence, a wholesale loss of faith in the American project seemed a salient possibility. The extraordinary jeopardy that Trump poses to the United States' constitutional democracy reinforces what would surely have been Agee's view: that disloyalty, in the first instance, is not a matter of moral or psychological weakness but rather is acutely contingent on particular circumstances. If they are dire enough to stay planted in moral memory, disloyalty becomes a habit of mind—that's the giddy line—and then a compulsion to act. Especially in ethically testing conditions, the boundary between loyalty and betrayal is inherently unstable to those who are truthful to themselves. What Pico Iyer said of Graham Greene applies equally to Agee: "Always there was a dance in him between evasion and an almost ruthless candor."[69] So he got used to walking that giddy line, and stayed, if barely, on his feet. This was not an entirely masochistic dispensation, of course. Iyer also said that Greene, and by extension Agee, "seemed to feast on confrontation, perverse of paradoxical positions, as if he would take any stance so long as it kept him apart from the crowd."[70] His turn, ever public, afforded Agee the psychological satisfaction of being unique. Perhaps several dozen disgruntled intelligence officers have followed his lead, but few if any of them have equaled his level of commitment or so obstructed the system they had once sustained.[71] How many more, girded by Agee's survival and circulation as a turncoat and disillusioned by a fallen America, might now emulate him?

Acknowledgments

Timothy Mennel has been a superb editor both intellectually and practically, providing incisive thematic guidance, a judicious red pen, and a sympathetic ear. Susan Olin did a remarkably deft job of copyediting, clearly having mastered Occam's razor. More broadly, Susannah Marie Engstrom, Rachel Kelly, and Kristen Raddatz assured me at various stages of the editorial process that the University of Chicago Press was indeed paying close attention.

Flip Brophy, my agent, crucially encouraged me to move forward with the Agee project after it had lain dormant for several years. The staff of the Tamiment Library and Robert F. Wagner Labor Archive at New York University, which hold the Philip Agee Papers, were as amiable as they were efficient in procuring the many files I pored over for months.

In 2016–17, I was afforded the privilege of being the Gilder Lehrman Fellow at the Dorothy and Lewis B. Cullman Center for Scholars and Writers at the New York Public Library. There could have been no better platform for researching and writing this book. That year's political events were, to say the least, highly distracting. But the Cullman Center's crack staff—led by Jean Strouse in her valedictory year as director there—and the other fellows struck a galvanizing balance between spirited dialogue and disciplined work. I am also grateful to the NYPL for furnishing me with a research carrel in the Allen Room after the fellowship ended—and for repeatedly extending it, no less—and to library staff for their patience. During that period, the Cullman Center's Paul Delaverdac generously provided important and much-appreciated research assistance.

Then there are the existential factors. In her determination, resolve, and fine spirit, Lena Curland, my stepdaughter, improved our lives and made it that much easier to concentrate. Finally, I thank my wife, Sharon Butler, whose love, wit, talent, and good cheer answer the question.

Any errors or infelicities, of course, are mine alone.

Notes

The Philip Agee Papers are held in the Tamiment Library and Robert F. Wagner Labor Archives at the Elmer Holmes Bobst Library at New York University. Citations follow this abbreviated form: [Description of item]; Agee Papers, [box number, folder number].

CHAPTER ONE

1. Author interview with Glenn Carle, March 9, 2016.

2. Author interview with David Corn, May 19, 2016.

3. See, in particular, *"Playboy* Interview: William Colby," *Playboy*, July 1978, 81.

4. Philip Agee, *On the Run* (London: Lyle Stuart, 1987), 288.

5. Malcolm Gladwell, "The Outsider," *New Yorker*, December 19 & 26, 2016. Ellsberg recounts his experiences in his *Secrets: A Memoir of Vietnam and the Pentagon Papers* (New York: Viking, 2002).

6. See Edward Snowden, *Permanent Record* (New York: Metropolitan, 2019).

7. Kaeten Mistry, "A Transnational Protest Against the National Security State: Whistle-Blowing, Philip Agee, and Networks of Dissent," *Journal of American History* 106, no. 2 (September 2019): 362–89.

8. For a similarly circumscribed view of what constitutes a whistleblower, see

Rahul Sagar, *Secrets and Leaks: The Dilemma of State Secrecy* (Princeton, NJ: Princeton University Press, 2013), 127–34.

9. See Lloyd C. Gardner, *The War on Leakers: National Security and American Democracy from Eugene V. Debs to Edward Snowden* (New York: New Press, 2016).

10. Victor Marchetti and John D. Marks, *The CIA and the Cult of Intelligence* (New York: Alfred A. Knopf, 1974). See Peter Singer, "Forswearing Secrecy," *Nation*, May 5, 1979, 488–91, for a worthwhile comparative perspective on books written by Agee, Marchetti/Marks, Snepp, and Stockwell.

11. Frank Snepp, *Decent Interval: An Insider's Account of Saigon's Indecent End as Told by the CIA's Chief Strategy Analyst in Vietnam* (New York: Random House, 1977).

12. John Stockwell, *In Search of Enemies: A CIA Story* (New York: W. W. Norton, 1978).

13. Glenn L. Carle, *The Interrogator: An Education* (New York: Nation Books, 2011).

14. Author interview with Glenn Carle, March 9, 2016.

15. Lawrence Osborne, "Agents of Betrayal," *Lapham's Quarterly* 9, no. 1 (Winter 2016): 217.

16. Agee, *On the Run*, 200.

17. Obituary of William Agee, *St. Petersburg Times*, September 30, 1994; Philip Agee Jr., e-mail to the author, February 8, 2010; Ye Mystic Krewe of Gasparilla webpage, https://ymkg.com/.

18. Florida Obituary and Death Notice Archive, http://www.genlookups.com/fl/webbbs_config.pl/read/361.

19. See, e.g., Hal Brands, *Latin America's Cold War* (Cambridge, MA: Harvard University Press, 2102), 24.

20. Jesuit High School Yearbook 1952, Senior History.

21. Author interview with Timothy Twomey, April 12, 2016.

22. Jesuit High School Yearbook 1952, Class Will.

23. Author interview with Timothy Twomey, April 12, 2016.

24. Author interview with Timothy Twomey, April 12, 2016.

25. Author interview with Donald Hess, April 2, 2016.

26. See generally Jonathan Stevenson, *Thinking Beyond the Unthinkable: Harnessing Doom from the Cold War to the Age of Terror* (New York: Viking, 2008).

27. See, e.g., Jennifer A. Delton, *Rethinking the 1950s: How Anticommunism and the*

Cold War Made American Liberal (Cambridge: Cambridge University Press, 2013). For the more standard, rose-colored view of the decade, see David Halberstam, *The Fifties* (New York: Ballantine, 1994).

28. Author interview with John Manion, April 19, 2016.

29. Author interview with Philip Agee Jr., May 6, 2015.

30. Tim Rutten, "A Spook's Faustian Bargain," *Los Angeles Times*, January 12, 2008, https://www.latimes.com/archives/la-xpm-2008-jan-12-oe-rutten12-story.html.

31. Author interview with Donald Brophy, April 21, 2016.

32. Author interview with Donald Brophy, May 11, 2016.

33. Author interview with Donald Brophy, April 21, 2016.

34. Author interview with Donald Brophy, May 11, 2016.

35. Karen M. Paget, *Patriotic Betrayal: The Inside Story of the CIA's Secret Campaign to Enroll American Students in the Campaign Against Communism* (New Haven, CT: Yale University Press, 2015), 31.

36. Agee, *On the Run*, 24.

37. Author interview with Donald Brophy, May 11, 2016.

38. See Linda Gordon, *The Second Coming of the KKK: The Ku Klux Klan of the 1920s and the American Political Tradition* (New York: W. W. Norton, 2017).

39. Author interview with Donald Brophy, May 11, 2016.

40. See Michael Graziano, *Errand into the Wilderness of Mirrors: Religion, American Intelligence, and National Security* (Chicago: University of Chicago Press, forthcoming), chap. 1; Steven Rosswurm, *The FBI and the Catholic Church, 1935–1962* (Amherst: University of Massachusetts Press, 2009), 44.

41. Philip Agee, *Inside the Company: CIA Diary* (London: Stonehill Publishing Co., 1975), 3–4.

42. Author interview with Timothy Twomey, April 12, 2016.

43. Author interview with John Manion, April 19, 2016.

44. Agee, *Inside the Company*, 3–9.

45. Author interview with Giselle Roberge Agee, July 15, 2016.

46. Author interview with Timothy Twomey, April 12, 2016.

47. Draft, "The CIA for Beginners: 100 Questions"; Agee Papers, box 17, folder 19.

48. See Tom Dooley, *Deliver Us From Evil: The Story of Vietnam's Flight to Freedom* (New York: Farrar, Straus and Cudahy, 1956).

49. See Jim Winters, "Tom Dooley: The Forgotten Hero," *Notre Dame Magazine*, May 1979, 10–17. See also "Dr. Tom Dooley's Ties to CIA Are Chronicled," Associated Press, July 4, 1979, https://www.cia.gov/library/readingroom/docs/CIA-RDP 89B00236R000500090010–9.pdf.

50. See Ralph W. McGehee, *Deadly Deceits: My 25 Years in the CIA* (New York: Sheridan Square Publications, 1983).

51. Diana Shaw, "The Temptation of Tom Dooley: He Was the Heroic Jungle Doctor of Indochina in the 1950s. But He Had a Secret, and to Protect it, He Helped Launch the First Disinformation Campaign of the Cold War," *Los Angeles Times*, December 15, 1991, https://www.latimes.com/archives/la-xpm-1991-12-15-tm-868 -story.html.

52. Agee, *Inside the Company*, 4.

53. CIA Training and Evaluation Report, July 1957 (obtained via Agee's FOIA request); Agee Papers, Box 5, Folder 42.

CHAPTER TWO

1. See Graziano, *Errand into the Wilderness of Mirrors*, chap. 1.

2. Tim Weiner, *Legacy of Ashes: The History of the CIA* (New York: Anchor Books, 2008), 78.

3. See Weiner, *Legacy of Ashes*, 52–53. See also Rhodri Jeffreys-Jones, *In Spies We Trust: The Story of Western Intelligence* (Oxford: Oxford University Press, 2013), 130.

4. Weiner, *Legacy of Ashes*, 158.

5. David Talbot, *The Devil's Chessboard: Allen Dulles, the CIA, and the Rise of America's Secret Government* (New York: Harper, 2015), 617.

6. Weiner, *Legacy of Ashes*, 152–54.

7. See Paget, *Patriotic Betrayal*, 26–42.

8. Agee, *Inside the Company*, 81–82.

9. Brands, *Latin America's Cold War*, 24–27. See also Michael Reid, *Forgotten Continent: A History of the New Latin America* (New Haven, CT: Yale University Press, 2009), 100–101.

10. Brands, *Latin America's Cold War*, 33.

11. Agee, *Inside the Company*, 82.

12. President John F. Kennedy's Inaugural Address, January 20, 1961; https://www.jfklibrary.org/Research/Research-Aids/Ready-Reference/JFK-Quotations/In augural-Address.aspx.

13. Quoted in Brands, *Latin America's Cold War*, 33.

14. Agee, *Inside the Company*, 113.

15. Reid, *Forgotten Continent*, 78.

16. Agee, *Inside the Company*, 116.

17. Agee, *On the Run*, 15.

18. Agee, *Inside the Company*, 119.

19. Agee, *Inside the Company*, 144.

20. Agee, *Inside the Company*, 237–38.

21. Agee, *Inside the Company*, 253.

22. Warren Hinckle and William W. Turner, *The Fish Is Red: The Story of the Secret War Against Castro* (New York: Harper & Row, 1981), 11–12.

23. Agee, *Inside the Company*, 270.

24. Penny Lernoux, *Cry of the People: The Struggle for Human Rights in Latin America—The Catholic Church in Conflict with U.S. Policy* (New York: Doubleday, 1980), 148.

25. Agee, *Inside the Company*, 163–64.

26. Agee, *Inside the Company*, 227.

27. Agee, *Inside the Company*, 140.

28. Bradley Earl Ayers, *The War That Never Was: An Insider's Account of C.I.A. Covert Operations Against Cuba* (Indianapolis, IN: Bobbs-Merrill, 1976), 216–17.

29. Richard H. Immerman, *The Hidden Hand: A Brief History of the CIA* (Malden, MA: Wiley-Blackwell, 2014), chap. 3.

30. See Frances FitzGerald, *Fire in the Lake: The Vietnamese and the Americans in Vietnam* (New York: Little, Brown, 1972).

31. Harry Maurer, *Strange Ground: An Oral History of Americans in Vietnam, 1945–1975* (Boston: Da Capo Press, 1998), 344.

32. Agee, *Inside the Company*, 19, 183.

33. CIA internal memorandum indicating that on February 16, 1967, an "informant" [name redacted] said Agee consulted a priest in connection with planned separation; Agee Papers, box 5, folder 8.

34. See the probing and comprehensive account of Militant Liberty during the Eisenhower administration in Graziano, *Errand into the Wilderness of Mirrors*, chap. 4.

35. See Graziano, *Errand into the Wilderness of Mirrors*, chap. 4.

36. Reid, *Forgotten Continent*, 82–83.

37. Weiner, *Legacy of Ashes*, 333.

38. Agee, *Inside the Company*, 202.

39. Agee, *Inside the Company*, 120, 143.

40. Agee, *Inside the Company*, 155–56.

41. Agee, *Inside the Company*, 215.

42. Agee, *Inside the Company*, 151, 183, 276.

43. Agee, *Inside the Company*, 377–78.

44. Agee, *Inside the Company*, 277.

45. Reid, *Forgotten Continent*, 69–70.

46. Reid, *Forgotten Continent*, 116–17, 126.

47. Agee, *Inside the Company*, 277–78.

48. Hinckle and Turner, *The Fish Is Red*, 42.

49. Agee, *Inside the Company*, 281.

50. See "Uruguay Breaks Tie With Cuba; Mexico Only Holdout in O.A.S.," *New York Times*, September 9, 1964, https://www.nytimes.com/1964/09/09/archives/uruguay-breaks-tie-with-cuba-mexico-only-holdout-in-oas.html.

51. Agee, *Inside the Company*, 285, 352.

52. Agee, *Inside the Company*, 339, 352.

53. Agee, *Inside the Company*, 321–24.

54. Reid, *Forgotten Continent*, 102.

55. Brands, *Latin America's Cold War*, 58; Reid, *Forgotten Continent*, 89, 102; Randall Bennett Woods, *Quest for Identity: America Since 1945* (Cambridge: Cambridge University Press, 2005), 238–41.

56. Agee, *Inside the Company*, 366.

57. Agee, *Inside the Company*, 378.

58. Agee, *Inside the Company*, 392.

59. Agee, *Inside the Company*, 383.

60. Agee, *Inside the Company*, 392–93.

61. See Michael Klare and Nancy Stein, "Police Terrorism in Latin America," *Latin*

America Documentation (U.S. Catholic Conference, 1974), 22, 26; Lernoux, *Cry of the People*, 188–91, 282; "Uruguay Police Agent Exposes U.S. Advisers," *NACLA Latin American Report*, July–August 1972.

62. Lernoux, *Cry of the People*, 281–83.

63. Brands, *Latin America's Cold War*, 105–6, 109; and A. J. Langguth, *Hidden Terrors: The Truth about U.S. Police Operations in Latin America* (New York: Pantheon, 1979), 8–43. The Mitrione episode is dramatized in Costa-Gavras's 1972 film *State of Siege*, which was filmed in Chile during the tenure of socialist president Salvador Allende.

64. Agee, *Inside the Company*, 371.

65. See Harold G. Moore and Joseph L. Galloway, *We Were Soldiers Once . . . and Young* (New York: Random House, 2004).

66. On the Bonaudi episode, see also Langguth, *Hidden Terrors*.

67. Agee, *Inside the Company*, 368.

68. Agee, *Inside the Company*, 412.

69. Ben Macintyre, *A Spy Among Friends: Kim Philby and the Great Betrayal* (New York: Crown, 2014), 133.

70. Agee, *Inside the Company*, 396.

71. Agee, *Inside the Company*, 404.

72. Maurer, *Strange Ground*, 350.

73. Agee, *Inside the Company*, 425.

74. Agee, *Inside the Company*, 432.

75. Agee, *Inside the Company*, 396.

76. Agee, *Inside the Company*, 425.

77. Agee, *Inside the Company*, 416–17.

78. Agee, *Inside the Company*, 527.

79. Agee, *Inside the Company*, 427.

80. Agee, *Inside the Company*, 432.

81. Agee, *Inside the Company*, 434.

82. Agee, *Inside the Company*, 435–38.

83. The celebrated British espionage novelist Len Deighton set the second of his famous *Game, Set, and Match* trilogy in Mexico City. See Len Deighton, *Mexico Set* (London: Hutchinson, 1984).

84. Brands, *Latin America's Cold War*, 85, 88; William C. Kelly, "Gustavo Díaz Ordaz's Foreign Policy: A Cold War Study," *Latin Americanist* 60, no. 3 (September 2016): 315–20; Reid, *Forgotten Continent*, 221. On National Security Doctrine, see Brands, *Latin America's Cold War*, 70–82.

85. Brands, *Latin America's Cold War*, 84–85.

86. Lernoux, *Cry of the People*, 444.

87. For a searching and sophisticated exploration of these themes, see Peter Cajka, *Follow Your Conscience: The Catholic Church, Sex, War, and the Transformation of American Freedom* (Chicago: University of Chicago Press, forthcoming), especially chap. 2.

88. Dorothy Day, "Theophane Venard and Ho Chi Minh," *Catholic Worker* (May 1954): 1–6.

89. Michael Harrington, *Fragments of the Century* (New York: Saturday Review Press, 1973).

90. Gustavo Guttiérez, *A Theology of Liberation: History, Politics, and Salvation*, trans. and ed. Sister Caridad Inda and John Eagleson (Maryknoll, NY: Orbis Books, 1995).

91. Brands, *Latin America's Cold War*, 90–100.

92. Guttiérez, *A Theology of Liberation*, 54 (citation omitted; emphasis in original).

93. Reid, *Forgotten Continent*, 261–62; Brands, *Latin America's Cold War*, 87.

94. Brands, *Latin America's Cold War*, 86–88.

95. Resignation papers; CIA memorandum, obtained via Agee's FOIA request; Agee Papers, box 5, folder 37.

96. Author interview with Philip Agee Jr., May 16, 2015.

97. Agee, *Inside the Company*, 473–76.

98. Agee, *Inside the Company*, 477–79.

99. Agee, *Inside the Company*, 479–81; Brands, *Latin America's Cold War*, 88–89; Reid, *Forgotten Continent*, 221–22.

100. Jefferson Morley, *Our Man in Mexico: Winston Scott and the Hidden History of the CIA* (Lawrence: University Press of Kansas, 2008), 265–71.

101. Brands, *Latin America's Cold War*, 89–90; Reid, *Forgotten Continent*, 222.

102. Brands, *Latin America's Cold War*, 93, 135, 142; Enrique Krauze, *Redeemers: Ideas and Power in Latin America* (New York: Harper Perennial, 2011), 217.

103. Brands, *Latin America's Cold War*, 90.

104. Brands, *Latin America's Cold War*, 87.

105. Agee, *Inside the Company*, 481–82.

106. Agee, *Inside the Company*, 2.

107. See, e.g., John Gerassi, "An Interview with Philip Agee: Confessions of an Ex-CIA Man," *The Real Paper*, February 19, 1975, 6–7, 10; located in Agee Papers, box 20, folder 1.

108. Agee, *Inside the Company*, 482.

109. Letter to director of personnel, Central Intelligence Agency, dated November 22, 1968; obtained via Agee's FOIA request; Agee Papers, box 5, folder 38.

110. Secrecy Agreement, dated November 22, 1968; obtained via Agee's FOIA request; Agee Papers, box 5, folder 38.

111. William Greider, "Ex-CIA Agent Was Friendlier in Resigning Than in Exposé," *International Herald Tribune*, March 10, 1975; located in Agee Papers, box 19, folder 9.

112. Marked-up galley, undated; Agee Papers, box 16, folder 38.

113. Author interview with Glenn Carle, March 9, 2016.

CHAPTER THREE

1. Graham Greene, foreword to *My Silent War*, by Kim Philby (New York: Modern Library, 2002).

2. See Agee, *Inside the Company*, 484–91.

3. "Proposal for the Establishment of a Sports Development Program," undated; obtained via Agee's FOIA request; Agee Papers, box 5, folder 37.

4. Agee, *Inside the Company*, 484–85. See Letter to Lawrence Grant (Agee's personal lawyer in the United Kingdom) from Agee's father, dated January 27, 1977; Agee Papers, box 12, folder 21.

5. Agee, *Inside the Company*, 485.

6. Review from *Studies in Intelligence*; https://www.cia.gov/library/center-for-the-study-of-intelligence/kent-csi/v0119n02/pdf/v19i2a06p.pdf.

7. Agee, *Inside the Company*, 486.

8. John Prados, *The Family Jewels: The CIA, Secrecy, and Presidential Power* (Austin: University of Texas Press, 2013), 246.

9. See William F. Parham, "Cuban Intelligence Gave Agee Help to Expose, Discredit CIA," *Norwich Bulletin*, August 31, 1981.

10. Agee, *Inside the Company*, 490.

11. Agee, *Inside the Company*, 491–94.

12. Agee, *On the Run*, 26–32.

13. Chris John Agee, "Bridging the Gap: Philip Agee, 1935–2008," *NACLA Reporting on the Americas*, January–February 2009, https://nacla.org/article/bridging-gap -philip-agee-1935%E2%80%932008.

14. Philip Agee Jr., e-mail to the author, January 20, 2010.

15. Mistry, "A Transnational Protest," 371, 388.

16. See Orlando Castro Hidalgo, *Spy for Fidel* (Miami, FL: E. A. Seemann, 1971), 60.

17. Michael J. Sulick, *American Spies: Espionage Against the United States from the Cold War to the Present* (Washington, DC: Georgetown University Press, 2013), 268.

18. Hidalgo, *Spy for Fidel*, 62.

19. Hidalgo, *Spy for Fidel*, 43–44.

20. See Hidalgo, *Spy for Fidel*, 62–63.

21. Jorge Masetti, *In the Pirates' Den: My Life as a Secret Agent for Castro* (San Francisco: Encounter Books, 1993), 37–38.

22. See Masetti, *In the Pirates' Den*, 70.

23. Agee, *Inside the Company*, 489–90.

24. Agee, *Inside the Company*, 490.

25. John Ranelagh, *The Rise and Decline of the CIA* (London: Weidenfeld & Nicholson, 1986), 471–73, 538.

26. Agee, *On the Run*, 31–32.

27. Agee, *Inside the Company*, 319.

28. Brands, *Latin America's Cold War*, 107–11; Reid, *Forgotten Continent*, 116–21.

29. Agee, *On the Run*, 32.

30. CIA memoranda to the file, undated, obtained via Agee's FOIA request; Agee Papers, box 5, folder 9.

31. "*Playboy* Interview: Philip Agee," *Playboy*, August 1975, 48–60.

32. Agee, *Inside the Company*, 486, 494–95; Agee, *On the Run*, 35–39.

33. David Corn, *Blond Ghost: Ted Shackley and the CIA's Crusades* (New York: Simon & Schuster, 1994), 230.

34. Agee, *Inside the Company*, 496.

35. Agee, *Inside the Company*, 496.

36. Agee, *Inside the Company*, 496–503.

37. Federal Tort Claims Act complaint, filed September 21, 1994; Agee Papers, box 2, folder 36. See also Agee, *Inside the Company*, 497.

38. Agee, *On the Run*, 123.

39. See Agee, *Inside the Company*, 432; and Agee, *On the Run*, 19–20.

40. Agee, *On the Run*, 22.

41. Agee, *On the Run*, 22.

42. CIA memorandum, undated; obtained via Agee's FOIA request; Agee Papers, box 5, folder 9; box 6, folder 63.

43. CIA memorandum, obtained via Agee's FOIA request; Agee Papers, box 5, folder 9.

44. CIA document entitled "CIRCUMSTANCES LEADING UP TO RESIGNATION," undated; obtained via Agee's FOIA request; Agee Papers, box 5, folder 10.

45. Agee, *On the Run*, 43–44.

46. CIA records, obtained via Agee's FOIA request; Agee Papers, box 5, folder 29.

47. "Talking paper" with transmittal slip from "Chief of Counterintelligence," undated, obtained via Agee's FOIA request; Agee Papers, box 6, folder 63.

48. CIA post-resignation evaluation, undated and partially redacted; obtained via Agee's FOIA request; Agee Papers, box 5, folder 32.

49. See Christopher Moran, *Company Confessions: Secrets, Memoirs, and the CIA* (New York: Thomas Dunne, 2015), 194; Ted Shackley, *Spymaster: My Life in the CIA* (Washington, DC: Potomac Books, 2005), xvii.

50. Prados, *Family Jewels*, 245.

51. Author interview with David Corn, May 19, 2016.

52. Author interview with Melvin Wulf, February 22, 2016.

53. Author interview with Melvin Wulf, February 22, 2016. Drew Days did not respond to a request for an interview.

54. CIA memorandum, undated, obtained via Agee's FOIA request; Agee Papers, box 5, folder 9.

55. Prados, *Family Jewels*, 244.

56. Note to Philip Agee from Philip Agee Jr., dated October 16, 1972; Agee Papers, box 15, folder 24 (typographical errors corrected). The note is reproduced in *Inside the Company* on page 498.

57. CIA Request for Personnel Action, dated November 18, 1968; obtained by author via FOIA request to Central Intelligence Agency, Reference No. F-2010–00430, Document C05651167.

58. Agee, *Inside the Company*, 498.

59. Agee, *Inside the Company*, 503.

60. Biographical Statement of Angela Camargo Seixas; Agee Papers, box 1A, folder 3.

61. See, e.g., FBI communication re: Philip Agee, dated March 27, 1992; obtained by author via FOIA request to Federal Bureau of Investigation, FOIPA Request No. 1141978–000.

62. The seminal articles were Seymour Hersh, "Censored Matter in Book about C.I.A. Said to Have Related Chile Activities," *New York Times*, September 11, 1974, https://www.nytimes.com/1974/09/11/archives/censored-matter-in-book-about-cia -said-to-have-related-chile.html (relating to Marchetti's redacted book); "Huge C.I.A. Operation Reported in U.S. against Antiwar Forces, Other Dissidents in Nixon Years," *New York Times*, December 22, 1974, https://www.nytimes.com/1974 /12/22/archives/huge-cia-operation-reported-in-u-s-against-antiwar-forces-other .html.

63. Agee, *On the Run*, 82.

64. John M. Crewdson, "CIA Agent Said to Give Secrets to Russia in 1972," *New York Times*, July 4, 1974, 1.

65. See especially Prados, *Family Jewels*, 245–48.

66. CIA document, substantially redacted, obtained via Agee's FOIA request; Agee Papers, box 5, folder 9. Described in Agee, *On the Run*, 91.

67. CIA memo, undated; obtained via Agee's FOIA request; Agee Papers, box 5, folder 37.

68. John M. Crewdson, "Ex-CIA Agent Denies He Gave Information to the Russians," *New York Times*, July 11, 1974, 9. See generally Agee, *On the Run*, 81–92.

69. Agee, *On the Run*, 92–96.

70. See, e.g., Yuval Rottenstreich and Christopher K. Hsee, "Money, Kisses, and Electric Shocks: On the Affective Psychology of Risks," *Psychological Science* 12, no. 3 (May 2001): 185–90.

71. Jeffreys-Jones, *In Spies We Trust*, 231.

72. See generally Daniel A. Sargent, *A Superpower Transformed: The Remaking of American Foreign Relations in the 1970s* (New York: Oxford University Press, 2015).

73. Agee, *Inside the Company*, 516.

74. FBI memorandum from W. B. Wanall to A. B. Fulton re: *Inside the Company* (BOOK REVIEW) RESEARCH MATTER, dated January 21, 1975; obtained via Agee's FOIA request; Agee Papers, box 6, folder 59.

75. USIA "review" of *Inside the Company*, dated (by transmittal memo) May 7, 1975; obtained via Agee's FOIA request; Agee Papers, box 6, folder 65.

76. Confidential cables to U.S. Embassy in The Hague from Secretary of State Henry A. Kissinger, dated July 1974 and January 1975, obtained via Agee's FOIA request; Agee Papers, box 6, folder 11.

77. Transmitted by State Department AIRGRAM to State Department HQ from US EC Mission in Brussels, dated March 24, 1975, obtained via Agee's FOIA request; Agee Papers, box 6, folder 16.

78. Cable to Secretary of State from U.S. Embassy in Ecuador, dated May 15, 1975, obtained via Agee's FOIA request; Agee Papers, box 6, folder 22. Cable to Secretary of State from U.S. Embassy in Mexico, dated September 18, 1975, obtained via Agee's FOIA request; Agee Papers, box 6, folder 19. Cable to Secretary of State from U.S. Embassy in Lisbon, dated January 16, 1977, obtained via Agee's FOIA request; Agee Papers, box 6, folder 45.

79. Gabriel García Márquez, "Crisis en la CIA," *Trifuno*, January 4, 1975.

80. Letter to Agee from Harcourt Brace Jovanovich, Inc., attaching galleys, dated January 9, 1976; Agee Papers, box 19, folder 53.

81. Transcript, Maury Povich interview with Agee, David Atlee Phillips and Harry Rositzke, WTTG TV, dated June 23, 1975; Agee Papers, box 18, folder 24.

82. Interview, *Literaturnaya Gazetta*, April 21, 1975; located in Agee Papers, box 18, folder 19.

83. Gabriel García Márquez, "The CIA in Latin America," review of *Inside the Company: CIA Diary*, by Philip Agee, trans. Gregory Rabasa, *New York Review of Books*, August 7, 1975.

84. See, e.g., Patrick Breslin, "The CIA and the Guilt of Intelligence," review of *Inside the Company: CIA Diary*, by Philip Agee, Book World, *Washington Post*, February 23, 1975; Walter Pincus, "Is There a Secret Police of American Capitalism?," review of *Inside the Company: CIA Diary*, by Philip Agee, *New York Times*, August 3, 1975.

85. Richard R. Lingeman, "The Unmaking of a Spy," review of *Inside the Company: CIA Diary*, by Philip Agee, *New York Times*, July 31, 1975.

86. See clippings on liaison services; Agee Papers, box 14, folder 47.

87. Marked-up galley, undated; Agee Papers, box 16, folder 38.

88. "Exposing the CIA," *CounterSpy* 2 (Winter 1975).

89. "Agee Goes on Naming CIA Agents," *Washington Star*, January 16, 1976, 1.

90. Garry Wills, "The CIA from Beginning to End," *New York Review of Books*, January 22, 1976.

91. A. Stepanov, "Agent Drops Out of the Game: How Philip Agee Broke With the CIA," *Pravda*, February 12, 1976, translation obtained via Agee's FOIA request; Agee Papers, box 5, folder 30.

92. Agee's 1976 datebook, entries for July 24 through August 2; Agee Papers, box 3.

93. CIA document, undated, obtained via Agee's FOIA request; Agee Papers, box 5, folder 9.

94. Colin Smith, *Carlos: Portrait of a Terrorist* (London: Andre Deutsch, 1976), 15–18.

95. On the U.S. intelligence community's underperformance against the DGI, see, e.g., Scott W. Carmichael, *True Believer: Inside the Investigation and Capture of Ana Montes, Cuba's Master Spy* (Annapolis, MD: Naval Institute Press, 2007), 151–52, 176. On the DGI's formation and operations in general, and in particular the ease with which it has infiltrated, operated in, and recruited in the United States, see Hidalgo, *Spy for Fidel*, appendix, 92–110.

96. Cable to Department of State et al. from US Embassy Jamaica re: Philip Agee Allegations Headlines by Jamaican Press, dated September 17, 1976; https://wiki leaks.org/plusd/cables/1976KINGST03978_b.html.

97. Press clippings, obtained via Agee's FOIA request; Agee Papers, box 6, folder 38.

98. Telegram 4183 From the Embassy in Jamaica to the Department of State, September 28, 1976, Office of the Historian, Bureau of Public Affairs, US Department of State, https://history.state.gov/historicaldocuments/frus1969–76ve11p1/d470.

99. *CounterSpy* 3, no. 1 (Spring 1976) and no. 3 (December 1976). Copies held by CIA obtained via Agee's FOIA request; Agee Papers, box 5, folder 33.

100. Agee, *On the Run*, 159–60.

101. Agee, *On the Run*, 160.

102. Cable to Secretary of State from U.S. Embassy in London, dated November 18, 1976, obtained via Agee's FOIA request; Agee Papers, box 6, folder 29.

103. Ramsey Clark noted these features of the case in "England Revives the Star Chamber," *Nation*, March 5, 1977, 261–63.

104. Agee Papers, box 12, folder 25.

105. "Draft Defense Statement," dated January 11, 1977; Agee Papers, box 12, folder 16.

106. Agee Papers, box 13, folder 1. The articles were Philip Agee, "Why I Split the CIA and Spilled the Beans," *Esquire*, June 1975, and "Rendezvous in Geneva: My Spy Exposed," *CounterSpy* 3, no. 2 (1976) (concerning the Ferrara/Donegan operation).

107. UK Country Files; Agee Papers, box 11, folder 9.

108. Agee Papers, box 12, folder 31.

109. Agee, *On the Run*, 169–73, 185; Agee Papers, box 11.

110. E. P. Thompson, letter to the editor, *The Times* (London), November 22, 1976.

111. Agee Papers, box 12, folders 22–24.

112. Cable to Secretary of State from U.S. Embassy in London, dated February 24, 1977, obtained via Agee's FOIA request; Agee Papers, box 6, folder 25.

113. Agee Papers, box 12, folder 17.

114. Agee Papers, box 18, folder 30.

115. Letter to Merlyn Rees from Ramsey Clark, dated February 7, 1977; Agee Papers, box 12, folder 22.

116. Clark, "England Revives the Star Chamber," pp. 261–63.

117. "Bobby Fischer's Mother Tries the Sleep-in Gambit to Harass the British Government," *People* (March 21, 1977), https://people.com/archive/bobby-fischers-mother-tries-the-sleep-in-gambit-to-harass-the-british-government-vol-7-no-11/; Albin Krebs, "Notes on People," *New York Times*, June 28, 1977, https://www.nytimes.com/1977/06/28/archives/notes-on-people.html.

118. Parliamentary Debate (Hansard), vol. 931, no. 98, Wednesday, May 4, 1977, pp. 368–401; located in Agee Papers, box 11, folder 11.

119. Letters, dated May 26, 1977; Agee Papers, box 13, folder 7.

120. Agee Papers, box 12, folder 21.

121. Agee Papers, box 15, folder 29.

122. Philip Agee, "Exiled: Agee's Amsterdam Letter," *Leveller*, July/August 1977, 12. See materials in Agee Papers, box 13, folder 10.

123. See, e.g., Karl van Meter, "Man Without a Country," *Paris Metro*, August 2, 1977; Philip Agee, "How I Was Kicked Out of France—and Why," *Paris Metro*, Sep-

tember 14, 1977; Therese Roberge, letter to the editor, *Paris Metro*, November 9, 1977.

124. Agee datebook, 1979; Agee Papers, box 3.

125. Agee, *On the Run*, 253–54, 270–76, 291–92, 372; Letter to Lynne Bernabei from Agee dated November 29, 1995; Agee Papers, box 7, folder 2.

126. See James H. Critchfield, *Partners at the Creation: The Men Behind Postwar Germany's Defense and Intelligence Establishments* (Annapolis, MD: Naval Institute Press, 2003).

127. See Tony Judt, *Postwar: A History of Europe Since 1945* (New York: Penguin, 2006), 497–98. See also David Calleo, *Beyond American Hegemony: The Future of the Western Alliance* (New York: Basic Books, 1987).

128. See, e.g., Dana H. Allin, *Cold War Illusions: America, Europe, and Soviet Power, 1969–1989* (New York: St. Martin's Press, 1997).

129. See generally Judt, *Postwar*, 496–503.

CHAPTER FOUR

1. Miles Copeland, book review of *Inside the Company*, *Spectator*, January 11, 1975.

2. See Agee, *On the Run*, 123.

3. Agee, *On the Run*, 351.

4. Corn, *Blond Ghost*, 232–35, 237–40; Agee, *On the Run*, passim.

5. *Covert Action Information Bulletin*, Premier Issue, July 1978, http://covertaction magazine.com/wp-content/uploads/2018/08/CAIB01.pdf.

6. Agee Papers, box 19, folder 31. See, e.g., Laurence Stern, "Ex-Agent Identified in 'Flap,'" *Washington Post*, July 7, 1974.

7. Letter to DCI William Colby from Attorney General Edward H. Levi, dated March 1975, obtained via Agee's FOIA request; Agee Papers, box 5, folder 48.

8. Edwin Warner, "New Day for the CIA," *Time*, January 19, 1981.

9. See Murray Seeger, "Agee's Archive: The Truth Unredacted?," *Washington Decoded*, November 11, 2010, https://www.washingtondecoded.com/site/2010/11/agee.html. See also Agee, *Inside the Company*, 456, 523. On Pawlowski and other pro-Western Polish spies, see "A Top Fencer Reported Jailed by Warsaw as Spying Suspect," *New York Times*, August 15, 1975, https://www.nytimes.com/1975/08/15/archives/a-top-fencer-reported-jailed-by-warsaw-as-spying-suspect.html; Benjamin Weiser, *A Secret Life: The Polish Officer, His Covert Mission, and the Price He Paid to Save His Country* (New York: PublicAffairs, 2004).

10. See Rhodri Jeffreys-Jones, *The CIA and American Democracy* (New Haven, CT: Yale University Press, 1989), 211.

11. Letter to the editor, "Philip Agee on Exposing CIA Agents," *Washington Post*, February 22, 1976.

12. Morley Safer interview with David Atlee Phillips, *60 Minutes, CBS*, January 25, 1976.

13. See, e.g., David Atlee Phillips, "Mr. Philip Agee, Jet-Set Benedict Arnold," *Eagle*, December 1981.

14. Norman Kempster, "Identity of U.S. Spies Harder to Hide, Colby Says," *Los Angeles Times*, December 28, 1977.

15. See Bill Gertz, "Ex-CIA Officials Blast 'Defector' Agee," *Washington Times*, June 11, 1987, 4-D.

16. Memorandum for the Record re: Meeting in Plains, Georgia, dated November 22, 1976; www.foia.ciagov/browse_docs_full.asp.

17. See Jeffreys-Jones, *The CIA and American Democracy*, 211–12; G. J. A. O'Toole, *Honorable Treachery: A History of U.S. Intelligence, Espionage, and Covert Action from the American Revolution to the CIA* (New York: Atlantic Monthly Press, 1991), 492–93.

18. Rick Perlstein, *The Invisible Bridge: The Fall of Nixon and the Rise of Reagan* (New York: Simon & Schuster, 2014), 575–78, 598.

19. Gary Hart, e-mail to the author, December 7, 2009.

20. See Barbara Bush, *Barbara Bush: A Memoir* (New York: Scribner, 1994).

21. George H. W. Bush, "Luncheon Remarks," presented at Conference on U.S. Intelligence and the End of the Cold War, Texas A&M University, November 19, 1999; https://www.cia.gov/news-information/speeches-testimony/1999/dci_spee ch_111999bushremarks.html.

22. Author interview with Glenn Carle, March 9, 2016.

23. See Eva Dillon, *Spies in the Family: An American Spymaster, His Russian Crown Jewel, and the Friendship That Helped End the Cold War* (New York: HarperCollins, 2017).

24. See, e.g., Jeff Stein, "The Trenchcoats Retrench," *Mother Jones*, February/March 1981.

25. *Progressive*, June 1982; located in Agee Papers, box 14, folder 1.

26. Walter James McIntosh, e-mail to the author, March 26, 2016.

27. Memorandum for the President from George Bush, dated January 3, 1976; www.foia.cia.gov/browse_docs_full.asp.

28. Memorandum for Deputy Director for Administration re: Civil Suit for Wrongful Death/Dick Welch, dated January 19, 1976; obtained by author via FOIA request to Central Intelligence Agency, Reference No. F-2010–00430, Document C00022097.

29. Victor Marchetti, "CIA Able to Gag Defector," *Spotlight*, July 27, 1987.

30. Author interview with Melvin Wulf, February 22, 2016.

31. Affidavit of DCI Stansfield Turner in *Agee vs. CIA*, dated January 29, 1980; Agee Papers, box 7, folder 28.

32. Bob Woodward, *Veil: The Secret Wars of the CIA* (New York: Simon & Schuster, 2005), 383–84n.

33. See George Lardner Jr., "CIA Uses Agee Case in War on Freedom of Information Act," *Washington Post*, March 15, 1980.

34. Order, *Agee v. CIA*, dated October 2, 1980; located in Agee Papers, box 8, folders 16 and 21.

35. "Former Agent Exposes Colleagues," *Tampa Times*, January 16, 1976.

36. See Adam Goldman, "Ex-CIA Officer Suspected of Compromising Chinese Informants Is Arrested," *New York Times*, January 16, 2018; Mark Mazzetti, Adam Goldman, Michael S. Schmidt, and Matt Apuzzo, "Killing C.I.A. Informants, China Crippled U.S. Spying Operations," *New York Times*, May 20, 2017.

37. Gerassi, "An Interview with Philip Agee. See also Agee, "Why I Split the CIA."

38. See, e.g., John M. Crewdson, "Covers for C.I.A. Growing Problem," *New York Times*, January 16, 1976.

39. "*Playboy* Interview: Philip Agee." Comparably incisive was Fred Fiske's "Empathy" show, WWDC Radio (Washington, DC), August 1, 1975.

40. Jane Friedman, "'I Don't Care About Vulnerability,'" *Newsweek*, August 12, 1977.

41. Philip Agee, "Why the CIA Should be Exposed," unpublished paper, undated; Agee Papers, box 18, folder 6.

42. Philip Agee Jr., e-mail to the author, December 21, 2009.

43. Philip Berrigan (with Fred A. Wilcox), *Fighting the Lamb's War: Skirmishes with the American Empire—The Autobiography of Philip Berrigan* (Monroe, ME: Common Courage Press, 1996), 95.

44. See Daniel Berrigan, *The Trial of the Catonsville Nine* (New York: Fordham Uni-

versity Press, 2004); Shawn Francis Peters, *The Catonsville Nine: A Story of Faith and Resistance in the Vietnam Era* (Oxford: Oxford University Press, 2012).

45. Berrigan, *Fighting the Lamb's War*, 93.

46. See Anne Klejment and Nancy L. Roberts, "The Catholic Worker and the Vietnam War," in Klejment and Roberts, eds., *American Catholic Pacifism: The Influence of Dorothy Day and the Catholic Worker Movement* (Westport, CT: Praeger, 1996), 153–69.

47. Birthday card to Agee from "Patty," undated; Agee Papers, box 3, folder 1.

48. Letter from Agee to Wolfgang Ludwig, undated; Agee Papers, box 2.

49. See "Rev. Philip Berrigan and Pulitzer Prize-winning author [*sic*] Philip Agee at Greens Party Nuremberg Tribunal," photo by Sahm Doherty, Getty Images, 1983, https://www.gettyimages.com/detail/news-photo/rev-philip-berrigan-and-pulitzer-prize-winning-author-news-photo/50541397.

50. Redacted CIA document; obtained via Agee's FOIA request, undated; Agee Papers, box 5, folder 32.

51. Cable to FBI Director from FBI Legat (legal attaché) in Mexico City, dated July 22, 1974, obtained via Agee's FOIA request; Agee Papers, box 6, folder 58.

52. Book contract between Agee and Stonehill Publishing Company, dated October 6, 1975; Agee Papers, box 1A, folder 2. Letter to Agee from Melvin Wulf; Agee Papers, box 2, folder 33.

53. CIA Notification of Personnel Action, effective date November 22, 1968; obtained by author via FOIA request to Central Intelligence Agency, Reference No. F-2010–00430, Document C05651166.

54. Author interview with Melvin Wulf, February 22, 2016.

55. FBI communication re: Philip Agee, dated December 16, 1992; obtained by author via FOIA request to Federal Bureau of Investigation, FOIPA Request No. 1141978–000.

56. Author interview with Michael Opperskalski, July 16, 2016.

57. Invoices and financial statements, Agee Papers, box 18, folder 22.

58. Agee, *On the Run*, 11.

59. Agee, *On the Run*, 18–23.

60. Biographical Statement of Angela Camargo Seixas; Agee Papers, box 1A, folder 3.

61. Langguth, *Hidden Terrors*, 197, 207.

62. Langguth, *Hidden Terrors*, 42–43.

63. For an especially emphatic recent example, see Christopher Moran, "Turning against the CIA: Whistleblowers during the 'Time of Troubles,'" *Journal of the Historical Association* 100 (April 2015). For a considerably more measured, probing, and sympathetic assessment, see Mistry, "A Transnational Protest."

64. CIA memorandum for the record, undated; obtained via Agee's FOIA request; Agee Papers, box 5, folder 32.

65. Memorandum to Director, FBI, from FBI Special Agent in Charge, Washington Field Office, unredacted, dated July 31, 1975; obtained via Agee's FOIA request; Agee Papers, box 6, folder 59. See also the heavily redacted memo, dated December 23, 1975, suggesting that the FBI was investigating whether a U.S. citizen had contact with Agee while traveling overseas; obtained via Agee's FOIA request; Agee Papers, box 6, folder 61.

66. Agee, *On the Run*, 218.

67. Friedman, "'I Don't Care About Vulnerability.'"

68. Agee datebooks, 1975–77; Agee Papers, box 3.

69. Agee, *On the Run*, 222.

70. Agee, *On the Run*, 273.

71. Agee, *On the Run*, 252–54.

72. Agee, *On the Run*, 227.

73. Author interview with Michael Opperskalski, July 16, 2016.

74. Author interview with Giselle Roberge Agee, July 15, 2016.

75. Agee datebooks, 1978–2007; Agee Papers, boxes 3 and 4.

76. See generally Agee datebook, 1978; Agee Papers, box 3. Author interview with Gselle Roberge Agee, July 15, 2016.

77. Agee, *On the Run*, 299.

78. Agee datebook, September 28, 1978; Agee Papers, box 3.

79. Author interview with Giselle Roberge Agee, July 15, 2016; letter to the author from Giselle Roberge Agee, dated February 20, 2019.

80. Author interview with Giselle Roberge Agee, July 15, 2016.

81. Author interview with Michael Opperskalski, July 16, 2016.

82. Author interview with Giselle Roberge Agee, July 15, 2016.

83. Agee, *On the Run*, 314.

84. "CIA Defector May Judge Hostages," *New York Post*, December 17, 1979; located in Agee Papers, box 20, folder 4.

85. Letter to Agee from Robert C. Stebbins, Consulate General of the United States of America, Hamburg, dated December 23, 1979; obtained by author via FOIA request to U.S. Department of State, Case No. 201000351, Document B1. See generally Agee, *On the Run*, 314–19.

86. Author interview with Giselle Roberge Agee, July 15, 2016.

87. Conservatives tended to applaud the decision as a national security constraint on the first amendment, while liberals condemned it as a diminution of the first amendment and of the structural constitutional right to travel. The case generated several passionate law review articles, notes, and comments challenging its holding. See, e.g., Joy Beane, "Passport Revocation: A Critical Analysis of *Haig v. Agee* and the Policy Test," *Fordham International Law Journal* 5, no. 1 (1981); Joan R. M. Bullock, "National Security Interests vs. The First Amendment: *Haig v. Agee*," *University of Toledo Law Review* 13, no. 4 (Summer 1982); Steven B. Kaplan, "The CIA Responds to Its Black Sheep: Censorship and Passport Revocation—The Case of Philip Agee," *Connecticut Law Review* 13, no. 2 (Winter 1981); Brad R. Roth, "The First Amendment in the Foreign Affairs Realm: Domesticating the Restrictions on Citizen Participation," 2 *Temple Political & Civil Liberties Law Review* 255 (Spring 1993). Agee himself maintained a defiant posture, highlighting the capriciousness of the decision and its implication that he was a highly effective and successful counterspy. See Philip Agee, "I Don't Need a Passport," *New York Times*, July 27, 1981. The Obama administration followed the *Haig v. Agee* precedent in depriving Edward Snowden of his passport in 2013.

88. *Haig v. Agee*, 453 U.S. 280 (1981).

89. Author interview with Melvin Wulf, February 22, 2016.

90. See Agee datebook, entry for December 24, 1979; Agee Papers, box 3.

91. "Trial By Agee," *New York Times*, January 7, 1980.

92. Philip Agee, unpublished letter to the editor of the *New York Times*, dated January 9, 1980, received January 21, 1980; New York Times Company records, Autograph file, Manuscripts and Archives Division, New York Public Library, Astor, Lenox, and Tilden Foundations.

93. Application for absentee ballot, commonwealth of Virginia, 1984; Agee Papers, box 1A, folder 5A.

94. Author interview with Giselle Roberge Agee, July 15, 2016.

95. Various travel-related documents; obtained by author via FOIA request to US Department of State, Case No. 201000351.

96. Author interview with Michael Opperskalski, July 16, 2016.

97. Author interview with Giselle Roberge Agee, July 15, 2016.

98. Agee datebooks, 1976–2007; Agee Papers, boxes 3 and 4.

99. See, e.g., Agee datebook, entry for January 8, 1978; Agee Papers, box 3.

100. Agee datebooks, 1976–2007; Agee 1992 datebook, entry for February 13, 1992; Agee Papers, boxes 3 and 4.

101. Letters to Dale and Corinne Wiehoff and to Annie Hess from Agee; Agee Papers, box 2, folder 49.

102. Letter to Dale Wiehoff, dated December 14, 1984; letter to Agee from Christopher Agee, dated January 24, 1988; Agee Papers, box 2, folder 49.

103. See, e.g., Philip Agee Jr., "UConn Dean Reports of CIA Attempt to Gain Info on Foreign Students," *Campus Watch* 2, no. 2 (Fall 1990); located in Agee Papers, box 14, folder 2.

104. Materials dated October 1989; Agee Papers, box 14, folder 5.

105. Author interview with Philip Agee Jr., May 6, 2015; Chris John Agee. "Bridging the Gap: Philip Agee, 1935–2008," *NACLA Reporting on the Americas*, no. 42, January–February 2009.

106. Agee 1979 datebook, entry for January 1, 1980; Agee Papers, box 3.

107. Memorandum from CIA Assistant General Counsel, undated; obtained via Agee's FOIA request; Agee Papers, box 5, folder 25.

108. Agee datebook, entry for September 14, 1980; Agee Papers, box 3.

109. Agee datebook, entry for September 7, 1988; Agee Papers, box 4.

110. Author interview with Giselle Roberge Agee, July 15, 2016.

111. Author interview with Giselle Roberge Agee, July 15, 2016.

112. Agee datebooks, 1978–2007; Agee Papers, boxes 3 and 4.

113. Letter to Ronald Weber from Agee, dated April 20, 1980; Agee Papers, box 2, folder 42.

114. Letter to John Wilkinson from Agee, dated June 1, 1982; Agee Papers, box 2, folder 43. Letter to Agee from Webster A. Stone, dated September 25, 1983; Letter to Stone from Agee, dated October 12, 1983; Agee Papers, box 2, folder 46. Letter to Agee from Joel Schechter, dated October 18, 1984; Agee Papers, box 2, folder 49; see Joel R. Schechter, *Durov's Pig: Clowns, Politics and Theatre* (New York: Theatre Communications Group, 1985). Letter to Douglas Valentine from Agee, dated March 30, 1985; Agee Papers, box 2, folder 50; see Douglas Valentine, *The Phoenix Program* (New York: William Morrow, 1990).

115. Author interview with Giselle Roberge Agee, July 15, 2016.

116. Letter to Agee from Rose Smart, dated February 5, 1982; Agee Papers, box 2, folder 42

117. Letter to Mr. and Mrs. Edward Horman from Agee, dated October 3, 1986; Agee Papers, box 2, folder 43.

118. Various letters, Agee Papers, box 1A.

119. Letter to Jon Peters, Barwood Productions, from Agee, dated October 31, 1975; Agee Papers, box 2, folder 40. Letter to Agee from Oliver Stone, dated March 3, 1988; Agee Papers, box 3, folder 3.

120. Memorandum to Agee from Jamie Otis, dated August 14, 1996; Agee Papers, box 3, folder 9. Invitation to fundraiser on October 26, 1996; Agee Papers, box 15, folder 23.

121. Letter to Agee from Sean MacBride, dated April 2, 1987; Agee Papers, box 2, folder 53. Letter to Agee from Howard Zinn; Agee Papers, box 3, folder 4.

122. Letter to Agee from Stephen Elliot Wilmer; Agee Papers, box 1A. Stephen Elliot Wilmer, e-mail to author, February 15, 2016.

123. See Roger Worthington, "Man Without a Country," *Chicago Tribune*, March 26, 1981. See also Frank Snepp, *Irreparable Harm: A Firsthand Account of How One Agent Took on the CIA in an Epic Battle over Secrecy and Free Speech* (New York: Random House, 1999), 12.

124. Author interview with Giselle Roberge Agee, July 15, 2016.

125. See Jonathan Kwitny, *Endless Enemies: The Making of an Unfriendly World* (New York: Penguin, 1986).

126. Letter to Agee from Bill Blum, arrived January 25, 1988; Agee Papers, box 3, folder 1.

127. Agee datebook, entry for December 9, 1981; Agee Papers, box 3. Letter to Daniel Ellsberg from Agee, dated January 14, 1982, Agee Papers, box 2, folder 42. Author interview with Giselle Roberge Agee, July 15, 2016.

128. Agee datebooks, entries for February 15, 1980, September 30 through November 26, 1987, early 1988; Agee Papers, boxes 3 and 4.

129. Letter to Petra Kelly from Agee, dated March 29, 1985; Agee Papers, box 2, folder 50.

130. Press release, Agee Papers, box 19, folder 13. See also "Former CIA Agents Call For End to Covert Operations," UPI, October 29, 1987, https://www.upi.com/Archi ves/1987/10/29/Former-CIA-agents-call-for-end-to-covert-operations/96915624 82000/.

131. See "Three Old Spies Out in the Cold," *Newsweek*, April 6, 1981; located in Agee Papers, box 17, unnumbered folder.

132. Letter to Ralph McGehee from Agee, dated April 21, 1981; Agee Papers, box 2, folder 31; box 14, folder 7.

133. Agee-McGehee correspondence, 1984–93; Agee Papers, box 14, folder 59.

134. Letter to Agee from Louis Wolf, dated October 22, 1989; Agee Papers, box 2, folder 31.

135. Agee datebooks, 1978–2007; Agee Papers, boxes 3 and 4.

136. Author interview with Giselle Roberge Agee, July 15, 2016.

137. "Open Letter," dated October 22, 1980; Agee Papers, box 17, folder 49A.

138. Philip Agee and Stephen Weissman, "CIA vs. USA—The Agency's Plot to Take Over America," *Oui*, September 1975; located in Agee Papers, box 18, folders 11 and 12.

139. *Garage Dibune* 1, no. 2 (December 1987): 6–7; located in Agee Papers, box 1A, folder 2.

CHAPTER FIVE

1. See John Patrick Diggins, *The Rise and Fall of the American Left* (New York, W. W. Norton, 1975), 254–65.

2. Diggins, *Rise and Fall*, 242–48.

3. Diggins, *Rise and Fall*, 275.

4. Bryan Burrough, *Days of Rage: America's Radical Underground, the FBI, and the Forgotten Age of Revolutionary Violence* (New York: Penguin, 2015), 69–71.

5. Daniel Berrigan, "Letter to the Weathermen," in Daniel Berrigan, *Essential Writings* (Maryknoll, NY: Orbis Books, 2009), 154–57.

6. Burrough, *Days of Rage*, 448.

7. Philip Jenkins, *Decade of Nightmares: The End of the Sixties and the Making of Eighties America* (Oxford: Oxford University Press, 2006), 243.

8. See, e.g., Rhodri Jeffreys-Jones, *The American Left: Its Impact on Politics and Society Since 1900* (Edinburgh, UK: Edinburgh University Press, 2013), 120–23.

9. Robert W. Marks, *The Meaning of Marcuse* (New York: Ballantine, 1970), 92, 97. See also Diggins, *Rise and Fall*, 274–75.

10. Perlstein, *Invisible Bridge*, 18–20.

11. See, e.g., Jenkins, *Decade of Nightmares*, 4.

12. Jenkins, *Decade of Nightmares*, 9.

13. Jenkins, *Decade of Nightmares*, 27.

14. For a comprehensive look at economic influences and the crisis of capitalism, see Niall Ferguson et al., eds., *The Shock of the Global: The Seventies in Perspective* (Cambridge, MA: Harvard University Press, 2010).

15. See Bruce J. Schulman, *The Seventies: The Great Shift in American Culture, Society, and Politics* (New York: Free Press, 2001).

16. Thomas Borstelmann, *The 1970s: A New Global History from Civil Rights to Economic Inequality* (Princeton, NJ: Princeton University Press, 2012), 12.

17. See, e.g., Poul Villaime, Rasmus Mariager, and Helle Porsdam, eds., *The "Long 1970s": Human Rights, East-West Détente, and Transnational Relations* (Abingdon, UK: Routledge, 2016).

18. Perlstein, *Invisible Bridge*, 20–21, 322–25.

19. See Loch K. Johnson, *A Season of Inquiry Revisited: The Church Committee Confronts America's Spy Agencies* (Topeka: University of Kansas Press, 2015), 89.

20. See generally Rick Perlstein, *Nixonland: The Rise of a President and the Fracturing of America* (New York: Scribner, 2008); Perlstein, *Invisible Bridge*.

21. See generally Duco Hellema, *The Global 1970s: Radicalism, Reform, and Crisis* (Abingdon, UK: Routledge, 2019); Judt, *Postwar*; Villaime, Mariager, and Porsdam, eds., *The "Long 1970s."*

22. Judt, *Postwar*, 469.

23. See especially Judt, *Postwar*, 1–10.

24. Sarah Bakewell, *At the Existentialist Café: Freedom, Being, and Apricot Cocktails* (New York: Other Press, 2016), 292.

25. Judt, *Postwar*, 504.

26. Judt, *Postwar*, 504–23.

27. Agee datebook, entries for November 25 and 27, 1975; Agee Papers, box 3.

28. Agee datebook, 1976; Agee Papers, box 3.

29. Cable to State Department from U.S. Embassy in Lisbon, dated January 11, 1977; obtained via Agee's FOIA request; Agee Papers, box 6, folder 45.

30. Philip Agee, "The American Factor in Greece: Old and New," *Anti*, May 1977. See also Mary Anne Weaver, "CIA Critic Publishes List of 64 CIA 'Agents' in Greece," *Washington Post*, June 13, 1977; and Mary Anne Weaver manuscript, undated; Agee Papers, box 6, folder 34.

31. Lernoux, *Cry of the People*, 145, 190, 282, 288–89, 298, 309, 338.

32. Quoted in Jack Nelson-Pallmeyer, *The Politics of Compassion* (Maryknoll, NY: Orbis Books, 1986), 57.

33. See Theodore Draper, *Castro's Revolution: Myth and Realities* (New York: Praeger, 1962). See also Diggins, *Rise and Fall*, 226.

34. CIA memorandum, undated; obtained via Agee's FOIA request; Agee Papers, box 5, folder 9.

35. CIA cable, undated; obtained via Agee's FOIA request; Agee Papers, box 5, folder 34.

36. Letter to Melvin Wulf from Attorney General Benjamin Civiletti, dated March 18, 1977; Agee Papers, box 2, folder 34.

37. Letter to Agee from Melvin Wulf, dated March 18, 1981; Agee Papers, box 2, folder 32. See also Letter to Agee from Melvin Wulf, dated May 23, 1980; Agee Papers, box 5, folder 50.

38. Letter to William French Smith, Attorney General, from William J. Casey, Director of Central Intelligence, dated September 3, 1982; obtained by author via FOIA request to Central Intelligence Agency, Reference No. F-2010–00430, Document C01250582.

39. See clippings; Agee Papers, box 14, folder 1.

40. Author interview with David Corn, May 19, 2016.

41. E.g., Jenkins, *Decade of Nightmares*, 11.

42. Judt, *Postwar*, 469.

43. Judt, *Postwar*, 464–77.

44. Judt, *Postwar*, 471.

45. Judt, *Postwar*, 473.

46. E.g., Jonathan Stevenson, *"We Wrecked the Place": Contemplating an End to the Northern Irish Troubles* (New York: Free Press, 1996).

47. Judt, *Postwar*, 474.

48. Judt, *Postwar*, 484–86.

49. See, e.g., Tom Buckley, "Film: C.I.A. Pro and Con in 'Company Business,'" *New York Times*, April 15, 1980, C12.

50. "Secrecy Is Not the Only Security," *New York Times*, July 21, 1981.

51. Smith, *Carlos: Portrait of a Terrorist*, 42, 88–89, 149–65.

52. John Follain, *Jackal: The Secret Wars of Carlos the Jackal* (London: Weidenfeld & Nicholson, 1998), 1.

53. Follain, *Jackal*, 51, 113–17.

54. Follain, *Jackal*, 77–98, 130.

55. Follain, *Jackal*, 182–84.

56. Patrick Seale, *Abu Nidal: A Gun for Hire* (New York: Random House, 1992), 105.

57. Seale, *Abu Nidal*, 265.

58. Author interview with Melvin Wulf, February 22, 2016.

59. Robert Moss, "Philip Agee Rides Again," *Daily Telegraph*, April 23, 1979; located in Agee Papers, box 14, folder 1.

60. Agee, *On the Run*, 306. See also Christopher Andrew and Vasili Mitrokhin, *The Sword and the Shield: The Mitrokhin Archive and the History of the KGB* (New York: Basic Books, 1999), 233–34.

61. See manuscript titled "Destabilization in Jamaica," Agee Papers, box 17, folder 32; and Agee-Wulf correspondence; Agee Papers, box 2, folder 33.

62. Author interview with Melvin Wulf, February 22, 2016.

63. Philip Agee Jr., e-mail to the author, December 21, 2009.

64. Written Statement After Caution of Kevin McGrady, dated January 14, 1982; Agee Papers, Box 14, Folder 60.

65. Letter to Kathy Boudin from Agee, dated October 11, 1984; Agee Papers, box 2.

66. Draft proposal for article on "The Trial of the Red Army Fraction [*sic*]: Modern Democracy, German Style," undated; Agee Papers, box 16, folder 67.

67. Transcript of "A Woman in the Grenadian Nightmare: An Interview with Regina Fuchs," undated; Agee Papers, box 18, folder 7.

68. Robert Scheer and Warren Hinckle, "The 'Vietnam Lobby,'" *Ramparts*, July 1965.

69. Donald Duncan, "'The Whole Thing Was a Lie,'" *Ramparts*, February 1966.

70. Agee Papers, box 2, folder 42.

71. David Armstrong, *A Trumpet of Arms: Alternative Media in America* (Boston: South End Press, 1981), 24.

72. Armstrong, *A Trumpet of Arms*, 158–59.

73. "*Playboy* Interview: Jimmy Carter," *Playboy*, November 1976.

74. See Armstrong, *A Trumpet of Arms*, 161–223.

75. See Joe Hagan, *Sticky Fingers: The Life and Times of Jann Wenner and Rolling Stone Magazine* (New York: Knopf, 2017).

76. Armstrong, *A Trumpet of Arms*, 257.

77. Armstrong, *A Trumpet of Arms*, 295.

78. See Hinckle and Turner, *The Fish Is Red*, 267–306.

79. See Agee's letter to the editor of *Ethnos*; Agee Papers, box 19, folder 21.

80. Author interview with Michael Opperskalski, July 16, 2016.

81. "Interview: Miles Copeland—The Puppet Master," *Penthouse*, August 1978.

82. See, e.g., Bill Greeley, *Variety*, January 28, 1976.

83. Correspondence and related materials; Agee Papers, box 15, folder 27.

84. Philip Agee, "Liberté, Egalité, Torture," review of *Torture: The Role of Ideology in the French-Algerian War*, by Rita Maran, *Nation*, May 21, 1990.

85. Agee-Wulf correspondence; Agee Papers, box 2, folder 33.

86. Letter to Kathy Boudin from Agee, dated June 1, 1984; Agee Papers, box 2, folder 48.

87. Letter to Agee from Kathy Boudin, dated August 10, 1984; Agee Papers, box 2, folder 48.

88. Letter to David Truong from Agee, dated March 5, 1984; Agee Papers, box 2, folder 31.

89. William Ayers, e-mail message to the author, August 16, 2016.

90. Letter to Iranian consulate from Agee, dated April 21, 1982; Agee Papers, box 2, folder 42.

91. Author interview with Michael Opperskalski, July 16, 2016.

92. Stephen Weissman, "Philip Agee on the Run," *Inquiry*, July 10, 1978. See documents in Agee Papers, box 16, folder 22.

93. See James M. Markham, "Green Party Puts Nuclear Arms before Nuremburg 'Jury,'" *International Herald Tribune*, February 22, 1983, 2.

CHAPTER SIX

1. See, e.g., David C. Martin, *Wilderness of Mirrors* (Harper and Row, 1980); David Wise, *Molehunt: The Secret Search for Traitors That Shattered the CIA* (New York: Random House, 1992).

2. CIA memorandum, obtained via Agee's FOIA request; Agee Papers, box 5, folder 9.

3. Walter Pincus, e-mail to the author, March 17, 2009.

4. Winn L. Taplin, "To Die in Bed," *Intelligence Quarterly* 13, no. 2 (Fall 1987): 5–6; located in Agee Papers, box 18, folder 42.

5. Weiner, *Legacy of Ashes*, 575.

6. See Jeffreys-Jones, *The CIA and American Democracy*, 172.

7. Adam Roberts, "The C.I.A.: Reform Is Not Enough," *Millennium: Journal of International Studies* 6 (Spring 1977).

8. Philip Agee, "Introduction: When Myths Lead to Murder," in Ellen Ray, William Schaap, Karl Van Meter, and Louis Wolf, eds., *Dirty Work 2: The CIA in Africa* (New York: Lyle Stuart, 1979).

9. See letter from Agee to Ralph McGehee, dated April 21, 1981; Agee Papers, box 2.

10. See, e.g., James M. Scott, *Deciding to Intervene: The Reagan Doctrine and American Foreign Policy* (Durham, NC: Duke University Press, 1996).

11. Daniel T. Rodgers, *Age of Fracture* (Cambridge, MA: Belknap Press, 2011), 37.

12. Scott, *Deciding to Intervene*, 5. See also Stephen G. Rabe, *The Killing Zone: The United States Wages Cold War in Latin America* (New York: Oxford University Press, 2011).

13. Christian Smith, *Resisting Reagan: The U.S. Central America Peace Movement* (Chicago: University of Chicago Press, 1996), 21.

14. Brands, *Latin America's Cold War*, 184–87.

15. Author interview with Michael Opperskalski, July 16, 2016.

16. Philip Agee, "The CIA's Blueprint for Nicaragua," *Covert Action Information Bulletin*, no. 6 (October 1979). See documents in Agee Papers, box 16, folder 16.

17. Agee, "My Stake in Jamaica's Elections." *Free West Indian (Grenada)* 1, no. 46 (January 20, 1980): 12–13.

18. Later embodied in "Critique of State Department White Paper" in Philip Agee, *White Paper Whitewash: Interviews with Philip Agee on the CIA and El Salvador*, ed. Warner Poelchau (New York: Deep Cover Publications, 1981), 75–101. The White Paper itself is reprinted in the appendix. See "U.S. State Department White Paper" in Agee, *White Paper Whitewash*, A-1–A-87.

19. "Critique of State Department White Paper" in Agee, *White Paper Whitewash*, 101.

20. See Robert G. Kaiser and Karen De Young, "White Paper on El Salvador Is

Faulty," *Washington Post*, June 9, 1981, https://www.washingtonpost.com/archive /politics/1981/06/09/white-paper-on-el-salvador-is-faulty/e17adfa2-3763-42b4 -a1f6-1c641ecfd72f/; Jonathan Kwitny, "Apparent Errors Cloud 'White Paper' on Reds in El Salvador," *Wall Street Journal*, June 8, 1981.

21. Brands, *Latin America's Cold War*, 198–99.

22. See Nick Witham, *The Cultural Left and the Reagan Era: U.S. Protest and the Central American Revolution* (London: I. B. Tauris, 2015).

23. Smith, *Resisting Reagan*, xvi.

24. Jessica Stites Mor, "Introduction: Situating Transnational Solidarity Within Critical Human Rights Studies of Cold War Latin America," in Jessica Stites Mor, ed., *Human Rights and Transnational Solidarity in Cold War Latin America* (Madison: University of Wisconsin Press, 2013), 15.

25. See Jan Hansen, Christian Helm, and Frank Reichherzer, eds., *Making Sense of the Americas: How Protest Related to America in the 1980s and Beyond* (Frankfurt: Campus Verlag GmbH, 2015).

26. See Kim Christiaens, "Between Diplomacy and Solidarity: Western European Support Networks for Sandinista Nicaragua," *European Review of History* 21 (July 2014): 620.

27. Christiaens, "Between Diplomacy and Solidarity," 625–27.

28. See Brian Barger, "CIA Manual Said Aimed at Contra Abuses," *Washington Post*, October 31, 1984.

29. See manuscript titled "Bringing in the Coffee — Nicaragua's Wartime Harvest;" Agee Papers, box 16, folder 36.

30. See Chris John Agee, "Bridging the Gap: Philip Agee, 1935–2008."

31. Agee Papers, box 1A.

32. Agee Papers, box 1A.

33. Brands, *Latin America's Cold War*, 210–16.

34. Jeffreys-Jones, *American Left*, 152–53.

35. Agee, "My Stake in Jamaica's Elections."

36. Author interview with Michael Opperskalski, July 16, 2016.

37. Agee datebook, January 7, 1983; Agee Papers, box 3.

38. Letter to Melvin Wulf from Agee, dated August 26, 1984; Agee Papers, box 2.

39. Author interview with Michael Opperskalski, July 16, 2016.

40. Clippings; Agee Papers, box 14, folder 47.

41. Philip Agee, "Uncloaking the CIA," unpublished paper; Agee Papers, box 17, folder 68.

42. Agee datebooks; Agee Papers, box 4.

43. Agee Papers, box 1A.

44. Agee Papers, box 2.

45. Agee datebooks; Agee Papers, box 3. Letter from Agee to Melvin Wulf, dated July 23, 1984; Agee Papers, box 2.

46. See *Agee v. Baker*, 753 F. Supp. 373 (D.D.C. 1990).

47. Letter to Agee from Clyde Wells, dated April 8, 1982; Agee Papers, box 2.

48. "Intrigue Follows Spy to His Death in Miami," *International Herald Tribune*, February 10, 1983.

49. See Agee Papers, box 2.

50. Letter to C. Phillip Liechty from Agee, dated October 8, 1984; Agee Papers, box 2.

51. Agee datebook, March 30, 1985; Agee Papers, box 4.

52. Author interview with Ron Ridenour, August 16, 2016.

53. Author interview with Ron Ridenour, August 16, 2016.

54. Author interview with Ron Ridenour, August 16, 2016.

55. See Ron Ridenour, *Yankee Sandinistas* (Willimantic, CT: Curbstone Press, 1986).

56. Author interview with Ron Ridenour, August 16, 2016.

57. See John Lofton, "NBC's Strange Link with Philip Agee," *Washington Times*, January 13, 1984.

58. Agee, *Inside the Company*, 563–64.

59. See Richard J. Aldrich, "American Journalism and the Landscape of Secrecy: Tad Szulc, the CIA and Cuba," *History* (Special Issue: The CIA and American Foreign Policy) 100, no. 346 (April 2015): 189–209, https://onlinelibrary.wiley.com /doi/full/10.1111/1468-229X.12101. See also Emma Best, "One of the CIA's Private Press Contacts Was a Suspected Soviet Spy," *MuckRock*, June 14, 2017, https://www .muckrock.com/news/archives/2017/jun/14/cia-szulc/.

60. Agee Papers, box 2.

61. Agee Papers, box 2.

62. Author interview with Marc Cooper, February 19, 2016.

63. Agee-Wulf correspondence; Agee Papers; box 2, folder 33.

64. Author interview with Marc Cooper, February 19, 2016.

65. Agee-Wulf correspondence; Agee Papers, box 2, folder 34.

66. Agee datebooks; Agee Papers, box 4.

67. See Planned Tour to Australia and New Zealand, Agee Papers, box 1A, folder 8.

68. Letter to Agee from Murray Horton, dated March 30, 1987; Agee Papers, box 1A, folder 8.

69. Agee datebook, September 1, 1987; Agee Papers, box 4.

70. Author interview with Frank Deese, February 22, 2016; Letter to Agee from Frank Deese, Agee Papers, box 1A.

71. Author interview with Frank Deese, February 22, 2016.

72. Author interview with Frank Deese, February 22, 2016.

73. Frank Deese, e-mail to the author, June 29, 2017.

74. Author interview with Frank Deese, February 22, 2016.

75. Author interview with Frank Deese, February 22, 2016.

76. Transcript of Agee interview with Franklin Deese [hereafter abbreviated "Agee/Deese interview"], April 3, 1986, tape 1A, p. 8; in author's possession.

77. Agee/Deese interview, April 3, 1986, tape 1A, p. 13.

78. Agee/Deese interview, April 3, 1986, tape 1A, p. 13.

79. Agee/Deese interview, April 3, 1986, tape 1B, p. 19.

80. Agee/Deese interview, April 3, 1986, tape 2A, p. 5.

81. Agee/Deese interview, April 3, 1986, tape 2B, pp. 9–12.

82. Agee/Deese interview, April 3, 1986, tape 4B, p. 11.

83. Agee/Deese interview, April 3, 1986, tape 4B, p. 9.

84. Agee/Deese interview, April 3, 1986, tape 5B, pp. 5–6.

85. Agee/Deese interview, April 3, 1986, tape 4B, p. 12.

86. Agee/Deese interview, April 3, 1986, tape 5A, p. 6.

87. Agee/Deese interview, April 3, 1986, tape 5B, p. 3.

88. Agee/Deese interview, April 3, 1986, tape 5B, pp. 11–12.

89. Agee/Deese interview, April 3, 1986, tape 6A, pp. 3–5.

90. Agee/Deese interview, April 3, 1986, tape 6A, p. 12.

91. Agee/Deese interview, April 3, 1986, tape 7A, p. 6.

92. Agee/Deese interview, April 3, 1986, tape 7A, p. 9.

93. Agee/Deese interview, April 3, 1986, tape 7A, p. 11.

94. Agee/Deese interview, April 3, 1986, tape 7B, p. 6.

95. Agee/Deese interview, April 3, 1986, tape 7B, p. 9.

96. Agee/Deese interview, April 3, 1986, tape 7B, p. 10.

97. Agee/Deese interview, April 3, 1986, tape 7B, p. 12.

98. Frank Deese, e-mail to the author, June 29, 2017.

99. Letter to Melvin Wulf from Assistant Attorney General Stephen Trott, dated February 5, 1985; Agee Papers, box 2, folder 34.

100. Agee-Wulf correspondence; Agee Papers, box 2, folder 34.

101. Unsigned memo re: PHILIP AGEE, dated August 28, 1991; obtained by author via FOIA request to US State Department, Case No. 201000351.

102. See Thomas Powers, "The Enemy of the Agency," *New York Times*, August 2, 1987.

103. Agee Papers, box 4.

104. Agee Papers, box 18, folder 41.

105. See Beth Rhea, "Former Agent Condemns CIA Actions," *Daily Tar Heel*, November 18, 1988, 1.

106. Agee Papers, box 9, folder 28.

107. Agee Papers, box 1A.

108. Letter to Charles Betz from Agee, dated April 19, 1988; Agee Papers, box 2, folder 34.

109. Agee Papers, boxes 1A and 3.

110. Agee datebooks; Agee Papers, box 4.

111. Philip Agee, "How to Become a Non-ND Alumnus," *Common Sense*, February 1989; Agee Papers, box 1A.

112. See Keith Smart, "Agee Not the Martyr He Claims to Be," *Observer*, March 14, 1989, 8.

113. Letter to Agee from Roger K. O'Reilly, dated April 17, 1989; Agee Papers, box 3.

114. Agee Papers, box 3.

115. Letter to Michael Mooney from Daniel M. Boland, dated June 11, 1988; Agee Papers, box 3.

116. See William H. Wild, "Unmasking Agee is a Difficult Task," *Dayton Daily News*, October 15, 1988, 11.

117. Letter to Agee from Eliot Cohen, dated July 9, 1987; Agee Papers, box 3.

118. Letter to Agee from James E. Koveky, dated April 30, 1988; Agee Papers, box 3.

119. Agee Papers, box 15, folder 28.

120. Agee Papers, box 9, folder 28.

121. Article dated November 17, 1989; Agee Papers, box 14, folder 30.

122. Agee Papers, box 18, folder 23.

123. Agee Papers, box 3.

124. Agee Papers, box 14, folder 5.

125. Agee Papers, box 17, folder 24.

126. See letter to Agee from Christine Kelly, dated January 15, 1989; Agee Papers, box 3.

127. Agee Papers, box 1A.

CHAPTER SEVEN

1. See Francis Fukuyama, "The End of History?," *National Interest*, no. 16 (Summer 1989): 3–18; Francis Fukuyama, *The End of History and the Last Man* (New York: Free Press, 1992).

2. Duncan Campbell, "The Spy Who Stayed Out in the Cold," *Guardian*, January 9, 2007, https://www.theguardian.com/world/2007/jan/10/usa.duncancampbell.

3. Letter to Anthony Lewis from Melvin Wulf, dated October 12, 1990; Agee Papers, box 2.

4. "Producing the Proper Crisis: A Talk by Philip Agee," *Z Magazine*, November 1990.

5. See Russell Crandall, *Gunboat Diplomacy: U.S. Interventions in the Dominican Republic, Grenada and Panama* (Lanham, MD: Rowman & Littlefield, 2006), 197–215; Reid, *Forgotten Continent*, 106.

6. See Charles Maechling Jr., "Washington's Illegal Invasion," *Foreign Policy*, no. 79 (Summer 1990): 113–31.

7. Draft speech; Agee Papers, box 18, folder 25.

8. Philip Agee, "The CIA's Prospects in Eastern Europe," *Covert Action Information Bulletin*, no. 35, Fall 1990.

9. Unpublished manuscript, "The CIA for Beginners"; Agee Papers, box 16, folder 40.

10. Agee, *On the Run*, 24.

11. Draft, "The CIA for Beginners: 100 Questions," undated; Agee Papers, box 17, folder 13.

12. Robert Stone, *A Flag for Sunrise* (New York: Knopf, 1981), 170.

13. Draft, "The CIA for Beginners: 100 Questions," undated; Agee Papers, box 17, folder 13.

14. Agee Papers, box 14, folder 2A.

15. Draft, "The CIA for Beginners: 100 Questions," undated; Agee Papers, box 17, folder 19.

16. Agee's copy of the article was more heavily highlighted than virtually any other piece in Agee's possession. See Agee Papers, box 14, folder 8.

17. Martin A. Lee, "Their Will Be Done," *Mother Jones*, July/August 1983.

18. James Carroll, *An American Requiem: God, My Father, and the War That Came Between Us* (Boston: Houghton Mifflin, 1996).

19. Author interview with Giselle Roberge Agee, July 15, 2016.

20. Author interview with Glenn Carle, March 9, 2016.

21. Agee Papers, box 16, folder 51.

22. Agee datebooks; Agee Papers, box 4.

23. See, e.g., Carl Bernstein, "The CIA and the Media," *Rolling Stone*, October 20, 1977, 55–67.

24. Datebook entry for November 20, 1990; Agee Papers, box 4.

25. See Philip Agee, manuscript of article entitled "The CIA at Fifty"; Agee Papers, box 16, folder 39.

26. Agee Papers, box 16, folder 31.

27. Agee Papers, box 14, folder 62.

28. Daniel Patrick Moynihan, "*JFK* Nonsense: Belief of Conspiracy Was to Be Expected," *International Herald Tribune*, December 31, 1991–January 1, 1992, 5.

29. Agee Papers, box 15, folder 21.

30. Agee datebooks; Agee Papers, box 4.

31. Datebook entry for March 2, 1992; Agee Papers, box 4.

32. Rutten, "A Spook's Faustian Bargain."

33. Author interview with Michael Opperskalski, July 16, 2016.

34. See Agee Papers, box 16.

35. Agee Papers, box 15, folder 48.

36. Agee Papers, box 16, folder 10.

37. See, e.g., Rick Atkinson, "Racing With the Grim Reaper to Unmask Nazis," *International Herald Tribune*, August 29, 1995.

38. See Agee Papers, box 15, folders 35–36.

39. Agee Papers; box 14, folder 66.

40. See Agee Papers, box 15, folders 40–42.

41. Agee Papers, box 16, folders 15–17, 54.

42. See Agee Papers, box 16.

43. See Agee Papers, box 15, folders 43–45.

44. Agee Papers, box 10, folder 18.

45. See, e.g., Janet Reitman, "U.S. Law Enforcement Failed to See the Threat of White Nationalism; Now They Don't Know How to Stop It," *New York Times Magazine*, November 3, 2018, https://www.nytimes.com/2018/11/03/magazine/FBI-charlottesville-white-nationalism-far-right.html.

46. Agee Papers, box 15, folder 46.

47. Agee Papers, box 15.

48. Agee Papers, box 15, folder 53.

49. Agee Papers, box 13, folder 17.

50. See *Congressional Record*, vol. 141, no. 1, S. 387, January 4, 1995.

51. Agee datebooks; Agee Papers, box 4.

52. See, e.g., "Philip Agee: A Profile," *Common Sense*, March 1996, 7.

53. Agee Papers, box 13, folder 23.

54. Agee Papers, box 15, folder 4.

55. Rick Atkinson and Steve Vogel, "Accused Spy Says He Was U.S. Double Agent," *Washington Post*, September 23, 1994.

56. See Mary Williams Walsh, "U.S. Professor Guilty in German Spy Case," *Los Angeles Times*, November 11, 1995.

57. Letter to Johanna Lawrenson from Agee, dated September 6, 1994; Agee Papers, box 13, folder 16.

58. Agee Papers, box 13, folder 34.

59. Agee datebooks; Agee Papers, box 4.

60. Agee Papers, box 14, folder 17.

61. Agee Papers, box 16, folder 33.

62. Complaint; located in Agee Papers, box 7, folder 9.

63. Barbara Bush, *Barbara Bush: A Memoir* (New York: Guideposts, 1994).

64. Author interview with Lynne Bernabei, May 18, 2016.

65. Author interview with Lynne Bernabei, May 18, 2016.

66. Author interview with Lynne Bernabei, May 18, 2016.

67. Author interview with Lynne Bernabei, May 18, 2016.

68. Author interview with Lynne Bernabei, May 18, 2016.

69. Letter to Razi Mireskandari from Agee, dated January 18, 1995; Agee Papers, box 7, folder 2.

70. Agee Papers, box 7, folder 2.

71. See Christopher Hitchens, "So Typically George," *Nation*, February 19, 1996. See also datebook entry for December 23, 1994; Agee Papers, box 4.

72. Agee Papers, box 7, folder 2.

73. Correspondence; Agee Papers, box 7, folder 2.

74. Agee Papers, box 7, folder 1.

75. Letter to Agee from Lynne Bernabei, dated March 27, 1997; Agee Papers, box 7, folder 3. Author interview with Lynne Bernabei, May 18, 2016.

76. John Barron, *The KGB Today: The Hidden Hand* (New York: Reader's Digest, 1983), 228.

77. Author interview with Michael Opperskalski, July 16, 2016.

78. John J. Dziak, *Chekisty: A History of the KGB* (Lexington, MA: Lexington Books, 1988), 163–64.

79. Author interview with Glenn Carle, March 9, 2016.

80. Brian Latell, *Castro's Secrets: The CIA and Cuba's Intelligence Machine* (New York: Palgrave Macmillan, 2012), 1–2.

81. Latell, *Castro's Secrets*, 9.

82. Author interview with Glenn Carle, March 9, 2016.

83. Card of Identity valid 1989–1994; Cards of Identity and Registration permitting short-term travel Agee issued 1989 and 1996; obtained by author via FOIA request to US State Department, Case No. 201000351.

84. Copy of Agee's Cuban passport, no. 91495, issued October 8, 1990; copy of Agee's World Service Authority "passport," issued February 11, 1991; obtained by author via FOIA request to US State Department, Case No. 201000351.

85. Memorandum to Director of Central Intelligence/Counterintelligence Center, Counterespionage Group from FBI Assistant Director in Charge, Intelligence Division, dated January 16, 1992; FBI communication re: Philip Agee, dated December 16, 1992; obtained by author via FOIA request to Federal Bureau of Investigation, FOIA Request No. 1141978–000.

86. Communication to Director, FBI, from FBI New York, dated August 14, 1991; obtained by author via FOIA request to Federal Bureau of Investigation, FOIA Request No. 1141978–000.

87. Federal Bureau of Investigation—INS Lookout Notice, date of request February 27, 1992; obtained by author via FOIA request to Federal Bureau of Investigation, FOIA Request No. 1141978–000.

88. Memorandum to Director of Central Intelligence/Counterintelligence Center, Counterespionage Group from FBI Assistant Director in Charge, Intelligence Division, dated April 22, 1992; obtained by author via FOIA request to Federal Bureau of Investigation, FOIA Request No. 1141978–000.

89. Cable to Director, FBI, from FBI Tampa, dated May 1992; obtained by author via FOIA request to Federal Bureau of Investigation, FOIA Request No. 1141978–000.

90. Cable to Director, FBI, from FBI Tampa, dated May 1992; obtained by author via FOIA request to Federal Bureau of Investigation, FOIA Request No. 1141978–000.

91. FBI New York document, dated December 16, 1992; obtained by author via FOIA request to Federal Bureau of Investigation, FOIA Request No. 1141978–000.

92. Communication to Director, FBI, from FBI New York, dated February 11, 1993; obtained by author via FOIA request to Federal Bureau of Investigation, FOIA Request No. 1141978–000.

93. Memorandum to Director, FBI, from Assistant Director in Charge, New York,

dated December 21, 1993; obtained by author via FOIA request to Federal Bureau of Investigation, FOIPA Request No. 1141978-000.

94. Cable to Director, FBI, from FBI New York, dated September 14, 1994; obtained by author via FOIA request to Federal Bureau of Investigation, FOIA Request No. 1141978-000.

95. Cable to FBI New York from Department of Justice, dated November 10, 1994; obtained by author via FOIA request to Federal Bureau of Investigation, FOIA Request No. 1141978-000.

96. Cable to Director, FBI, from FBI New York, dated June 29, 1995; cable to FBI Director from FBI Alexandria, dated Jun 27, 1984; cable to FBI Alexandria from Director, FBI, re: Philip B. G. [sic] Agee—Intelligence Identities Protection Act, dated June 28, 1984; memorandum to [redacted] from John E. Otto, Acting Director, FBI, re: PHILIP AGEE, dated June 10, 1987; obtained by author via FOIA request to Federal Bureau of Investigation, FOIA Request No. 1141978-000.

97. Communication to Director, FBI, from FBI New York, dated August 22, 1995; obtained by author via FOIA request to Federal Bureau of Investigation, FOIA Request No. 1141978-000.

98. Communication to Director, FBI, et al., from FBI New York, dated November 9, 1995; obtained by author via FOIA request to Federal Bureau of Investigation, FOIA Request No. 1141978-000.

99. Oleg Kalugin, *Spymaster: My 32 Years in Intelligence and Espionage Against the West* (London: Smith Gryphon, 1994), 191–92.

100. FBI communication to Director, FBI, from FBI New York, dated November 2, 1994; Communication to Director, FBI, from Deputy Assistant Director in Charge, New York, dated February 13, 1995; obtained by author via FOIA request to Federal Bureau of Investigation, FOIA Request No. 1141978-000.

101. FBI communication to Director, FBI, from FBI New York, dated November 12, 1996; obtained by author via FOIA request to Federal Bureau of Investigation, FOIA Request No. 1141978-000.

102. Edward Jay Epstein, *Deception: The Invisible War between the KGB and the CIA* (New York: Simon & Schuster, 1989), 281.

103. See Agee, *Inside the Company*, 374. Epstein's proffer of Angleton's case, however baseless, has caught light in stiltedly praetorian, flagrantly pro-CIA publications. See, e.g., Laughlin Campbell, "Agee At It Again," *Foreign Intelligence Literary Scene* 8 (1989). Campbell was a former CIA station chief.

104. Andrew and Mitrokhin, *The Sword and the Shield, 230.*

105. See Seeger, "Agee's Archive: The Truth Unredacted?"

106. Author interview with Michael Opperskalski, July 16, 2016.

107. Andrew and Mitrokhin, *The Sword and the Shield*, 617 n. 44.

108. Andrew and Mitrokhin, *The Sword and the Shield*, 231.

109. Christopher Andrew and Vasili Mitrokhin, *The World Was Going Our Way: The KGB and the Battle for the Third World* (New York: Basic Books, 2005), 103–4.

110. See generally Tim Weiner, David Johnston, and Neil A. Lewis, *Betrayal: The Story of Aldrich Ames, An American Spy* (New York: Random House, 1995).

111. Agee Papers, box 13, folders 24–28.

112. See Adam Gopnik, "Spy vs. Spy vs. Spy," *New Yorker*, September 2, 2019.

113. Author interview with David Corn, May 19, 2016.

114. Andrew and Mitrokhin, *The Sword and the Shield*, 385.

115. Conference transcript, "U.S. Intelligence and the End of the Cold War," Texas A&M University, November 18–20, 1999, Panel III3—Espionage and Counterintelligence; www.cia.gov/library/reading room.

116. Agee Papers, box 3.

117. See Agee Papers, box 15, folder 23.

118. Agee Papers, box 16, folder 4.

119. Agee Papers, box 15, folder 8.

120. Agee Papers, box 18, folder 4.

121. Jim Lobe, "U.S.–Cuba: Contradictions Plague a Largely Improvised Policy," *Inter Press Service*, August 29, 1994.

122. Agee Papers, box 3.

123. Agee Papers, box 2.

124. Agee Papers, box 15, folder 53.

125. Agee Papers, box 17, folder 26.

126. Agee Papers, box 17, folder 40.

127. Sandra Grimes and Jeanne Vertefeuille, *Circle of Treason: A CIA Account of Traitor Aldrich Ames and the Men He Betrayed* (Annapolis, MD: Naval Institute Press, 2012), 115–16.

128. James Risen, "Once Again, Ex-Agent Eludes Grasp of the CIA," *Los Angeles Times*, October 14, 1997, A2.

129. Julia Preston and Tim Weiner, "A Document by Cuban Spy Talks of Acts Against C.I.A.," *New York Times*, October 8, 2000.

130. Agee datebooks; Agee Papers, box 4.

131. Agee Papers, box 18.

CHAPTER EIGHT

1. Author interview with Giselle Roberge Agee, July 15, 2016.

2. See Teishan A. Latner, *Cuban Revolution in America: Havana and the Making of a United States Left, 1968–1992* (Chapel Hill: University of North Carolina Press, 2018).

3. See Mistry, "A Transnational Protest," 387–88.

4. *United States Air Force 58B Officer Candidate School*, Officer Candidate Agee, USAF Class 58-B, https://sites.rootsweb.com/˜ocs58b/wg-staff/agee.html (accessed January 14, 2020).

5. *United States Air Force 58B Officer Candidate School*, Messages posted by Phil Agee, https://sites.rootsweb.ancestry.com/˜ocs58b/notes-comments/agee.html (accessed February 22, 2015).

6. Tracey Eaton, "Defiant Ex-Spy Runs Travel Agency in Cuba," *Dallas Morning News*, April 14, 2001, 15A.

7. Letter to CNN from Agee, dated December 16, 2000; Agee Papers, box 3.

8. Plaque with inscription: "In appreciation for hosting the MIT Sloan School of Management, Mexico-Cuba Trip, March, 2003"; Agee Papers, box 1A.

9. Letter to the author from Giselle Roberge Agee, dated July 29, 2016.

10. See, e.g., A. L. Bardach, "Jerry Brown's Castro Trouble on 2000 Cuba Trip," *Daily Beast*, October 4, 2010; Kevan Blanche, "The Red Side of Brown," *Weekly Standard*, October 26, 2006.

11. Letter to U.S. Interests Section from Agee, dated June 13, 2005; Agee Papers, box 1A.

12. Agee Papers, box 4.

13. Eulogy by Len Weinglass in "Remembering Philip Agee," *Socialism and Democracy Online*, March 6, 2011, http://sdonline.org/51/remembering-philip-agee/.

14. Letter to the author from Giselle Roberge Agee, dated February 20, 2019.

15. Agee Papers, box 17, folder 72.

16. Agee Papers, box 14, folder 76–77.

17. Agee datebook entries for August 10 and 11, 2004; Agee Papers, box 4.

18. See Campbell, "The Spy Who Stayed Out in the Cold."

19. Agee datebook entries for May 19 and July 10–12, 2006; Agee Papers, box 4.

20. Agee datebooks; Agee Papers, box 4.

21. Kenneth R. Timmerman, "The Ghost of Philip Agee," *FrontPageMagazine*, November 30, 2006.

22. Letter to Agee from Assistant Secretary of State for Consular Affairs, dated February 2, 2007; Agee Papers, box 1A.

23. Philip Agee, "Terrorism and Civil Society as Instruments of U.S. Policy in Cuba," *Socialism and Democracy* 34 (Summer–Fall 2003): 1–25.

24. See "Press Release Announcing the Visit to Ireland of Philip Agee," *IndyMedia Ireland*, March 12, 2007; https://www.indymedia.ie/article/81448.

25. Campbell, "The Spy Who Stayed Out in the Cold."

26. Philip Agee, "A Shameful Injustice," *Guardian*, March 10, 2007.

27. Agee datebooks; Agee Papers, box 4.

28. See Anonymous, *Imperial Hubris: Why the West Is Losing the War on Terror* (Washington, DC: Potomac Books, 2004). The book was first published anonymously because Scheuer was then still in the CIA, though it was widely suspected that he was the author. When he resigned from the agency in 2004, he acknowledged his authorship.

29. Michael Scheuer, *Marching Toward Hell: America and Israel After Iraq* (New York: Free Press, 2008).

30. Agee datebooks; Agee Papers, box 4.

31. Agee datebooks; Agee Papers, box 4.

32. Author interview with Giselle Roberge Agee, July 15, 2016; author interview with Philip Agee Jr., May 16, 2015.

33. Anthony Boadle, "CIA Whistle-blower Philip Agee Dies in Cuba," Reuters, January 9, 2008, https://www.reuters.com/article/us-cuba-usa-spy/cia-whistle-blower-philip-agee-dies-in-cuba-idUSN0959077820080109.

34. Author telephone interview with Giselle Roberge Agee, August 14, 2020.

35. George Will, "Philip Agee: No Passport, Less Trouble," *Washington Post*, July 8, 1981.

36. Author telephone interview with Giselle Roberge Agee, August 14, 2020.

37. Lawrence Osborne, *Hunters in the Dark* (London: Hogarth, 2015), 155.

38. Philip Agee Jr., e-mail to the author, February 8, 2010.

39. Author interview with Giselle Roberge Agee, July 15, 2016.

40. See Alyse Myers, "I'm Honoring the Dead (and Look at These Great Seats)," *New York Times*, July 2, 2009.

41. Author interview with Giselle Roberge Agee, July 15, 2016.

42. Michael Weiss, "Tea Now Being Served in the Guy Burgess Reading Room," *New Criterion*, Dispatch, May 6, 2009, https://www.newcriterion.com/blogs/dispatch/tea-now-being-served-in-the-guy-burgess-reading-room.

43. Eulogy by Melvin Wulf, "Remembering Philip Agee."

44. Letter to the author from Giselle Roberge Agee, dated February 20, 2019.

45. Sam Jones, "Cyber Espionage: A New Cold War?," *Financial Times*, August 19, 2016.

46. Steven T. Usdin, "The Forgotten Story of the Julian Assange of the 1970s," *Politico*, November 28, 2018, https://www.politico.com/magazine/story/2018/11/28/assange-wikileaks-prosecute-agee-covert-action-cia-222693.

47. Author telephone interview with Giselle Roberge Agee, August 14, 2020.

48. See, e.g., Charlie Savage, "Expansion of Secrecy Law for Intelligence Operatives Alarms Free Press Advocates," *New York Times*, July 10, 2019, https://www.nytimes.com/2019/07/10/us/politics/cia-operatives-secrecy-law.html; Gabe Rottman, "Congress Should Think Twice Before Expanding the Intelligence Identities Protection Act," *Lawfare*, July 16, 2019, https://www.lawfareblog.com/congress-should-think-twice-expanding-intelligence-identities-protection-act; Bruce W. Sandford and Bruce D. Brown, "Why Are We Expanding the Covert Agent Secrecy Law Now?," *Washington Post*, July 17, 2019, https://www.washingtonpost.com/opinions/2019/07/17/why-are-we-expanding-covert-agent-secrecy-law-now/.

49. See Victor Bulmer-Thomas, *Empire in Retreat: The Past, Present, and Future of the United States* (New Haven, CT: Yale University Press, 2018); David C. Hendrickson, *Republic in Peril: American Empire and the Liberal Tradition* (New York: Oxford University Press, 2018). See also Andrew J. Bacevich, *The Limits of Power: The End of American Exceptionalism* (New York: Holt, 2009); Paul Kennedy, *The Rise and Fall of the Great Powers* (New York: Vintage, 1989).

50. See Genevieve Redsten, "Incendiary Rhetoric, Impeachment, Protests: Attorney General William Barr Visits Campus," *Scholastic*, November 19, 2019, https://scholastic.nd.edu/issues/incendiary-rhetoric-impeachment-and-protests-attorney-general-william-barr-visits-campus/; David Rohde, "Sword and Shield," *New Yorker*, January 20, 2020; Michael Sean Winters, "Notre Dame Had a Right to Host Barr—But His Talk Was Ridiculously Stupid," *National Catholic Reporter*, Octo-

ber 18, 2019, https://www.ncronline.org/news/opinion/distinctly-catholic/notre
-dame-had-right-host-barr-his-talk-was-ridiculously-stupid.

51. The acclaimed film *A Twelve-Year Night*, Uruguay's submission for the 2018 Academy Award for Best Foreign-Language Film, chronicles Mujica's experiences. See Reid, *Forgotten Continent*, 2, 301–28.

52. See, e.g., Jeff Sparrow, "If It No Go So, It Go Near So: *A Brief History of Seven Killings*," *Sydney Review of Books*, March 3, 2015.

53. Marlon James, *A Brief History of Seven Killings* (New York: Riverhead, 2014), 20.

54. James, *A Brief History of Seven Killings*, 20.

55. James, *A Brief History of Seven Killings*, 20, 21.

56. James, *A Brief History of Seven Killings*, 95.

57. James, *A Brief History of Seven Killings*, 173.

58. James, *A Brief History of Seven Killings*, 318.

59. James, *A Brief History of Seven Killings*, 326.

60. Eulogy by Len Weinglass in "Remembering Philip Agee."

61. Boadle, "CIA Whistle-blower Philip Agee Dies in Cuba."

62. Rebecca West, *The New Meaning of Treason* (New York: Open Road Media, 2010), 154, Kindle.

63. See, e.g., Scott Shane, "A Spy's Motivation: For Love of Another Country," *New York Times*, April 20, 2008.

64. Moran, *Company Confessions*, 112–13.

65. Greg Grandin, *The Last Colonial Massacre: Latin America in the Cold War*, 2nd ed. (Chicago: University of Chicago Press, 2011), 17.

66. Witham, *The Cultural Left and the Reagan Era*.

67. Snepp, *Irreparable Harm*, 12, 102, 362.

68. "Five Years Later, Many Say Snowden Is Neither Hero Nor Traitor," Rasmussen Reports, August 15, 2018, http://www.rasmussenreports.com/public_content/politics/general_politics/august_2018/five_years_later_many_say_snowden_is_neither_hero_nor_traitor. See also Nate Fick, "Was Snowden a Hero or Traitor? Perhaps a Little of Both?," *Washington Post*, January 19, 2017.

69. Pico Iyer, *The Man Within My Head* (New York: Knopf, 2012), 73.

70. Iyer, *The Man Within My Head*, 116.

71. See Moran, *Company Confessions*, 218.

Selected Bibliography

This bibliography is substantial but not exhaustive. It lists published books, magazine articles, and newspaper articles that informed the book. Most, but not all, of these sources are also cited in endnotes to specific passages.

Adams, James. *Sellout: Aldrich Ames and the Corruption of the CIA*. New York: Viking, 1995.

"Agee Goes on Naming CIA Agents." *Washington Star*, January 16, 1976.

Agee, Chris John. "Bridging the Gap: Philip Agee, 1935–2008." *NACLA Reporting on the Americas*, no. 42 (January–February 2009). https://nacla.org/article/bridging-gap-philip-agee-1935%E2%80%932008.

Agee, Philip. "The American Factor in Greece: Old and New." *Anti* (May 1977).

———. "The CIA's Blueprint for Nicaragua." *Covert Action Information Bulletin*, no. 6 (October 1979).

———. "The CIA's Prospects in Eastern Europe." *Covert Action Information Bulletin*, no. 35 (Fall 1990).

———. "Exiled: Agee's Amsterdam Letter." *Leveller* (July/August 1977).

———. "Exposing the CIA." *CounterSpy* 2, no. 2 (Winter 1975).

———. "How I Was Kicked Out of France—and Why." *Paris Metro*, September 14, 1977.

———. "How to Become a Non-ND Alumnus." *Common Sense*, February 1989.

———. "I Don't Need a Passport." *New York Times*, July 27, 1981, A15.

———. *Inside the Company: CIA Diary*. New York: Stonehill, 1975.

———. "Liberté, Egalité, Torture." Review of *Torture: The Role of Ideology in the French-Algerian War*, by Rita Maran. *Nation*, May 21, 1990, 712–13.

———. "My Stake in Jamaica's Elections." *Free West Indian (Grenada)* 1, no. 46 (January 20, 1980).

———. *On the Run*. Secaucus, NJ: Lyle Stuart, 1987.

———. "Philip Agee on Exposing CIA Agents." Letter to the editor. *Washington Post*, February 22, 1976.

———. "Producing the Proper Crisis: A Talk by Philip Agee." *Z Magazine* (November 1990).

———. "Rendezvous in Geneva: My Spy Exposed." *CounterSpy* 3, no. 2 (December 1976): 18–20.

———. "A Shameful Injustice." *Guardian*, March 10, 2007. https://www.theguardian.com/commentisfree/2007/mar/10/comment.cuba.

———. "Terrorism and Civil Society as Instruments of U.S. Policy in Cuba." *Socialism and Democracy* 17, no. 2 (Summer–Fall 2003): 1–25.

———. *White Paper Whitewash: Interviews with Philip Agee on the CIA and El Salvador*. Edited by Warner Poelchau. New York: Deep Cover Publications, 1981.

———. "Why I Split the CIA and Spilled the Beans." *Esquire*, June 1975.

Agee, Philip, and Stephen Weissman. "CIA vs. USA—The Agency's Plot to Take Over America." *Oui*, September 1975.

Agee, Philip, and Louis Wolf. *Dirty Work: The CIA in Western Europe*. Secaucus, NJ: Lyle Stuart, 1978.

Agee, Philip, Jr. "UConn Dean Reports of CIA Attempt to Gain Info on Foreign Students." *Campus Watch* 2, no. 2 (Fall 1990).

"AHR Forum: Transnational Lives in the Twentieth Century." *American Historical Review* 118, no. 1 (February 2013): xiii–xvi.

Aldrich, Richard J. "American Journalism and the Landscape of Secrecy: Tad Szulc, the CIA and Cuba." Special Issue: The CIA and American Foreign Policy, *History* 100, no. 340 (April 2015): 189–209.

Allin, Dana H. *Cold War Illusions: America, Europe, and Soviet Power, 1969–1989*. New York: St. Martin's Press, 1997.

Anderson, Jon Lee. "A New Cuba." *New Yorker*, October 3, 2016. https://www
.newyorker.com/magazine/2016/10/03/a-new-cuba.

Andrew, Christopher. *The Secret World: A History of Intelligence*. New Haven,
CT: Yale University Press, 2018.

Andrew, Christopher, and Vasili Mitrokhin. *The Sword and the Shield: The
Mitrokhin Archive and the Secret History of the KGB*. New York: Basic
Books, 1999.

———. *The World Was Going Our Way: The KGB and the Battle for the Third
World*. New York: Basic Books, 2005.

Anonymous. *Imperial Hubris: Why the West Is Losing the War on Terror*. Washington, DC: Potomac Books, 2004.

Armstrong, David. *A Trumpet to Arms: Alternative Media in America*. Boston:
South End Press, 1981.

Atkinson, Rick. "Racing With the Grim Reaper to Unmask Nazis." *International Herald Tribune*, August 29, 1995.

Atkinson, Rick, and Steve Vogel. "Accused Spy Says He Was U.S. Double
Agent." *Washington Post*, September 23, 1994. https://www.washington
post.com/archive/politics/1994/09/23/accused-spy-says-he-was-us
-double-agent/59bb5d16-4715-40e5-87e1-ff7a0f1a905a/.

Ayers, Bradley Earl. *The War That Never Was: An Insider's Account of C.I.A.
Covert Operations Against Cuba*. Indianapolis, IN: Bobbs-Merrill, 1976.

Bacevich, Andrew J. *The Limits of Power: The End of American Exceptionalism*. New York: Holt, 2009.

Baer, Robert. *See No Evil: The True Story of a Ground Soldier in the CIA's War
on Terrorism*. New York: Broadway Books, 2003.

Bakewell, Sarah. *At the Existentialist Café: Freedom, Being and Apricot Cocktails*. New York: Other Press, 2016.

Bardach, A. L. "Jerry Brown's Castro Trouble on 2000 Cuba Trip." *Daily
Beast*, October 4, 2010. https://www.thedailybeast.com/jerry-browns
-castro-trouble-on-2000-cuba-trip.

Barger, Brian. "CIA Manual Said Aimed at Contra Abuses." *Washington Post*,
October 31, 1984. https://www.washingtonpost.com/archive/politics/19
84/10/31/cia-manual-said-aimed-at-contra-abuses-cia-book-seen-aimed
-at-abuses/54aacc31-3501-4337-afaa-52e16a152d00/.

Barron, John. *KGB Today: The Hidden Hand*. New York: Reader's Digest
Press, 1983.

Bernstein, Carl. "The CIA and the Media" *Rolling Stone*, October 20, 1977, 55–67.

Berrigan, Daniel. *Essential Writings*. Maryknoll, NY: Orbis Books, 2009.

———. *The Trial of the Catonsville Nine*. New York: Fordham University Press, 2004.

Berrigan, Philip (with Fred A. Wilcox). *Fighting the Lamb's War: Skirmishes with the American Empire — The Autobiography of Philip Berrigan*. Monroe, ME: Common Courage Press, 1996.

Best, Emma. "One of the CIA's Private Press Contacts Was a Suspected Soviet Spy." *MuckRock*, June 14, 2017, https://www.muckrock.com/news /archives/2017/jun/14/cia-szulc/.

Biden, Joseph R., Jr. "A Spy That Harms National Security." *Christian Science Monitor*, April 6, 1982. https://www.csmonitor.com/1982/0406/040622 .html.

Blanche, Kevan. "The Red Side of Brown." *Weekly Standard*, October 26, 2006.

Blum, William. *Killing Hope: US Military and CIA Interventions Since World War II*. London: Zed Books, 2004.

Boadle, Anthony. "CIA Whistle-blower Philip Agee Dies in Cuba." Reuters, January 9, 2008. https://www.reuters.com/article/us-cuba-usa-spy/cia -whistle-blower-philip-agee-dies-in-cuba-idUSN0959077820080109.

Boot, Max. *The Road Not Taken: Edward Lansdale and the American Tragedy in Vietnam*. New York: Liveright, 2018.

———. *The Savage Wars of Peace: Small Wars and the Rise of American Power*. Rev. ed. New York: Basic Books, 2014.

Borstelmann, Thomas. *The 1970s: A New Global History from Civil Rights to Economic Inequality*. Princeton, NJ: Princeton University Press, 2012.

Brands, Hal. *Latin America's Cold War*. Cambridge, MA: Harvard University Press, 2012.

Braudy, Susan. *Family Circle: The Boudins and the Aristocracy of the Left*. New York: Knopf, 2003.

Breslin, Patrick. "The CIA and the Guilt of Intelligence." Review of *Inside the Company: CIA Diary*, by Philip Agee. Book World, *Washington Post*, February 23, 1975.

Buckley, Tom. "Film: C.I.A. Pro and Con in 'Company Business.'" *New York Times*, April 15, 1980.

Bulmer-Thomas, Victor. *Empire in Retreat: The Past, Present, and Future of the United States.* New Haven, CT: Yale University Press, 2018.

Burrough, Bryan. *Days of Rage: America's Radical Underground, the FBI, and the Forgotten Age of Revolutionary Violence.* New York: Penguin Press, 2015.

Bush, Barbara. *Barbara Bush: A Memoir.* New York: Guideposts, 1994.

Calleo, David. *Beyond American Hegemony: The Future of the Western Alliance.* New York: Basic Books, 1987.

Campbell, Duncan. "The Spy Who Stayed Out in the Cold." *Guardian,* January 9, 2007. https://www.theguardian.com/world/2007/jan/10/usa.dun cancampbell.

Campbell, Laughlin. "Agee At It Again." *Foreign Intelligence Literary Scene* 8 (1989).

Carle, Glenn L. *The Interrogator: An Education.* New York: Nation Books, 2011.

Carmichael, Scott W. *True Believer: Inside the Investigation and Capture of Ana Montes, Cuba's Master Spy.* Annapolis, MD: Naval Institute Press, 2007.

Carroll, James. *An American Requiem: God, My Father, and the War That Came Between Us.* Boston: Houghton Mifflin, 1996.

Cep, Casey. "A Radical Faith: The Life and Legacy of Dorothy Day." Review of *Dorothy Day: Dissenting Voice of the American Century*, by John Loughery and Blythe Randolph. *New Yorker*, April 13, 2020. https://www.newyorker .com/magazine/2020/04/13/dorothy-days-radical-faith.

Christiaens, Kim. "Between Diplomacy and Solidarity: Western European Support Networks for Sandinista Nicaragua." *European Review of History* 21, no. 4 (July 2014): 617–34.

"CIA Defector May Judge Hostages." *New York Post*, December 17, 1979.

Clark, Ramsey. "England Revives the Star Chamber." *Nation* (March 5, 1977).

Coll, Steve. *Directorate S: The C.I.A. and America's Secret Wars in Afghanistan and Pakistan.* New York: Penguin, 2018.

———. *Ghost Wars: The Secret History of the CIA, Afghanistan, and Bin Laden, from the Soviet Invasion to September 10, 2001.* New York: Penguin, 2004.

Copeland, Miles. Book review of *Inside the Company. Spectator* (January 11, 1975).

Corn, David. *Blond Ghost: Ted Shackley and the CIA's Crusades*. New York: Simon & Schuster, 1994.

Crandall, Russell. *Gunboat Diplomacy: U.S. Interventions in the Dominican Republic, Grenada and Panama*. Lanham, MD: Rowman & Littlefield, 2006.

Crewdson, John M. "CIA Agent Said to Give Secrets to Russia in 1972." *New York Times*, July 4, 1974, 1.

———. "Ex-CIA Agent Denies He Gave Information to the Russians." *New York Times*, July 11, 1974, 9.

Crile, George. *Charlie Wilson's War: The Extraordinary Story of How the Wildest Man in Congress and a Rogue CIA Agent Changed the History of Our Times*. New York: Atlantic Monthly Press, 2003.

Critchfield, James H. *Partners at the Creation: The Men Behind Postwar Germany's Defense and Intelligence Establishments*. Annapolis, MD: Naval Institute Press, 2003.

Day, Dorothy. "Theophane Venard and Ho Chi Minh." *Catholic Worker* (May 1954): 1–6.

de Borchgrave, Arnaud, and Robert Moss. *The Spike*. London: Weidenfeld & Nicholson, 1980.

Deighton, Len. *Mexico Set*. London: Hutchinson, 1984.

Delton, Jennifer A. *Rethinking the 1950s: How Anticommunism and the Cold War Made American Liberal*. Cambridge: Cambridge University Press, 2013.

Diggins, John Patrick. *The Rise and Fall of the American Left*. New York: W. W. Norton, 1975.

Dillon, Eva. *Spies in the Family: An American Spymaster, His Russian Crown Jewel, and the Friendship That Helped End the Cold War*. New York: HarperCollins, 2017.

Dooley, Tom. *Deliver Us From Evil: The Story of Vietnam's Flight to Freedom*. New York: Farrar, Straus and Cudahy, 1956.

Draper, Theodore. *Castro's Revolution: Myth and Realities*. New York: Praeger, 1962.

"Dr. Tom Dooley's Ties to CIA Are Chronicled." Associated Press, July 4, 1979.

Duncan, Donald. " 'The Whole Thing Was a Lie.' " *Ramparts* (February 1966): 12–24.

Dyson, Freeman. "Scientist, Spy, Genius: Who Was Bruno Pontecorvo?" Review of *Half-Life: The Divided Life of Bruno Pontecorvo, Physicist or Spy*, by Frank Close. *New York Review of Books*, March 5, 2015.

Dziak, John J. *Chekisty: A History of the KGB*. Lexington, MA: Lexington Books, 1988.

Earley, Pete. *Confessions of a Spy: The Real Story of Aldrich Ames*. New York: G. P. Putnam's Sons, 1997.

Eaton, Tracey. "Defiant Ex-Spy Runs Travel Agency in Cuba." *Dallas Morning News*, April 14, 2001.

Eder, Richard. "The Disillusion of a CIA Man: 12 Years from Agent to Radical." *New York Times*, July 12, 1974, 4.

Epstein, Edward Jay. *Deception: The Invisible War Between the KGB and the CIA*. New York: Simon & Schuster, 1989.

Escalante, Fabian. *The Secret War: CIA Covert Operations Against Cuba, 1959–62*. Translated by Maxine Shaw. Melbourne, Australia: Ocean Press, 1995.

Evans, Rowland, and Robert Novak. "CIA's First Defector?" *New York Post*, March 12, 1977.

Fagen, Richard R. "A Death in Uruguay" Review of *Hidden Terrors*, by A. J. Langguth. *New York Times*, Book Review, June 25, 1978, 4.

Feinberg, Richard E., ed. *Central America: International Dimensions of the Crisis*. New York: Holmes & Meier, 1982.

Ferguson, Niall, et al., eds. *The Shock of the Global: The Seventies in Perspective*. Pts. 1, 2. Cambridge, MA: Harvard University Press, 2010.

FitzGerald, Frances. *Fire in the Lake: The Vietnamese and the Americans in Vietnam*. New York: Little, Brown, 1972.

Follain, John. *Jackal: The Secret Wars of Carlos the Jackal*. London: Weidenfeld & Nicholson, 1998.

"Former Agent Exposes Colleagues." *Tampa Times*, January 16, 1976.

"Former CIA Agents Call For End to Covert Operations." UPI, October 29, 1987. https://www.upi.com/Archives/1987/10/29/Former-CIA-agents-call-for-end-to-covert-operations/9691562482000/.

Frank, Marc. *Cuban Revelations: Behind the Scenes in Havana*. Miami: University Press of Florida, 2015.

Fraser, Steve. *Age of Acquiescence: The Life and Death of American Resistance to Organized Wealth and Power*. New York: Little, Brown, 2015.

Friedman, Jane. "'I Don't Care About Vulnerability.'" *Newsweek*, August 12, 1977.

Fukuyama, Francis. "The End of History?" *National Interest*, no. 16 (Summer 1989): 3–18.

———. *The End of History and the Last Man*. New York: Free Press, 1992).

García Márquez, Gabriel. "The CIA in Latin America." Review of *Inside the Company: CIA Diary*, by Philip Agee. Translated by Gregory Rabasa. *New York Review of Books*, August 7, 1975.

Gardner, Lloyd C. *The War on Leakers: National Security and American Democracy from Eugene V. Debs to Edward Snowden*. New York: New Press, 2016.

Garrard-Burnett, Virginia, Mark Atwood Lawrence, and Julio E. Moreno. *Beyond the Eagle's Shadow: New Histories of Latin America's Cold War*. Albuquerque: University of New Mexico Press, 2013.

Gerassi, John. *The Great Fear in Latin America*. New York: Macmillan, 1965.

———. "An Interview with Philip Agee: Confessions of an Ex-CIA Man." *Real Paper*, February 19, 1975.

Gertz, Bill. "Ex-CIA Officials Blast 'Defector' Agee." *Washington Times*, June 11, 1987

Gitlin, Todd. *The Sixties: Years of Hope, Days of Rage*. New York: Bantam, 1993.

Gladwell, Malcolm. "The Outside Man." *New Yorker*, December 19 and 26, 2016.

Goldman, Adam. "Ex-CIA Officer Suspected of Compromising Chinese Informants Is Arrested." *New York Times*, January 16, 2018.

Goodman, Melvin A. *Whistleblower at the CIA: An Insider's Account of the Politics of Intelligence*. San Francisco: City Lights Books, 2017.

Gopnik, Adam. "Kill Box." *New Yorker*, August 29, 2016.

———. "Spy vs. Spy vs. Spy." Review of *The Secret World: A History of Intelligence*, by Christopher Andrew. *New Yorker*, September 2, 2019.

Gordon, Linda. *The Second Coming of the KKK: The Ku Klux Klan of the 1920s and the American Political Tradition*. New York: W. W. Norton, 2017.

Grace, Thomas M. *Kent State: Death and Dissent in the Long Sixties*. Amherst, MA: University of Massachusetts Press, 2016.

Grandin, Greg. *Empire's Workshop: Latin America, the United States, and the Rise of the New Imperialism*. New York: Metropolitan Books, 2006.

———. *The Last Colonial Massacre: Latin America in the Cold War*. 2nd ed. Chicago: University of Chicago Press, 2011.

Greene, Graham. *A Sort of Life*. London: Bodley Head, 1971.

———. *Ways of Escape*. New York: Simon & Schuster, 1980.

Greider, William. "Ex-CIA Agent Was Friendlier in Resigning Than in Exposé." *International Herald Tribune*, March 10, 1975.

Grimes, Sandra, and Jeanne Vertefeuille. *Circle of Treason: A CIA Account of Traitor Aldrich Ames and the Men He Betrayed*. Annapolis, MD: Naval Institute Press, 2012.

Guttiérez, Gustavo. *A Theology of Liberation: History, Politics, and Salvation*. Translated and edited by Sister Caridad Inda and John Eagleson. Maryknoll, NY: Orbis Books, 1995.

Hagan, Joe. *Sticky Fingers: The Life and Times of Jann Wenner and Rolling Stone Magazine*. New York: Knopf, 2017.

Halberstam, David. *The Best and the Brightest*. New York: Random House, 1972.

———. *The Fifties*. New York: Ballantine, 1994.

Hansen, Jan, Christian Helm, and Frank Reichherzer, eds. *Making Sense of the Americas: How Protest Related to America in the 1980s and Beyond*. Frankfurt: Campus Verlag GmbH, 2015.

Haslam, Jonathan. *Near and Distant Neighbors: A New History of Soviet Intelligence*. New York: Farrar, Straus and Giroux, 2015.

Hellema, Duco. *The Global 1970s: Radicalism, Reform, and Crisis*. Abingdon, UK: Routledge, 2019.

Hendrickson, David C. *Republic in Peril: American Empire and the Liberal Tradition*. New York: Oxford University Press, 2018.

Hersh, Seymour. "Censored Matter in Book About C.I.A. Said to Have Related Chile Activities." *New York Times*, September 11, 1974, 14.

———. "Huge C.I.A. Operation Reported in U.S. Against Antiwar Forces, Other Dissidents in Nixon Years." *New York Times*, December 22, 1974, 1.

Hidalgo, Orlando Castro. *Spy for Fidel*. Miami, FL: E. A. Seemann, 1971.

Hinckle, Warren, and William W. Turner. *The Fish Is Red: The Story of the Secret War Against Castro*. New York: Harper & Row, 1981.

Hitchens, Christopher. "So Typically George." *Nation*, February 19, 1996.

Iber, Patrick. *Neither Peace Nor Freedom: The Cold War in Latin America*. Cambridge, MA: Harvard University Press, 2015.

Ignatieff, Michael. "Messianic America: Can He Explain It?" Review of

American Foreign Policy and Its Thinkers, by Perry Anderson, and *World-making: The Art and Science of American Diplomacy*, by David Milne. *New York Review of Books*, November 19, 2015.

Immerman, Richard H. *The Hidden Hand: A Brief History of the CIA*. Malden, MA: Wiley-Blackwell, 2014.

"Interview: Miles Copeland—The Puppet Master." *Penthouse* (August 1978).

"Intrigue Follows Spy to His Death in Miami." *International Herald Tribune*, February 10, 1983.

Iyer, Pico. *The Man Within My Head*. New York: Knopf, 2012.

James, Marlon. *A Brief History of Seven Killings*. New York: Riverhead, 2014.

Jeffreys-Jones, Rhodri. *The American Left: Its Impact on Politics and Society Since 1900*. Edinburgh, UK: Edinburgh University Press, 2013.

———. *The CIA and American Democracy*. New Haven, CT: Yale University Press, 1989.

———. *In Spies We Trust: The Story of Western Intelligence*. Oxford: Oxford University Press, 2013.

Jenkins, Philip. *Decade of Nightmares: The End of the Sixties and the Making of Eighties America*. Oxford: Oxford University Press, 2006.

Johnson, Loch K. *A Season of Inquiry Revisited: The Church Committee Confronts America's Spy Agencies*. Topeka: University of Kansas Press, 2015.

Jones, Sam. "Cyber Espionage: A New Cold War?" *Financial Times*, August 19, 2016.

Judt, Tony. *Postwar: A History of Europe Since 1945*. New York: Penguin, 2006.

Kaiser, Robert G., and Karen De Young. "White Paper on El Salvador Is Faulty." *Washington Post*, June 9, 1981. https://www.washingtonpost.com/archive/politics/1981/06/09/white-paper-on-el-salvador-is-faulty/e17 adfa2-3763-42b4-a1f6-1c641ecfd72f/.

Kalman, Laura. *Right Star Rising: A New Politics, 1974–1980*. New York: W. W. Norton, 2010.

Kalugin, Oleg. *Spymaster: My 32 Years in Intelligence and Espionage Against the West*. London: Smith Gryphon, 1994.

Karnow, Stanley. *Vietnam: A History*. New York: Viking, 1983.

Kelly, William C. "Gustavo Díaz Ordaz's Foreign Policy: A Cold War Study." *Latin Americanist* 60, no. 3 (September 2016): 347–69.

Kempster, Norman. "Identity of U.S. Spies Harder to Hide, Colby Says." *Los Angeles Times*, December 28, 1977.

Kennedy, Paul. *The Rise and Fall of the Great Powers*. New York: Vintage, 1989.

"Kidnapped U.S. Official Found Slain in Uruguay." *New York Times*, August 11, 1970, 1.

Kiriakou, John. *Doing Time Like A Spy: How the CIA Taught Me to Survive and Thrive in Prison*. Los Angeles: Rare Bird Books, 2017.

———. *The Reluctant Spy: My Secret Life in the CIA's War on Terror*. New York: Bantam, 2010.

Klare, Michael, and Nancy Stein. "Police Terrorism in Latin America." *Latin America Documentation*. US Catholic Conference, 1974.

Klejment, Anne, and Nancy L. Roberts. "The Catholic Worker and the Vietnam War," in *American Catholic Pacifism: The Influence of Dorothy Day and the Catholic Worker Movement*, ed. Anne Klejment and Nancy L. Roberts. Westport, CT: Praeger, 1996.

———, eds. *American Catholic Pacifism: The Influence of Dorothy Day and the Catholic Worker Movement*. Westport, CT: Praeger, 1996.

Krauze, Enrique. "The New Cuba?" Review of *Cuban Revelations: Behind the Scenes in Havana*, by Marc Frank. *New York Review of Books*, March 19, 2015.

———. *Redeemers: Ideas and Power in Latin America*. New York: Harper, 2011.

Kwitny, Jonathan. "Apparent Errors Cloud 'White Paper' on Reds in El Salvador." *Wall Street Journal*, June 8, 1981.

———. *Endless Enemies: The Making of an Unfriendly World*. New York: Congdon & Weed, 1984.

LaFeber, Walter. *Inevitable Revolutions: The United States in Central America*. New York: W. W. Norton, 1993.

Langguth, A. J. *Hidden Terrors: The Truth about U.S. Police Operations in Latin America*. New York: Pantheon, 1979.

Lardner, George, Jr. "CIA Uses Agee Case in War on Freedom of Information Act." *Washington Post*, March 15, 1980. https://www.washingtonpost.com /archive/politics/1980/03/15/cia-uses-agee-case-in-war-on-freedom-of -information-act/c3186ce7-8888-49d3-97f2-781d73951921/.

Lardner, James. "The Years of Rage." Review of, inter alia, *Days of Rage: America's Radical Underground, the FBI, and the Forgotten Age of Revolu-*

tionary Violence, by Bryan Burrough. *New York Review of Books*, September 24, 2015.

Latell, Brian. *Castro's Secrets: The CIA and Cuba's Intelligence Machine*. New York: Palgrave Macmillan, 2012.

Latner, Teishan A. *Cuban Revolution in America: Havana and the Making of a United States Left, 1968–1992*. Chapel Hill: University of North Carolina Press, 2018.

Lears, Jackson. "Imperial Exceptionalism." Review of *Empire in Retreat: The Past, Present, and Future of the United States*, by Victor Bulmer-Thomas, and *Republic in Peril: American Empire and the Liberal Tradition*, by David C. Hendrickson. *New York Review of Books*, February 7, 2019.

le Carré, John. *The Spy Who Came in from the Cold*. London: Victor Gollancz & Pan, 1963.

Lee, Martin A. "Their Will Be Done." *Mother Jones*, July/August 1983. https://www.motherjones.com/politics/1983/07/their-will-be-done/.

Lernoux, Penny. *Cry of the People: The Struggle for Human Rights in Latin America—The Catholic Church in Conflict with U.S. Policy*. New York: Doubleday, 1980.

Lethem, Jonathan. "Snowden in the Labyrinth." Review of *Permanent Record*, by Edward Snowden. *New York Review of Books*, October 24, 2019.

Lingeman, Richard R. "The Unmaking of a Spy." Review of *Inside the Company: CIA Diary*, by Philip Agee. Books of the Times, *New York Times*, July 31, 1975, 25.

Lobe, Jim. "U.S.–Cuba: Contradictions Plague a Largely Improvised Policy." *Inter Press Service*, August 29, 1994.

Lofton, John. "NBC's Strange Link with Philip Agee." *Washington Times*, January 13, 1984, A-3.

Loughery, John, and Blythe Randolph. *Dorothy Day: Dissenting Voice of the American Century*. New York: Simon & Schuster, 2020.

Maas, Peter. *Killer Spy: The Inside Story of the FBI's Pursuit and Capture of Aldrich Ames, America's Deadliest Spy*. New York: Warner Books, 1995.

Macintyre, Ben. *A Spy Among Friends: Kim Philby and the Great Betrayal*. New York: Crown, 2014.

———. *The Spy and the Traitor: The Greatest Espionage Story of the Cold War*. New York: Crown, 2018.

Mackenzie, Angus. *Secrets: The CIA's War at Home*. Berkeley: University of California Press, 1997.

Maechling, Charles, Jr. "Washington's Illegal Invasion." *Foreign Policy*, no. 79 (Summer 1990): 113–31.

Marchetti, Victor. "CIA Able to Gag Defector." *Spotlight* (July 27, 1987).

Marchetti, Victor, and John D. Marks. *The CIA and the Cult of Intelligence*. New York: Knopf, 1974.

Markham, James M. "Green Party Puts Nuclear Arms Before Nuremburg 'Jury.'" *International Herald Tribune*, February 22, 1983; reprinted as "The A-Bomb Is 'Convicted' in Nuremburg," *New York Times*, February 23, 1983, A5.

Marks, John. "How to Spot a Spook." *Washington Monthly*, November 1974.

Marks, Robert W. *The Meaning of Marcuse*. New York: Ballantine, 1970.

Marsh, James L., and Anna J. Brown. *Faith, Resistance, and the Future: Daniel Berrigan's Challenge to Catholic Social Thought*. New York: Fordham University Press, 2012.

Martin, Bradford. *The Other Eighties: A Secret History of America in the Age of Reagan*. New York: Hill & Wang, 2011.

Martin, David C. *Wilderness of Mirrors*. New York: Harper and Row, 1980.

Masetti, Jorge. *In the Pirates' Den: My Life as a Secret Agent for Castro*. San Francisco, CA: Encounter Books, 1993.

Maurer, Harry. *Strange Ground: An Oral History of Americans in Vietnam, 1945–1975*. Boston: Da Capo Press, 1998.

Mazzetti, Mark, Adam Goldman, Michael S. Schmidt, and Matt Apuzzo. "Killing C.I.A. Informants, China Crippled U.S. Spying Operations." *New York Times*, May 20, 2017. https://www.nytimes.com/2017/05/20/world/asia/china-cia-spies-espionage.html.

McCoy, Alfred W. *A Question of Torture: CIA Interrogation from the Cold War to the War on Terror*. New York: Holt, 2006.

McGehee, Ralph W. *Deadly Deceits: My 25 Years in the CIA*. New York: Sheridan Square Publications, 1983.

Menand, Louis. "A Friend of the Devil." Review of *Patriotic Betrayal, by Karen M. Paget. New Yorker*, March 23, 2015.

Mickolus, Edward, ed. *Stories from Langley: A Glimpse Inside the CIA*. Lincoln: University of Nebraska Press, 2014.

Mistry, Kaeten. "A Transnational Protest Against the National Security State: Whistle-Blowing, Philip Agee, and Networks of Dissent." *Journal of American History* 106, no. 2 (September 2019): 362–89.

Mistry, Kaeten, and Hannah Gurman, eds. *Whistleblower Nation: The History of National Security Disclosures and the Cult of State Secrecy*. New York: Columbia University Press, 2020.

Mor, Jessica Stites, ed. *Human Rights and Transnational Solidarity in Cold War Latin America*. Madison: University of Wisconsin Press, 2013.

Moran, Christopher. *Company Confessions: Secrets, Memoirs, and the CIA*. New York: Thomas Dunne Books, 2015.

———. "Turning Against the CIA: Whistleblowers During the 'Time of Troubles.'" *Journal of the Historical Association* 100, no. 340 (April 2015): 251–74.

Morley, Jefferson. *The Ghost: The Secret Life of CIA Spymaster James Jesus Angleton*. New York: St. Martin's Press, 2017.

———. *Our Man in Mexico: Winston Scott and the Hidden History of the CIA*. Lawrence: University Press of Kansas, 2008.

Moss, Robert. "Philip Agee Rides Again." *Daily Telegraph*, April 23, 1979.

Moynihan, Daniel Patrick. "JFK Nonsense: Belief of Conspiracy Was To Be Expected." *International Herald Tribune*, December 31, 1991–January 1, 1992, 5

Myers, Alyse. "I'm Honoring the Dead (and Look at These Great Seats)." *New York Times*, July 2, 2009. https://www.nytimes.com/2009/07/05/fashion/05crashers.html.

Nelson-Pallmeyer, Jack. *The Politics of Compassion*. Maryknoll, NY: Orbis Books, 1986.

Obituary of William Agee, *St. Petersburg Times*, September 30, 1994.

Olmsted, Kathryn S. *Challenging the Secret Government: The Post-Watergate Investigations of the CIA and FBI*. Chapel Hill: University of North Carolina Press, 1996.

Osborne, Lawrence. "Agents of Betrayal." *Lapham's Quarterly* 9, no. 1 (Winter 2016): 213–19.

———. *Hunters in the Dark*. London: Hogarth, 2015.

O'Toole, G. J. A. *Honorable Treachery: A History of U.S. Intelligence, Espionage, and Covert Action from the American Revolution to the CIA*. New York: Atlantic Monthly Press, 1991.

Paget, Karen M. *Patriotic Betrayal: The CIA's Secret Campaign to Enroll American Students in the Crusade Against Communism.* New Haven, CT: Yale University Press, 2015.

Parham, William F. "Cuban Intelligence Gave Agee Help to Expose, Discredit CIA." *Norwich Bulletin*, August 31, 1981.

Perlstein, Rick. *The Invisible Bridge: The Fall of Nixon and the Rise of Reagan.* New York: Simon & Schuster, 2014.

———. *Nixonland: The Rise of a President and the Fracturing of America.* New York: Scribner, 2008.

Peters, Shawn Francis. *The Catonsville Nine: A Story of Faith and Resistance in the Vietnam Era.* Oxford: Oxford University Press, 2012.

Philby, Kim. *My Silent War.* New York: Modern Library, 2002.

"Philip Agee: A Profile." *Common Sense*, March 1996.

"Philip Agee: Man Without a Country." *Covert Action Information Bulletin*, no. 8 (March–April 1980): 4–7.

Phillips, David Atlee. "Mr. Philip Agee, Jet-Set Benedict Arnold." *Eagle* (December 1981).

Pincus, Walter. "Is There a Secret Police of American Capitalism?" Review of *Inside the Company: CIA Diary*, by Philip Agee. Book Review, *New York Times*, August 3, 1975. https://www.nytimes.com/1975/08/03/archives/is-there-a-secret-police-of-american-capitalism-inside-the-company.html.

"*Playboy* Interview: Philip Agee." *Playboy* August 1975, 48–60.

"*Playboy* Interview: William Colby." *Playboy*, July 1978, 69–81, 164–66, 209–16.

Polner, Murray, and Jim O'Grady. *Disarmed and Dangerous: The Radical Lives and Times of Daniel and Philip Berrigan.* New York: Basic Books, 1997.

Powers, Thomas. "The Enemy of the Agency." Review of *On the Run*, by Philip Agee. Book Review, *New York Times*, August 2, 1987, 7.

Prados, John. *The Family Jewels: The CIA, Secrecy, and Presidential Power.* Austin: University of Texas Press, 2013.

———. *The Ghosts of Langley: Into the CIA's Heart of Darkness.* New York: New Press, 2017.

Preston, Julia, and Tim Weiner. "A Document By Cuban Spy Talks of Acts Against C.I.A." *New York Times*, October 8, 2000, 9.

Rabe, Stephen G. *The Killing Zone: The United States Wages Cold War in Latin America*. New York: Oxford University Press, 2011.

Rafalko, Frank G. *MH/CHAOS: The CIA's Campaign Against the Radical New Left and the Black Panthers* (Annapolis, MD: Naval Institute Press, 2011).

Ranelagh, John. *The Agency: The Rise and Decline of the CIA*. London: Weidenfeld & Nicholson, 1986.

Ray, Ellen, William Schaap, Karl Van Meter, and Louis Wolf. *Dirty Work 2: The CIA in Africa*. Secaucus, NJ: Lyle Stuart, 1979.

Redsten, Genevieve. "Incendiary Rhetoric, Impeachment, Protests: Attorney General William Barr Visits Campus." *Scholastic*, November 14, 2019. https://scholastic.nd.edu/issues/incendiary-rhetoric-impeachment-and-protests-attorney-general-william-barr-visits-campus/.

Reid, Michael. *Forgotten Continent: The Battle for Latin America's Soul*. 2nd ed. New Haven, CT: Yale University Press, 2017.

Reitman, Janet. "U.S. Law Enforcement Failed to See the Threat of White Nationalism. Now They Don't Know How to Stop It." *New York Times Magazine*, November 3, 2018. https://www.nytimes.com/2018/11/03/magazine/FBI-charlottesville-white-nationalism-far-right.html.

"Remembering Philip Agee." *Socialism and Democracy Online*, March 6, 2011. http://sdonline.org/51/remembering-philip-agee/.

Rhea, Beth. "Former Agent Condemns CIA Actions." *Daily Tar Heel*, November 18, 1988.

Richardson, Peter. "The Perilous Fight: The Rise of Ramparts Magazine, 1965–1966." *California History* 86, no. 3 (2009): 22–43, 68–69.

Ridenour, Ron. *Yankee Sandinistas*. Willimantic, CT: Curbstone Press, 1986.

Risen, James. "Once Again, Ex-Agent Eludes Grasp of the CIA." *Los Angeles Times*, October 14, 1997. https://www.latimes.com/archives/la-xpm-1997-oct-14-mn-42699-story.html.

Roberge, Therese. Letter to the editor. *Paris Metro*, November 9, 1977.

Roberts, Adam. "The C.I.A.: Reform Is Not Enough." *Millennium: Journal of International Studies* 6, no. 1 (Spring 1977).

Rodgers, Daniel T. *Age of Fracture*. Cambridge, MA: Harvard University Press, 2011.

Rohde, David. "Sword and Shield." *New Yorker*, January 20, 2020.

Rosswurm, Steven. *The FBI and the Catholic Church, 1935–1962*. Amherst: University of Massachusetts Press, 2009.

Rottenstreich, Yuval, and Christopher K. Hsee. "Money, Kisses, and Electric Shocks: On the Affective Psychology of Risks." *Psychological Science* 12, no. 3 (May 2001): 185–90.

Rottman, Gabe. "Congress Should Think Twice Before Expanding the Intelligence Identities Protection Act." *Lawfare*, July 16, 2019, https://www.lawfareblog.com/congress-should-think-twice-expanding-intelligence-identities-protection-act.

Rutten, Tim. "A Spook's Faustian Bargain." *Los Angeles Times*, January 12, 2008. https://www.latimes.com/archives/la-xpm-2008-jan-12-oe-rutten12-story.html.

Sagar, Rahul. *Secrets and Leaks: The Dilemma of State Secrecy*. Princeton, NJ: Princeton University Press, 2013.

Sandford, Bruce W., and Bruce D. Brown. "Why Are We Expanding the Covert Agent Secrecy Law Now?" *Washington Post*, July 17, 2019. https://www.washingtonpost.com/opinions/2019/07/17/why-are-we-expanding-covert-agent-secrecy-law-now/.

Sargent, Daniel A. *A Superpower Transformed: The Remaking of American Foreign Relations in the 1970s*. New York: Oxford University Press, 2015.

Savage, Charlie. "Expansion of Secrecy Law for Intelligence Operatives Alarms Free Press Advocates." *New York Times*, July 10, 2019. https://www.nytimes.com/2019/07/10/us/politics/cia-operatives-secrecy-law.html.

Scheer, Robert, and Warren Hinckle. "The 'Vietnam Lobby.'" *Ramparts* (July 1965).

Scheuer, Michael. *Marching Toward Hell: America and Israel After Iraq*. New York: Free Press, 2008.

Schiller, Lawrence. *Into the Mirror: The Life of Master Spy Robert L. Hanssen*. New York: HarperCollins, 2002.

Schlosser, Eric. "Break-in at Y-12." *New Yorker*, March 9, 2015.

Schulman, Bruce J. *The Seventies: The Great Shift in American Culture, Society, and Politics*. New York: Free Press, 2001.

Scott, James M. *Deciding to Intervene: The Reagan Doctrine and American Foreign Policy*. Durham, NC: Duke University Press, 1996.

Seale, Patrick. *Abu Nidal: A Gun for Hire*. New York: Random House, 1992.

"Secrecy Is Not the Only Security." *New York Times*, July 21, 1981, A14.

Seeger, Murray. "Agee's Archive: The Truth Unredacted?" *Washington De-*

coded, November 11, 2010. https://www.washingtondecoded.com/site
/2010/11/agee.html.

Shackley, Ted. *Spymaster: My Life in the CIA*. Washington, DC: Potomac
Books, 2005.

Shane, Scott. "A Spy's Motivation: For Love of Another Country." *New York
Times*, April 20, 2008. https://www.nytimes.com/2008/04/20/weekinre
view/20shane.html.

Shaw, Diana. "The Temptation of Tom Dooley: He Was the Heroic Jungle
Doctor of Indochina in the 1950s. But He Had a Secret, and to Protect
It, He Helped Launch the First Disinformation Campaign of the Cold
War." *Los Angeles Times*, December 15, 1991. https://www.latimes.com
/archives/la-xpm-1991-12-15-tm-868-story.html.

Sheehan, Neil. *A Bright Shining Lie: John Paul Vann and America in Vietnam*.
New York: Random House, 1988.

Siegel, Lee. "Means of Dissent: America's Lost Culture of Opposition."
Harper's, October 2015. https://harpers.org/archive/2015/10/means-of
-dissent/.

Singer, Peter. "Forswearing Secrecy." *Nation*, May 5, 1979, 488–91.

Sklar, Holly. *Washington's War on Nicaragua*. Cambridge, MA: South End
Press, 1988.

Smart, Keith. "Agee Not the Martyr He Claims to Be." *Observer*, March 14,
1989.

Smith, Christian. *Resisting Reagan: The U.S. Central America Peace Movement*. Chicago: University of Chicago Press, 1996.

Smith, Colin. *Carlos: Portrait of a Terrorist*. London: Andre Deutsch, 1976.

Snepp, Frank. *Decent Interval: An Insider's Account of Saigon's Indecent End
as Told by the CIA's Chief Strategy Analyst in Vietnam*. New York: Random
House, 1977.

———. *Irreparable Harm: A Firsthand Account of How One Agent Took on the
CIA in an Epic Battle over Secrecy and Free Speech*. New York: Random
House, 1999.

Snowden, Edward. *Permanent Record*. New York: Metropolitan, 2019.

Sparrow, Jeff. "If It No Go So, It Go Near So: *A Brief History of Seven Killings*."
Sydney Review of Books, March 3, 2015. https://sydneyreviewofbooks
.com/review/marlon-james-brief-history-seven-killings/.

"Statement of *CAIB* Before House Committee, Jan. 31, 1980." *Covert Action Information Bulletin*, no. 8 (March–April 1980): 16.

Stein, Jeff. "The Trenchcoats Retrench." *Mother Jones* (February/March 1981), 55–57.

Stepanov, A. "Agent Drops Out of the Game: How Philip Agee Broke With the CIA." *Pravda*, February 12, 1976.

Sterling, Jeffrey. *Unwanted Spy: The Persecution of an American Whistle-blower*. New York: Bold Type Books, 2019.

Stevenson, Jonathan. *Thinking Beyond the Unthinkable: Harnessing Doom from the Cold War to the Age of Terror*. New York: Viking, 2008.

———. *"We Wrecked the Place": Contemplating an End to the Northern Irish Troubles*. New York: Free Press, 1996).

Stockwell, John. *In Search of Enemies: A CIA Story*. New York: W. W. Norton, 1978.

Stone, Robert. *Dog Soldiers*. Boston: Houghton Mifflin, 1974.

———. *A Flag for Sunrise*. New York: Knopf, 1981.

Strain, Christopher B. *The Long Sixties: America, 1955–1973*. Hoboken, NJ: Wiley-Blackwell, 2016.

Sulick, Michael J. *American Spies: Espionage Against the United States from the Cold War to the Present*. Washington, DC: Georgetown University Press, 2013.

Talbot, David. *The Devil's Chessboard: Allen Dulles, the CIA, and the Rise of America's Secret Government*. New York: Harper, 2015.

Taplin, Winn L. "To Die in Bed." *Intelligence Quarterly* 13 (Fall 1987).

"Three Old Spies Out in the Cold." *Newsweek*, April 6, 1981.

Timmerman, Kenneth R. "The Ghost of Philip Agee." *FrontPageMagazine*, November 30, 2006.

"A Top Fencer Reported Jailed By Warsaw as Spying Suspect." *New York Times*, August 15, 1975.

"Trial By Agee." *New York Times*, January 7, 1980.

Troy, Thomas F. *Donovan and the CIA: A History of the Establishment of the Central Intelligence Agency*. Frederick, MD: University Publications of America, Inc., 1981.

"Uruguay Breaks Tie With Cuba; Mexico Only Holdout in O.A.S." *New York Times*, September 9, 1964. https://www.nytimes.com/1964/09/09/archi ves/uruguay-breaks-tie-with-cuba-mexico-only-holdout-in-oas.html.

"Uruguay Police Agent Exposes U.S. Advisers." *NACLA Latin American Report* 6, no. 6 (July–August 1972): 20–25.

Usdin, Steven T. "The Forgotten Story of the Julian Assange of the 1970s." *Politico*, November 28, 2018. https://www.politico.com/magazine/story/2018/11/28/assange-wikileaks-prosecute-agee-covert-action-cia-222693.

Van Meter, Karl. "Man Without a Country." *Paris Metro*, August 2, 1977.

Villaime, Poul, Rasmus Mariager, and Helle Porsdam, eds. *The "Long 1970s": Human Rights, East-West Détente, and Transnational Relations*. Abingdon, UK: Routledge, 2016.

Walsh, Mary Williams. "U.S. Professor Guilty in German Spy Case." *Los Angeles Times*, November 11, 1995. https://www.latimes.com/archives/la-xpm-1995-11-11-mn-1937-story.html.

Warner, Edwin. "New Day for the CIA." *Time*, January 19, 1981, 21.

Weaver, Mary Anne. "CIA Critic Publishes List of 64 CIA 'Agents' in Greece." *Washington Post*, June 13, 1977, A20. https://www.washingtonpost.com/archive/politics/1977/06/13/cia-critic-publishes-list-of-64-agents-in-greece/75d660da-1ead-4515-b8f0-3e1815930595/.

Webb, Gary. *Dark Alliance: The CIA, the Contras, and the Crack Cocaine Explosion*. New York: Seven Stories Press, 2011.

Weiner, Tim. *Legacy of Ashes: The History of the CIA*. New York: Anchor Books, 2008.

Weiner, Tim, David Johnston, and Neil A. Lewis. *Betrayal: The Story of Aldrich Ames, An American Spy*. New York: Random House, 1995.

Weiser, Benjamin. *A Secret Life: The Polish Officer, His Covert Mission, and the Price He Paid to Save His Country*. New York: PublicAffairs, 2004.

Weiss, Michael. "Tea Now Being Served in the Guy Burgess Reading Room." *New Criterion*, Dispatch, May 6, 2009. https://www.newcriterion.com/blogs/dispatch/tea-now-being-served-in-the-guy-burgess-reading-room.

Weissman, Stephen. "Philip Agee on the Run." *Inquiry*, July 10, 1978.

West, Rebecca. *The Meaning of Treason*. London: Phoenix Press, 1982.

———. *The New Meaning of Treason*. New York: Open Road Media, 2010, Kindle.

Westad, Odd Arne. *The Cold War: A World History*. New York: Basic Books, 2018.

Whipple, Chris. *The Spymasters: How the CIA Directors Shape History and the Future*. New York: Scribner, 2020.

Wild, William H. "Unmasking Agee Is a Difficult Task." *Dayton Daily News*, October 15, 1988, 11.

Will, George. "Philip Agee: No Passport, Less Trouble." *Washington Post*, July 8, 1981.

Williams, William Appleman. *The Tragedy of American Diplomacy*. New York: W. W. Norton, 2009.

Wills, Garry. "The CIA from Beginning to End." *New York Review of Books*, January 22, 1976.

Winters, Jim. "Tom Dooley: The Forgotten Hero" *Notre Dame Magazine*, May 1979, 10–17.

Winters, Michael Sean. "Notre Dame Had a Right to Host Barr—But His Talk Was Ridiculously Stupid." *National Catholic Reporter*, October 18, 2019. https://www.ncronline.org/news/opinion/distinctly-catholic/notre -dame-had-right-host-barr-his-talk-was-ridiculously-stupid.

Wise, David. *Molehunt: The Secret Search for Traitors That Shattered the CIA*. New York: Random House, 1992.

———. *Nightmover: How Aldrich Ames Sold the CIA to the KGB for $4.6 Million*. New York: HarperCollins, 1995.

———. *Spy: The Inside Story of How the FBI's Robert Hanssen Betrayed America*. New York: Random House, 2002.

Witham, Nick. *The Cultural Left and the Reagan Era: U.S. Protest and the Central American Revolution*. London: I. B. Tauris, 2015.

Woods, Randall Bennett. *Quest for Identity: America Since 1945*. Cambridge: Cambridge University Press, 2005.

———. *Shadow Warrior: William Egan Colby and the CIA*. New York: Basic Books, 2013.

Worthington, Roger. "Man Without a Country." *Chicago Tribune*, March 26, 1981.

Wright, Peter, with Paul Greengrass. *Spycatcher: A Candid Autobiography of a Senior Intelligence Officer*. New York: Viking, 1987.

Index

Abu Nidal Organization, 160
Acheson, Dean, 15
Afghanistan, 177
African National Congress, 184
Agee, Christopher, 4n, 42, 73, 84, 135–36, 182, 205, 238, 245
Agee, Giselle Roberge, 4n, 23, 104, 124, 127–30, 136–37, 141, 164, 199, 205, 211, 239, 240–41, 245, 246
Agee, Helen (née O'Neill), 11, 205
Agee, Janet (née Wasserberger), 22, 39, 42, 51–52, 60, 61, 77, 84, 86, 126, 135–36, 205
Agee, Nancy, 136–37, 205
Agee, Philip: alleged operation against CIA in Mexico City, 234–36; as basis for "Bill Adler" in James's *A Brief History of Seven Killings*, 250–53; Catholic beliefs, 11, 16, 25, 39, 64, 69, 209–11, 256; CIA evaluations, 26, 80–82; CIA promotions, 35, 80, 234; CIA recruitment, 21–23; CIA resignation, 65; compliance with 1980 US district court injunction, 162–63, 189, 236; in Cuba, 72–73, 78–79, 148, 172, 212, 224–25, 235, 237–45; death, 244–45; in Denmark, 188; deportation from United Kingdom, 97–104; DGI and KGB, relationship with, 222–32; on Eastern Europe and the Soviet Union after 1989, 208; in Ecuador, 31–37, 41–42, 51; exposure of CIA officers and assets, 5, 80, 89, 94, 95–96, 109–16, 153, 250; finances, 69–70, 78–79, 85, 123–25, 237, 246; fondness for intelligence tradecraft, 193; in France, 77–86; in Grenada, 179–80; on the Gulf War, 208; at Hamburg University, 213–15, 232; health, 215, 236, 243; in historical Cold War and intelligence context, 255–56; interview with Frank Deese, 191–99; in Ireland, 242–43, 244; in Jamaica, 95–97, 99, 162, 183; justification for exposure of CIA, 118–21; memorial service in New York, 246–47; mercenary impulses, 220–21; in Mexico, 53–65, 69–70; in the Netherlands, 104; in Nicaragua, 181–82, 186; pride in performance as CIA case officer, 197–99; rehabilitation of reputation at Notre Dame, 201–2, 205–7; in the Soviet Union, 94, 95; in Spain, 135, 186, 199; State Department revocation of US passport, 131–32, 172, 186, 239–40, 242, 247; sympathy for, 219–20; in the United Kingdom, 86–104, 154, 233; in the United States, 199, 201–4, 225; as unreliable narrator, 70–72; in Uruguay, 42–53, 54, 76, 77, 115, 227; in West Germany/Germany, 105–6, 129–35, 141, 156
Agee, Philip, Jr., 4n, 39, 73, 84, 121, 135–36, 163, 204, 205, 245, 246

Prebisch, Raul, 59
Progressive Student Organization, 202
Prohibition, 28
Protestantism, evangelical, 60
Prouty, L. Fletcher, 98
Provisional Irish Republican Army (IRA), 144, 149, 156–57, 161, 164
Purdue University, appreciation for Agee, 216

Quadragesimo Anno (papal encyclical, 1931), 56
Quiet American, The (Greene), 24

Rabe, David, 146
Radford, Arthur, 39–40
Ramirez, Roberto, 47–48
Ramparts (magazine), 35, 165–66, 168
Ray, Ellen, 115n
Reader (newspaper), 167
Reagan, Ronald, 147, 177
Reagan administration, 20, 155, 177, 183, 196, 207
Reagan Doctrine, 177
Real Paper (newspaper), 119, 167
Rebel (magazine), 171, 189–90
Red Brigades (Italy), 144, 149, 157, 158, 161
Redford, Robert, 219
Redmond, Paul, 231
Reed, Jim, 203
Rees, Merlyn, 102, 103
Reforma (newspaper), 235
Rerum Novarum (papal encyclical, 1891), 56
Reserve Officers Training Corps (ROTC), 18, 176
Revolutionary Cells, 159–60
Reynolds, Kevin, 191–92n
Ridenhour, Ronald, 187n
Ridenour, Ron, 187–88
Riera Escalante, Pedro, 235–36
Rio Protocol, 33
Risen, James, 234–35
Roberge, Therese, 85, 104
Roberts, Adam, 176
Robeson, Paul, 135
Rodgers, Daniel T., 177
Rodriguez, Ventura, 47–48
Roettinger, Philip, 140, 232
Rolling Stone (magazine), 167, 170, 213
Rosenberg, Ethel, 17–18
Rosenberg, Julius, 17–18
Rositzke, Harry, 93

Russia, 9; hacking of 2016 US presidential election, 9
Rutten, Tim, 16, 213

Safer, Morley, 170, 220
Sahl, Mort, 93
Salazar, Antonio, 152
Sandinista National Liberation Front (FSLN), 153, 162, 177–78, 179, 180, 182, 202, 203
Sartre, Jean-Paul, 92
Saturday Night Live, 148
Savimbi, Jonas, 177
Schaap, William, 115n, 246
Scheuer, Michael, 244
Schevitz, Jeffrey, 217
Schleyer, Hans Martin, 157–58
Schmidt, Helmut, 105
Schneider, René, 91
Schorr, Daniel, 113
Scott, Winston, 61, 63, 80
Seaga, Edward, 250
Seale, Bobby, 142
Seale, Patrick, 160
Second Vatican Council (Vatican II), 16, 58
Seeger, Murray, 110–11, 115n, 228
Seixas, Angela Camargo, 86, 88, 94, 125–27, 153, 171; torture by Brazilian security services, 86, 94, 125
September 11 terrorist attacks, 8
Shackley, Theodore George ("Ted"), 30, 82, 119
Shaw, Diana, 25
Sheehan, Neil, 165
Shining Path, 153
60 Minutes (TV news magazine), 170, 220
Sloan School of Management (Massachusetts Institute of Technology), 239
Smith, Christian, 180
Smith, Tommie, 56
Smith, Walter Bedell, 29
Smith, William French, 155
Snepp, Frank, 7, 39, 51, 108, 139, 140, 176, 255, 256
Sniffen, Michael, 88
Snowden, Edward, 5–8, 188, 247, 256
Soares, Mario, 152
Soberanta (magazine), 182
Social Christian movement (Ecuador), 34
Socialist Press (magazine), 169
Soderbergh, Steven, 146
Solidarity Movement, 180–81, 256
Somoza Debayle, Anastasio, 177–78

Vietnam War, 2, 5, 7, 16, 24, 37–38, 39, 49, 53, 54–55, 57, 66, 67, 68, 122–23, 144, 145, 147, 154, 165, 170, 176, 187n, 193–94, 197, 211; coup against Diem (1963), 37–38; Gulf of Tonkin incident (1964), 38; My Lai massacre (1968), 187n; Paris Accords (1973), 67, 123, 145; Phoenix Program, book on, 137–38

Voice of America, 212

Wall Street Journal (newspaper), 179
Washington Post (newspaper), 175, 179
Washington Times (newspaper), 188
Watergate scandal, 8, 88, 90, 145
Weather Underground (Weathermen), 143–45, 164
Weatherwax, Robert ("Bob"), 33
Webster, William, 234
Welch, Joseph, 14, 17
Welch, Richard: and Agee's lawsuit against Barbara Bush, 218–22, 232; assassination of, 111–16, 153, 170, 201, 218–22, 232, 239, 248, 250, 251–53; in Marlon James's *A Brief History of Seven Killings*, 251–53
Weinglass, Len, 246, 254
Weissman, Stephen, 169
Wells, Clyde, 186
West, Rebecca, 254
West Germany/Germany, 105, 149, 156, 247; *Ostpolitik* policy, 105, 149, 156
Whistleblower Protection Act of 1989, 6
whistleblowers, 6–7

Whitlam, Gough, 191
Whole Earth Catalog (magazine), 167
Wiehoff, Corinne, 136
Wiehoff, Dale, 136
Will, George F., 245
Wills, Garry, 95
Willson, Brian, 203
Wilmer, Stephen Elliott, 139
Wilson, Harold, 69
Wilson, Joseph, 184–85n
Wilson, Woodrow, 45
Wilson, Valerie Plame, 184–85n
Winner, Reality, 9
Winterbottom, Michael, 242
Winters, Jim, 24
Wisner, Frank, 25, 28, 40
Witham, Nick, 256
Wolf, Louis, 115–16, 115n, 141, 176–77
Woodstock music festival (1969), 68
Woolsey, James, 231
World Service Authority, 224–25
Wormwood (docudrama), 150n
Wright, Peter, 209n
Wulf, Melvin, 83–84, 99–100, 102, 116–17, 124, 131–32, 134, 155, 162, 190, 206, 218, 246–47

Yankee Sandinistas (Ridenour), 188
Yugoslavia, 52

Zed Books, 189
Zinn, Howard, 138